Classroom Communication and Instructional Processes

Advances Through Meta-Analysis

LEA'S COMMUNICATION SERIES
Jennings Bryant/Dolf Zillmann, General Editors

For a complete list of titles in LEA's Communication Series, please contact Lawrence Erlbaum Associates, Publisher at www.erlbaum.com

Classroom Communication and Instructional Processes

Advances Through Meta-Analysis

Edited by

Barbara Mae Gayle
Saint Martin's University

Raymond W. Preiss
University of Puget Sound

Nancy Burrell
Mike Allen
University of Wisconsin–Milwaukee

LEA
2006

LAWRENCE ERLBAUM ASSOCIATES, PUBLISHERS
Mahwah, New Jersey   London

Lawrence Erlbaum Associates, Inc., Publishers
10 Industrial Avenue
Mahwah, New Jersey 07430
www.erlbaum.com

Cover design by Kathryn Houghtaling Lacey

Library of Congress Cataloging-in-Publication Data

Classroom communication and instructional processes : advances
through meta-analysis / edited by Barbara Mae Gayle ... [et al.].
p. cm. — (LEA's communication series)
Includes bibliographical references and index.
ISBN 0-8058-4423-6 (cloth : alk. paper)
ISBN 0-8058-4424-4 (paper : alk. paper)
1. Communication in education. 2. Meta-analysis. I. Gayle, Barbara
Mae. II. Series.
LB1033.5.C59 2006
371.102'2—dc22   2005046277
                                                        CIP

Books published by Lawrence Erlbaum Associates are printed on acid-
free paper, and their bindings are chosen for strength and durability.

Printed in the United States of America
10 9 8 7 6 5 4 3 2 1

Contents

III   Classroom Interactions

Preface

Barbara Mae Gayle
Saint Martin's University

When I entered college as a nontraditional student, I was acutely aware that my intellectual development often depended on the teaching strategies my professors employed. When I began teaching my own courses, I sought to understand the "essential" elements I should include in my classes to promote student understanding and deep learning. I explored theoretically based research, collections of class exercises and projects, and books offering "teaching tips." I was looking for methods to engage and challenge students to increase the likelihood that they would be active contributors in their own intellectual development. In conversations with colleagues, I have learned that my search is a rather common occurrence. Professional educators are continuously monitoring the literature for developments in their disciplines, sorting through competing claims about a new theory, and searching for new ways to convey this information to students. The evolution of content and pedagogy is a normal aspect of our lives.

Educators understand that a healthy discussion is underway about the effectiveness of specific teaching practices and techniques to promote student performance outcomes. There is no shortage of experimental literature on these issues, and the research on creating learning-conducive environments may seem contradictory or uneven. The editors of this book believe that meta-analysis is a useful tool for summarizing many experiments and determining how and why particular teaching and learning experiences are associated with positive student outcomes. In later chapters, we develop the logic of aggregating study effects and offer useful advice regarding instructional strategies.

The findings addressed in this volume focus on classroom communication and instructional processes. The sheer number of studies in this area prompted us to establish criteria for including topics in this volume. In this unit, we articulate our inclusion criteria and discuss the logic for organizing and grouping the collection of meta-analyses. Prior to each upcoming unit, we provide a framework or overview for considering relevant educational issues and classroom practices. Our goal is to make meta-analytic findings accessible and relevant.

SELECTION CRITERIA AND ORGANIZATION

Preiss and Allen (1995) recommended that domains of experimental literature merit empirical aggregation if they meet the criteria of uniqueness or suitability. Consistent with this logic, we selected broad topic areas that address student learning, and oral and online communication. If an area or question has never been empirically assessed, if earlier meta-analyses are controversial or equivocal, or if a great deal of research has been completed since a previous meta-analysis in that area, a new meta-analytic review may be considered unique. A meta-analysis may also be unique if it explores a theoretical model or identifies a moderator variable that helps clarify a theoretical proposition. Suitability is primarily an issue of variability where the meta-analysis is used to explicate a large number of inconsistent experimental findings or to estimate the magnitude of a particular effect. A meta-analysis is suitable for aggregation if the review illuminates theoretical processes or specifies theoretical implications.

When selecting and arranging the meta-analytic summaries for this volume, we were mindful of both the uniqueness and suitability criteria. First, we identified major issues associated with communication in the classroom that contribute to student learning. We isolated broad domains of literature, including teacher effectiveness in the classroom, practices employed to enhance learning, and the impact of student–teacher interpersonal interactions. Next, we examined the available empirical summaries in each of the three areas that focused on oral communication practices. Topics included in the area of teacher effectiveness focused on such areas as humor use and question asking. Meta-analyses on areas such as computer-assisted instruction or critical thinking are found in the classroom practices section, and race, sex equity, and teacher immediacy were included in the section dealing with classroom interaction.

CONTENT OF THE BOOK

In selecting and arranging chapters in this volume, we sought topics that were meaningful and relevant to classroom processes. In Part I of this volume, "Classroom Communication and Instructional Processes," we explore the intersections between meta-analysis and instructional practices. Chapter 1 by Preiss and Allen explains how meta-analysis may be an appropriate tool for exploring inconsistencies in educational research. The authors consider how meta-analytic investigations may be a credible source of claims about instructional practices. McCroskey, Richmond, and McCroskey (chap. 2) summarize traditions of instructional communication research, describe measurement and design issues, and pose questions stimulating future research.

Part II, "Educational Practices in the Classroom," provides meta-analytic investigations on issues associated with learning-conducive classroom environments. Two chapters focus on the role of computers in enhancing student understanding. Timmerman and Kruepke (chap. 6) investigate the efficacy of computer-assisted instruction in enhancing student performance, and Shapiro, Kerssen-Griep, Gayle, and Allen (chap. 5) examine the ability of PowerPoint presentations to increase student learning and recall. Three chapters focus on enhancing student performance capabilities. Preiss, Gayle, and Allen (chap. 7) summarize the evidence for a relationship between test anxiety and study behaviors. Burrell, Zirbel, and Allen (chap. 8) review the evidence for peer mediation of conflict in educational settings. Finally, Berkowitz (chap. 4) investigates if competitive forensics can enhance critical thinking and improve student performance.

Part III, "Classroom Interactions," emphasizes student–teacher contact as the basis for positive academic outcomes. Witt, Wheeless, and Allen's (chap. 10) meta-analysis reviews the relationship between teachers' verbal and nonverbal behaviors and student learning. Bradford, Cooper, Allen, Stanley, and Grimes (chap. 11) summarize studies on the student–teacher relationships of underrepresented populations. Jones, Dindia, and Tye's (chap. 12) meta-analysis examines the outcomes of sex equity in the classroom. The importance of teacher–student interactions is illustrated by Bourhis, Allen, and Bauman's (chap. 13) meta-analysis on communication apprehension and the Allen, Bourhis, Mabry, Burrell, & Timmermann (chap. 14) meta-analysis on the success of distance education programs.

Part IV, "Teacher Effectiveness and Communicative and Instructional Processes," investigates the nature, antecedents, and outcomes of teacher effectiveness. These behaviors are thought to elicit perceptions of teacher competence, clarity, and effectiveness. A meta-analysis by Gayle, Preiss, and Allen (chap. 17) examines the role of oral questions in enhancing students' learning and their ability to apply course material. In a separate meta-analysis, Preiss and Gayle (chap. 20) study the use of oral advanced organizers to promote learning, recall, and the understanding of subsequent information on complex educational topics. In other meta-analyses selected for this section, Preiss and Gayle (chap. 19) examine the relationship between lecture speed and student recall of lecture material. Also, Martin, Preiss, Gayle, and Allen (chap. 18) investigate the role of humor in facilitating the affective, perceived, and objective learning. Finally in this section, Allen's (chap. 21) meta-analysis considers whether student evaluations of faculty teaching effectiveness are associated with the faculty member's record of scholarly productivity.

In Part V, "Meta-Analysis and Interactional and Instructional Processes in the Classroom," contributors consider whether the meta-analyses in this volume provide a platform for the next generation of classroom interaction research. Young, Plax, and Kearney (chap. 23) examine how meta-analysis might best be used to interpret communicative processes in the classroom. Applegate (chap. 24), on the other hand, considers extending the information gained from the meta-analyses presented in this volume to clarify communication processes in the classroom for individual professors. Finally, Allen, Preiss, and Burrell (chap. 25) analyze educational textbooks to assess the advice on teaching strategies and classroom behaviors and Gayle (chap. 22) discusses the contribution of the scholarship of teaching and learning (SoTL).

CONCLUDING REMARKS ABOUT AVERAGE EFFECTS

Taken together, the chapters in this volume are intended to enhance our understanding of behaviors, practices, and processes that promote positive student outcomes. Meta-analysis is one of many tools used to unravel these complex issues. The average effect is a powerful concept because it describes a distribution of outcomes, rather than a single finding from a single study. Also, it focuses our attention on the historical record of research and the findings that have been replicated in that record. Although the meta-analyses selected for this volume are not an exhaustive roster of the historical record, they are representative of the enduring and current controversies found there. Our hope is that the empirical summaries presented in this book will lead to new questions and new levels of inquiry. Over time, meta-analysis will help us understand the outcomes of classroom communication and instructional processes. As the historical record of studies accumulates, new questions will be posed and new primary investigations will be designed. Scientific progression is the foundation for advances through meta-analysis. As these studies are empirically summarized, interlocking meta-analytic reviews will provide a more complete set of generalizations related to instructional contexts.

ACKNOWLEDGMENT

The author wishes to express her gratitude to The University of Portland for contributing time and resources in the earlier stages of this entire project.

REFERENCE

Preiss, R. W., & Allen, M. (1995). Understanding and using meta-analysis. *Evaluation & The Health Professions, 18,* 315–335.

I

Classroom Communication and Instructional Processes

1

Meta-Analysis, Classroom Communication, and Instructional Processes

Raymond W. Preiss
University of Puget Sound

Mike Allen
University of Wisconsin–Milwaukee

Classroom Communication and Instructional Processes: Advances Through Meta-Analysis is primarily a collection of investigations related to effective instructional practices. In addition to offering generalizations bearing on classroom communication and instructional techniques, the meta-analyses included in this book reflect our commitment to designing curriculum and pedagogy based on the "best available evidence." In an era of high-stakes testing and intense competition for resources, the criteria for what constitutes "best" evidence merits consideration. At issue are the qualities of research that make advice about educational techniques and strategies believable. In this chapter, we review one exchange between researchers regarding credible evidence, advance the rationale for meta-analytic summaries of instructional research, and consider the various audiences that will assess the believability of meta-analytic claims. Our goal is to illustrate the contributions meta-analysis can make to the development of curriculum, pedagogy, and educational policy.

THE SEARCH FOR CREDIBLE SCIENTIFIC EVIDENCE
REGARDING INSTRUCTION

The issue of what constitutes powerful evidence for scientific claims about instructional practices is a reoccurring topic in the scholarly literature. Although this discussion takes several forms and advances a variety of issues, there is a general dissatisfaction with the quality of instructional research and the generalizability of findings to policy decisions or classroom applications. One example of the controversy is found in Levin and O'Donnell's (1999) compelling critique of educational research's credibility gaps. The discussion centered on the nature of the purposes, methods, and conclusions of educational research. Of special concern was the nature of evidence documenting claims regarding educational processes and outcomes. To oversimplify the thesis, the authors advanced the notion of "credible evidence" and advocated research that is theory driven, rigorous, and empirical. In addition to advancing a framework for conducting these investigations, Levin and O'Donnell considered technological advances, methodological training, and policy contexts. They made a case for persuading the public, the press, and policymakers about the viability of educational research. Responding authors advocated competition among methods and philosophies (Winne, 1999), balanced sources of educational research (Corno, 1999), best practices (Stanovich, 1999), the relevance of scientific evidence (Mayer, 1999), problems beside methodological rigor (Benton, 1999), and renewed emphasis on scientific credibility (Carlson, 1999). This is not a unique exchange and readers may have observed many of these discussions between scholars from many disciplines. One would be hard-pressed, however, to identify instances in which instructional research practices have been altered by this, or other, critiques of the educational research enterprise.

Meta-Analysis and Less-Than-Perfect Instructional Research

We begin this book by showcasing the call for rigorous instructional research for pragmatic reasons. Clearly, these concerns are raised routinely across the social sciences, and there is little doubt that improved standards for quality research are desirable and necessary. This tautology is troubling, however, as adopting the thesis leaves the impression that more than 60 years of instructional research have made few contributions to classroom practices. The easy path is to affirm both the thesis and the implication that less-than-perfect research is suspect. We are concerned that this hasty conclusion violates basic standards for scientific burden of proof. When researchers review literature, pose hypotheses, design and execute tests, and report plausible findings, we conclude the basic burden for proof has been established. Dismissing evidence, even evidence that contradicts many other studies, is not a decision to be made casually. Of course, those advocating quality tend to favor methodology, design, and sample factors as a way to resolve competing claims. We respect this view by seeking to establish credible evidence by drawing on the "best" and the "less-than-perfect" experimental findings. However, not everyone would agree on what the "best" design requires and the necessary elements of a design change over time. The result is that investigations deemed "state of the art" by today's standards are considered deficient 20 years later and necessary requirements for empirical research existing 40 years ago seem silly today. The standards of quality are dynamic and not fixed, therefore appealing as a fix to "quality" in methods and design may be elusive, if not impossible.

Granting the fact that many—perhaps far too many—investigations are flawed, it is also true that researchers make design, sample, and comparison decisions for many reasons. For example, the nature of existing assignments may make it difficult to use some procedures, or busy class schedules may limit the use of lengthy measurement instruments. Instructors may wisely decide that certain topics are at odds with community sensibilities, electing to use less volatile subjects that address theoretical issues unobtrusively. Similarly, some school institutional review boards may not approve a protocol that dramatically alters standard testing, writing, or lecturing practices. A researcher might reasonably decide to explore these issues in subtle ways that avoid placing students in experimental conditions where little learning might occur. The point here is that the use of rigorous scientific methods should be applauded and the results from investigations should be studied carefully. The question remains regarding what should be done with less-than-perfect research.

The best practices view brands all investigations that do not employ the most appropriate experimental designs and statistical comparisons as being suspect. Although endorsing the need for enhancing the quality (e.g., validity) of research, we also see the need to comb through the existing body of educational literature and salvage the evidence that is available there. Not all research using less-than-ideal methods produces invalid results, as robust effects may be observed by methods that are practical and feasible, but not perfect. In the following chapters, the authors offer meta-analytic findings as a parallel option for closing the credibility gap and advancing powerful claims about instructional practices. We seek generalizations that unify and illuminate the educational enterprise.

Assessing large bodies of literature is a complicated task. It is helpful to conceptualize the corpus of literature not as hundreds of studies differing in levels of quality, but as evidence (more or less credible) related to questions and theories that researchers believe are central (more or less) to understanding how learning occurs or how classroom techniques achieve learning objectives. In this view, existing studies can be viewed as domains of research related to a question or theory. Although every theory or question is assessed by its ability to produce valid, reliable, and meaningful generalizations, there are many theories and questions to consider and many experimental findings to evaluate. As the authors discuss, researchers may approach this task by employing narrative or empirical reviews. It is important to remember, however, that the goal is to assess the domain of literature bearing on the theory or question of interest. This can be accomplished by impeaching (or venerating) design and statistical decisions, but an alternative is to describe and probe the body of research in the domain. This is the approach we pursue in this volume.

A second complicating factor involves the nature of the theories and questions that govern the domains. Many educational processes and outcomes are subject to healthy interrogation, and advocates (also critics) offer important observations and key findings that are consistent with their perspectives. We view these controversies as consistent with the scientific enterprise. Given the need to discover what works and the disparate theoretical approaches, assumptions, and methods for why it works, it is not surprising that scientific progress has been uneven and that some questions resist simple interpretations. We argue that this is precisely the reason to examine all available existing evidence related to a question while improving the "quality" of new investigations. It is a false dichotomy to suggest that only one path can be explored.

We believe that social scientific progress in understanding educational practices would be served best if the literature could be simultaneously summarized and expanded. Before educators accept claims regarding the effectiveness of a lecture technique, the impact of distance learning, or the outcome of teacher–student interactions, research bearing on the question should be systematically gathered and summarized. These summaries should include studies using best and less-than-perfect designs and methods. The summary should identify voids in the literature, draw attention to accepted issues that are supported by only a limited number of findings, and assess the sophistication of design and comparison decisions. In short, a comprehensive review of the classroom communication and instructional processes literature should assess the existing domain of research, consider strengths and weaknesses, and provide conclusions that offer fertile soil for the next generation of studies. As research accumulates, the new primary research should be folded into ever-widening reviews of the issues dominating the domain. Two methods for summarizing literature and reviewing findings are currently being used: narrative summaries and meta-analysis.

The Logic of Narrative Summaries

The narrative review is the traditional verbal description of a body of literature (Pillemer, 1984) and the qualitative method for evaluating research on a given topic (Rosenthal, 1984). In most instances, the narrative reviewer explicates a basic assumption or question and classifies existing research using a vote counting system. The narrative reviewer samples relevant experimental evidence and tallies results related to expected outcomes. Questions in the narrative summary might include these: Do the studies on the roster of germane experiments detect a significant effect? Is the significant effect in the predicted direction? Is the significant effect plausibly attributable to a competing theory or perspective? In their narrative summary, Levin and O'Donnell (1999) argued for the vote count to be based primarily on "scientifically credible" methods and statistical procedures. After discarding studies that do not meet the criteria, readers are asked to tally the votes (confirming or nonconfirming tests) and render a judgment regarding the question of interest.

The outcome of a narrative review may range from strong support (a uniform confirming vote count) for some proposition to no support (the failure to detect confirming votes). Of course, interesting and complex questions about educational processes and outcomes rarely produce a clear-cut vote count. If 60% or 70% of the votes confirm a proposition, the narrative reviewer may question the robustness of the relationship or provide a rationale for nonconfirming outcomes. If 30% or 40% of the votes are confirming, the reviewer may impugn the relationship and express the concern that little progress has been made in understanding such an important issue. In either outcome, more research will certainly be required and best practices research will be more credible than less-than-perfect evidence.

One difficulty with the narrative review process involves confusion about what counts as a qualifying vote. The idea here is that a best practices study is 100% accurate. Levin and O'Donnell (1999) advanced a system for improving the rigor of educational experiments as a way to improve the accuracy of the tally regarding educational policies. Thus, methodological rigor becomes the pivotal point of scientific credibility. This is problematic because empirical findings are assessed probabilistically and it is a tautology that the findings of any one study may be the result of sampling error. Usually, narrative reviewers do not consider the possibility of Type I (false positive) or Type II (false negative) error as factors influencing trends in primary research. Instead, experts tend to introduce intervening variables that explain apparent inconsistencies in the experimental record. In instances where less-than-perfect studies produce discrepancies, narrative reviewers may assess sample characteristics, research designs, or statistical methods as the source of contradictory findings. If scientifically perfect studies produce discrepancies, narrative reviewers introduce new theories or variables as an explanation for the unexpected vote tally. The new variable allows the narrative reviewer to "connect the dots" consistently by discounting nonconfirming studies. This practice can produce a web of issues, theoretical and methodological, that tend to deflect attention away from hypothesized relationships.

We believe that expert narrative reviews are essential components of the scientific enterprise, as they provide an avenue for subjective interpretation, reformulation, and reappraisal. If the goal is to assess the domain of evidence, however, this approach may possess the liability of nonrepresentativeness. In the course of making the case for an innovative interpretation or conclusion, the reviewer elevates certain studies as exemplars of the outcome of interest. The difficulty here is that narrative reviews usually do not employ explicit rules or specify the methods used to locate primary evidence. The reader is not privy to judgment calls regarding why one of several "perfect" studies is counted whereas a second "perfect" study is not. The reader is asked to consider the exemplar studies in the context of a theoretical narrative or story that explains what the findings mean.

The narrative review offers an important venue for experts to advance their informed conclusions about a domain of literature. The risk is that while making the case for one interpretation the ballot box for the vote count can be "stuffed" with nonrepresentative example studies. When nonconforming studies are mentioned, new variables may be introduced to explain discrepancies. Often, the intervening variable has been studied in only a limited number of investigations, and applying them to the entire domain runs the risk of overgeneralization. For this reason, it is difficult for the vote-counting method used by narrative reviewers to present a balanced portrayal of a large domain of literature.

The Logic of Meta-Analytic Summaries

The term *meta-analysis* (Hedges & Olkin, 1985; Hunter, Schmidt, & Jackson, 1982) refers to a cluster of research procedures for aggregating primary research findings and estimating the direction and magnitude of effects. The discussion regarding the virtues and limitations of meta-analytic procedures has waxed and waned for more than 20 years (see Rosenthal & DiMatteo, 2001) and educators were among the first groups to use these techniques to assess instructional practices. By coding and transforming individual study outcomes into a common metric, it is possible to average results across studies, estimate average effects, and detect moderator variables. In this book, we use variance-centered forms of meta-analysis (Hunter & Schmidt, 1990). This procedure requires the calculation of a weighted average correlation that is tested for homogeneity of the sample. The homogeneity test, using the chi-square statistic, compares the expected variability in the sample of correlations to the actual variability in the observed correlations. A significant chi-square indicates the existence of greater variability than would be expected due to random sampling error. This would be a sign of the probable existence of a moderator variable and a reason to interpret the average effect cautiously.

Because researchers share the goal of establishing credible evidence, it is not possible to ignore the quality issue. Meta-analysis provides many advantages over narrative reviews when the goal of the researcher is to describe the quality of a domain of experimental findings. The average effect will display a direction (positive, zero, or negative), a magnitude (small, moderate, or large), and a level of stability across individual study effects. These characteristics are markers of replication (Allen & Preiss, 1993), a fundamental hallmark of scientific knowledge. The stability of the direction and magnitude of an effect across many studies indicates a level of replication meriting confidence in any particular finding. This logic returns us to the notion of best evidence and less-than-perfect evidence for claims about instructional methods and processes. If an average effect is consistent in direction and meaningful in degree, the finding is credible even if the method, sample, or comparison employed in an individual study is not ideal. Furthermore, if a researcher is convinced that a meta-analytic finding is distorted or biased, the investigator can code individual studies in the domain for scientific quality and empirically assess the average effects associated with sample, design, or comparison decisions. In either case, the credibility of a claim shifts from any single study to the effect associated with the domain of studies.

Replicating an existing meta-analysis provides a second avenue for establishing the credibility of educational evidence. Unlike narrative reviews, meta-analytic summaries are inherently public activities. Interested readers can quickly identify the way studies were located, procedures for computing study effects, and decision rules for coding information. Any skeptic can follow the search regimen described in the original meta-analysis, locate the studies listed in the reference section, add any new studies conducted since the meta-analysis was published, or capture experiments missed by the original search procedures. Thus, the replicating meta-analysis updates the original summary, expands the database for claims, and validates (or disputes) the existence of moderator variables. To the extent that multiple meta-analyses affirm findings, confidence in the claim increases as a function of new studies (samples) employed and as a function of increased power (sample size) to detect effects. The quality of any single experiment plays a lesser role in this process. The credibility of meta-analytic evidence is rooted in independent assessments of the research domain and critical revaluation of coding decisions. These assessments involve the context governing a policy change and the audiences judging the clash of competing issues.

THE CONTEXT FOR CREDIBLE CLAIMS ABOUT INSTRUCTIONAL PRACTICES

Debates about educational practices exist within a social context. Some debates are quite narrow and specific, perhaps involving an administrator's decision to adopt a peer tutoring model. Other contexts can be wide-ranging and involve many stakeholders. An example of this context might involve changing the general education curriculum or cutting funding for athletics and the arts. On one level, there may be agreement that a problem exists and a large body of research may address the problem. If so, it would be an error to assert that all audiences would agree if they just understood the scientific evidence. The reality is that even scientists disagree on what the scientific record means! Both narrative and meta-analytic reviewers can quantify the seriousness of a problem, identify why the problem exists, and propose needed changes. Advocates for all positions on a policy will have credible evidence for making a change. In this instance, quality credible evidence may well carry the day. Nevertheless, a meta-analysis that quantifies the direction, degree, and magnitude of a problem may significantly increase the persuasiveness of a proposal to change policies.

More commonly, educational debates involve competing positions and perspectives. In this case, the scientific record may be extensive, but ideologues may not be interested in compromises or solutions that violate their values. One possibility is that people disagree about the nature of an educational problem or the seriousness of the problem. If there is no agreement, each side may be able to produce exemplar studies and narratives that bolster its position in the dispute. In this case, a meta-analysis can be a valuable tool, as the average effect will trump example studies in the same way that a case study is trumped by a sample-based experiment. Of course, the advocate has the option of presenting case study examples, exemplar experiments, and meta-analyses! In this instance, meta-analyses can be a persuasive instrument for advocating policy changes.

A third possibility is that the public and stakeholders agree that a policy change must be made, but the scientific evidence about the causes and outcomes of the problem is unclear. In this case the advantages gained by adopting a new policy may appear ambiguous or even counterproductive. Narrative reviewers are likely to experience difficulties in this environment. When each side provides example studies and narratives, listeners may become confused or frustrated. Also, the introduction of new variables to explain discrepancies between experiments is likely to fragment and dilute the basic positions. Meta-analyses are powerful sources of evidence in this situation. If the average results (positive, zero, or negative) are meaningful (small, moderate, or large) based on scores of studies (stable or unstable) involving thousands of participants, listeners are likely to be persuaded that a change is warranted. If there are no moderator variables, the advocate can press for a policy change based on best evidence. If a moderator variable is isolated, the debate moves to its causes, not the significance of the problem.

In a final context, the public may disagree over the need for a policy change and the scientific record may be fractured or inconsistent with regard to the causes of a problem and outcomes of existing policies. This is the most difficult (and perhaps the most common) situation facing educators today. Few educators and members of the public agree on the nature and magnitude of harm associated with deficits in student knowledge of mathematics, much less geography. Everyone would like students to solve equations and identify land masses, but few have evidence that this goal should be accomplished using tests, written papers, or oral presentation. The point here is that complex problems involving polarized (or apathetic) constituencies produce the most intractable disputes. It is unclear that narrative or meta-analytic reviews will decisively alter these debates. It is also unrealistic to expect credible scientific evidence to win the day. In this context, advocates must employ all of their resources for building audiences and persuading listeners.

THE AUDIENCE FOR CREDIBLE CLAIMS ABOUT INSTRUCTIONAL PRACTICES

An important aspect of credibility is rarely mentioned in exchanges about educational practices and processes: Judgments of believability are made by the audience considering the evidence. This audience-centered approach has a long and respected history. Aristotle reasoned that believability was rooted in perceptions of a source's expertise and trustworthiness. Contemporary social scientific studies have isolated other dimensions (factor structures) of these perceptions: competence, character, dynamism, similarity, and sociability. The point here is that trained scientists are likely to respond to experimental evidence differently than other audiences. Moreover, some audiences may be alienated or apathetic and thus are unresponsive to any evidence from any source that contradicts privately held beliefs. It behooves advocates for an educational reform to adapt their evidence to the intended audience.

There are at least three primary audiences for educational claims: Professional educators, policy makers, and citizens. Of course, there are subcategories within each grouping and overlaps across groupings. Professional educators may include teachers, department chairs, and principals. A principal, however, may also be a policymaker. Other policymakers include members of the state or federal legislature and members of a local school board. Needless to say, school board members may also be parents and tax-payers, categories we associate with private citizens who vote on school bonds and levies. The list of overlapping audiences is further complicated by the role of planning consultants, educational service district employees, deans, and staff trainers. The advocate of credible evidence must navigate these audiences as she or he makes the case for policy changes.

As we consider these audiences, it is important to remember that narrative reviews and meta-analyses are not mutually exclusive approaches to presenting evidence. In fact, both strategies combine numbers and narratives as they summarize evidence and explain rationales for policy approaches. The issue is one of emphasis. It is clear that meta-analysis provides additional credible evidence that an advocate can use to convince an audience that a change in policy is needed. Figure 1.1 provides examples of how meta-analysis can supplement narrative reviews to support policy claims.

This breakdown is not exhaustive, but it does illustrate that meta-analysis increases the rhetorical options available to policy advocates. For example, citizens may not understand the virtues of a Solomon four-group design, but they may understand the power of a study employing 40,000 participants or the increase of a learning outcome by 40%. Policymakers may be much more interested in the consistency and magnitude of an effect than in the findings of all controlled studies on a topic. Professional educators are likely to respond to evidence that one theory is consistent with a pattern of outcomes. Rather than prescribe the issues to emphasize, we recognize that different audiences are likely to respond to a variety of arguments and different combinations of arguments.

	Type of Review	
Audience	Narrative Review	Meta-Analytic Review
Professional Educator	Stress scientific quality Stress application of a study	Stress consistency of direction Stress magnitude of average effect Stress sample size Stress number of studies Stress quality moderators
Policymaker	Stress most appropriate studies Stress feasibility of best studies	Stress magnitude of average effect Stress number of studies Stress sample size Stress sample moderators
Public Citizen	Stress the logic of a study Stress examples from the best studies	Stress sample size Stress ability of the average effect to discriminate between causes Stress consistency of outcomes

FIG. 1.1.   Examples of audience-centered issues by type of review.

CONCLUSIONS

In the chapters that follow, readers are invited to consider the clash of theoretical positions embedded in the scientific record. In spite of the complexity of some issues, many readers will conclude that rather obvious policies flow from the meta-analytic findings. Some policy changes may prompt educators to change their lesson plans; other findings may suggest institutional changes. We acknowledge the fact that some readers may object to our interpretations and insist that average effects do not match their experiences in the classroom. We encourage educators (and others) to look closely at the primary studies and reexamine our methods and conclusions. Meta-analysis is an inherently public enterprise, and all meta-analysts explicitly state search procedures, study inclusion standards, coding rules, and aggregation formulas. Any informed reader from any theoretical or ideological persuasion is welcome to sort through the primary literature and add, recode, reformulate, or reinterpret findings. When readers accept our invitation to replicate, interlock, and extend empirical summaries, we believe that educators and policymakers will indeed see advances through meta-analysis.

REFERENCES

Allen, M., & Preiss, R. W. (1993). Replication and meta-analysis: A necessary connection. *Journal of Social Behavior and Personality, 8,* 9–20.

Benton, S. L. (1999). The Levin and O'Donnell proposal is a good first step. *Issues in Education, 5,* 231–238.

Carlson, J. S. (1999). What to do about educational research's credibility gap?: Become more scientific. *Issues in Education, 5,* 239–245.

Corno, L. (1999). It's the accumulated evidence and the argument. *Issues in Education, 5,* 247–253.

Hedges, L. V., & Olkin, I. (1985). *Statistical methods of meta-analysis.* Orlando, FL: Academic.

Hunter, J. E., & Schmidt, F. (1990). *Methods for meta-analysis.* Newbury Park, CA: Sage.

Hunter, J. E., Schmidt, F. L., & Jackson, G. B. (1982). *Meta-analysis: Cumulating findings across research.* Beverly Hills, CA: Sage.

Levin, J. R., & O'Donnell, A. M. (1999). What to do about educational research's credibility gaps? *Issues in Education, 5,* 177–229.

Mayer, R. E. (1999). To foster meaningful learning: Is science relevant? *Issues in Education, 5,* 255–260.

Pillemer, D. (1984). Conceptual issues in research synthesis. *Journal of Special Education, 18,* 27–40.

Rosenthal, R. (1984). *Meta-analytic procedures for social research.* Beverly Hills, CA: Sage.

Rosenthal, R., & DiMatteo, M. R. (2001). Meta-analysis: Recent developments in quantitative methods for literature reviews. *Annual Review of Psychology, 52,* 59–82.

Stanovich, K. E. (1999). Educational research at a choice point. *Issues in Education, 5,* 267–272.

Winne, P. H. (1999). How to improve the credibility of research in education. *Issues in Education, 5,* 273–278.

2

The Role of Communication in Instruction: The First Three Decades

James C. McCroskey
Virginia P. Richmond
West Virginia University

Linda L. McCroskey
California State University, Long Beach

An interest in research on teaching in the field of communication traces back to the earliest beginnings of the field. When the first professional association in the field (what is now known as the Eastern Communication Association) was founded in 1909 it was founded by college teachers of speech. When the first journal (Quarterly Journal of Speech) in the field was published by our first national association (now known as the National Communication Association) shortly after its founding in 1914, the primary focus of the journal was teaching. The founding fathers of the field held teaching as a high priority and devoted considerable scholarly attention to it.

Whereas the discipline of communication, at an age approaching 100 years, is a youngster compared to most of its sister disciplines in the arts and sciences, the study of instructional communication is much younger. For most of its history, communication and its predecessor, speech, have focused on the teaching of speech (more recently the teaching of communication) not the role of communication in instruction across academic fields. Whereas the formal research on stage fright, and later communication apprehension and reticence, dates back at least to the 1930s, it was the 1970s before scholarship in this area directed attention beyond the speech classroom to its likely impact on instruction across disciplines. Similarly, whereas books and courses related to teaching communication and later books concerned with speech for teachers (usually public speaking or voice and articulation) were widely used by the 1950s, the first book concerned with communication in the classroom (Hurt, Scott, & McCroskey, 1978) did not appear until the late 1970s. It is not an exaggeration, therefore, to describe the study of communication in instruction as currently still in its infancy.

Although several professional communication associations had interest groups concerned with teaching speech, it was not until 1972 that a professional association established an instructional communication subgroup. In that year, due primarily to the efforts of Barbara Lieb Brilhart of the Speech Communication Association's national office and Robert Kibler of Florida State University, the International Communication Association (ICA) established the Instructional Communication Division. The establishment of this division validated the legitimacy of instructional communication research in the field. It provided convention space for presentation of papers reporting this kind of research and, in 1977 it provided a publication outlet for this research in ICA's *Communication Yearbook* series. For the 15-year period of 1972 to 1986 the professional home of virtually all instructional communication scholars was ICA, and much of the best scholarship in the area was published in the *Communication Yearbook* series.

Unfortunately for instructional communication researchers, the nature of ICA's *Communication Yearbook* series was changed so that top convention papers in the various divisions of the association no longer were published. Fortunately, however, by this time the third oldest journal published by the National Communication Association, *Communication Education,* had broadened its perspective to include instructional communication research as well as scholarship devoted to teaching speech and communication. Several of the journals sponsored by the regional professional associations, particularly *Communication Quarterly* and *Communication Research Reports* published by the Eastern Communication Association, also had become open to submission of papers devoted to instructional communication. Because most of the founders of the instructional communication division were from the "human communication" side of the field, these scholars found new professional homes in the National Communication Association and the various regional associations because all of these had established subdivisions that were open to research in this area. Many of the mass communication scholars continued to consider the ICA to be their primary professional affiliation, as did scholars whose focus was on intercultural aspects of instruction or communication development. However, those with split loyalties retained affiliations with both professional associations. These af-filiations continue at present.

DEFINING THE FIELD OF INSTRUCTIONAL COMMUNICATION

In the early days of instructional communication research there was consid-erable confusion as to what composed scholarship in instructional commu-nication as opposed to scholarship in speech (later, communication) education. As noted previously, a major area within the field of speech had always been speech education. Many observers simply assumed that these two areas of scholarship were the same thing under different names. This misconception probably was fostered by the fact that many of the early re-searchers in instructional communication also published work in communi-cation education.

This concern was addressed in the first article on instructional communi-cation that was published in the *Communication Yearbook* series (Scott & Wheeless, 1977). The authors established the distinction in terms of desired outcomes. They indicated that communication education is scholarship di-rected toward "finding ways to facilitate the acquisition of communication skills among students" (p. 495). In contrast, scholarship in instructional communication is directed toward discovering the ways in which communi-cation variables impact the learning process. Thus, instructional communi-cation is concerned broadly with the role of communication in the teaching–learning process in all fields of education and training, not just in the teaching of speech or communication. It is an applied subdiscipline within the larger communication discipline—much like other applied areas such as organizational communication, health communication, political communication, relational communication, and so on. Hence, it draws its theoretical foundation primarily from the discipline of communication, not the discipline of education.

Instructional communication scholars see their contributions to the fields of education and training as forming the third leg of three-legged stool that provides the foundation for effective teaching and training. The three legs are competence in the subject matter to be taught, competence in peda-gogy, and competence in instructional communication (McCroskey, Rich-mond, & McCroskey, 2002). All are seen as critical aspects of effective teaching and training, and each as representing an independent, but not un-related, scholarly discipline. Thus, instructional communication research-ers do not study education in general or in any specific content field; they study the workings of communication in the instructional process across all disciplines and contexts, including both traditional classroom instruction and training in a variety of contexts.

MEASUREMENT AND DESIGN

During the first few years of active research in the area of instructional communication, most of the investigations involved variables or theories that had originally been advanced in the areas of general communication theory, interpersonal communication, or rhetorical communication. Very little attention was directed toward mass communication or instructional technology. Research designs typically reflected approaches currently in use in other areas of communication. Scholarship in the field of educational psychology also had a major impact on this early research, particularly writings about the multidimensional nature of learning. On the basis of this work, much of the early instructional communication research focused on affective and cognitive learning. Psychomotor learning received then, as well as more recently, much less attention. Because many of the courses taught at the high school and college levels do not involve psychomotor learning, few of the research designs employed have permitted meaningful data collection in this arena.

Measures of affective and cognitive learning presented problems in the early research. In many of the studies of affective learning, measures incorporated items related to affect toward the instructor as well as affect toward the content of the course. This resulted in inflated estimates of affective learning. Later measures have distinguished between affect for instructor and affect for content. As a result, many of the subsequent studies found the impact of instructors' communication behaviors was strongest for instructor affect, but still strong for content affect.

Measuring cognitive learning presented an even more difficult problem. Although valid learning measures can be developed for tightly controlled experiments, very few of these were reported in the early years of research on instructional communication, and very few are being reported currently. The few that have been reported have consistently found cognitive learning effects attributable to instructor communication behaviors. However, most of the studies have been naturalistic observations or questionnaire surveys. In several of the early studies of instructors' communication behaviors impact on learning, the design of the studies included graduate teaching assistants all teaching individual sections of the same course (usually a freshman speech or interpersonal communication course). These multisection courses typically used common teacher-made tests (of low or unknown reliability and validity), common sets of learning objectives (provided to the students as well as the instructors), common textbooks, and common syllabi. Typically, the graduate teaching assistants were carefully trained and permitted very little flexibility in content presented or style of instruction. Not surprisingly (in retrospect), these studies found virtually no association between instructor communication behaviors reported by observers (or by the students) and the students' scores on the tests. The courses were designed to be "teacher proof," and that goal apparently was achieved. Although this research still is frequently cited by critics of newer measurement approaches, it was clear that the designs of these early studies were defective and provided no valid evidence for either the presence or absence of effects of instructors' communication behavior on cognitive learning.

It was also determined that using intact classes in research designs for this type of research was severely limiting in terms of generalizability. Only a few instructors were involved, and they were all teaching communication classes. Although a new design for instructional communication research (asking research participants to respond to an instructor they had before the class in which the data were collected—instead of the instructor in the class in which the data were being collected) overcame this design flaw (Richmond, McCroskey, Kearney, & Plax, 1987), it only aggravated the problem of measuring cognitive learning. No test could be designed that could measure learning in a variety of courses spread throughout the university. Similarly, standardized tests could not be obtained for all classes, but even if they could they would certainly be highly variable in their difficulty level and there was no certainty that the individual course instructor had even attempted to teach what the standardized test measured. Unfortunately, some studies with these design flaws are still being published in our journals and present a serious threat to meta-analyses of the effects on cognitive learning.

Researchers recognizing these problems determined that only two other options for measuring cognitive learning remained open. The most obvious was using final grades as an indicant of cognitive learning. This option has been rejected for good reasons by most researchers. Even if we were to discount the extreme impact on final grades from grade inflation over the past three decades and potential instructor bias, there are many other validity problems with final grades. Grading involves much more than just test scores.

Many courses have homework requirements. Evaluation of such work is probably a better estimate of student motivation and effort than actual learning. Similarly, syllabi indicate that many courses base as much as half of the final grade on participation rather than learning achievement—and others do not include this factor at all. In addition, attendance is a frequent factor in final grades, even though bright students may learn as much from the textbook as they do from attending classes. In sum, grades can be indicants of many things, only one of which might be cognitive learning—and we have no way of knowing what any specific grade may indicate.

As a last resort, researchers have chosen to use student reports of learning. Although no one to our knowledge has argued that this is an ideal method of measuring cognitive learning in the classroom, it has become the most often used method in the instructional communication research literature. Although few, if anyone, would choose this method for determining final grades for a course or for college admission, this method may be acceptable for this kind of research. First, any student is likely to have a pretty good idea what he or she has learned in a course—a view that we hear from students, particularly nontraditional students, regularly. This, of course, does not mean that the student's view and the instructor's grade are in agreement. Again, many things go into determining grades. Second, carefully designed studies can remove most of the self-serving bias that might cause students to inflate their learning estimate by ensuring the students' anonymity and removing any opportunity for students to benefit from exaggerating (or diminishing) their learning estimates. Third, some governmental agencies have used this approach to obtain an estimate of how well schools are achieving their goals, and the goals of their students, with considerable success.

Although many valid criticisms of this approach can and have been made by critics, no better method has been advanced, and no substantive evidence of invalidity has been provided, only speculations. Over time it will be possible to determine with confidence the validity of this approach. The best evidence is comparing the self-report results with the results of carefully designed experiments. So far, the few comparisons available have been very supportive of this approach (Chesebro & McCroskey, 2000; Kelley & Gorham, 1988). However, there is far too little experimental research available to make firm decisions one way or the other. Future meta-analyses of both approaches may be able to provide the critical evidence for the decision in this matter. However, it is important that such studies clearly distinguish studies that have a possibility of finding relationships from those that employ teacher-proof classes or measures from testing and grading systems that do not measure elements that are actually taught in the classroom.

As research in instructional communication has evolved, new concerns with research designs have come to the forefront. Most important of these has been a concern that halo effects might result in artificially high relationships being observed when the same participants are asked to complete both the measures of instructor communication behavior and the measures of learning. This is of particular concern with the design that was developed to attain more generalizability of results. This design asks participants to respond to an instructor the participant has had prior to the class in which the data are collected. Fortunately, even though this concern continues to be expressed (Feeley, 2002), inflation of effect sizes in research employing this research design have been demonstrated not to exist. In fact, the exact opposite has been found to be the case.

The gold standard of research involving instruction is the split-class design, in which students are randomly assigned to complete different measures rather than all students responding to all of the measures employed.

The drawback to this design is that it mandates a by-class analysis of the data rather than a by-student analysis. Hence, the unit of analysis is not the individual student participant but the aggregated data for all of the students in the class. The degrees of freedom for statistical tests are based on the number of classes studied, not the number of individual students who participate in the data collection, hence the power of the data analyses is determined by the number of classes and instructors involved, not the number of students involved. Halo effects on individual student responses are prevented by correlating the mean responses of Group A (who respond to predictor variable measures) with the mean responses of Group B (who respond to criterion variable measures). Obviously, this design requires far more data collection and the involvement of far more participants, both students and instructors, than designs that have all participants completing all measures. As a function of the difficulty in implementing this design and obtaining the participation of the numbers of instructors and students needed, it has been used rarely in instructional communication research.

Fortunately, Christophel (1990) reported landmark research in which the split-class design was used in one study and the class-before-this-one design in another study. The studies were conducted simultaneously with different samples from the same student population. Participant instructor and student samples were drawn from the same population in both studies. The results indicated higher correlations between predictor and criterion variables, and variance accounted for, in the split-class study compared to the class-before-this-one study. Using the latter design resulted in more conservative estimates of the relationships between instructor communication variables and student learning, not higher estimates, which would be expected if halo effects on measurement were present. Although the split-class design is still the best available for instructional communication research, researchers need not discount the use of the class-before-this-one design because of its potential for halo effects (Type I error). It can be criticized, however, for its conservative estimate of observed relationships between instructor communication behaviors and learning outcomes (Type II error). As more research employing the split-class design is reported, meta-analyses of the results of research relating to instructor communication behaviors and student learning need to recognize the potential moderating impact of these design differences.

TARGETS OF STUDY

As the variety of topics represented in the chapters in this book would suggest, research in instructional communication has come to be very diverse over the years since the inception of this scholarly area. Although the initial focus of scholars launching this area was on teacher communication behaviors and their impact on student learning, many aspects of instructional communication, now more broadly defined, have received attention.

Student Factors

One stream of research that began even before professional associations acknowledged instructional communication research has continued to the present: research on communication apprehension (CA). The initial research on CA began long before CA was conceptualized in 1970. In the middle 1930s research on public speaking anxiety, one aspect of CA, was initiated in the speech field. The focus was on speech education, however, not instructional communication. Research on CA generally has examined it as an individual's trait reaction to either actual or anticipated communication. This is a trait that can have many social consequences, only one of which is interference with student learning (see Bourhis, Allen, & Bauman, chap. 13, this volume).

Research by instructional communication scholars has confirmed that CA can cause a wide variety of problems for students in classes across the curriculum, not just those speech or communication classes that require speaking activities. In fact, it is not an exaggeration to conclude from this research that CA may be the most serious learning disability a student can have, both in terms of its severity and its prevalence in approximately 20% of the student body at all levels. As a result, considerable attention from both instructional communication researchers and others with a broader focus has been directed toward discovering means by which CA may be reduced in students and nonstudents alike. Meta-analyses have confirmed a modest level of success for several of these methods. Recent research has implicated genetic factors as causal elements in the development of CA, which may help explain the difficulty researchers have had finding effective methods of reducing it.

Although most of the research on CA and student learning has focused on CA as a student trait, some of the attention of instructional communication researchers has been directed toward CA in teachers. Although specific effects of instructor CA on student learning have not been thoroughly explored, it has been learned that instructors who have a high level of CA are much more likely to teach at the lower elementary (K–5) school level. It is presumed that this is because little children are perceived as less threatening than older learners. Actual study of CA on instructional behaviors of instructors has been very rare, but may be an area that will receive attention in the future. Given the powerful impact that CA has been found to have on communication generally, such research is likely to identify impacts that could be serious in the instructional arena.

CA, of course, has not been the only student communication factor studied. Recent research has indicated that gender (see Jones, Dindia, & Tye, chap. 12, this volume) and culture or ethnicity (see Bradford, Cooper, Allen, Stanley, & Grimes, chap. 11, this volume) of learners can be an important factor in the instructional communication process. Males and females within the U.S. culture have been found to involve themselves in the classroom to different degrees and in different ways. Similarly, the classroom communication behaviors of students from different cultures have been found to be quite different, both with regard to large national cultures as well as cocultures within the larger U.S. culture. Each of these differences has the potential to have a major impact on the instructional communication process in diverse instructional environments and, as a result, each is likely to receive greater attention in the future.

Instructor Factors

For the most part, the central focus of instructional communication research in the recent past has been on instructor communication behaviors. Included among these are instructor use of power strategies, use of affinity-seeking strategies, use of nonverbal immediacy cues, use of assertiveness cues, use of responsiveness cues, use of humor, use of verbal aggression, communicating clearly, use of argument or encouraging disagreement, use of self-disclosures, and engaging in teacher misbehaviors. Although this list certainly does not exhaust all of the topics on which research has been reported, it does represent a cross-section of that work. A simple summary of the results of this work could be that effective teachers use prosocial (but not anti-social) power strategies and a wide variety of affinity-seeking strategies; are nonverbally immediate, assertive, and responsive; are tolerant of disagreement but restrain their use of argument directly with the learner; use humor; use positive (but not negative) self-disclosures; make what they are saying clear to the learner; and avoid both verbal aggression and teacher misbehaviors.

None of these conclusions are particularly surprising (at least to us). Most, if not all, of these conclusions could apply within most communication contexts. In fact, some might even suggest that these behaviors could be used to operationalize the construct of communication competence generally. When we examine the research literature more closely, however, we find much less simplicity in the results than is initially obvious. Several controversies have emerged.

Some of the questions that have arisen probably will stimulate future research. A listing of such questions, and our best guesses (some based on research, others not) as to what might be found follows.

1. Should instructors always avoid use of the antisocial power strategies? For the most part, we think yes. Use of such strategies reduces an in-

structor's ability to subsequently employ the prosocial power strategies, tends to produce students who have negative affect toward both the instructor and the content taught, and lowers students' perceptions of what they have learned in the class. However, when severe circumstances are present, such as a student physically or verbally abusing another student or threatening to do so, an instructor may need to change priorities and employ verbal or even physical behaviors, which would normally be considered off limits, to regain control and prevent harm to students. Such circumstances, of course, are very rare in most instructional environments. Does the necessity of the negative power use negate the normal negative impacts on learning and teacher evaluation in these rare situations? We do not know.

2. Is "the more, the better" the case with use of affinity-seeking strategies? Although the research so far would suggest a positive answer, it is far from proven. We think there probably is a limit to how much use of affinity-seeking strategies can increase positive outcomes. At some point, increased use of affinity-seeking strategies probably levels off. That is, the optimum level of affinity seeking has been reached and using more will not produce continued increases in positive outcomes. However, we do not know whether continued increases in use would result in an actual decline in positive outcomes. We can imagine such a situation as one in which the receivers get tired of gratuitous affinity seeking and see the source as a sycophant. Whether this actually happens in instructional environments is open to future research.

3. Can an instructor be too nonverbally immediate? In a sense, the answer to this question is clearly no. By definition, immediacy is one of the steps along a relational continuum ranging from physical violence to intimacy. Immediacy is the step just before intimacy. So long as an instructor stays at that step, there is no problem. However, moving to the intimacy level of a relationship generally is seen as out of bounds in instructional settings. It is, of course, possible to engage in behaviors that at one level or in one context are seen as immediate and at another level or in another context are seen as intimate. Touch provides an obvious example: Where you touch, who you touch, and how you touch are very different in immediacy than intimacy, but not everyone is sensitive to these differences. At the practical level, we have seen in a number of data sets an indication that the relationship between instructor nonverbal immediacy and positive outcomes is not completely linear. When we have plotted our data, it has been common to observe a strong positive linear relationship up moderately high levels of nonverbal immediacy, and then to note a flattening of the relationship. That is, there is no increase or decrease of positive outcomes when immediacy increases beyond that point. It would appear that in most circumstances more is better when

considering nonverbal immediacy, and when it is not, more still is not worse. Inappropriate intimate behavior, of course, almost always produces negative outcomes.

4. Although both assertiveness and responsiveness of teachers have been found to be positively related to instructional outcomes, is it possible to be too assertive or too responsive? We believe that an instructor can be either too high or too low on either of these behaviors. Although assertiveness and responsiveness are not meaningfully correlated with each other, they seem to work together in instructional environments. Clearly, it is best to be both assertive and responsive, and worst to be neither assertive nor responsive. However, high assertiveness teamed with low responsiveness may result in an instructor being perceived as overly dominant, or even verbally aggressive. Similarly, high responsiveness teamed with low assertiveness may result in an instructor being perceived as an "easy touch," or not in control of the classroom. More research is needed to confirm (or disconfirm) these hypotheses.

5. Is using humor always good? We know that certain kinds of humor do seem to consistently produce positive results. However, not all humor is alike. Humor that makes a student the target of laughter, to mention just one type of humor, is very likely to be seen as inappropriate, particularly by the student who is the target, and may be seen by students as verbally aggressive. Researchers need to develop a clear typology of humor in instruction. This will open the way to determining the limitations of humor in this context.

6. Are verbal aggression and argument ever positive in the instructional context? At this point research has not been able to confirm a positive impact for either of these. However, highly argumentative instructors tend also to be very open to disagreement on the part of their students. Such tolerance for disagreement does seem to be a positive factor in instruction: Instructors with high tolerance for disagreement may encourage more participation and questioning on the part of their students, whereas instructors with lower tolerance may discourage such activity. It may be that it is only when an instructor initiates disagreement or argument with students that negative outcomes occur. Much more research is needed in this area.

7. Is an instructor self-disclosing information about herself or himself while teaching a positive behavior? Although this is a common instructor behavior, there has been little research into its value. The largest study in this area (Sorensen, 1989) determined that positive self-disclosures, particularly those positively worded ones, generated desired outcomes. However, negatively worded self-disclosures did not. It appears that the answer to the question of the value of self-disclosures may be quite complicated. It would seem reasonable that if an instructor discloses "I hate

cats," this might have a positive impact in a class of students who all hate cats, but a negative impact if the class were a group of cat lovers. However, at this point it appears wording disclosures in a positive way is as important as the substance of the disclosure. "I hate cats" is negatively received, whereas "I love cats" is positively received, regardless of the students' views on cats. We believe something is missing here. Future research is needed to clarify this issue.

8. How important is clarity in instruction? It is critical. To date, virtually every study of instructor clarity has pointed to it as one of the most important factors in effective instruction. It may be as important as immediacy (which has received more attention and extremely strong results) to generating positive affect toward both the instructor and the content taught. It may even be more important for cognitive learning. Lack of clarity can prevent cognitive learning or even lead to learning things incorrectly. Future research is likely to refine our understanding of what leads to clarity or the lack of it.

9. How important are instructor misbehaviors? It appears that the answer to this question is "very important." Although there are categories of instructor misbehaviors (incompetence, indolence, and offensiveness) that range in severity, it appears that any behavior on the part of the instructor that students perceive as misbehavior is a serious problem. Even though an instructor may engage in many positive behaviors, it appears that students tend to focus attention on even a single misbehavior. The research in this area is still quite new, so we anticipate future research will refine our current answer to this question.

10. Why are foreign instructors perceived to be so bad? To begin with, not all foreign instructors are perceived to be bad. Some are seen by their students to be as good as, or even better than, their domestic colleagues (McCroskey, 2003). Nevertheless, a negative reaction to foreign instructors in general is common in U.S. colleges and universities. The belief that undergraduate students in the United States generally evaluate their foreign instructors less positively than they evaluate their domestic instructors is correct. This has led to the conclusion that these students are biased against foreign instructors and their bias is the factor producing such evaluations. However, this has been found not to be the case; student ethnocentrism has been found to not be meaningfully related to student evaluations of foreign instructors (McCroskey, 2002, 2003). Rather, it has been found that U.S. students evaluate their foreign instructors on the same bases as they rate their domestic instructors—on such things as assertiveness, responsiveness, immediacy, and so on (McCroskey, 2003). Some, but not all, foreign instructors have previously been enculturated to engage in instructional communication behaviors that are accepted in their home culture but are not considered by students raised in the U.S.

culture to be appropriate. Some, but not all, foreign instructors are able to adapt to the instructional communication behaviors that are effective in this culture.

Although a small amount of instructional communication research has examined instruction in other cultures, we cannot at this time judge whether instructors acculturated in the U.S. culture would be received more or less positively by students in other cultures. On the one hand, the research that has been done in other cultures suggests that the same factors that are associated with effective instruction in the United States (e.g., nonverbal immediacy) are associated with effective instruction in some other cultures. On the other hand, we must never forget the old adage told to sojourners over the centuries: "When in Rome, do as the Romans do." It probably is wise to assume that effective instructional communication is culturally determined, at least until proven otherwise.

The issues raised by these questions are a very important concern to the use of meta-analyses to summarize and interpret the findings of a body of research. Not all effects are reflected as main effects in research. Many effects are a function of a combination (or interaction) of multiple variables. In an area of study such as instructional communication, where relatively few true replications have been conducted (or reported), it is often difficult to tease out these combinations or interactions. Hence, at this point we are often left to speculate about relationships (as we did in several of our answers to the preceding questions) that have not yet received sufficient attention from researchers to enable the appropriate use of meta-analyses. As research in instructional communication grows, however, meta-analyses will become an increasingly important tool.

REFERENCES

Chesebro, J. L., & McCroskey, J. C. (2000). The relationship between students' reports of learning and their actual recall of lecture material: A validity test. *Communication Education, 49,* 297–301.

Christophel, D. M. (1990). The relationships among teacher immediacy behaviors, student motivation, and learning. *Communication Education, 39,* 323–340.

Feeley, T. H. (2002). Evidence of halo effects in student evaluations of communication instruction. *Communication Education, 51,* 225–236.

Hurt, H. T., Scott, M. D., & McCroskey, J. C. (1978). *Communication in the classroom.* Reading, MA: Addison-Wesley.

Kelley, D. H., & Gorham, J. S. (1988). The effects of immediacy on the recall of information. *Communication Education, 37,* 198–207.

McCroskey, L. L. (2002). Domestic and international college instructors: An examination of perceived differences and their correlates. *Journal of Intercultural Communication Research, 31,* 63–83.

McCroskey, L. L. (2003). Relationships of instructional communication styles of domestic and foreign instructors with instructional outcomes. *Journal of Intercultural Communication Research, 32,* 75–96.

McCroskey, L. L., Richmond, V. P., & McCroskey, J. C. (2002). The scholarship of teaching and learning: Contributions from the discipline of communication. *Communication Education, 51,* 383–391.

Richmond, V. P., McCroskey, J. C., Kearney, P., & Plax, T. G. (1987). Power in the classroom VII: Linking behavior alteration techniques with cognitive learning. *Communication Education, 36,* 1–12.

Scott, M. D., & Wheeless, L. R. (1977). Instructional communication theory and research: An overview. In B. D. Ruben (Ed.), *Communication yearbook I* (pp. 495–511). New Brunswick, NJ: Transaction.

Sorensen, G. (1989). The relationships among teachers' self-disclosive statements, students' perceptions, and affective learning. *Communication Education, 38,* 259–277.

II

Educational Practices in the Classroom

3

Pedagogical Issues Underlying Classroom Learning Techniques

Craig Rich
University of Utah

Barbara Mae Gayle
Saint Martin's University

Raymond W. Preiss
University of Puget Sound

Thousands of essays have been devoted to investigating the classroom behaviors associated with student learning. A substantial portion of this body of literature has focused on classroom communication and instructional processes. In this first overview chapter, we preview the organization of meta-analyses presented in this part of the volume and provide the context for the section theme, pedagogy and classroom learning techniques. We believe that all teachers may benefit from studying the literature on instructional theory and practice. Sometimes, "faculty are constrained in their knowledge of teaching by not being aware of alternatives and options" (Kreber & Cranton, 2000, p. 484). Pedagogical, instructional, and curricular knowledge are all needed to engage students in the rigorous challenges involved in course work and to strengthen the educator's own reflections on the success or failure of this endeavor.

PEDAGOGICAL ISSUES AND CLASSROOM PRACTICES

Kreber and Cranton (2000) provided three levels of knowledge associated with instructional practices: pedagogical knowledge, instructional knowledge, and curricular knowledge. *Pedagogical knowledge* encompasses an understanding of the cognitive and affective processes involved in student learning. *Instructional knowledge* involves weighing the advantages and disadvantages of various teaching methods. *Curricular knowledge* is centered on the premise that examining how a course contributes to students' overall knowledge helps educators become more cognizant of the relationship between course design and student learning. Kreber and Cranton (2000) contended that the scholarship of teaching and learning (SoTL) provides educators with an opportunity to demonstrate the convergence of their pedagogical, instructional, and curricular knowledge, affording teachers an opportunity to reflect on the instrumental (learning that is task oriented or problem solving), communicative (understanding what others mean), and emancipatory (overcoming the limitations of self-knowledge and social constraints) learning in that occurs in their classrooms (see chap. 22, this volume, for further discussion). In essence, Kreber and Cranton (2000) conceptualized the types of knowledge required to engage in researching and assessing effective teaching practices. Their framework serves as the organizing principle of this overview chapter.

PEDAGOGICAL KNOWLEDGE

Pedagogical knowledge involves "how to teach the content of a discipline, how to assist students in solving the learning tasks associated with understanding concepts within the discipline, and how to facilitate critical thinking and self-directed learning beyond the discipline" (Kreber & Cranton, 2000, p. 480). Brandt and Perkins (2000) reasoned that pedagogical knowledge must be part of every instructor's professional preparation so that educators are fully versed in how students learn and how to select the most effective teaching techniques possible. A brief review of approaches to the learning literature reveals three learning themes: behaviorism, cognitivism, and constructivism.

Approaches to Learning and Comprehension

A vast body of literature examines how people learn and how to facilitate the learning process. The study of learning is not unified by one explanation for how people learn (Brandt & Perkins, 2000; Grippin & Peters, 1984); rather, the disciplines of education, psychology, and communication studies offer educators multiple views of the mind and learning. The result is that new educational theories often compete with other, more established traditions (Brandt & Perkins, 2000; Grippin & Peters, 1984). Instructors seeking to build pedagogical knowledge must consider multiple ideas and internally inconsistent explanations and propositions of how people learn (Bigge & Shermis, 1992; Brandt & Perkins, 2000). To facilitate educators' understanding of learning theories, many experts group learning theories into paradigms that share a common foundational worldview (Marsick, 1988). Although not comprehensive, the pedagogical literature often includes the behaviorist, cognitivist, and constructivist paradigms of learning as the most salient and informative platforms for instructional practices.

Behaviorism. Often treated as the primary paradigm of learning, behaviorism provides an overarching explanation of the learning process. Rooted in psychology and empiricism and based on works by scientists like Skinner and Pavlov, behaviorism conceptualizes learning as a process of forming connections between stimuli and responses (Bransford, Brown, & Cocking, 2000), or "any more or less permanent change in behavior which is the result of experience" (Borger & Seaborne, 1966, p. 16). In the behaviorism paradigm, learning is an observable outcome or product (a changed behavior) and the expansion of a learner's behavioral repertoire resulting from environmental factors (Brandt & Perkins, 2000; Grippin & Peters, 1984; Williams, 1999). Behaviorist thinking focuses on observable and measurable behavior changes to assess learning (Brandt & Perkins, 2000; Jarvis, Holford, & Griffin, 1998) and maintains that the environment structures and influences a student's learning by garnering attention or eliciting a response (Grippin & Peters, 1984). Thus, the learner's action produces change within the environment and the consequence can either positively reinforce (reward) the behavior, strengthening it, or negatively reinforce (punish) the behavior, weakening it (Brandt & Perkins, 2000; Jarvis et al., 1998; Ulman, 1998). The instructor becomes part of the learner's environment, creating and controlling the learning experience by providing feedback, or positive or negative reinforcement, to externally motivate the learner (Bransford et al., 2000; Grippin & Peters, 1984; Williams, 1999). From this view, the strategies or techniques used to structure the classroom environment affect and are affected by the student learner.

Behaviorists approach learning through the process of accretion. For example, complex behaviors or skills are broken into parts or rough approximations of the target behavior (Brandt & Perkins, 2000). Each task or skill is taught to the learner by reinforcing the appropriate behaviors. After mastery of a prerequisite skill, other graduated steps are added until the complete target behavior is achieved (Brandt & Perkins, 2000; Grippin & Peters, 1984; Ulman, 1998). Frequent and appropriate learning assessment allows instructors to ascertain learner skill mastery, to determine if the learner is ready for the next graduated step, or to determine if instructional procedures need to be altered to avoid learner failure (Ulman, 1998).

Cognitivism.   An alternative paradigm to behaviorism, cognitivism concentrates on the process of knowing (Brandt & Perkins, 2000). Cognitivists focus on changes in the way people conceptualize, organize, and understand their environment (Grippin & Peters, 1984) or the "acquisition of knowledge and cognitive structures due to information processing" (Schunk, 1991, p. 337). Cognitivists contend that "the skills which the learner has may or may not change significantly, but the way in which the learner is now able to use the skills may be totally different from the way she [sic] used them before the learning (reorganization) took place" (Grippin & Peters, 1984, p. 10).

Most cognitive theories of learning focus on the learner's internal structure or mind using central metaphors for learning such as information processing (Brandt & Perkins, 2000). For example, internal structures (psychological structures or schemata) are symbolic representations of past experiences that are systematically or procedurally linked. The learner uses these infrastructures to interpret future experiences, reduce environmental ambiguity, create stability, and select from available environmental stimuli (Grippin & Peters, 1984). As a result, learning is conceptualized as the modification of the learner's internal structure, such that a new experience alters the internal structure (Grippin & Peters, 1984). When a learner is confronted with stimuli that her or his existing structure cannot process, disequilibrium occurs, and to re-create balance, the learner modifies or adds to her or his internal structure (Grippin & Peters, 1984). Overall, cognitivists treat the mind as a rule-governed conceptual device, and the educator's job is to identify how the learner manipulates symbols to arrive at specific learning objectives (Brandt & Perkins, 2000).

In addition to focusing on cognitive structures, some educators link learning to human development (Jarvis et al., 1998; Rideout, 2002). For example, Bruner and Piaget (Vaccaro, 2002) maintained that the stages of human cognitive development change as learners grow older and their abilities to conceptualize their environment evolve. Thus, learning is effective when the content is matched to the learner's cognitive developmental stage, resulting in better learning outcomes (Rideout, 2002). Taken together, the existing cognitive research indicates that educators should employ strategies and techniques in the classroom that simultaneously address developmental stages and cognitive structures of the learner.

Constructivism.   Rather than follow the reasoning of behaviorism or cognitivism, some educators embrace a more contemporary paradigm of learning known as constructivism. According to Williams (1999), constructivism overlaps elements of earlier learning paradigms such as cognitivism and humanism and is a movement highlighting the importance of affective learning, personal meaning and choice, and intrinsic motivation. Thus in the constructivist paradigm, knowledge is impermanent, developmental, subjective, internally constructed, and socially and culturally mediated (Fosnot, 1996). Constructivists "construe learning as an interpretive, recursive, building process by active learners interacting with the physical and social world" (Fosnot, 1996, p. 30). Learning is seen as a constructive, self-regulated activity or process of human meaning making. Learners are thought to struggle with existing personal models of the world and discrepant new ideas as they construct new models of reality (Fosnot, 1996; von Glaserfeld, 1996). Consistent with constructivist thinking, Marlowe and Page (1998) argued that learning occurs when students are active (mentally and physically) and when they build knowledge structures by discovering their own answers and solutions. In addition, active learning occurs when students create their own interpretations and integrate current experiences with past knowledge about a given concept.

Constructivists associate learning with student-centered classrooms. These environments are thought to encourage active learning and critical reflection, as well as a deep understanding of course content. The role of the teacher is viewed as being facilitative, encouraging learners to take ownership of the material and become autonomous in their learning regimen (Fosnot, 1996; Marlowe & Page, 1998). Learning is not tested through repetition of pertinent information, but through learners summarizing ideas in their own words. Students may develop new, critical questions or put their knowledge into action through creative and practical projects (Marlowe & Page, 1998). Although the efficacy of constructivism has been documented by relatively few empirical studies (e.g., Brown & Campione, 1994; Maypoole & Davies, 2001; Palincsar & Brown, 1984), proponents maintain that constructivism promotes an active, student-centered learning environment that engages students in discourse, critical thinking, reflection, and discovery that is informed by a facilitating teacher (Fosnot, 1996; Marlowe & Page, 1998).

Taken together, these three major paradigms (behaviorism, constructivism, and cognitivism) offer educators insights into the way students learn and new avenues to increase their pedagogical knowledge. These understandings allow educators to motivate students with different teaching materials, guide student collaborations, encourage student critical thinking, and promote reflection on the success of teaching practices in terms of student learning.

INSTRUCTIONAL KNOWLEDGE

Not only should educators be mindful of how students learn, but Kreber and Cranton (2000) believed that educators need to enhance their instructional knowledge to "develop teaching materials, ... organize or sequence instruction, ... prepare a lecture, ... construct good tests, ... facilitate discussion" and employ a "variety of instructional methods" (pp. 486–487). Thus, instructional knowledge requires the ability to enhance learning in a classroom setting, design environments that foster student-centered classrooms, and implement active learning processes.

Classroom Learning

According to Bransford et al. (2000), reflection on the learning process influences the choices professors make in selecting strategies and techniques for classroom instruction. An educator's pedagogical knowledge informs her or his instructional knowledge as she or he considers the task or learning at hand, what learning practice is consistent with the task, and what materials are at her or his disposal (Bransford et al., 2000). The connection between learning goals and learning practice affects students' abilities to accomplish course goals (Bransford et al., 2000), and although lecture or text-based methods still have their place as learning practices, contemporary instructional practices suggest that successful learning environments are more student centered, active, and contextually based to allow students to transfer knowledge to new problems, concepts, and settings (Nelson, 1996).

Student-Centered Classrooms.   Lambert and McCombs (1998) reasoned that learning practices should be informed not only by an understanding of the learning process, but also by considering the individual learner. Creating student- or learner-centered classrooms demands that educators focus on individual learners, their experiences, backgrounds, and needs, as well as on the pedagogical knowledge needed to guide learning practices and instructional decision making (McCombs & Whisler, 1997). Land and Hannafin (2000) maintained that engaging and respecting a learner's preexisting perspectives, beliefs, experiences, and differences fosters learner responsibility, promotes deeper understanding, and allows for greater transfer of knowledge to new situations.

Learner-centered instruction employs a diagnostic teaching strategy to discover students' prior knowledge and experience (Bell, 1982a, 1982b). Through observation, dialogue, or assessment of students' work, instructors actively engage learners in constructing new, relevant, and contextually meaningful knowledge (Lambert & McCombs, 1998). To facilitate learner-centered instruction, educators need to be aware of learner differences, such as learning styles, stages of development, or emotional states, and incorporate this knowledge into their classroom practice (Lambert & McCombs, 1998). More broadly, learner-centered classrooms may be seen as communities of discourse (Fosnot, 1996) where instructors facilitate positive, face-supportive, interpersonal classroom interactions. The dialogue fostered in learning-centered classrooms is supportive of students' individual efforts to construct new knowledge through active and authentic activities and learning (Lambert & McCombs, 1998).

Active Learning.   Another instructional practice that goes beyond the learning-by-transmission method requires a commitment to action and opportunities to learn by doing. Child (1991) contended that active learning builds on prior knowledge as students gain new intellectual structures and understanding. Active learning does not simply involve hands-on activity and a lack of teacher involvement (Marlowe & Page, 1998; Mayer, 1998); rather, students are given opportunities to engage in activities with an instructor, fellow classmates, and selected materials that facilitate sense-making and the ability to test cognitive structures and schemata (Marlowe & Page, 1998; Mayer, 1998; Meyers, 1993).

An instructor employing active learning methods seeks "to engage the learner's cognitive processes, such as helping the learner select relevant information, organize that information into a coherent representation, and integrate that representation into existing knowledge" (Mayer, 1998, p. 368). Thus, in active learning classrooms, instructors give a portion of their power and control over the learning process to students, allowing students to take responsibility for their learning and making instructors take on roles of facilitators, designers, or managers of the classroom community (Meyers, 1993).

As a construct, active learning encompasses a variety of strategies and techniques and has been categorized according to those practices. For example, trial-and-error or discovery learning involves using universal instances to create general cases with little instruction (Child, 1991; Jarvis et al., 1998). Experiential learning focuses on the experience of learners in creating and transforming their previous encounters with a topic into knowledge or cognitive structures (Jarvis et al., 1998). Problem-based learning involves using problems or conundrums as the motivation for student activity and learning (Boud & Feletti, 1991). In these instances, the instructor encourages students with support and specific resource material. Additional instruction may be provided in specific areas of learning (Jarvis et al., 1998), or learners may become proficient at working with little instruction (Child, 1991). The goal is for learners to transform experience into knowledge or cognitive structures, work collaboratively in groups and teams to solve problems, and gather the resources needed to succeed (Boud & Feletti, 1991; Child, 1991; Jarvis et al., 1998).

Overall, an educator's instructional knowledge should enhance her or his ability to design a classroom environment that increases the likelihood of student learning, develop learner-centered activities that motivate both teacher and student, and implement active learning processes that promote deeper understanding. Thus, educators can use their pedagogical and instructional knowledge to provide guidance, motivation, and reinforcement to improve student learning.

CURRICULAR KNOWLEDGE

Not only should educators understand the nature of student learning (pedagogical knowledge) and identify the teaching practices that are likely to enhance student learning (instructional knowledge), they must also know how to clearly articulate and measure course objectives and determine whether their courses fit into the existing sequence of courses (curricular knowledge). This curricular knowledge was described by Kreber and Cranton (2000) as enabling educators to "judge the quality of their course goals"; identify how their course enhances students' knowledge, skills, and abilities; and make meaningful adaptations to their course design to meet the academic challenge of a specific major or program (p. 480). Additionally, curricular knowledge helps educators make the pedagogical underpinnings of their course design visible, specify the learning outcomes desired, and identify what would constitute evidence that student learning had occurred. In essence, educators use curricular knowledge to investigate the intersection among pedagogical knowledge, instructional practices, and curricular design to engage in what that Hutchings (1999) called the "richer conversation about educational purposes and processes" (p. 207).

At the core of curricular knowledge is an emphasis on assessing student learning and deep understanding. What constitutes good assessment practices—those that are systematic, continuous, and crafted to produce constructive information used to improve student learning—is the subject of numerous published essays and books. At the very heart of the curricular knowledge discussion is whether assessment results will be used summatively to make judgments about the success or failure of specified courses and programs, or whether the process will be used formatively to engage in ongoing improvements to the teaching and learning process. Regardless of the approach employed, curricular knowledge should be used to establish "an improvement process not just a measuring process" (Shavelson & Huang, 2003, p. 14). In other words, educators must know how to "conduct research on student learning, interpret the results of the assessment, and reflect on those interpretations to advance" their own teaching and curricular design (Maki, 2002, p. 5).

The focus of most assessment research has been on course outcomes and the measurement techniques that best helped institutions or programs determine whether student performance is meeting expectations. Recently, a shift has occurred that refocuses assessment procedures "from measuring teaching by what is taught or other teacher behaviors to measuring what is learned" (Nelson, 1996, p. 172). Maki (2002) believed that a "good practice in assessment involves using multiple methods to assess student learning" (p. 31). Banta (1993) and Palomba and Banta (1999) discussed a variety of approaches to assessment, including developing institution-specific tools such as capstone courses and senior projects, to gain a more holistic view of the efficacy of the curriculum. On the other hand, Davis and Wavering (1999) advocated alternative assessment methods such as cooperative learning groups and peer teaching protocols to link teaching and assessment. These measures should "involve students in real world challenges and increase graduates' potential for becoming active contributors to society" (Davis & Wavering, 1999, p. 55).

Other approaches to curricular knowledge suggest that good assessment practices are not only closely aligned with what we would consider good teaching practices, but also provide a more unified approach to assessment. Holistic assessment produces a wealth of information that can illuminate learning outcomes. Hutchings (1999) advised educators to concentrate on the learning process, explore what students are learning from a variety of points of view and in multiple settings, and put student learning into context to understand how the specified outcomes occur. She advised educators to increase their curricular knowledge by studying what is known about students entering an institution or program, student course-taking patterns, how those patterns are related to learning outcomes, and how students experience the institution. She also suggested that putting curricular knowledge into a context requires identifying what students are contributing to their own learning, what students are able to do with what they know, what patterns characterize successful students moving through the institution, and what judgments students make about their overall learning. This view stresses the instructor's obligation to use assessment as a vehicle for modifying and improving pedagogical practices.

Other voices are also beginning to shift curricular knowledge into the arena of student involvement in assessment practices. Gregory (2001) believed that all educators need to remember that "exposing students to a well-thought out curriculum is not the same thing as educating them" (p. 69). His approach supports Boud's (2000) reasoning that students should be active participants in the assessment and learning conversation. Involving students in their own assessment helps them plan a lifelong assessment strategy. Boud (2000) advised educators to "focus as much on the judgments they make about learning as on [the] learning tasks themselves" (p. 154), abandon normed assessment methods that measure students against one another, and adopt a standards-based approach that helps students know whether they have achieved the desired outcome. He also urged that feedback on learning be separated from grading and that it be private and linked to opportunities for improvement, so that students recognize the external cues they might employ to emphasize learning rather than performance. Essentially, Boud (2000) reasoned that engaging students in frequent self- and peer assessment enhances their own sense of what they are learning, encourages self-initiated behaviors, and prepares students for the ongoing assessment activities they will perform during the rest of their lives.

Taken together, these approaches to enhancing an instructor's curricular knowledge frame assessment as part of a broader educational conversation. This discussion stresses the interdependence of curricular, pedagogical, and instructional knowledge. Because assessment is also an act of communication about what is valued, it conveys institutional commitments about what we think is important to be learned and how disciplinary content should be learned. Boud (2000) argued that curricular knowledge should focus both "on the immediate task and on the implications for equipping students for lifelong learning in an unknown future" (p. 160).

Overall, an instructor's pedagogical, instructional, and curricular knowledge will maximize student learning. The ability to create classroom cultures that nurture deep understanding and learning is likely to occur because of systematically combining the most prevalent features in each of the knowledge areas.

CONCLUSION

The meta-analyses in this section illuminate basic issues associated with creating a learning-conducive classroom environment. Timmerman and Kruepke (chap. 6, this volume) used pedagogical knowledge to investigate the efficacy of computer-assisted instruction in enhancing student performance. Preiss, Gayle, and Allen (chap. 7, this volume) and Shapiro, Kerssen-Griep, Gayle, and Allen (chap. 5, this volume) investigate aspects of instructional capabilities in increasing student learning outcomes, and Berkowitz (chap. 4, this volume) and Burrell, Zirbel, and Allen (chap. 8, this volume) explore curricular processes in enhancing student learning. Preiss et al. explore the relationship between test anxiety and study skills, and Shapiro et al. investigate the ability of Microsoft PowerPoint to promote learning. Berkowitz investigated whether developing critical thinking through forensics can enhance student learning, and Burrell et al. evaluated the curricular success of peer mediation in an educational setting. Taken together, these studies weigh the efficacy of using specific ideas to construct effective preclass, in-class, and postclassroom experiences. Our intent is to initiate a conversation about learner-conducive classrooms, and the discussion must involve teachers assessing their classrooms by reflecting on the available literature. This process assures advances through meta-analysis.

REFERENCES

Banta, T. W. (1993). *Making a difference: Outcomes of a decade of assessment in higher education.* San Francisco: Jossey-Bass.

Bell, A. W. (1982a). Diagnosing student misconceptions. *The Australian Mathematics Teacher, 1,* 6–10.

Bell, A. W. (1982b). Treating students' misconceptions. *The Australian Mathematics, 2,* 11–13.

Bigge, M. L., & Shermis, S. S. (1992). *Learning theories for teachers* (5th ed.). New York: HarperCollins.

Borger, R., & Seaborne, A. E. M. (1966). *The psychology of learning.* Harmondsworth, UK: Penguin.

Boud, D. (2000). Sustainable assessment: Rethinking assessment for the learning society. *Studies in Continuing Education, 22,* 151–167.

Boud, D., & Feletti, G. (1991). *The challenge of problem based learning.* London: Kogan Page.

Brandt, R. S., & Perkins, D. N. (2000). The evolving science of learning. In R. S. Brandt (Ed.), *Yearbook/Association for Supervision and Curriculum Development* (pp. 159–183). Alexandria, VA: Association for Supervision and Curriculum Development.

Bransford, J. D., Brown, A. L., & Cocking, R. R. (Eds.). (2000). *How people learn: Brain, mind, experience, and school: Expanded edition.* Washington, DC: National Academy Press.

Brown, A. L., & Campione, J. C. (1994). Guided discovery in a community of learners. In K. McGilly (Ed.), *Classroom lessons: Integrating cognitive theory and classroom practice* (pp. 229–270). Cambridge, MA: MIT Press.

Child, D. (1991). *Psychology and the teacher* (6th ed.). London: Cassell.

Davis, M. A., & Wavering, M. (1999). Alternative assessment: New directions in teaching and learning. *Contemporary Education, 71,* 49–56.

Fosnot, C. T. (1996). Constructivism: A psychological theory of learning. In C. T. Fosnot (Ed.), *Constructivism: Theory, perspectives, and practice* (pp. 8–33). New York: Teachers College Press.

Gregory, M. (2001). Curriculum, pedagogy, and teaching ethos. *Pedagogy, 1,* 69–89.

Grippin, P., & Peters, S. (1984). *Learning theories and learning outcomes: The connections.* Lanham, MD: University of America Press.

Hutchings, P. (1999). Behind outcomes: Contexts and questions for assessment. In B. A. Pescosolido & R. Aminzade (Eds.), *The social worlds of higher education: Handbook for teaching in the new century* (pp. 206–217). Thousand Oaks, CA: Pine Forge Press.

Jarvis, P., Holford, J., & Griffin, C. (1998). *The theory and practice of learning.* London: Kogan Page.

Kreber, C., & Cranton, P. A. (2000). Exploring the scholarship of teaching. *The Journal of Higher Education, 71,* 476–495.

Lambert, N. M., & McCombs, B. L. (1998). Introduction: Learner-centered schools and classrooms as a direction for school reform. In N. M. Lambert & B. L. McCombs

(Eds.), *How students learn: Reforming schools through learner-centered education* (pp. 1–22). Washington, DC: American Psychological Association.

Land, S. M., & Hannafin, M. J. (2000). Student-centered learning environments. In D. H. Jonassen & S. M. Land (Eds.), *Theoretical foundations of learning environments* (pp. 1–23). Mahwah, NJ: Lawrence Erlbaum Associates.

Maki, P. (2002). Moving from paperwork to pedagogy: Channeling intellectual curiosity into a commitment to assessment. *Bulletin, 54*(9), 3–5.

Marlowe, B. A., & Page, M. L. (1998). *Creating and sustaining the constructivist classroom.* Thousand Oaks, CA: Corwin.

Marsick, V. J. (1988). Learning in the workplace: The case for reflectivity and critical reflectivity. *Adult Education Quarterly, 38*(4), 187–198.

Mayer, R. E. (1998). Cognitive theory for education: What teachers need to know. In N. M. Lambert & B. L. Combs (Eds.), *How students learn: Reforming schools through learner-centered education* (pp. 353–377). Washington, DC: American Psychological Association.

Maypoole, J., & Davies, T. G. (2001). Students' perceptions of constructivist learning in a communication college American history II survey course. *Community College Review, 29*(2), 54–79.

McCombs, B. L., & Whisler, J. S. (1997). *The learner-centered classroom and school: Strategies for enhancing student motivation and achievement.* San Francisco: Jossey-Bass.

Meyers, C. (1993). *Promoting active learning: Strategies for the college classroom.* San Francisco: Jossey-Bass.

Nelson, C. E. (1996). Student diversity requires different approaches to college teaching, even in math and science. *American Behavioral Scientist, 40,* 165–175.

Palincsar, A. S., & Brown, A. L. (1984). Reciprocal teaching of comprehension-fostering and comprehension-monitoring activities. *Cognition and Instruction, 1,* 117–175.

Palomba, C. A., & Banta, T. W. (1999). *Assessment essentials: Planning, implementing and improving assessment in higher education.* San Francisco: Jossey-Bass.

Rideout, R. R. (2002). Psychology and music education. *Music Educators Journal, 89*(1), 33–37.

Schunk, D. H. (1991). *Learning theories: An educational perspective.* New York: Macmillan.

Shavelson, R. J., & Huang, L. (2003, January-February). Responding responsibly: To the frenzy to assess learning in higher education. *Change,* pp. 11–19.

Ulman, J. D. (1998). Applying behaviorological principles in the classroom: Creating responsive learning environments. *The Teacher Educator, 34,* 144–156.

Vaccaro, V. (2002). Summaries of various educational philosophers. *National Teaching and Learning Forum, 11*(4), 2.

von Glaserfeld, E. (1996). Introduction: Aspects of constructivism. In C. T. Fosnot (Ed.), *Constructivism: Theory, perspectives, and practice* (pp. 8–33). New York: Teachers College Press.

Williams, R. L. (1999). The behavioral perspective in contemporary education. *The Teacher Educator, 35*(2), 44–60.

4

Developing Critical Thinking Through Forensics and Communication Education: Assessing the Impact Through Meta-Analysis

Sandra J. Berkowitz
University of Maine

We all want our students to be critical thinkers, define who "we" is but what do we mean when we say that? The importance of critical thinking is borne out by continuing discussions in everyday life. Managers and CEOs argue for the importance of critical thinking and decry the lack of attention given to it in schools; "We need to refocus on content in our communications. What we communicate and how well we communicate will always be more important than the medium of communication" (Dilenschneider, 2001, p. 26). In our increasing technological age, critical thinking remains central; "At the heart of design and engineering is critical thinking. The ability to separate what is worthwhile from what isn't is the hallmark of the best in many fields, from film directors to project managers, programmers to designers" (Berkun, 2001). Critical thinking is an important issue of discussion in multiple disciplines including communication, education, nursing, and psychology. There are debates over definition (e.g., Facione, 1998) and discussions about specific teaching strategies (e.g., Fritz & Weaver, 1986: Garside, 1996; Palmerton, 1992; Powell, 1992).

One question that combines issues of definition and teaching strategy is whether specific communication courses and activities, such as forensics and debate, improve the critical thinking of participants. In a time of cost consciousness in schools and colleges, being able to document such an impact is particularly important. Because this chapter is based on previously published meta-analyses of the impact of forensics and communication education courses on critical thinking (M. Allen, Berkowitz, Hunt, & Louden, 1999; M. Allen, Berkowitz, & Louden, 1995), the focus is on considering current discussions about critical thinking, reviewing the results of the meta-analyses, and drawing implications for forensics and debate activities, curriculum development and teaching strategies, and for other areas of communication theory.[1]

WHAT IS CRITICAL THINKING?

Critical thinking is a contested term. There is no single accepted meaning for the term within the discipline, and certainly not without. The purpose of this section is to provide a context for understanding what a critical thinking meta-analysis measures and why those assessments are significant.

Most people would agree with O'Keefe's (1986) description that critical thinking is "thought processes which involve more abstract operations" (p. 4). Paul and Elder (1999) argued that "it is part of many teachers' mind sets that students cannot learn abstract ideas and that abstract ideas are, therefore, not very 'practical.' Not so. 'Abstractions' are often the key to the most powerful 'learning'" (p. 34). They went on to outline a set of important ideas about learning generated by critical thinking:

1. Look for interrelationships (try to connect everything together).
2. Solidify your learning goals (what exactly is your purpose?).
3. Ask yourself what the question (or problem or issue) is you are trying to answer.
4. Clarify the information you need (to answer the question or solve the problem).
5. Figure out what the information is telling you (what inferences you can legitimately make).
6. Trace (and assess) the implications of your thinking (what follows from thinking this rather than that).
7. Figure out the key ideas that will help you answer the question or solve the problem.
8. Make sure you are adopting the most reasonable point of view with respect to the issue.

---

[1]The findings reported in this chapter are summaries of the major findings in the original meta-analysis. For more detailed information about methods and findings, please see the original meta-analysis and the studies coded therein.

9. Check your assumptions (should you be taking this or that for granted?). (p. 34)

Such an outline provides a useful checklist for both students and instructors.

However, it does not provide a list of specific skills and aptitudes, which teachers of communication, argumentation, and debate need. Facione (1998), summarizing the results of a consensus of experts, indicated that the core cognitive skills of critical thinking are interpretation, analysis, evaluation, and inference. He continued,

> Beyond being able to interpret, analyze, evaluate and infer, good critical thinkers can do two more things. They can explain what they think and how they arrived at that judgment. And, they can apply their powers of critical thinking to themselves and improve on their previous opinions. These two skills are called "explanation" and "self-regulation." (p. 5)

In total, these six skills help us to not only understand and interact with the world, but also keep our learning organized (Paul & Elder, 1999), creating what a consensus of experts describes as the ideal critical thinker:

> The ideal critical thinker is habitually inquisitive, well-informed, trustful of reason, open-minded, flexible, fair-minded in evaluation, honest in facing personal biases, prudent in making judgments, willing to reconsider, clear about issues, orderly in complex matters, diligent in seeking relevant information, reasonable in the selection of criteria, focused in inquiry, and persistent in seeking results which are precise as the subject and the circumstances of inquiry permit. (1994 statement, cited in Facione, 1998, p. 14)

As educators, we read in our communication and argumentation and debate textbooks about the importance of critical thinking. Many of the exercises and assignments indicate that they improve students' critical thinking abilities: Exercise A strengthens Skill X, and so on. Clearly, critical thinking is a goal of most communication and argumentation classes and forensic activities. But what impact do communication and argumentation classes and forensics and debate activities have on critical thinking, on the creation of the ideal critical thinker? And How can we maximize critical thinking in our classes and activities?

THE IMPACT OF FORENSICS AND COMMUNICATION CLASSES ON CRITICAL THINKING

Studies of the impact of forensics, debate, and communication courses on critical thinking have been done for a number of decades. Most often a

group of students—forensics or debate participants or students in classes—
have been selected for testing. Some studies used a longitudinal design, in
which a pretest and posttest were done with the same group, comparing results over time. The conclusion is that the greater the change, the greater
the improvement in critical thinking. Other studies utilized a cross-sectional design, whereby a static posttest was used, comparing the group who
received training with a group who did not. Again, because each group presumably begins at the same level, the greater the change in the end, the
greater the improvement in critical thinking prompted by forensics activities and communication and argumentation classes. The number of unpublished reports has grown over time and has not been accounted for in the
published research. Thus, as the numbers of studies of critical thinking and
communication activities have grown, so has the diversity of those studies.

In addition to the growth in the number of studies, there has been growing criticism of the research focused in two areas: critiques of how critical
thinking is measured and critiques of the samples used for analysis. The
Watson–Glaser test (in all its variety of forms) is the predominant test form
used. Questions remain as to whether these types of paper-and-pencil tests
can really measure critical thinking. A second criticism is that forensics participants are self-selecting, thus making comparisons between forensics participants and nonparticipants unfair, as forensics participants may choose
the activity because of preexisting higher levels of critical thinking.
Although these problems have been identified with various individual longitudinal and cross-sectional studies, they become reasons to do a meta-
analysis: "The advantage of meta-analysis as a literature summarization
technique is that the arguments about measurement and design become the
sources and reasons for conducting the analysis rather than for a rejection of
the conclusions" (M. Allen et al., 1999, p. 20).

After a literature search for both published and unpublished manuscripts, 23 were coded. Longitudinal, cross-sectional, and combination
studies were included. A variety of communication skill experiences were
investigated, including public speaking, argumentation, debate, and discussion classes, and competitive forensics participation, including debate, individual events, discussion, mock trial, and other forms of competitive events.
Watson–Glaser and the other measures were investigated and reported separately. Although the meta-analysis could not adequately address continuing questions about the reliance on Watson–Glaser as opposed to other
measures, it did provide important insights into the relationship between
critical thinking and communication skill experiences.

Perhaps the most important finding was that regardless of measure, design, or communication skill taught, critical thinking improved as a result of
communication training. Specifically, participation in public speaking
courses increased critical thinking skills (average $r = .145$, variance $= .066$,

$k = 6$, N = 531, 95% CI $\pm$ .082), participation in argumentation-type classes increased critical thinking skills (average r = .129, variance = .012, $k = 5$, N = 549, 95% CI $\pm$ .081), and participation in various types of competitive forensics improved critical thinking (average r = .203, variance = .010, $k = 8$, N = 1,577, 95% CI $\pm$ .047). In addition, all methods of communication skills training stimulate gains in critical thinking. The largest effect was gains in competitive forensics compared with public speaking classes (d = .89) or argumentation classes (d = 1.14). Finally, cross-sectional data fostered a number of comparisons. Compared to a control group, the communication skills group demonstrated larger gains in critical thinking (average r = .241, variance = .025, k = 10, N = 1,526, 95% CI $\pm$ .047). Participants in competitive forensics demonstrated greater gains compared with participants in argumentation or public speaking classes (average r = .271, variance = .015, $k = 5$, N = 455, 95% CI $\pm$ .084). And, finally, participants in argumentation or "enhanced" public speaking classes demonstrated greater gains in critical thinking compared with "normal" public speaking classes (average r = .364, variance = .022, $k = 5$, N = 362, 95% CI $\pm$ .086). Clearly, the results demonstrate gains in critical thinking with participation in communication skills activities.

The implications of these results for communication education are significant. First, for the forensics and debate communities, these findings provide justification for the continuation of current programs and development of new courses. In a recent sociological analysis, Fine (2001) examined the world of high school debate and described not only the culture, but also the citizenship skills that are developed. This meta-analysis provides important empirical data about the specific critical thinking skills that are part and parcel of the development of citizenship. In an era of cost consciousness, directors of debate and forensic programs need empirical data to demonstrate educational accountability. Forensic programs can meet educational goals of developing the critical thinking ability of students. Second, the results of this meta-analysis address questions about accountability in public speaking and argumentation classes. Such classes provide opportunities for more than the mere practice of speaking and arguing. Public speaking and argumentation classes provide significant instruction in the skills of critical thinking as well as important opportunities to hone the skills through research, listening, and speaking exercises. The results are demonstrated in improvements in critical thinking measures.

At the same time, these results raise questions. Should more aspects of argumentation be incorporated in public speaking classes? Into other courses? Are the critical thinking categories currently developed sufficient? The original article focuses on the how the results can be used to answer calls for educational accountability, but the analysis can be extended into additional areas.

CRITICAL THINKING AND EDUCATION

Critical thinking is central to what we understand as education:

> Liberal education is about learning to learn, to think for yourself, on your own and in collaboration with others. Liberal education leads us away from naïve acceptance of authority, above self-defeating relativism, and beyond ambiguous contextualism. It culminates in principled reflective judgment. Learning critical thinking, cultivating the critical spirit, is not just a means to this end, it is part of the goal itself. People who are poor critical thinkers, who lack the dispositions and skills described, cannot be said to be liberally educated, regardless of the academic degrees they may hold. (Facione, 1998, p. 12)

In the continuing debates over curriculum development and teaching practices, we need to consider critical thinking once again. It is not just a means, a skill, and a strategy. It is a goal, and as such we should be thinking about how and why particular activities are effective in developing critical thinking.

In a recent issue of *Communication Education* devoted to a discussion of communication curriculum, authors gleaned sets of expectations or core skills. Morreale and Backlund (2002) provided a historical overview of the developments of communication curricula. There are several different ways that core skills have been identified. They have been described as speaking and listening competencies; as essential communication skills in areas such as public speaking and interpersonal and group contexts; as basic skills for persuading, informing, and relating; as expectations for speaking and listening; and as communication competencies. Critical thinking is identifiable in some of these competencies. For example, the Standards for General Education Speech Communication Courses in Maryland Higher Education Institutions includes these statements:

> Competent communicators can:
>
> a. distinguish among statements of fact, inference, and opinion; between emotional and logical arguments; and between objective and biased messages,
>
> b. effectively analyze and evaluate the content and delivery of verbal and nonverbal messages, and
>
> c. express opinions and ask questions constructively. (Morreale & Backlund, 2002, p. 17)

Elements of critical thinking are contained in the competency, including interpretation, evaluation, and a level of explanation. Similarly, Rosenthal (2002) outlined curricular goals and competencies with suggested methods by which to achieve those competencies. For example, to fulfill a competency in "reflective construction and analysis of arguments" (p. 23), one could take an argument course, complete a significant assignment in reflective construction and analysis of arguments, or complete a capstone experience or scholarly service learning project. Developments such as these are welcome, not necessarily as a way to come to consensus, but as ways to operationalize goals and competencies.

These efforts reflect the idea articulated in the original study for the need to better understand the impact of specific techniques, assignments, and activities on the development of critical thinking skills. However, it would be useful to attend more to the specific outcomes of critical thinking. Framing these discussions in terms of measurable aspects of critical thinking can provide another level of accountability for such curricular developments. For example, one specific issue that continues to be discussed on myriad college campuses is communication courses as general education requirements. Because communication courses tend to be included among those students may take to fulfill general education requirements, assessment remains at issue. The acknowledgment of critical thinking components or foundations in existing courses, and the inclusion of critical thinking in other courses, can help answer the question "What is the role of communication curriculum in general education?" (T. H. Allen, 2002, p. 37).

Curriculum and content development is only one issue when addressing the role of communication education. Without effective instructors, the development of critical thinking in students will be impaired. Students need to become aware of the complexity of ideas, have frequent direct opportunities to practice skills of analysis and evaluation, and have opportunities to engage conflicting perspectives and information (Browne, 2000). This requires not only time, but also awareness and commitment of the instructor:

> Teachers in higher education often have a single clear model of their instructional role. They are experts about a body of knowledge; the students are seeking that knowledge. Thus, the one with the knowledge speaks; the one seeking the knowledge listens. The clarity of this model, however, should not be confused with its effectiveness. Lectures, even at their most eloquent and persuasive, possess a major inadequacy, viz., they fail to provide the learner with the opportunity to practice using the knowledge under the guidance of a skilled mentor. (Browne, 2000, p. 303)

These weaknesses do not mean that one should never lecture. Rather, lecturers need to realize that they can model critical thinking skills and balance lecturing with other teaching techniques. Similarly, we need to reconsider how discussions are led. Are we modeling critical thinking skills through the use of combinations of open-ended, probing, divergent, and higher order questions?[2] If we advocate training our students to be more critical consumers of information and better and more critical participants in society, shouldn't we be more self-reflexive about these issues, especially as we enact them in the classroom? A recent section of *Communication Studies* devoted to a discussion of teaching philosophies (Burrell, 2001; Simonds, 2001; Turman, 2001; Turner, 2001; Worley, 2001) illustrates the advantages of being self-reflexive about teaching. By focusing on critical thinking issues in a statement of teaching philosophy, one can move beyond an individualized statement to a philosophy of teaching that is grounded in specific concepts, with specific goals. At a time when many instructors are required to teach disparate courses, a focus on critical thinking can provide a common, positive theme.

As we consider teaching philosophies and curriculum development, we must ask this: In what courses should critical thinking be developed? Or, perhaps, in what courses is critical thinking already being incorporated? The original study focused on forensics activities and public speaking and argumentation courses. That is neither surprising nor unwarranted. It is important to assess critical thinking developments in areas that are so directly associated with critical thinking. There are significant gains made in each area; but the results of the meta-analysis also point to the fact that as we move to incorporate activities and teaching strategies into other classes, we need to inquire about the effects on critical thinking. When a small group textbook (Harris & Sherblom, 2002) incorporates an activity of a "non-debate," an assignment in which students must choose sides on a controversial topic, and while one side presents their arguments the other must listen, take notes, and then paraphrase the position, it is an illustration of the integration of critical thinking and listening into the class. Critical listening and critical thinking are not relegated to a single obligatory chapter. Critical thinking becomes the foundation for effective group interactions.

Understanding critical thinking and lived experiences means that critical thinking activities occur in seemingly unrelated courses and issues. For example, when a public service campaign to reduce drug use suggests that we "ask where your kids are" (National Youth Anti-Drug Media Campaign, n.d.), public relations, advertising, media, and persuasion classes may engage in interpretation, evaluation, and critical reflective judgment. Similarly, critical thinking impacts our everyday experiences. So, a discussion of uncertainty reduction in the context of family communication can also be an opportunity for discussion and development of critical thinking skills. Finally, there is the example of critical thinking and ethics. Kienzler (2001) ar-

---

[2]There are a number of useful Web sites that provide resources for leading discussions, including those of the Center for Teaching Excellence, University of Kansas, the College Writing Program, Vanderbilt University, the Teaching and Learning Center, University of Nebraska, at Lincoln, and the Teaching Resources Center at Indiana University.

gued that critical thinking pedagogy creates a supportive environment in which ethics can be effectively engaged. She identified four characteristics of critical thinking that promote ethical discussion and behavior: "identifying and questioning assumptions, seeking a multiplicity of voices and alternatives on a subject, making connections, and fostering active involvement" (p. 319). What critical thinking creates is an entire context:

> Perhaps the biggest advantage of the critical thinking environment is that its ethics permeate the entire course, not just a discrete unit on ethics. The critical thinking environment focuses not on a right answer or document but on an extensive collection of ethical procedures for both instructors and students. It adds ethics to audience, context, and purpose as a basic part of rhetorical analysis for all communication. It adds ethics to classroom interaction, including information gathering, collaboration, and communicating. (p. 336)

Critical thinking can be identified in a variety of classes and ways. I am not arguing that the results of the original meta-analysis can be extrapolated to all other contexts and courses. However, if we begin to see critical thinking along a continuum rather than as merely equated with traditional contexts and understandings of argument, we can open up new avenues for research. In what classes, besides public speaking and argument, is critical thinking foundational, and is it therefore advisable to measure the development of critical thinking? For what activities should gains in critical thinking be measured? In asking these questions, we can develop additional ways of understanding how critical thinking works in our everyday lives and in our own academic classes.

Not only does the meta-analysis prompt new questions and research areas, but it also provides a model for how we can test the outcomes of different tests and teaching strategies. When the original meta-analysis was done, the majority of studies coded used Watson–Glaser as the measure. As indicated in the discussion in the original study, further meta-analyses of studies using additional measures are necessary to address any weaknesses in the use of Watson–Glaser. Recent U.S. Department of Education (2000a, 2000b) documents outline the number of tests that are now being used to measure gains in critical thinking, as shown in Table 4.1.

The U.S. Department of Education (2000a) further provides 12 pages of tables listing the skills and subskills for each of seven categories of critical thinking: interpretation, analysis, evaluation, inference, presenting arguments, reflection and dispositions, and correlating those with the tests. For example, under inference, one of the skills is drawing conclusions and a subskill is developing and using criteria for making judgments. That subskill is measured by 6 of the 12 tests, whereas the subskill of reasoning well with divergent points of view is only measured by one test. This type of information

TABLE 4.1
A Sample of Critical Thinking Tests

Acronym	Test Name
A. Profile	Academic Profile
CAAP	Collegiate Assessment of Academic Proficiency
CCTDI	California Critical Thinking Dispositions Inventory
CTAB	CAAP Critical Thinking Assessment Battery
CCTST	California Critical Thinking Skills Test
CCTT	Cornell Critical Thinking Test
COMP	College Outcomes Measures Program—Objective Test
ETS TASKS	ETS Tasks in Critical Thinking
MID	Measure of Intellectual Development
PSI	Problem Solving Inventory
RJI	Reflective Judgment Inventory
WGCTA	Watson–Glaser Critical Thinking Appraisal

Note. Adapted from U.S. Department of Education (2000a).

might be useful in helping to determine which measure of critical thinking development one might use in a specific setting. However, it continues to treat measures and the studies that use them as separate entities. The critical thinking meta-analysis can serve as a model for how to test across different articulations of critical thinking skills and across different measures.

Meta-analysis is not only a tool to deal with measurement differences; it can also provide a way to investigate interdisciplinary issues. One such issue is communication across the curriculum or speaking across the curriculum. Morello (2000) argued that such programs need to establish themselves as valuable in their own right so that they will not be perceived as not having their own theoretical base. Dannels (2002) concurred and suggested further that given that communication across the curriculum is done in and with specific disciplines, it is important to learn about the specific disciplines' cultures. One of her conclusions is that theoretical depth of communication across the curriculum can be found in that orality is a site for disciplinary knowledge construction:

> The oral presentations became sites for reproducing the norms, epistemologies, and values of that particular discipline. As more and more communication departments engage in interdisciplinary outreach in the name of improving commu-

nication competence—whether it be through the basic course or CXC programs —it is important to consider that oral communication is not simply an add-on to the discipline, but rather a potentially critical part of the way in which students and faculty construct and negotiate disciplinary epistemologies, discourses and practices. (p. 265)

The language Dannels used is quite reminiscent of the idea that critical thinking creates a context for the engagement of ethics. In this case, is it critical thinking that provides an environment for disciplinary knowledge construction? Is the negotiation of disciplinary epistemologies, discourses, and practices enabled through critical thinking strategies? These are questions worth investigating.

In the continuing conversations about curriculum development, teaching strategies, and interdisciplinary issues, an ideal communication curriculum (Morreale & Backlund, 2002) or set of teaching strategies is elusive at best. Assessing improvements in critical thinking positions critical thinking as a goal and not merely as a means to another end. Thus, it provides accountability data and much more.

CRITICAL THINKING AND CRITICAL THINKERS

In focusing on critical thinking, we want to teach our students to recognize the layered meanings of language.

> If we are committed to helping students think well with concepts, we must teach them how to strip off surface language and consider alternative ways to talk and think about things. This includes teaching them how to closely examine the concepts they have personally formed as well as those into which they have been socially indoctrinated. (Elder & Paul, 2001b, p. 43)

It is a challenging way to teach, to teach empowerment through critical thinking.

Is this too grandiose a goal, to teach empowerment? Does the development of critical thinking through communication classes and activities serve only more modest goals? The answer to both questions is no. As demonstrated in discussions about academic debate, empowerment is a realistic and even necessary goal. Warner and Bruschke (2001) argued that "empowerment is the ability to change one's own life and one's community, empowerment occurs at both individual and community levels, and the most crucial role education can play in relation to empowerment is teaching students the skills of critical intellectual engagement" (p. 5).

To enact empowerment, Warner and Bruschke (2001) contended that there are three requirements for an empowering education: that students learn to engage knowledge in a critical way, that students be social critics, and that students be agents of change. The final requirement may seem elusive. By its very nature, developing critical thinking skills positions students to engage knowledge critically and to become social critics. Yet, critical thinking also positions students to become agents of change. Debate is a competitive, time-pressured event in which students must be prepared and unafraid to engage (Warner & Bruschke, 2001). Beyond the nature of debate, when argumentative agency becomes a central goal outside of winning rounds and tournaments, they look to become involved more directly in public affairs and social change, which works to improve their argumentative agency (Mitchell, 1998). As Mitchell (1998) noted, "argumentative agency involves the capacity to contextualize and employ the skills and strategies of argumentative discourse in fields of social action, especially wider spheres of public deliberation" (p. 4). So, "when debaters reconfigure themselves as producers of knowledge, rather than passive consumers of it, it becomes easier to cultivate senses of personal agency" (p. 5). The proof is in the actions of the debaters. From working with underserved Urban Debate Leagues to engaging in public advocacy, through public debates and public policy engagement, debaters are enacting their argumentative agency.[3]

Critical thinking meta-analyses can play an important role in developing our understanding of how empowerment takes place. After taking note of the findings in the original meta-analysis that debate improves critical thinking, Warner and Bruschke (2001) explained:

> This paper seeks not simply to prove that debate can improve traditional student performance, but that debate is the sort of activity that can lead to student empowerment in a way that traditional education fails to encourage. In other words, academic debate has tremendous value quite apart from its ability to improve achievement. (p. 8)

The values of debate are myriad, and many have been overlooked. However, if techniques are available through the use of meta-analysis to document the skills that lead to empowerment, should they not be used? Conversely, if skills and strategies that are being developed through academic debate are not included in our articulation of the skills of critical thinking, should we not revise those skills and characteristics?

What about classroom teaching and research practices? Are there other issues about critical thinking that are being overlooked? For exam-

---

[3]Another interesting project is the Student Voices Project that encourages empowerment through civic engagement by studying local campaigns in high school classes. Through research, engagement with the candidates, and interactions with media and the public, students make their voices heard. This might well be another example of developing argumentative agency and brings media into the study of critical thinking. Information on the Student Voices Project can be found at http://student-voices.org/

ple, does critical thinking compete with the disciplinary knowledge we seek to impart?

> Is persuasion a justifiable means to the critical thinking/emancipatory ends? If my goal is to develop thinkers who can engage in critical analysis, then won't using persuasive tactics undermine the accomplishment of that goal? If not, how do I get students to meet these new goals without using persuasion? The disparate goals of learning disciplinary information and processes and understanding and acting upon the nature of knowledge seem to be in competition. Paradoxically, however, I cannot think of a way to meet any of the goals I have mentioned without being persuasive. (Hynd, 2001, p. 275)

These questions have particular resonance for communication educators, for we teach not only skills but also theoretical and conceptual knowledge about communication practices. So, must we enact through persuasion the very qualities that are counter to critical thinking? The question assumes a particular and negative view of persuasion as counter to critical thinking. However, we can use persuasion to outline different arguments, to point out the multiple sides of issues, and to explore the different contexts and lines of argument. In doing so, we open up new avenues for research. For example, we can connect critical thinking and message sidedness research (M. Allen et al., 1990) and find additional ways of understanding specific strategies and teaching strategies. Or, we might want to examine the links between critical thinking and cooperative argumentation. As compared with competitive argumentation, Makau and Marty (2001) indicated that cooperative argumentation "calls upon us to view those who disagree with us as resources rather than rivals" (p. 88). For the formation of deliberative communities, critical thinking is absolutely necessary. In reframing notions of argument and persuasion we do not need to throw out critical thinking. We have opportunities to assess the ways in which such skills can be learned and enacted in different contexts.

Although critical thinking and persuasion are not incompatible, theoretical questions remain. If developing critical thinking skills positions us to critique dominant discourses and ideologies, then we must be prepared to examine the intersection of critical thinking and critical theories. As one example, let us examine the intersection of critical thinking, persuasion, and feminist theory.

Feminist communication scholars developed invitational rhetoric as a challenge to traditional conceptions of persuasion as focused on domination and coercion. "Invitational rhetoric is an invitation to understanding as a means to create a relationship rooted in equality, immanent value, and self-determination. Invitational rhetoric constitutes an invitation to the audience to enter the rhetor's world and see it as the rhetor does" (Foss &

Griffin, 1995, p. 5). Similarly, the conception of critical thinking used throughout this chapter has been challenged by feminist scholars as biased and limited: "[Critical thinking] is limited in that vital tools that help us to be critical thinkers are ignored or diminished, such as our tools of imagination, intuition, and emotional feelings, while our reasoning tool is highlighted and underscored" (Thayer-Bacon, 1998, p. 125). The argument is that traditional conceptions of persuasion and critical thinking tend to bifurcate reason and emotion. Reading the responses of Foss and Griffin and Thayer-Bacon independently of one another, one may read each essay as turning the traditional relationship on its head and privileging emotion over reason. However, read in combination, these essays open possibilities to reconceptualize the very nature of critical thinking and persuasion without having to discard either concept.

Thayer-Bacon (1998) redescribed the theory of critical thinking as constructive thinking:

> Constructive thinking views knowledge as personal and public. As a model for thinking, it stresses the impossibility of separating the self from the object, the knower from the known. This description of thinking allows that there is an interaction between subjectivity and objectivity, and "assigns equal rights to both factors in experience—objective and internal conditions." I use the term "construction" in a public, sociopolitical manner, while at the same time questioning the distinction between a public and private self. I mean for "construction" to underscore a view of knowledge as something knowers create through a transactive sociopolitical process with others. I seek to emphasize that constructing knowledge is an activity that must be viewed from many angles, including epistemological, sociopolitical, and educational. (pp. 137–138)[4]

And, as Thayer-Bacon concluded, "without intuition, imagination, emotional feelings, *and* reasoning, one cannot hope to be a good constructive thinker" (p. 143). Foss and Griffin (1995) also reconfigured the strategies used to invite consideration of a position, highlighting the willingness to yield and the use of re-sourcement:

> In using re-sourcement, the rhetor deliberately draws energy from a new source—a source other than the individual or system that provided the initial frame for the issue. It is a means, then, of communicating a perspective that is different from that of the individual who produced the message to which the rhetor is responding. (Foss & Griffin, 1995, p. 9)

---

[4]The discussion of critical thinking and constructive thinking is necessarily limited in this chapter. For additional discussions of revisions of critical thinking see Alston (2001).

In both reconceptions, the skills and strategies that we usually think of as exemplars of critical thinking and persuasion are revised and expanded to include and account for emotional and contextual elements.

Both Foss and Griffin (1995) and Thayer-Bacon (1998) argued for transformation of conceptions of persuasion and critical thinking. Reading together the ideas of constructive thinking and invitational rhetoric, we can see that we do not need to eliminate traditional notions of either persuasion or critical thinking. Scholars can revisit the skills and subskills of critical thinking and then use them to revisit persuasion. Do measurement tools include measures of intuition, imagination, and emotional feelings, as well as reason? Are strategies such as willingness to yield, resourcement, and external conditions included? If not, can they be developed? If they cannot be developed, what are we measuring in critical thinking tests? What are we teaching?

It may be argued that such issues muddy the waters and educators should concentrate on issues of reasoning. However, these are conversations that are going on around us, and as scholars of critical thinking and communication, we have unique perspectives to offer. Connecting seemingly disparate threads of the conversation, as meta-analysis as a method and interdisciplinary interpretation does, can yield new insights (M. Allen, 1999).

CONCLUSIONS

The results of the meta-analysis confirm what many of us already know: Training in forensics, debate, public speaking, and argumentation courses has clear and demonstrable effects on critical thinking development. Experience is useful, but the meta-analysis provides data that can be used to answer calls for educational accountability for our extracurricular programs and our courses.

As the discipline continues to debate the definition of critical thinking, we need to consider many questions: What is noncritical thinking? Is complex thinking a better conceptualization of critical thinking? Is meta-thinking (critical thinking about thinking) a better conceptualization? These questions do not give way to mere definitional mental gymnastics. They are central to curriculum development, teaching strategies, research, and theorizing. I am not suggesting that we abandon the term critical thinking, for whatever term is used will carry its own definitional and ideological baggage. Rather, it is important for us to understand that how we define the term impacts how we can test it. So, although meta-analysis can serve as a model for testing critical thinking, how we define critical thinking will significantly affect what and how we test. In any event, testing should continue. The skills of critical thinking are integral to our everyday, lived experiences, and the more we know about those skills the better our teaching and our lives will be.

REFERENCES

Allen, M. (1999). The role of meta-analysis for connecting critical and scientific approaches: The need to develop a sense of collaboration. *Critical Studies in Mass Communication, 16,* 373–378.

Allen, M., Berkowitz, S., Hunt, S., & Louden, A. (1999). A meta-analysis of the impact of forensics and communication education on critical thinking. *Communication Education, 48,* 18–30.

Allen, M., Berkowitz, S., & Louden, A. (1995). A study comparing the impact of communication classes and competitive forensic experience on critical thinking improvement. *The Forensic, 81,* 1–7.

Allen, M., Hale, J., Mongeau, P., Berkowitz, S., Stafford, R. S., Shanahan, W., et al. (1990). Testing a model of message sidedness: Three replications. *Communication Monographs, 57,* 275–291.

Allen, T. H. (2002). Charting a communication pathway: Using assessment to guide curriculum development in a re-vitalized general education plan. *Communication Education, 51,* 26–39.

Alston, K. (2001). Re/thinking critical thinking: The seductions of everyday life. *Studies in Philosophy and Education, 20,* 27–40.

Berkun, S. (2001, May). Issue #14: Critical thinking in Web and interface design. *UIWEB.COM.* Retrieved July 30, 2002, from http://www.uiweb.com/issues/issue14.htm

Browne, M. N. (2000). Distinguishing features of critical thinking classrooms. *Teaching in Higher Education, 5,* 301–310.

Burrell, N. A. (2001). Central States Outstanding Teacher Award—Winners recognizing the importance of teaching: An introduction to our very best! *Communication Studies, 52,* 257–259.

Dannels, D. P. (2002). Communication across the curriculum and in the disciplines: Speaking in engineering. *Communication Education, 51,* 254–268.

Dilenschneider, R. (2001). The coming age of content and critical thinking. *Executive Speeches, 15*(5), 23–26.

Elder, L., & Paul, R. (2001). Critical thinking: Thinking to some purpose. *Journal of Developmental Education, 25,* 40–41.

Facione, P. A. (1998). *Critical thinking: What it is and why it counts.* Millbrae, CA: California Academic Press. Retrieved July 15, 2002, from www.calpress.com/pdf_files/what&why.pdf

Fine, G. A. (2001). *Gifted tongues: High school debate and adolescent culture.* Princeton, NJ: Princeton University Press.

Foss, S. K., & Griffin, C. L. (1995). Beyond persuasion: A proposal for an invitational rhetoric. *Communication Monographs, 62,* 2–18.

Fritz, P. A., & Weaver, R. L. (1986). Teaching critical thinking skills in the basic speaking course: A liberal arts perspective. *Communication Education, 35,* 174–182.

Garside, C. (1996). Look who's talking: A comparison of lecture and group discussion teaching strategies in developing critical thinking skills. *Communication Education, 45,* 212–227.

Harris, T. E., & Sherblom, J. C. (2002). *Small group and team communication* (2nd ed.). Boston: Allyn & Bacon.

Hynd, C. (2001). Persuasion and its role in meeting educational goals. *Theory Into Practice, 40,* 270–277.

Kienzler, D. (2001). Ethics, critical thinking, and professional communication pedagogy. *Technical Communication Quarterly, 10,* 319–340.

Makau, J. M., & Marty, D. L. (2001). *Cooperative argumentation: A model for deliberative community.* Prospect Heights, IL: Waveland.

Mitchell, G. R. (1998). Pedagogical possibilities for argumentative agency in academic debate. *Argumentation and Advocacy, 35,* 41–60.

Morello, J. T. (2000). Comparing speaking across the curriculum and writing across the curriculum programs. *Communication Education, 49,* 99–113.

Morreale, S. P., & Backlund, P. M. (2002). Communication curricula: History, recommendations, resources. *Communication Education, 51,* 2–18.

National Youth Anti-Drug Media Campaign. (n.d.). *The anti-drug.com.* Retrieved August 28, 2002, from http://www.theantidrug.com/advice/index.html

O'Keefe, V. P. (1986). *Affecting critical thinking through speech.* Annandale, VA: Speech Communication Association.

Palmerton, P. R. (1992). Teaching skills or teaching thinking? *Journal of Applied Communication Research, 20,* 335–341.

Paul, R., & Elder, L. (1999). Critical thinking: Teaching students to seek the logic of things. *Journal of Developmental Education, 23*(1), 34–35.

Powell, R. G. (1992). Critical thinking and speech communication: Our teaching strategies are warranted—Not! *Journal of Applied Communication Research, 20,* 342–347.

Rosenthal, A. (2002). Report of the Hope College Conference on designing the undergraduate curriculum in communication. *Communication Education, 51,* 19–25.

Simonds, C. J. (2001). Reflecting on the relationship between communication theory and instructional practices. *Communication Studies, 52,* 260–265.

Thayer-Bacon, B. (1998). Transforming and redescribing critical thinking: Constructive thinking. *Studies in Philosophy and Education, 17,* 123–148.

Turman, P. D. (2001). "Learn to play the game": Recommendations for being successful as a graduate teaching assistant. *Communication Studies, 52,* 266–271.

Turner, P. K. (2001). Eloquence, and a little bit of yourself: A philosophy for teaching. *Communication Studies, 52,* 272–277.

U.S. Department of Education, National Center for Education Statistics. (2000a). *The NPEC sourcebook on assessment: Vol. I. Definitions and assessment methods for critical thinking, problem solving, and writing* (NCES 2000–172). Washington, DC: U.S. Government Printing Office. Retrieved July 30, 2002, from http://nces.ed.gov/pubs2000/2000195.pdf

U.S. Department of Education, National Center for Education Statistics. (2000b). *The NPEC sourcebook on assessment: Vol. II. Selected institutions utilizing assessment results* (NCES 2000–172). Washington, DC: U.S. Government Printing Office. Retrieved July 30, 2002, from http://nces.ed.gov/pubs2000/2000196.pdf

Warner, E., & Bruschke, J. (2001). *"Gone on debating": Competitive debate as a tool of empowerment for urban America.* Paper presented at the Western States Communication Association Convention, Coeur d'Alene, ID. Retrieved August 28, 2002, from http://commfaculty.fullerton.edu/jbruschke/Papers/Debate%20as%20a%20Tool%20of%20empowerment.htm

Worley, D. W. (2001). A teaching philosophy. *Communication Studies, 52,* 278–283.

5

How Powerful Is PowerPoint? Analyzing the Educational Effects of Desktop Presentational Programs in the Classroom

Elayne J. Shapiro
Jeff Kerssen-Griep
University of Portland

Barbara Mae Gayle
Saint Martin's University

Mike Allen
University of Wisconsin–Milwaukee

Instructional technologies have played a prominent role for decades in public and private discourse about education. Each technological advance from instructional radio through interactive digital video technology has generated a related debate about its use, effects, and costs for schools, teachers, students, and society (see Ehrmann, 1999, for a recent example). Over the years those debates have spurred hundreds of studies about technology's educational impacts, many of which have been summarized in meta-analytic research studies (e.g., C.-L. C. Kulik, Kulik, & Cohen, 1980; J. Kulik, Kulik, & Cohen, 1979) and extensive literature reviews (e.g., Clark, 1983; Clark &

61

Salomon, 1986; Jamison, Suppes, & Wells, 1974; Kozma, 1991; Levie & Dickie, 1973; Mielke, 1968; Schramm, 1977; Wetzel, Radtke, & Stern, 1994). This chapter reviews theories and findings associated with classroom use of presentational media technologies, then applies those understandings and issues to a meta-analysis of experimental studies about desktop presentational programs' (DPP) instructional effects. Studies of computer-aided instruction and distance learning technologies are meta-analyzed elsewhere in this volume (Allen, Bourhis, Mabry, Burrell, & Timmerman, chap. 14; Timmerman & Kruepke, chap. 6), and thus are not included in this chapter.

PREVIOUS INSTRUCTIONAL MEDIA THEORY AND RESEARCH

Educational research presents a mixed bag of findings about classroom media's effects on student achievement. Instructional media studies generally support either a weak or a strong media theory (Clark & Craig, 1992), although newer media theorizing attempts focus more on cognition and learning (Kozma, 1994).

Strong Media Research

Advocates of this approach argue that each medium produces unique psychological changes that vary from the effects produced by a different medium. For example, one meta-analysis found ($d = .15$) that students learned slightly more from visual-based instruction (e.g., instructional television) than from a conventional lecture approach (Cohen, Ebeling, & Kulik, 1981), thus supporting the notion that instructional television brings something unique to student learning that is unreachable via a different medium. A broader meta-analytic review of 312 instructional technology studies found positive effects for technology on student achievement ($ES = .28$) and ratings of course quality ($ES = .10$; C.-L. C. Kulik et al., 1980).

Many of these strong media studies have been relatively pragmatic in their design, often simply contrasting the effects of instruction with and without particular instructional technology. Paivio's (1971, 1991) dual coding theory drives much of the research seeking direct connections between specific forms of media and particular learning outcomes. The theory claims that cognitive knowledge is represented both in words and in pictures simultaneously, and that the two systems are accessed differently: Words are recalled sequentially, whereas images can be scanned from a variety of spatial perspectives. According to the theory, memory works most efficiently when the two systems can be cross-referenced.

Extended into classroom practice, this conception has been used to support the importance of congruent text and images as helpful to retrieving and generating knowledge. Salomon (1979) further argued that media differ in the complexity of their symbol systems and in the complexity of the coding by which information is conveyed. Salomon (1984) argued that the nature of the medium itself changes the information processing required from students (e.g., learners exposed to a medium they deem difficult will exert more effort than learners involved in media they perceive as easier). Park and Hannafin (1993) helpfully taxonomized many additional psychological, pedagogical, and technological theories that underlie other aspects of this strong instructional media research.

Many studies mirror these assumptions in their methodologies, often treating each form of media as having a unique influence on learners. Clark and Craig (1992) called attention to the "additive" and "multiplicative" logic of such research about classroom media effects. Following dual coding theory, an additive assumption presumes that instruction produces more learning when it is presented using two or more media. The multiplicative assumption suggests that different media are likely to combine into something greater than the sum of their individual benefits. If either presumption holds true, students viewing presentational media as supplements to their face-to-face instruction should experience greater learning outcomes than they do when confronted with only one mode of instruction.

Weak Media Research

According to critics of the strong media research, available evidence does not support the classroom application of dual coding theory assumptions that "words plus pictures" enhance instruction (Anderson, 1985; Clark & Craig, 1992). Weak media proponents instead tout only the economic advantages of instructional media, claiming that technologies have no distinct psychological influences on learning but that they can reduce the cost and improve the rate of student learning. Beginning with an influential 1983 article and continuing since then, researcher Richard Clark has argued that most contemporary media comparison research summaries and meta-analyses continually show that media "do not influence learning under any conditions," attributing any positive educational media outcomes to "uncontrolled effects of instructional method and novelty" (Clark, 1994, p. 457). That is, learning was affected by the novelty of new technologies or the (often active) instructional strategies that accompanied them, not by the technology itself. Clark (1983) claimed that "media are vehicles that deliver instruction but do not influence student achievement any more than the truck that delivers our groceries causes changes in our nutrition" (p. 445). Weak media proponents continue offering evidence that instructional media should be studied for its economic benefits (i.e., cost and speed of learning) rather than for any gains in learning itself, which they argue are unsupported by the overall research evidence (Clark & Craig, 1992).

Cognitive Processing

Whereas earlier theorizing about instruction media presumed a "trucks to market" view of teaching (i.e., bringing information to students), newer media theorizing attempts to account for more constructivist and distributed views of cognition and learning (see Kozma, 1994). These newer media theorists acknowledge that student interaction with various agents, tools, and media affects their learning processes. Cobb's (1997) theory of cognitive efficiency, for example, provided a softer version of the strong media approach. He suggested that "while different media may not create different cognitive products, such as concepts, schemas, and mental models ... they clearly create different cognitive processes at different levels of efficiency (with regard to speed, ease, effectiveness)" (Cobb, 1997, p. 27).

The debate remains vigorous and no consensus has been reached. Researchers do not agree regarding whether, or how, instructional media interact with students' interests, motivations, cognitions, and learning.

USING VISUAL ILLUSTRATIONS IN TEACHING

One principle of a strong media approach rooted in dual coding theory (Paivio, 1971) is that learning will improve with the number of complementary stimuli used to represent the information to be learned (Park & Hannafin, 1993). This idea is supported by at least one narrative review (Levie & Lentz, 1982) and reflected in the advice given by popular visual consultants (see, e.g., Tufte, 1997). Levin, Anglin, and Carney (1987), for example, argued that graphic illustrations can function to decorate, represent, transform (e.g., create a mnemonic device to aid students' memory), organize, and interpret knowledge for learners. They found beneficial educational effects for graphics that illustrated concepts, organized information, and transformed or interpreted information for learners; only purely "decorative" graphics did not benefit learning. These studies suggest that visual illustrations affect student cognition and achievement.

On the other hand, the achievement found in the visual studies may be artifactual due to graphic technology's novelty to the students or its role in an innovative instructional method, as "weak media" proponents would assert (see Clark, 1994). Students in Nowaczyk, Santos, and Patton's (1998) semester-long study, for example, preferred the instructor's Microsoft PowerPoint additions to lectures but showed no significant relationships between the numbers of PowerPoint text, graphics, and limited-animation slides shown each day and their demonstrated understanding of course materials. These students reported feeling that classroom interactions suffered somewhat due to the dimly lit room and perceived formality of PowerPoint presentations. Thus, when novelty was controlled via semester-long data collection, PowerPoint technology showed no significant psychological effects on students' understanding of course materials.

PowerPoint Use in the Classroom

Defining PowerPoint. PowerPoint presentation software, designed by Microsoft, has the capability to integrate text, sound, color, and animation. Although PowerPoint prevails as the dominant presentation software, other options exist, such as Corel Presentations or Lotus Freelance Graphics. This study uses the term desktop presentation program (DPP) to allow for the variety of software. Where studies make clear that PowerPoint was the program employed, the terms are used interchangeably. We first describe some of the advantages and disadvantages of presentation software and then review research that attempted to measure actual outcomes.

Advantages and Disadvantages of Presentation Software. Many published studies discussing PowerPoint use in the classroom focus on case study reports of successful usage (Fifield & Peifer, 1994; Hutchinson; 2001; Marr, 2000; Mason & Hlynka, 1998; McAdams & Duclos, 1999; Pauw, 2002) or discuss strategies for using PowerPoint in the classroom (Downing & Garmon, 2001; Harrison, 1999; Hodges, 1999; Kelly, 1999; Sammons, 1995). Effective technology usage reinforces and takes into account instructional objectives, the types of subject matter, and important learner characteristics (Clark, 1983). DPPs are relatively easy to learn and use and can provide a gateway for instructors newly incorporating computer technology into their classrooms (Downing & Garmon, 2001; Larson, 2001). Because slides can be colorful, incorporate animated graphics, and include sound, DPPs offer visual appeal and potentially more ease of understanding for students than chalkboard visual aids (Daniels, 1999). If instructors choose to upload slides to the World Wide Web, students may also be able to access live links to related sites. Teachers can review their previous class by quickly clicking through their previous presentation and can provide notes in addition to their slides (Daniels, 1999). However, as Pauw (2002) claimed, the benefits can be outweighed without carefully considering "PowerPoint's tendency to produce disembodied, decontextualized learning environment" (p. 39).

On the downside, preparing effective presentations requires time and effort. McAdams and Duclos (1999) found that developing a "lengthy lesson required hundreds of hours, substantial hardware/software and a high tolerance for frustration" (p. 57), and Daniels (1999) suggested there may be a startup cost for projection equipment. Additionally, the hardware and software needed to create a variety of interface possibilities can cause both expense and compatibility challenges (Hutchinson, 2001). Currently, little empirically based research provides guidance as to the most effective way to use slides. Most tips and tricks are offered based on personally oriented use (Harrison, 1999; Hodges, 1999; Kelly, 1999).

Challenges to Comparing DPP Studies. According to Clark (1983) and others, overall narrative conclusions about media effectiveness can be confounded by methodological inconsistencies. A number of researchers have conducted studies attempting to find out what benefits, if any, DPPs provide. The basic model for these studies includes using control groups that receive traditional lectures supplemented with overheads, chalkboard, or handouts, and test groups that use a form of DPP. A variety of instruments are then used to evaluate differences. Time frames for studies vary greatly. In some instances, participants consist of traditional classes over a several-year period (Daniels, 1999; Mantei, 2000) and test groups revisited in subsequent years. In other studies, groups are given one treatment for a few weeks followed by the other treatment in the subsequent few weeks (Larson, 2001). In a third type of study, within the same semester, some sections of a particular course receive traditional treatment, and other sections receive the test treatment (Carrell & Menzel, 2001). The preponderance of studies used college-aged students as participants, with subject matter that ranged from the theoretical to the practical. No study assessed the quality of teaching independently of the supplementary materials. One study took into account the learning style of the students (Daniels, 1999). Plainly, there is variation in how this phenomenon has been investigated by researchers.

Student Learning and DPPs. The major focus of studies investigating the impact of DPPs is on assessing student learning. Typically, these studies rely on two types of measures: grades and self-reports. Other indicators such as absences or students seeking additional help occasionally appear as well.

Several studies used grading to assess student learning. For example, Avila, Biner, Bink, and Dean (1995) found that with the use of DPPs exam scores in a "Professional Selling" class were no different relative to those in classes that used conventional graphics. However, when students were exposed to DPP and then went back to conventional graphics, exam scores decreased; when they moved from conventional graphics to DPP, their scores increased, but the results were not at acceptable levels of significance. In a course designed to improve library research skills, Bushong (1998) found that no significant difference in grades occurred between groups that were exposed to DPPs and those provided oral instruction by the librarian. Ahmed (1998), in a teacher education program, found very little difference between groups exposed to traditional overheads and those exposed to DPP. Similarly, Carrell and Menzel (2001) reported no significant difference between traditional presentations and use of DPP in a freshman communication class and Szabo and Hastings (2000), teaching in sports science classes, did not find that DPP made any difference in grades. Comparable results were reported by Daniels (1999) in teaching economics.

However, Nowaczyk et al. (1998), teaching honor students in an introductory psychology class, found that students who did better on the test thought PowerPoint had helped them learn, even though the findings only approached statistical significance. Luttig (1998) discovered that students in a college-prep chemistry class were helped in their understanding of chemistry through PowerPoint. In a study with upperclassmen, Carrell and Menzel (2001) found short-term learning increased with DPP, but not long-term learning, although the results approached significance. Mantei (2000) discovered that students with DPPs received better exam scores and semester letter grades than those without DPPs, and Siegle and Foster (2001) found students' grades did improve significantly in a year-long study in which the students developed PowerPoint presentations. However, students in both Mantei's (2000) and Siegle and Foster's (2001) studies could augment their learning with additional technology, so results could not be interpreted as a consequence of DPPs alone.

Interestingly, three studies undertaken by Szabo and Hastings (2000) revealed conflicting results. The authors found no significant differences in their first study when they compared grades with two different classes 1 year apart. In their second study, they discovered that PowerPoint usage resulted in higher test scores. In their third study, Szabo and Hastings attempted to control for extraneous variables they felt were present in the first two experiments and found a significant difference in test scores, but this time the students who received traditional methods of presentation had higher test scores. They suggested that the efficacy of DPP lectures may be more course specific than universal.

Taken together, these studies raise significant questions concerning DPP usage and its effect on student grades. A few researchers investigated whether students felt that DPPs improved learning. Atkins-Sayre, Hopkins, Mohundro, and Sayre (1998) reported that frequency of DPP use contributed to the perception that PowerPoint affected retention of information. Likewise, Mantei's (2000) students believed that they could learn material better with DPPs because notes accompanied slides. A student in Siegle and Foster's (2001) study who produced his or her own PowerPoint presentation claimed that "creating the story board resulted in putting more time into the presentation" and another one reported "you have to review the information so frequently that it is implanted in your memory" (p. 34).

Students' perceptions that they learn better with DPPs may also be related to their levels of interest and motivation. A number of studies looked at students' attitudes related to DPPs. Atkins-Sayre et al. (1998) found that 73% of participants in their large study felt that PowerPoint helped them maintain interest. Bushong (1998) found that attitudes toward library sessions were more positive when DPPs were not used. In contrast, Daniels (1999) noted that 76% to 80% of students found slides somewhat to extremely useful. In Mantei's (2000) physical geography class, students said that PowerPoint was more interesting than traditional lectures and they could listen more intently. Szabo and Hastings's (2000) sport science students preferred PowerPoint lectures to traditional lectures. Carrell and Menzel's (2001) study with freshmen communication students, however, found that state motivation was no different with or without PowerPoint. Clearly, this research does not provide conclusive findings on the efficacy of PowerPoint to enhance interest or motivation to learn any more than it evaluates whether DPPs improve student learning.

In addition to learning and attitudes toward subject matter, researchers also explore the relationship between DPP usage and perceptions of teacher immediacy. Atkins-Sayre et al. (1998) found that the majority of their students felt that PowerPoint enhanced instructor delivery and credibility, as did Mantei (2000). Bushong's (1998) library students felt that the presenter was more energetic without PowerPoint. Thus, results were mixed and confounded because teacher immediacy and expertise were not assessed before the concurrent use of DPPs.

In general, studies done thus far question whether or not the use of DPPs improves grades or enhances learning. The impact of DPPs in making a course more interesting or in enhancing the perception of teacher immediacy produced mixed findings. Thus, aggregating all available current data about PowerPoint's effectiveness (relative to conventional instruction) may enable a greater degree of certainty about any of its unique educational effects.

METHOD

Narrative literature review of PowerPoint research yields mixed findings about the technology's effects on student attitudes and performance. By collecting quantitative research studies about a phenomenon and converting their results into a common metric, meta-analysis allows the determination of an average effect size across a group of studies (Glass, 1976). This process can help resolve statistical inconsistencies and test for the homogeneity of effects.

Literature Search

Experimental studies of instructional PowerPoint use were retrieved using the computer-based retrieval systems ERIC, Education Abstracts, Academic Universe, PsychINFO, Business Abstracts, and Communication Index. ERIC was the only database of unpublished manuscripts searched. The reference section of each manuscript collected also was searched for additional experiments involving PowerPoint's instructional effects.

Selecting Studies

Four criteria commonly used for meta-analytic reviews guided the selection of works included in this study (Bourhis & Allen, 1998). Acceptable manuscripts had to: (a) investigate some aspect of PowerPoint use in an instructional context, (b) contain a quantitative analysis of PowerPoint's effect on one or more dependent measures, (c) provide enough information to allow conversion of results into a common metric for comparison, and (d) be accessible to these investigators. The 12 manuscripts with 16 separate studies that met these criteria are displayed in Table 5.1. Each manuscript was coded for the year completed, types of learners tested, number of participants, publication status, and student learning.

Statistical Analysis

The summary statistics of each study were converted to correlations so that the magnitude of outcomes attributable to student learning with DPPs could be quantified.

The correlations were weighted for sample size and then averaged. Each average correlation was assessed to determine if the variance in the observed sample correlations was larger than expected by random sample error (Hedges & Olein, 1985). To detect a moderator variable, the sum of the squared error was tested using a chi-square test. A nonsignificant chi-square indicates that the amount of variability is probably the result of chance, whereas a significant chi-square indicates that the amount of variability is probably the result of some type of moderating variable.

RESULTS

The individual analysis of the 12 studies with 16 separate data points produced generally small effect sizes (see Table 5.1). The overall results with 1,778 participants revealed a small, average effect size ($r = .128$) suggesting that PowerPoint presentations do have a slight effect on student learning. Using a binomial effect size display (Rosenthal & Rubin, 1982), this analysis reveals an increase in learning or comprehension success from 44% to 56% based on DPP usage.

These general results should be interpreted with caution, however, because each of these samples was found to be heterogeneous (overall

TABLE 5.1
Manuscripts Used in the Analysis

Authors	Year	N	Published	Effect Size	Significance
Ahmed	1998	143	No	−.060	No significant difference
Atkins-Sayre et al.	1998	485	No	.135	Improved with DPP
Avila et al.	1995	56	Yes	.000	No significant difference
Bushong	1998	65	No	−.187	No significant difference
		55	No	.258	No significant difference
Carrell & Menzel 1	2001	120	Yes	−.118	No significant difference
Carrell & Menzel 2	2001	49	Yes	.000	Short term improved
				.324	Long term almost significant
Daniels Class 1	1999	50	Yes	.000	No significant difference
Daniels Class 2	1999	49	Yes	.000	No significant difference
Larson	2001	48	Yes	.217	No significant difference
Luttig	1998	52	No	.270	Improved with DPP
Mantei	2000	248	Yes	.188	Improved with DPP
Nowaczyk et al.	1998	83	Yes	.200	Almost significant with DPP
Siegle & Foster	2001	27	Yes	.395	Improved with DPP
Szabo & Hastings 1	2000	155	Yes	.056	No significant difference
Szabo & Hastings 2	2000	25	Yes	.861	Improved with DPP
Szabo & Hastings 3	2000	69	Yes	.650	Traditional method works

Note. DPP = desktop presentational programs.

$\chi^2 = 47.377.492$, $p < .05$), indicating the possibility of one or more moderator variables. In an effort to search for the moderators, two categories were separately considered. The publication status revealed a somewhat smaller effect size for nonpublished studies ($r = .092$, $k = 5$, $N = 799$) than for published studies ($r = .158$, $k = 5$, $N = 979$). The subject matter of the class also revealed some differences in the average effect sizes.

DISCUSSION

Results of this analysis provide limited support for the role of DPPs in improving students' comprehension and learning, with science courses appearing to benefit the most by a small degree. Students sometimes—

although not always—preferred the use of DPP software, occasionally even perceiving that they learned more from it (Atkins-Sayre et al., 1998). That perception may be a simple result of PowerPoint's organizing feature, or its novelty to the student group (Clark, 1994). According to Szabo and Hastings (2000), students' five most appreciated features of PowerPoint were: (a) variation of fonts, (b) use of illustrations, (c) a preference for light background, (d) use of colors, and (e) line-by-line projection of lecture concepts. Importantly, though, two of Szabo and Hastings's (2000) studies found that although students felt DPPs helped them learn more, their test scores did not reflect any actual differences in learning. Other studies did find increases in learning associated with DPP usage. Clearly this analysis encompasses a wide range of assumptions, research practices, and results.

We forward two explanations for the findings. On one hand, the use of DPPs may instigate dual coding from students as strong media advocates argue: The additive use of aural and visual stimuli may increase cognitive processing (Paivio, 1971, 1991). Depending on the elaborateness of usage (animation, quality of presentation, etc.), more cognitive processing may be evoked via use of this medium. Alternatively, findings here instead may support only the weak media position that DPPs can increase the efficiency of information sharing even though they create no distinct psychological changes for learners.

Analysis of the studies themselves shows that the strong media position can be supported only with caution because the studies analyzed here varied widely in how they investigated DPPs' influence. Very few of them accounted for many of the social and instructional variables occurring around the DPP vs. conventional teaching relationship being tested. For example, Luttig (1998) gave students a quiz, used DPP in a presentation, and then gave another quiz. It is difficult to know what role the presentation had versus the repeated quizzes. Similarly, his students had the option to review with slides. It is not clear what role the structured review had versus the medium of DPP. The absence of non-DPP control groups clouds the claim that the DPP presentation itself was responsible for the learning gains reported in the study. This and similar research designs call into question whether overall significant gains are attributable to the DPP or to the uncontrolled effects of other classroom variables (Clark, 1994). Several such variables are present within this corpus of studies.

Active, Constructivist Teaching Practices

What can be learned from those studies where DPP use was associated with learning improvements in students? In most instances where learning increased, DPPs were used in conjunction with constructivist learning activities. For example, in the Carrell and Menzel (2001) study in which short-term learning improved, research assistants reported that the only students who took notes were in the PowerPoint sections. Siegle and Foster (2001) had their students create their own slides and do extensive planning, which reinforced the concepts being learned. Mantei (2000) incorporated DPPs with animation into a physical geology class. Students, however, also could access lecture notes online before class (most did), visit other Web sites related to the class, and try practice exams online. Luttig's (1998) results also may be due to similar student-centered teaching strategies. Szabo and Hastings (2000) found, in part, that students' information retention increased with DPP, a result the authors partly attributed to the better structuring of the lectures that accompanied the DPP condition. In each case these more active teaching practices may have affected the outcomes attributed to PowerPoint usage.

Setting and Subject Matter Variables

Some research suggests that DPPs' efficacy may be more course or topic specific than universal across teaching–learning situations. Szabo and Hastings (2000), for example, found that conventional teaching produced higher test scores than DPPs did once the researchers managed to control for other variables they felt were present in the learning situation. Our own results here suggest that scientific subject matter may be better suited than other disciplines to DPP use.

Teacher and Learner Variables

Findings also may be confounded due to the influence of unexamined but relevant teacher and learner characteristics. Teacher expertise was not assessed in these studies. Only one study, Carrell and Menzel (2001), looked at immediacy and motivation. Daniels (1999) highlighted students' learning styles as worth including in analyses of DPPs' effectiveness. Further research on DPP effects clearly needs to accommodate more of the personal variables that impact learning and achievement.

CONCLUSION

We cannot tell from these studies the extent to which active instructional strategies, settings, subjects, personal variables, or other factors affected the DPP contribution to outcomes, so even the slight gains reported here must be interpreted with caution. Regarding limitations, meta-analysis is bounded by the quality of the studies it aggregates (Bourhis & Allen, 1998). Relatively few studies comprise this body of literature; clearly the technology has been described and touted much more often than it has been analyzed. Additional research assessing the quality of DPPs, the types and amounts of cognitive processing stimulated by particular DPP uses, the contributions made by instructional strategies that accompany DPP use, and the usefulness of DPPs for different types of teachers and learners will help clarify the many ambiguities that remain in this body of research.

REFERENCES

References marked with an asterisk indicate studies included in the meta-analysis.

*Ahmed, C. (1998, November). *PowerPoint versus traditional overheads: Which is more effective for learning?* Paper presented at the South Dakota Association for Health, Physical Education and Recreation, Sioux Falls, SD. (ERIC Document Reproduction Service No. ED429037)

Anderson, J. R. (1985). *Cognitive psychology and its implications* (2nd ed.). New York: Freeman.

*Atkins-Sayre, W., Hopkins, S., Mohundro, S., & Sayre, W. (1998, November). *Rewards and liabilities of presentation software as an ancillary tool: Prison or paradise?* Paper presented at the annual convention of the National Communication Association, New York. (ERIC Document Reproduction Service No. ED430260)

*Avila, R. A., Biner, P. M., Bink, M. L., & Dean, R. S. (1995). Course materials presentation using video-based technologies: An evaluation study of college student performance and attitudes. *Psychology in the Schools, 12,* 38–45.

*Bourhis, J., & Allen, M. (1998). The role of videotaped feedback in the instruction of public speaking: A quantitative synthesis of published empirical research. *Communication Research Reports, 15,* 256–261.

*Bushong, S. (1998). *Utilization of PowerPoint presentation software in library instruction of subject specific reference sources.* Unpublished master's thesis, Kent State University, Kent, OH.

*Carrell, L. J., & Menzel, K. E. (2001). Variations in learning, motivation, and perceived intimacy between live and distance education classrooms. *Communication Education, 50,* 230–240.

Clark, R. E. (1983). Reconsidering research on learning from media. *Review of Educational Research, 53,* 445–459.

Clark, R. E. (1994). Media will never influence learning. *Educational Technology Research and Development, 42,* 21–29.

Clark, R. E., & Craig, T. G. (1992). Research and theory on multi-media learning effects. In M. Giardina (Ed.), *Interactive multimedia learning environments: Human factors and technical considerations on design issues* (pp. 19–30). New York: Springer-Verlag.

Clark, R. E., & Salomon, G. (1986). Media in teaching. In M. Wittrock (Ed.), *Handbook of research on teaching* (3rd ed., pp. 464–478). Chicago: Rand McNally.

Cobb, T. (1997). Cognitive efficiency: Toward a revised theory of media. *Educational Technology Research and Development, 45,* 21–35.

*Cohen, P. A., Ebeling, B. J., & Kulik, J. A. (1981). A meta-analysis of outcome studies of visual-based instruction. *Educational Communication and Technology Journal, 29,* 26–36.

*Daniels, L. (1999). Introducing technology in the classroom: PowerPoint as a first step. *Journal of Computing in Higher Education, 10,* 42–56.

Downing, J., & Garmon, C. (2001). Teaching students in the basic course how to use presentation software. *Communication Education, 50*, 218–229.

Ehrmann, S. C. (1999, March –April). Asking the hard questions about technology use and education. *Change*, 25–29.

Fifield, S., & Peifer, R. (1994). Enhancing lecture presentations in introductory biology with computer-based multimedia. *Journal of College Science Teaching, 23*(4), 235–239.

Glass, G. V. (1976). Primary, secondary, and meta-analysis of research. *Educational Researcher, 10*, 3–8.

Harrison, A. (1999). Power up! Stimulating your students with PowerPoint. *Learning and Leading With Technology, 26*, 6–9.

Hedges, L., & Olein, I. (1985). *Statistical methods for meta-analysis.* Orlando, FL: Academic.

Hodges, B. (1999). Electronic books: Presentation software makes writing more fun. *Learning and Leading With Technology, 27*, 18–21.

Hutchinson, V. V. (2001). Dance appreciation: Enhancing the traditional classroom with technology. *Journal of Interactive Instruction Development, 13*(3), 24–28.

Jamison, D., Suppes, P., & Wells, S. (1974). The effectiveness of alternative instructional media: A survey. *Review of Educational Research, 44*(1), 1–67.

Kelly, R. (1999). Getting everybody involved: Cooperative PowerPoint creations benefit inclusion students. *Learning and Leading With Technology, 27*, 10–14.

Kozma, R. L. (1991). Learning with media. *Review of Educational Research, 61*, 179–211.

Kozma, R. L. (1994). Will media influence learning? Reframing the debate. *Educational Technology Research and Development, 42*, 7–19.

Kulik, C.-L. C., Kulik, J. A., & Cohen, P. A. (1980). Instructional technology and college teaching. *Teaching of Psychology, 7*, 199–205.

Kulik, J. A., Kulik, C.-L. C., & Cohen, P. A. (1979). Research on audiotutorial instruction: A meta-analysis of comparative studies. *Research in Higher Education, 11*, 321–341.

*Larson, T. D. (2001). *A comparison of fifth-grade children receiving both a traditional and a technology based means of instruction in social studies.* Unpublished master's action research project, Johnson Bible College. (ERIC Document Reproduction Service No. ED456090)

Levie, W. H., & Dickie, K. (1973). The analysis and application of media. In R. M. Travers (Ed.), *Second handbook of research on teaching* (pp. 858–882). Chicago: Rand McNally.

Levie, W. H., & Lentz, R. (1982). Effects of text illustrations: A review of research. *Educational Communication and Technology Journal, 30*, 195–232.

Levin, J. R., Anglin, G. J., & Carney, R. R. (1987). On empirically validating functions of pictures in prose. In D. M. Willows & H. A. Houghton (Eds.), *The psychology of illustration: Vol. I. Basic research* (pp. 51–85). New York: Springer-Verlag.

*Luttig, E. P. (1998). *Enhancing student learning with PowerPoint presentations.* Unpublished master's thesis, Michigan State University, East Lansing, MI.

*Mantei, E. J. (2000). Using Internet class notes and PowerPoint in the physical geology lecture. *Journal of College Science Teaching, 29*, 301–305.

Marr, P. M. (2000). Grouping students at the computer to enhance the study of British literature. *English Journal, 90*(2), 120–125.

Mason, R., & Hlynka, D. (1998). PowerPoint in the classroom: Where is the power? *Educational Technology, 38*(5), 42–45.

McAdams, T., & Duclos, L. K. (1999). Teaching business ethics with computer-based multimedia? A cautionary analysis. *Teaching Business Ethics, 3*, 57–67.

Mielke, K. W. (1968). Questioning the questions of ETV research. *Educational Broadcasting, 2,* 6–15.

*Nowaczyk, R. H., Santos, L. T., & Patton, C. (1998). Student perception of multimedia in the undergraduate classroom. *International Journal of Instructional Media, 25,* 367–382.

Paivio, A. (1971). Imagery and deep structure in the recall of English nominalizations. *Journal of Verbal Learning and Verbal Behavior, 10,* 1–12.

Paivio, A. (1991). Dual coding theory and education. *Educational Psychology Review, 3,* 149–210.

Park, I., & Hannafin, M. J. (1993). Empirically-based guidelines for the design of interactive media. *Educational Technology Research and Development, 41,* 63–85.

Pauw, A. P. (2002). Discoveries and dangers in teaching theology with PowerPoint. *Teaching Theology and Religion, 5*(1), 39–41.

Rosenthal, R., & Rubin, D. B. (1982). A simple general response display of the magnitude of experimental effect. *Journal of Educational Psychology, 74,* 166–169.

Salomon, G. (1979). *Interaction of media, cognition, and learning.* San Francisco: Jossey-Bass.

Salomon, G. (1984). Television is "easy" and print is "tough": The differential investment of mental effort in learning as a function of perceptions and attributions. *Journal of Educational Psychology, 74,* 647–658.

Sammons, M. C. (1995). Students assess computer-aided classroom presentations. *T.H.E. Journal, 22*(10), 66–69.

Schramm, W. (1977). *Big media, little media.* Beverly Hills, CA: Sage.

*Siegle, D., & Foster, T. (2001). Laptop computers and multimedia and presentational software: Their effects on student achievement in anatomy and physiology. *Journal of Research on Technology in Education, 34,* 29–37.

*Szabo, A., & Hastings, N. (2000). Using IT in the undergraduate classroom: Should we replace the blackboard with PowerPoint? *Computers & Education, 35,* 175–187.

Tufte, E. R. (1997). *Visual explanations: Images and quantities, evidence and narrative.* Cheshire, CT: Graphics Press.

Wetzel, C. D., Radtke, P. H., & Stern, H. W. (1994). *Instructional effectiveness of video media.* Hillsdale, NJ: Lawrence Erlbaum Associates.

6

Comparisons of College Student Performance Across Computer-Assisted and Traditional Instruction Formats

C. Erik Timmerman
University of Wisconsin–Milwaukee

Kristine A. Kruepke
US Cellular

The use of computer technology in college classrooms is at an all-time high (Morrison & Green, 2002). Analyses of instructional practices reveal that e-mail, Internet resources, course Web sites, computer simulations, presentation handouts, and course management tools are an increasingly central element among courses taught at postsecondary educational institutions (Green, 2002). Many instructors regularly use computer-based technology to replicate, supplement, or even replace their lectures, discussions, and assessments. Without question, educators in today's colleges and universities have more options for delivering and supplementing course content than ever before.

A sizeable body of research has emerged as instructors and researchers experiment with these new delivery options. Computer-assisted instruction (CAI) is the use of computer technology for delivering or supplementing content that is delivered in a traditional face-to-face classroom (Cotton, 1992). CAI includes a variety of different activities that may include tutorials, drill and practice assessments, simulations, and the use of course-specific software applications (Niemiec & Walberg, 1987). Research in this domain frequently compares CAI learning outcomes with those of more traditional instructional methods such as face-to-face lectures (e.g., Adams & Kandt, 1991) or hard-copy text (e.g., Fish & Feldmann, 1987). Extant reviews generally indicate that the use of CAI provides a slight degree of improvement in student performance when compared to traditional instruction (Kulik & Kulik, 1986; Niemiec & Walberg, 1987).

The breadth of CAI research spans across disciplines that range from education to computer science, but questions about the effectiveness of this delivery format are centered within the domain of communication research. The classroom context is a densely communicative environment in which instructors and students participate in the exchange of course-specific information. Clearly, comparisons of the effectiveness of CAI and traditional instruction methods deal with the effectiveness of a fundamental element of the information exchange process—communication media. Thus, by emphasizing the communication factors that may impact learning outcomes, it is possible to develop conclusions that may allow instructors and course designers to make informed choices about methods for delivering course material.

This study uses meta-analysis to summarize findings from quantitative studies that compare CAI to traditional instructional formats in postsecondary education. This research is designed to extend a meta-analysis by Kulik and Kulik (1986) that summarized comparative CAI studies in college classrooms from dates prior to 1969 until 1984. The chapter begins with a review of literature to identify conclusions from extant literature and point to key factors (CAI channel, CAI comparison group, and CAI course content) that may provide more insight into the relative effectiveness of CAI when compared to traditional forms of instruction. Then, the focus turns toward explaining the methods that were used for locating CAI studies and computing effect sizes. Subsequently, the results from the analyses are summarized. The chapter concludes by exploring conclusions from the study, limitations, future research directions, and practical implications.

A DEFINITION OF CAI

Before specifying the nature of CAI, it is necessary to provide a brief explanation of the terminology used by researchers for describing the different forms of technology used in educational contexts. Cotton (1992) explained that the most general term used to describe the concept is *computer-based education* (CBE), which is used to designate the general incorporation of computers into academic settings. CBE studies may range from explorations of how the use of electronic presentation software (e.g., Microsoft PowerPoint) can impact learning (e.g., Rankin & Hoaas, 2001) to examination of learning outcomes that result from courses offered in online formats (e.g., Neuhauser, 2002).

Within the rubric of CBE lie additional variations of classroom computer use. CAI is a more specific term representing the use of computer technology as a means to supplement or replace the delivery of course content that, without the technology, would be delivered via traditional means (usually lecture, but also written hard-copy text; Cotton, 1992). Typically, CAI activities include instructor-led use of tutorials (brief explanations and description of new or previously reviewed course material), drill and practice activities (usually tutorials with some form of built-in feedback for self-assessment), and simulations of course content as depicted in class (e.g., the instructor using software to illustrate polynomial functions).

Two additional variations of CAI that are noted in the literature are computer-managed instruction (CMI) and computer-enriched instruction (CEI). CMI focuses on instructor or student use of the computer for organizing student records, grades, policies, and so forth. For example, instructors who incorporate CMI may provide students with a method for tracking their course grades as the semester progresses. CEI entails the use of various software applications that students utilize to perform activities that may include complex virtual simulations (e.g., simulated cadaver dissection for anatomy instruction), operation of computer programs (e.g., using a statistics program in a statistics course), or other unstructured activities that are designed to stimulate student thinking, awareness, or motivation (e.g., having students experiment with SimCity to prompt thinking about urban design).

Because there are not notable differences in learning outcomes across CAI, CMI, and CEI (Fletcher-Flinn & Gravatt, 1995; Kulik & Kulik, 1986), the different CBE formats can be categorized within the single domain of CAI. Although there are qualitative differences among these forms of CAI, all involve the use of computer technology for delivering course content. Importantly, all forms are used in classes that also have some real-time, face-to-face classroom component—they all supplement the traditional forms of classroom instruction. This feature distinguishes CAI from other instructional methods that rely exclusively on computer technology as the sole medium for delivering course content (online classes). Thus, this study defines CAI as instructional techniques that utilize instructor- or student-operated computer technology for delivering, supplementing, managing, illustrating, or applying content and are included in courses that also have regular, face-to-face instruction.

CAI RESEARCH FINDINGS

Extant meta-analyses have examined impacts of CAI in postsecondary educational settings and revealed a slight advantage of CAI over traditional instruction in terms of student achievement. Kulik and Kulik's (1986) analysis of 101 studies that were conducted prior to 1984 revealed an overall effect size (d) of .26 (r = .13). Their study suggested that college students who were in classes that used CAI would perform in the 60th percentile on examinations, whereas students in traditional courses would perform in the 50th percentile. A smaller scale, but more recent assessment by Fletcher-Flinn and Gravatt (1995) also revealed that CAI students have higher course achievement with a reported effect size (d) of .20 (r = .10) among 48 studies that were conducted in college or university classes. In an analysis of 47 studies from courses in health-related disciplines, Cohen and Dacanay (1992) also found that CAI has a positive impact on performance and reported a larger, medium-sized effect (d) of .41 (r = .20). Christmann and Badgett's (1999) analysis of CAI in science-based courses indicated an overall effect (d) of .27 (r = .13). Clearly, these findings suggest that CAI provides some potential benefits beyond traditional instruction formats when considering student performance.

Moderators of CAI Benefits

The extant meta-analyses that compare CAI to traditional formats illustrate the relative advantages of CAI, but they do not account for a variety of communication-based factors that may provide more information about why CAI increases student performance. Although these studies do consider a variety of study features (e.g., duration of instruction, subject assignment) and other theoretically relevant moderators (e.g., type of CAI, ability level of students), we believe that there are additional factors that may help to clarify why CAI does or does not provide performance above traditional instruction.

Three factors that we see as relevant moderators of CAI impacts on student performance are (a) the type of channel used by the CAI, (b) the comparison group against which CAI impacts are assessed, and (c) the content area of the CAI instruction. The factors identified here (and reviewed in more detail later) coincide with a study design that examines differences within a medium (channels), differences across media (comparison groups), and differences in the content or message that is conveyed with CAI. Analyzing this subset of moderators allows for heightened specificity in any recommendations that may emerge from the analyses. Specifically, the study seeks to determine (a) which CAI design maximizes performance by focusing on channel, (b) how much CAI may increase performance in comparison to traditional instruction formats, and (c) the types of courses that may benefit the most from the use of CAI.

   CAI Channel.   First, a communication medium is composed of a variety of features (Griffith & Northcraft, 1994). Channels are one such feature and consist of the delivery format used to convey information, such as video, audio, and text. Although all CAI is delivered via a single medium—a computer—CAI may vary in terms of the channels that are used. For example, CAI delivery systems may include video (e.g., Guy & Frisby, 1992), audio (e.g., Dalby, 1992), or text-based (e.g., Deardorff, 1986) channels.

There are theoretical arguments that identify the potential impact of CAI channel on performance, but none of the extant meta-analyses have considered this factor. Propositions of media richness theory suggest that a medium's capacity for reducing message ambiguity is a function of the number of cues (e.g., audio, visual) that a medium provides (Daft & Lengel, 1986; Lengel & Daft, 1988; Trevino, Daft, & Lengel, 1990). Richer media—those that convey messages with channels holding a greater number of cues—are thought to convey more information to recipients than lean media—those that may provide information via channels with fewer cues. From the media richness perspective, maximizing student performance would result when a medium has channels with a large capacity for conveying a variety of cues that clarify the content. High performance would come from the richest channels and lower performance from leaner ones.

CAI applications vary in the types of channels used. When a video channel is used, there are multiple additional channels (audio, text, captions, etc.) that are conveyed along with the moving visual image. Although an audio channel lacks moving visuals, it still conveys information via sound as well as any accompanying text and graphics that participants view or select to initiate the audio presentation. Moving toward the leaner end of the richness continuum, channels that provide textual information may or may not incorporate graphics to illustrate explanations. Because inclusion of graphics provides additional visual cues not found with text-only delivery, text with graphics can be classified as slightly richer than text alone. This rationale suggests that student performance will be highest when CAI uses a video channel, followed by audio, text with graphics, then text alone.

CAI Comparison Group. In addition to the potential for variation in the impact of CAI as a result of variations in channels, it is also likely that there are variations that result from the whole medium. As mentioned, media are collections of features (Griffith & Northcraft, 1994). Traditional lecture, for example, has features that include colocation of message sender and recipient and a variety of channels (visual, audio, tactile, etc.). Although all CAI is delivered with the same medium—a computer—comparative studies of CAI examine learning outcomes across different media. For instance, some studies compare CAI activities to similar activities that are delivered via face-to-face lecture or discussion (e.g., Chaparro & Halcomb, 1990; Garrett, Ashford, & Savage, 1987) or written, hard-copy text (Desch, Esquivel, & Anderson, 1991; Hawisher, 1987).

Fletcher-Flinn and Gravatt's (1995) meta-analysis of CAI effectiveness provides some precedent for analyzing the impact of a CAI medium in comparison to other media. In their study, they found that comparisons to traditional lecture provide an effect size (d) of .26 (r = .13), indicating that CAI increases performance to a higher degree than lecture. In contrast, paper versions of the CAI instruction decreased the overall effect (d) to .08 (r = .04), suggesting that performance improvements afforded by CAI are not as great when compared to paper. Unfortunately, this element of their study did not distinguish between postsecondary and elementary- or secondary-level instruction, so the generalizability of this finding to a sample of exclusively college-based students is not clear.

When interpreted within a media richness framework, Fletcher-Flinn and Gravatt's (1995) study suggests a need for modification of the media richness continuum. Media richness arguments suggest that when arranging media from rich to lean, written documents are close to the lean end of the richness continuum, computer-based media such as e-mail lie near the middle, and lecture and discussion is near the rich end (Trevino et al., 1990). However, Fletcher-Flinn and Gravatt's finding suggests that incorporation of classroom-based CAI on the richness continuum would set CAI as richest, followed by hard-copy text, then lecture. Essentially, the conclusion casts uncertainty on the location of CAI along the richness continuum.

To address this issue, this study seeks to more directly assess the validity of the richness continuum by testing a prediction that is derived from media richness tenets. Should the hypothesis receive support, it casts doubt on the validity of existing data. Should the null hold true, the study provides further evidence of a potential limitation in media richness theory. Thus, this study predicts that there will be a smaller effect in studies that compare CAI to lecture and discussion (indicating that lecture and discussion is more effective than CAI) and a larger effect when comparing CAI to hard-copy text (indicating that CAI is more effective than hard copy). Although this prediction is contrary to existing findings, it allows for a test of the media richness model and replicates extant research within a more theoretical framework.

CAI Course Content.   CAI is used across a variety of disciplines including physical sciences (e.g., Villareal & Seetharam, 1994), life sciences (e.g., Friedman, deBliek, Gilmer, Twarog, & File, 1992), social sciences (e.g., Reed-Sanders & Liebowitz, 1991), and languages and humanities (e.g., Kleinmann, 1987). Previous meta-analyses within specific postsecondary disciplinary areas indicate that within the physical sciences CAI results in an increase in performance above traditional media with an effect size (d) of .24 (r = .12) (Christmann & Badgett, 1999). Within the health professions CAI produces an effect size (d) of .41 (r = .20), indicating that CAI fares better than traditional lecture for courses in this area (Cohen & Dacanay, 1992). One meta-analysis that includes multiple disciplines reports that "hard" scientific disciplines (physical and life science) improve performance with an effect (d) of .15 ($r = .07$), and that soft disciplines (social sciences and language and humanities) produced a larger degree of improvement with an effect (d) of .35 ($r = .17$; Kulik & Kulik, 1986).

Although findings are mixed (as are the category systems), one fairly discernible pattern suggests that when harder science (physical science) disciplines are summarized, effect sizes tend to be comparatively lower than when softer disciplines (social sciences and language and humanities) are included. Although media richness theory argues that understanding complex information is facilitated by the use of richer media (Daft & Lengel, 1986), it is not possible to cleanly organize disciplines along a single continuum of their content or message complexity. On the one hand, some may argue that physical science content is more oriented toward clear-cut answers to problems, which may lessen the ambiguity experienced by students. On the other hand, these disciplines still have theories and propositions that are quite likely to be perceived as complex by developing college students. Thus, rather than propose a hypothesis to test the impact of CAI across disciplines, this study seeks to determine how CAI influences student performance across four disciplinary areas: (a) physical sciences, (b) life sciences, (c) social sciences, and (d) language and humanities.

METHODS

Although there are several existing meta-analyses of CAI impacts on student performance in postsecondary education, none have examined the communication-oriented moderators described earlier. Further, the most recent meta-analysis (Fletcher-Flinn & Gravatt, 1995) focuses across a variety of student levels rather than on college and university settings. The other studies are more narrowly focused on specific types of courses (Christmann & Badgett, 1999; Cohen & Dacanay, 1992). Although Kulik and Kulik's (1986) analysis contains a very thorough review of the literature, its review ends in 1984. Thus, this investigation seeks to identify comparative CAI research in college settings that has been published between 1985 and 2002.

Literature Search and Selection of Studies

Systematic searches of the Educational Research Information Clearinghouse (ERIC), ABI/Inform, Academic Search Elite, MEDLINE, and Health Source were initially conducted to locate CAI research studies published since 1984. Initial search terms used were computer-assisted instruction, computer-based education, computer-enriched instruction, comparative studies, and student achievement. A manual search of a variety of journals that were determined to contain a substantial amount of CAI research was also performed. These journals included *The Journal of Computer-Based Instruction, The Journal of Educational Technology Systems, The Journal of Educational Computing Research, Communication Education*, and *The Journal of Research on Computing in Education*. Finally, studies and meta-analyses were acquired from manuscript references.

To be included in this analysis, studies had to include quantitative research that compared student performance across CAI and a traditional instruction format (variations of lecture and discussion or hard-copy text) and were free from obvious methodological flaws. All studies had to include measures of student performance that included CAI-specific assessments, final examination scores, and final course grades. Studies that did not include a comparison group (Skinner, 1993; Turner, Evers, Wood, Lehman, & Peck, 2000) did not focus on student performance (Basile & D'Aquila, 2002; Leonard, 1989), or did not contain recoverable data (Kuehner, 1999; LaBonty, 1989; Nyamathi, Chang, Sherman, & Grech, 1989; Raidl, Wood, Lehman, & Evers, 1995) were excluded from the analysis. These procedures resulted in the location of 57 studies that compared CAI to traditional instructional formats. A list of these studies along with their moderator codes and effect sizes is available from the first author.

Moderator Coding

Three potential moderators were coded by the researchers for subsequent analysis. The first was the communication channel used by the CAI instruction. Four hierarchically organized channel categories were coded: text only, text with graphics, audio, and video. That is, video CAI also contains text, graphics, and audio channels. At the next level, audio-based studies also included text and graphics, and so forth. This category system assumes that higher level channels (i.e., video) are inclusive of lower categories and is consistent with previous meta-analyses of educational delivery formats (see Allen, Bourhis, Burrell, & Mabry, 2002).

The second moderator that was coded examined the medium used by the comparison group. Two general categories for comparison groups were identified after surveying the studies. Lecture and discussion encompassed any study that compared CAI to situations in which instructors delivered content via spoken presentation or more informal discussion. An initial attempt was made to distinguish lecture-only presentations from lectures that contained discussion as well. However, because students are usually free to ask questions and discuss topics during a lecture and may also discuss the lecture materials away from the confines of the lecture, such a distinction is artificial and potentially misleading. Thus, any form of traditional delivery that included face-to-face presentation was coded in the lecture and discussion category. Studies that provided material that paralleled the CAI instruction with a written, hard-copy document were coded in the written, hard-copy category.

The final moderator coded in this study was the content area of the CAI instruction. A review of extant meta-analyses that focused on course content distinctions indicated that there were no consistently used category schemes. Thus, the researchers devised a general, four-category scheme that distinguished between (a) physical sciences, (b) life sciences, (c) social sciences, and (d) language and humanities. The physical sciences category included studies of mathematics, statistics, engineering, and computer programming. Life sciences included studies in biology, anatomy, agriculture, and others connected to technical components of health and medical professions. The social sciences category included studies of psychology, sociology, business, telecommunications, criminal justice, education, and sports training. Finally, language and humanities studies included analyses of courses in reading, language learning, writing, and music.

Meta-Analysis Procedures

This study used a variance-centered form of analysis as developed by Hunter and Schmidt (1990). After manuscripts were gathered, mean scores from students in CAI groups and traditional formats were converted to a common, effect-size metric, in this case, Pearson's correlation coefficient. Any studies that included information about reliability of the performance measurement were then corrected for attenuation. Because a substantial number of studies did not include reliability indexes, the mean reliability from the studies that did contain such information was computed (.83) and used as a means to correct for measurement error. Subsequently, box and whisker plots were used to detect outliers and extreme data points. Effect sizes were then averaged using a weighting procedure that accounts for differences in individual study sample sizes. Finally, to determine whether additional moderators were present, tests for homogeneity of sample effects were calculated using chi-square.

RESULTS

Overall Effect

The overall analysis revealed a higher level of performance for the CAI groups than traditional groups (average $r = .12, k = 57, N = 6,206$), with a heterogeneous set of correlations, $\chi^2(57, N = 6,206) = 340.21, p < .05$ (see

Table 6.1). Because box and whisker plots detected several outliers (Watkins, 1998; Wiksten, Patterson, Antonio, De La Cruz, & Buxton, 1998), the average effect size was recomputed after excluding these studies. The resulting average effect was slightly larger (average $r = .14, k = 55, N = 6,024$) although the data were still heterogeneous, $\chi^2(55, N = 6,024) = 271.52, p < .05$. The significance of the chi-square tests for departure from homogeneity suggests that these findings should be interpreted cautiously, as it is likely that additional moderating variables may be present.

TABLE 6.1
Summary of Results

Effect	k	N	ES (r)	SD	χ^2
Overall	57	6,206	.1191	.24	340.21*
Outliers removed	55	6,024	.1377	.22	271.52*
CAI channel					
Text	23	2,816	.1572	.23	150.13*
Graphics	21	2,085	.0992	.23	105.35*
Outliers removed	16	1,722	.1015	.12	25.79
Audio	5	498	.1133	.18	15.17*
Outliers removed	3	375	.1454	.09	1.85
Video	6	652	−.0159	.25	39.13*
Comparison group					
CAI vs. lecture	45	5,134	.1557	.22	237.61*
Outliers removed	43	4,952	.1796	.18	160.12*
CAI vs. hard copy	12	1,072	−.0561	.25	64.46*
Course content					
Physical science	16	1,759	.1297	.20	66.15*
Life science	21	2,261	.0787	.24	126.56*
Outliers removed	18	1,999	.1498	.15	41.55*
Social science	13	1,692	.1895	.26	113.38*
Outlier removed	12	1,575	.2365	.21	64.50*
Language and Humanities	7	494	.0251	.20	18.31*
Outlier removed	6	454	−.0161	.15	9.51

*$p < .05$.

CAI Channel

Effect sizes for the four CAI channels were examined separately. First, the effect size for CAI studies that used a text-based channel was .16 ($k = 23$, $N = 2,816$), but the data were heterogeneous, indicating that additional moderators or undetected outliers may be present, $\chi^2(23, N = 2,816) = 150.13, p < .05$ (see Table 6.1). The effect size for CAI that used text with graphics was slightly smaller, indicating that effects of text-only CAI are larger than those for text with graphics (average $r = .10$, $k = 21$, $N = 2,085$). The test for homogeneity indicated that the set of effect sizes for the text with graphics studies was heterogeneous, $\chi^2(21, N = 2,085) = 105.35, p < .05$. A total of five studies were detected as outliers (Dalal, Haworth, Davis, Fowler, & Randolph, 1991–1992; Kiser, 1990; Palmiter, 1991; Reed-Sanders & Liebowitz, 1991; Watkins, 1998). The effect size without the outliers was .10 ($k = 16$, $N = 1,722$). The chi-square test was not significant, indicating that it is unlikely that additional moderators or outliers could account for variation in the effect sizes, $\chi^2(16, N = 1,722) = 25.79, p > .05$.

The effect size for studies that used an audio channel was .11 ($k = 5$, $N = 498$) with a heterogeneous set of correlations, $\chi^2(5, N = 498) = 15.17, p < .05$. Two outlier studies (Dalby, 1992; Prindle & McLaughlin, 1987) were detected and removed and then the average effect size was recomputed. After removing the outliers, the average r was .15 ($k = 3$, $N = 375$) and the set of correlations was homogenous, $\chi^2(3, N = 375) = 1.85, p > .05$. For CAI studies that used a video channel, the average effect size was –.02 ($k = 6$, $N = 652$), indicating that the use of CAI with a video channel slightly decreased student performance in comparison to traditional media. However, the data were heterogeneous, indicating that outliers or additional moderators may be present, $\chi^2(6, N = 652) = 39.13, p < .05$.

CAI Comparison Group

The two types of media that were compared against the computer-based medium of CAI were traditional lecture and discussion and hard-copy written. Studies that compared CAI to lecture and discussion yielded an average r of .16 ($k = 45$, $N = 5,134$) and the data were heterogeneous, $\chi^2(45, N = 5,134) = 237.61, p < .05$ (see Table 6.1). Subsequent analyses revealed two outliers (Watkins, 1998; Wiksten et al., 1998). The average r after removing outliers was slightly larger at .18 ($k = 43$, $N = 4,952$), but the data were heterogeneous, $\chi^2(43, N = 4,952) = 160.12, p < .05$, indicating that additional outliers or moderators may be present. When compared to traditional lecture and discussion, CAI results in an increase in student performance.

Effect sizes from studies that compared CAI to hard-copy text averaged to $-.06$ ($k = 12, N = 1,072$). Although box and whisker plots failed to reveal outliers, the data were heterogeneous, indicating that moderators may be present, $\chi^2(12, N = 1,072) = 64.46, p < .05$. The negative average correlation indicates that CAI decreases student performance when compared to hard-copy text.

CAI Course Content

The four types of CAI course content analyzed in this study were physical sciences, life sciences, social sciences, and language and humanities (see Table 6.1 for summary). Among the physical sciences, the average effect size was .13 ($k = 16, N = 1,759$) based on a heterogeneous set of correlations, $\chi^2(16, N = 1,759) = 66.15, p < .05$. Among the life sciences, the average effect size dropped to .08 ($k = 21, N = 2,261$) with a heterogeneous set of correlations. After removing three outliers (Vichitvejpaisal et al., 2001; Watkins, 1998; Wiksten et al., 1998), the average r jumped to .15 ($k = 18, N = 1,999$), but the data were heterogeneous, indicating continued presence of moderators, $\chi^2(18, N = 1,999) = 41.55, p < .05$. In the social sciences, there was an average r of .19 ($k = 13, N = 1,692$) with a heterogeneous set of correlations, $\chi^2(13, N = 1,692) = 113.38, p < .05$. After removing one outlier (Sawyer, 1988), the average r was .24 ($k = 12, N = 1,575$), with heterogeneous correlations, $\chi^2(12, N = 1,575) = 64.50, p < .05$. Finally, for the language and humanities studies, the average correlation was .03 ($k = 7, N = 494$) and the data were heterogeneous, $\chi^2(7, N = 494) = 18.31, p < .05$. After removing one outlier (Dalby, 1992), the average correlation was negative at $-.02$ ($k = 6, N = 454$), suggesting that the use of CAI in language and humanities decreases student performance. Additionally, the correlations were homogenous, $\chi^2(6, N = 454) = 9.51, p > .05$, indicating that additional outliers or moderators were unlikely.

DISCUSSION

This study used meta-analysis to determine the impact of CAI on student performance. Overall, it appears that there is a small performance improvement among students who receive CAI when compared to those who are taught with traditional instructional formats. With regard to channels, these data indicate that CAI that uses text, text with graphics, and audio channels tends to increase student performance, whereas the video channel leads to a very slight decrease. Comparisons across different media indicate that CAI leads to higher performance than lecture and discussion, but slightly lower performance than a written, hard-copy medium. Finally, this study indicates that CAI leads to performance increases in physical sciences, life sciences, and social sciences, but may lead to a small performance decrement for students in language and humanities disciplines.

Overall Effect of CAI

The findings from this investigation are largely consistent with extant meta-analyses (Christmann & Badgett, 1999; Cohen & Dacanay, 1992; Fletcher-Flinn & Gravatt, 1995; Kulik & Kulik, 1986) that examine the overall impact of CAI on student performance. After converting previous meta-analysis effect sizes to the common metric of Pearson's r, the average effect size from existing studies is .14, with a range from .10 to .20. This study found an overall effect size of .12, clearly within the range of previously reported effects. Thus, this study further contributes to the growing body of literature suggesting that CAI does provide a small increase in student performance when compared to traditional instructional formats.

CAI Channel

Arguments based on media richness theory (Daft & Lengel, 1986) suggested that student performance would be highest when CAI uses a video channel, followed by audio, text with graphics, then text alone. Surprisingly, the results of this investigation reveal that text leads to the greatest performance improvements, followed by audio, then text with graphics. CAI that uses a video channel actually appears to result in a small decrease in student performance. The findings are contrary to the arguments that richer channels will decrease ambiguity (Trevino, Lengel, & Daft, 1987) and thereby lead to improved performance.

It is possible that the increased quantity of information provided by CAI that uses video channels may limit student comprehension of material. In other words, video may provide more information than students need and result in a form of information overload. Because the ultimate factor that may influence student performance is the content of the CAI rather than the format of the presentation, additional video cues may distract students from focusing on the material that is needed to perform well on assessments. In contrast, audio- and text-based CAI provides fewer cues and leads to higher degrees of performance. Potentially, these leaner channels allow participants to focus more exclusively on the CAI content (whether it is spoken audio or written in text form) with fewer distractions. This idea is further supported by the fact that text with graphics resulted in lower performance than text alone. Well-designed written CAI with textual illustration may allow learners to process material, whereas graphics may serve as an additional distraction. Thus, these data point to the possibility that CAI using leaner channels may lead to greater performance improvements than CAI that uses rich channels.

CAI Comparison Group

The preceding section explained the relative effectiveness of various channels within a CAI presentation; however, it did not indicate how CAI fares
against different traditional instructional media. Direct consideration of the
type of traditional medium to which CAI was compared reveals that CAI
improves student performance above lecture and discussion, but may not
provide a performance increase above written, hard-copy text. This finding
is similar to Fletcher-Flinn and Gravatt's (1995) report that revealed that
CAI performance improvement was greater when the comparison group
was lecture than when it consisted of paper versions. Although this study revealed a slight negative effect for the written comparison, both studies
clearly indicate that paper versions of CAI are nearly equivalent to computer versions.

These findings challenge the arguments of media richness theory, which
suggested a smaller effect in studies that compare CAI to lecture and discussion and a larger effect when comparing CAI to hard-copy text. In fact, the
actual finding was the inverse. A plausible explanation for this effect lies in
the features afforded by the different media. Lecture and discussion is syn-
chronously delivered and limits the opportunity for students to review, focus
on, and analyze content. Once a lecture is complete, students must rely on
their ability to retain the information that was presented and may only review notes that were taken at the time. In contrast, hard-copy materials are
asynchronous and allow students time to closely examine and review material, perhaps until they are satisfied with their level of comprehension. With
the CAI medium, students have the exact, word-for-word content that was
eventually assessed on quizzes and exams.

CAI's computer-based features are more similar to the hard-copy medium than to lecture and discussion. Typically, the CAI implementations
found in the studies included in this data set allowed students to view material initially, and then review it if they wished to do so. Similar to hard copy, if
CAI material was not clear, students may have reviewed the presentation
until the material was understood. Unlike lecture and discussion, CAI features incorporate greater opportunity for students to reconsider the content
on which they were eventually assessed. Thus, the findings here suggest that
features of CAI media increase student performance to a higher degree than
lecture and discussion. However, CAI does not provide substantial
improvement in performance above written, hard-copy media.

CAI Course Content

Separate effect sizes were computed for four course content areas: physical
sciences, life sciences, social sciences, and language and humanities. Analy-

sis of average effect sizes for studies in each area suggest that social science courses benefit the most from CAI, followed by life sciences, then physical sciences. In the language and humanities disciplines, integration of CAI appears to lead to a small decline in student performance when compared to traditional instructional formats.

Although findings in extant meta-analyses are mixed, they have generally shown that hard science areas (i.e., physical sciences) tend to have lower CAI effect sizes than soft disciplines (i.e., social sciences and language and humanities; Kulik & Kulik, 1986). A separate study of the health professions (i.e., life sciences) yielded a medium-sized CAI effect (Cohen & Dacanay, 1992). This study indicates that social sciences did produce the greatest CAI effect and physical sciences were substantially lower. However, language and humanities, which is a soft discipline, did not appear to benefit from CAI. Further, the effect size for life science disciplines was the second largest in the study, but it was far from the overall effect size reported in Cohen and Dacanay's previous analysis.

Although there is no clearly articulated rationale to assist with the interpretation of discipline-based, CAI effect discrepancies, focusing on content characteristics or a match between user's technical skills and CAI requirements may provide some inroads. Arguments related to content characteristics imply that some materials may be more suited for CAI than others. This study would indicate that courses in languages, writing, and the arts (language and humanities) are not well suited for CAI. Claims related to potential performance improvements that result from a match between user skill and CAI requirements might suggest that certain disciplinary areas are more likely to include instructors and students that have technical abilities that may match technical skills required to effectively design and operate CAI. So, although there is no clearly articulated rationale for variations across disciplinary areas, it may be useful to focus on the data to date and more closely examine specific CAI variations to determine whether computer-based activities are more beneficial in specific content areas.

Limitations

Three limitations should be considered when interpreting the results from this research. First, as noted earlier, many of the effect sizes were computed based on a heterogeneous set of correlations. This suggests that there is a significant amount of variation in the correlations that is not explained. Typically, such variation is a result of outliers or additional moderators. Because this study utilized box and whisker plots to detect and exclude outliers, it is quite likely that additional moderator coding is needed to definitively identify the effect of CAI on course performance.

Second, three of the moderator codes substantially reduced the number of studies that were included in the computation of some of the effect sizes. Effects for audio channels, video channels, and language and humanities content were based on six or fewer studies after outliers were removed. For example, only five studies utilized audio channels and two of these were excluded because they were outliers. As a result, the effect size for audio CAI is based on a small number of studies ($k = 3, N = 375$). Thus, because of the small sample sizes, validity of the effect sizes in these areas is tenuous.

Third, the fundamental effect being considered here was performance. Studies in the sample measured performance differently, including CAI-specific assessments, final course grades, and final examination grades. Although these measures can be categorized within the general area of student performance, further analysis is required to determine whether there is a differential impact for different types of assessment.

Future Directions

In addition to efforts to resolve the limitations of this study, we believe that future meta-analyses of CAI research may benefit by pursuing additional research in four areas. First, future studies should look more closely at additional communication variables to determine how these factors may moderate effects. Assessments of the CAI interactivity and degree of audience focus are especially important. Interactivity deals with the degree to which a CAI task allows the user to become involved in dictating how the activity develops. Some CAI activities provide feedback to users as they progress through the lesson. In such cases, it is possible that this heightened involvement and feedback may assist students with further understanding of the material. Also, CAI implementations are generally of two types: those designed by an instructor for a specific course or those developed and sold by general publishers. Course-specific CAI tasks are likely to be designed with an emphasis on a specific audience, but CAI from general publishers may not have as clear a focus on specific types of students. Potentially, there may be some variation in the impact of CAI when a specific audience's needs are incorporated into CAI design that may differ from general audiences.

Second, CAI research must look more closely at additional outcomes. Student satisfaction with CAI may be especially important for determining the overall success of a CAI implementation. Determining which CAI features lead to the highest levels of satisfaction and performance are likely to be quite informative for instructors who design CAI work. Additionally, some studies suggest that CAI may shorten the amount of time that is required for students to effectively learn content (e.g., Garrett et al., 1987; Lamperti & Sodicoff, 1997). By more closely examining time requirements of students, further information may be gleaned about the efficiency, as well as effectiveness, of CAI methods.

Finally, future studies should begin to address individual differences among students who are taught with CAI. An emphasis on factors such as learning style and attitudes toward computers may allow CAI researchers to determine the type of student who may benefit the most from CAI instruction. As a result, it may be that CAI is not a general solution for improving student performance, but rather one option that is especially effective (or ineffective) depending on the characteristics of an individual student.

Practical Implications

In addition to the general information that suggests CAI may provide small improvements in student performance, this study has important implications for CAI designers and implementers. First, we recommend that CAI designers use video sparingly. This study revealed that CAI that includes video channels may not improve student performance and may even slightly reduce it (when compared to traditional instruction). Although it is likely that some forms of simulation or presentation require the use of video, these results suggest that it should not be the primary channel used. In circumstances where video can be avoided, audio- or text-only CAI may lead to greater increases in student performance.

Second, when considering whether to implement CAI, instructors should carefully consider whether switching to a computer-based medium holds advantages over previously used, traditional media. Although CAI may lead to some performance improvement over lecture and discussion, those considering a switch to CAI should assess whether the potentially small gain justifies the additional equipment, training, and effort needed to design CAI. If the activities that will be moved to CAI are already available via hard-copy text, the data reported here suggest that moving to CAI will offer no benefits at all. Thus, we believe that if equipment, training, or time are at a premium, instructors may benefit more by creating well-designed written, hard-copy documents rather than CAI. However, if content or other factors prevent the use of hard copy, instructors should recognize that potential CAI performance gains may be fairly small.

Finally, it would be premature to recommend that some disciplinary areas should or should not use CAI. Although the data suggest that there are variations across course content areas, we believe that any instructor in any content area can design effective CAI. However, regardless of discipline, potential CAI designers should pay close attention to fundamental instructional practices and ask whether CAI is in fact appropriate for a particular type of content. In circumstances in which computer-based technology may present an obstacle to student understanding, it should be avoided in favor of traditional formats. However, if instructors are careful to focus on well-designed content, CAI may lead to improvements in student learning.

CONCLUSION

It is safe to say that computer technology has changed the way that many instructors deliver course content. This study suggests that CAI can lead to a slight increase in student performance that is not found with traditional instructional formats. By focusing on communication-oriented variables (channel, medium, content), the data reported here provide additional information about how and why certain types of CAI may maximize student performance. In summary, findings indicate that (a) CAI that uses leaner channels is more effective than that using rich channels; (b) CAI offers improvement in performance above traditional lecture, but does not appear to improve performance above written hard copy; and (c) CAI leads to performance improvements in social sciences, life sciences, and physical sciences, but not for courses in language and humanities.

In closing, this research points to the fundamental importance of considering the method for delivering course content in relation to its potential for improving student performance. Even though research indicates that a wide range of technology is available in today's postsecondary institutions (Green, 2002), instructors would be ill advised to immediately assume that incorporating CAI will automatically improve student learning. Although well-designed CAI may increase student performance, poorly designed CAI will surely decrease it. CAI technologies are but one tool among many that can be used to complement effective instruction. Without sound instructional practices, even the most promising CAI possibilities may remain undiscovered.

REFERENCES

Adams, T. M., & Kandt, G. K. (1991). Computer-assisted instruction vs. lecture methods in teaching the rules of golf. *Physical Educator, 48,* 146–151.

Allen, M., Bourhis, J., Burrell, N., & Mabry, E. (2002). Comparing student satisfaction with distance education to traditional classrooms in higher education: A meta-analysis. *The American Journal of Distance Education, 16,* 83–97.

Basile, A., & D'Aquila, J. M. (2002). An experimental analysis of computer-mediated instruction and student attitudes in a principles of financial accounting course. *Journal of Education for Business, 177,* 137–143.

Chaparro, B. S., & Halcomb, C. G. (1990). The effects of computerized tutorial usage on course performance in general psychology. *Journal of Computer-Based Instruction, 17,* 141–146.

Christmann, E., & Badgett, J. L. (1999). A comparative analysis of the effects of computer-assisted instruction on student achievement in differing science and demographical areas. *Journal of Computers in Mathematics and Science Teaching, 18,* 135–143.

Cohen, P. A., & Dacanay, L. S. (1992). Computer-based instruction and health professions education. *Evaluation & the Health Professions, 15,* 259–281.

Cotton, K. (1992). SIRS Close-Up #10: *Computer-assisted instruction.* Retrieved December 28, 2002, from http://www.nwrel.org/scpd/sirs/5/cu10.html

Daft, R. L., & Lengel, R. H. (1986). Organizational information requirements: Media richness and structural design. *Management Science, 32,* 554–571.

Dalal, N. P., Haworth, D. A., Davis, M. A., Fowler, D. G., & Randolph, J. T. (1991–1992). Educational software—it isn't always. *Journal of Educational Technology Systems, 20,* 169–178.

Dalby, B. (1992). A computer-based training program for developing harmonic intonation discrimination skill. *Journal of Research in Music Education, 40,* 139–152.

Deardorff, W. W. (1986). Computerized health education: A comparison with additional formats. *Health Education Quarterly, 13,* 61–72.

Desch, L. W., Esquivel, M. T., & Anderson, S. K. (1991). Comparison of a computer tutorial with other methods for teaching well-newborn care. *American Journal of Diseases of Children, 145,* 1255–1258.

Fish, M. C., & Feldmann, S. C. (1987). A comparison of reading comprehension using print and microcomputer presentation. *Journal of Computer-Based Instruction, 14,* 57–61.

Fletcher-Flinn, C. M., & Gravatt, B. (1995). The efficacy of computer assisted instruction (CAI): A meta-analysis. *Journal of Educational Computing Research, 12,* 219–242.

Friedman, C. P., deBliek, R., Gilmer, J. S., Twarog, R. G., & File, D. D. (1992). Influence of a computer database and problem exercises on students' knowledge of bacteriology. *Academic Medicine, 67,* 332–338.

Garrett, T. J., Ashford, A. R., & Savage, D. G. (1987). A comparison of computer-assisted instruction and tutorials in hematology and oncology. *Journal of Medical Education, 62,* 918–922.

Green, K. C. (2002). *Campus computing, 2002: The national survey of computing and information technology in American higher education.* Encino, CA: Campus Computing.

Griffith, T. L., & Northcraft, G. B. (1994). Distinguishing between the forest and the trees: Media, features, and methodology in electronic communication research. *Organization Science, 5,* 272–285.

Guy, J. F., & Frisby, A. J. (1992). Using interactive videodiscs to teach gross anatomy to undergraduates at The Ohio State University. *Academic Medicine, 67,* 132–133.

Hawisher, G. E. (1987). The effects of word processing on the revision strategies of college freshmen. *Research in the Teaching of English, 21,* 145–159.

Hunter, J., & Schmidt, F. (1990). *Methods of meta-analysis: Correcting error and bias in research findings.* Newbury Park, CA: Sage.

Kiser, L. (1990). Interaction of spatial visualization with computer-enhanced and traditional presentation of linear absolute-value inequalities. *Journal of Computers in Mathematics and Science Teaching, 10,* 85–97.

Kleinmann, H. H. (1987). The effect of computer-assisted instruction on ESL reading achievement. *The Modern Language Journal, 71,* 267–276.

Kuehner, A. V. (1999). The effects of computer-based vs. text-based instruction on remedial college readers. *Journal of Adolescent & Adult Literacy, 43,* 160–168.

Kulik, C.-L. C., & Kulik, J. A. (1986). Effectiveness of computer-based education in colleges. *AEDS Journal, 19,* 81–108.

LaBonty, D. J. (1989). Computer-assisted homework in accounting: Effects on student achievement and attitude. *The Delta Pi Epsilon Journal, 31*(2), 47–55.

Lamperti, A., & Sodicoff, M. (1997). Computer-based neuroanatomy laboratory for medical students. *The Anatomical Record, 249*, 422–428.

Lengel, R. H., & Daft, R. L. (1988). The selection of communication media as an executive skill. *The Academy of Management Executive, 2*, 225–232.

Leonard, W. H. (1989). A comparison of student reactions to biology instruction by interactive videodisc or conventional laboratory. *Journal of Research in Science Teaching, 26*, 95–104.

Morrison, J. L. (1999). The role of technology in education today and tomorrow: An interview with Kenneth Green. *On the Horizon, 7*(1), 2–5.

Neuhauser, C. (2002). Learning style and effectiveness of online and face-to-face instruction. *The American Journal of Distance Education, 16*, 99–113.

Niemiec, R., & Walberg, H. J. (1987). Comparative effects of computer-assisted instruction: A synthesis of reviews. *Journal of Educational Computing Research, 3*, 19–37.

Nyamathi, A., Chang, B., Sherman, B., & Grech, M. (1989). Computer use and nursing research. *Western Journal of Nursing Research, 11*, 498–501.

Palmiter, J. R. (1991). Effects of computer algebra systems on concept and skill acquisition in calculus. *Journal for Research in Mathematics Education, 22*, 151–156.

Prindle, L., & McLaughlin, T. F. (1987). A computer spelling testing program with clerical English students: An empirical evaluation. *Journal of Computer-Based Instruction, 14*, 146–149.

Raidl, M. A., Wood, O. B., Lehman, J. D., & Evers, W. D. (1995). Computer-assisted instruction improves clinical reasoning of dietetics students. *Journal of the American Dietetic Association, 95*, 868–880.

Rankin, E. L., & Hoaas, D. J. (2001). The use of PowerPoint and student performance. *Atlantic Economic Journal, 29*(1), 113.

Reed-Sanders, D., & Liebowitz, S. (1991). An empirical test of integration of computers in introductory sociology. *Teaching Sociology, 19*, 223–230.

Sawyer, T. A. (1988). The effects of computerized and conventional study guides on achievement in college students. *Journal of Computer-Based Instruction, 15*(3), 80–82.

Skinner, M. E. (1993). The effects of computer-based instruction on the achievement of college students as a function of achievement status and mode of presentation. *Computers in Human Behavior, 6*, 351–360.

Trevino, L. K., Daft, R. L., & Lengel, R. H. (1990). Understanding managers' media choices: A symbolic interactionist perspective. In J. Fulk & C. Steinfield (Eds.), *Organizations and communication technology* (pp. 71–93). Newbury Park, CA: Sage.

Trevino, L. K., Lengel, R. H., & Daft, R. L. (1987). Media symbolism, media richness, and media choice in organizations. *Communication Research, 14*, 553–574.

Turner, R. E., Evers, W. D., Wood, O. B., Lehman, J. D., & Peck, L. W. (2000). Computer-based simulations enhance clinical experience of dietetics interns. *Journal of the American Dietetic Association, 100*, 183–190.

Vichitvejpaisal, P., Sitthikongsak, S., Preechakoon, B., Kraiprasit, K., Parakkanodom, S., Manon, C., et al. (2001). Does computer-assisted instruction really help to improve the learning process. *Medical Education, 35*, 983–989.

Villareal, S. S., & Seetharam, A. (1994, November). *The impact of CAI emphasizing visual feedback on industrial distribution students at Texas A&M.* Paper presented at the Frontiers in Education Conference, San Jose, CA.

Watkins, G. L. (1998). Achievement and attitudes with CD-ROM instruction. *College Student Journal, 32,* 293–302.
Wiksten, D. L., Patterson, P., Antonio, K., De La Cruz, D., & Buxton, B. P. (1998). The effectiveness of an interactive computer program versus traditional lecture in athletic training education. *Journal of Athletic Training, 33,* 238–243.

7

Test Anxiety, Academic Self-Efficacy, and Study Skills: A Meta-Analytic Review

Raymond W. Preiss
University of Puget Sound

Barbara Mae Gayle
Saint Martin's University

Mike Allen
University of Wisconsin–Milwaukee

Social scientists have studied the relationship between anxiety and performance for well over 50 years (Lazarus, Deese, & Osler, 1952). The motivational and interference qualities of anxiety have been demonstrated in diverse areas such as reaction time (Grice, 1955), persuasion (Janis, 1955), drive level (Spence, Farber, & McFann, 1956), performance under stress (Westrope, 1953), verbal conditioning (Spielberger, DeNike, & Stein, 1965), and learning (Nicholson, 1958; Sarason, Mandler, & Craighill, 1952). The negative relationship between anxiety and performance, especially on learning tasks, was the genesis of a rich line of educational research concerning psychological drives associated with learning situations and types of performance. Test anxiety (TA) investigations are the descendents of this tradition, and TA research embraces a range of issues from cognitive interference in processing information in testing situations (Sarason, 1986), to academic self-concept and achievement motivation (Marsh, 1993), to treatment protocols designed to improve educational performance (Hembree, 1988; Seipp, 1991).

The goal of this investigation is to examine the study behaviors and motivation of test-anxious students. Rather than focus on treatment therapies, we sought to understand the day-to-day behaviors students routinely use to prepare for educational assignments and examinations. Of course, these study skills have been the topic of numerous experiments over the years. However, previous meta-analytic reviews have emphasized test performance (i.e., the effect of study skills training on improved learning) or anxiety reduction (i.e., the effect of systematic desensitization therapy in reducing test anxiety). Hembree (1988), for example, reported only six effect sizes in two categories (study hours per week, good study habits) of study behaviors in his meta-analytic examination of TA levels (p. 64, Table 9).

Other meta-analyses have examined the ruminations associated with TA. For example, Seipp (1991) examined the stability of the TA—performance effect size, stressing cognitive components (worry and emotionality) associated with TA. Unfortunately, learning preparation variables have not been emphasized in these investigations. Treatments and cognitions are important aspects of understanding TA, and we endorse efforts to clarify these issues. It also seems prudent to explore the ways TA may play out in students' curricular and cocurricular activities. We opted to focus on the often mundane and routine study activities that provide a platform for learning. We offer this empirical review after summarizing the TA literature and discussing major findings related to study behaviors.

CONCEPTUALIZATIONS OF TEST ANXIETY

The precise nature and definition of TA is contested. Most would agree, however, that anxieties in testing situations may facilitate or debilitate task-directed behavior (Alpert & Haber, 1960), produce ruminations involving worry and emotionality (Liebert & Morris, 1967), and may involve skills associated with learning and testing such as test-wiseness (Benson, 1989) and study behaviors (Tobias, 1980). The generally accepted finding that TA is associated with lower academic performance has been confirmed by several meta-analyses (Hembree, 1988; Seipp, 1991). Also, reductions in TA have been associated with various therapies, including systematic desensitization (Osterhouse, 1972), cognitive restructuring (Gonzalez, 1987), hypnosis (Sapp, 1999), and study skills counseling (Culler & Holahan, 1980). Meta-analytic reviews indicate that programs combining anxiety reduction regimens with skills training offer greater improvements in academic performance (Hembree, 1988).

Although the TA–academic performance association is substantial ($r = -.21$; Seipp, 1991), the effect size would be classified as "small" using

Cohen's (1977) system. This is not to argue that the outcomes are minor. The number of proposed mechanisms for TA-related performance deficits and evidence that testing situations produce cognitive interference that can block processing (Covington & Omelich, 1987) or diminish on-task time is persuasive. It is possible that the effect size is reflecting a small part of the cluster of variables and systems in play.

Spielberger and Vagg (1995) proposed a transactional process model in an effort to broadly conceptualize TA. This approach is appealing because it acknowledges cognitive components (perceptions, ruminations, information processing, retrieval mechanisms) that operate in concert with performance-linked worry and emotionality. This perspective calls attention to the dynamic and continuous process of TA and emphasizes behaviors that may occur before and after performance is assessed. Spielberger and Vagg pointed to study skills, test-wiseness, testing skills, and study habits as variables central to understanding the TA construct.

The transactional process model of TA is also attractive due to its isomorphism. Test-taking is only one aspect of the educational enterprise and theories attempting to understand curricular and cocurricular outcomes should incorporate behaviors beyond classroom testing. The transactional process model addresses day-to-day educational tasks such as academic motivation, study skills and habits, procrastination, and test preparation and test-taking skills. There is evidence that TA is associated with patterns of these behaviors. Pintrich and De Groot (1990) and Zimmerman and Bandura (1994) found that TA and academic self-efficacy were negatively associated. Because self-efficacy is frequently associated with academic aspirations, researchers have explored the test-taking behaviors of high- and low-achieving students. Birenbaum and Nasser (1994) found that low-achieving students made more serious errors and errors indicating study deficits. High-achieving students, however, tended to make less serious errors and errors indicating task-irrelevant thoughts. This line of reasoning suggests that effort expended well before an examination, and behaviors and cognitions occurring during a test, are integral aspects of the TA construct.

Most TA research is compatible with this view and many TA studies implicitly acknowledge the motivational, behavioral, and cognitive aspects of the variable. For example, Cassady and Johnson (2002) developed an instrument measuring the worry dimension of TA. Scores on their scale were associated with self-reported procrastination prior to tests. Covington and Omelich (1987) found evidence of TA-associated blockage for performance on easy test items. Students who used effective study strategies were able to access previously blocked information. Considerable evidence exists that high-test-anxious and low-test-anxious students differ in study skills and exam-taking skills (Benjamin, McKeachie, Lin, & Holinger, 1981; Naveh-Benjamin, McKeachie, & Lin, 1987; Paulman & Kennelly, 1984).

Behaviors prior to testing have also received attention. Students with TA tend to exhibit poor study habits (Culler & Holahan, 1980; Kirkland & Hollandsworth, 1979, 1980) and to procrastinate regarding academic tasks (Rothblum, Solomon, & Murakami, 1986). Some researchers believe that students with TA are equipped and intend to study, but do not (Kalechstein, Hocevar, Zimmer, & Kalechstein, 1989). This relationship is somewhat complex, as one type of procrastinator tends to find the test material to be aversive, whereas another type disengages out of fear of failure (Solomon & Rothblum, 1984). In any event, few investigations have explored procrastination and test avoidance (Geen, 1985) and one researcher believes that students with TA avoid or attempt to escape the evaluation situation or do not persist at testing tasks, perhaps due to a "self-protective" process (Geen, 1987). Wishing to escape the testing situation is the most frequently experienced negative cognition students with TA report during testing situations (Galassi, Frierson & Sharer, 1981a, 1981b).

META-ANALYTIC SUMMARY

Our review of the TA literature revealed a formidable body of research organized around the themes of cognitive interference (facilitative and debilitative anxiety), personality characteristics (self-esteem, locus of control, dominance, fear of failure, etc.), and treatment programs (systematic desensitization, study skills training, relaxation training, etc.). To understand the day-to-day experience of TA, we found the transactional process model to be helpful. Following Spielberger and Vagg's (1995) reasoning, we sought to understand how routine and common student behaviors were associated with TA. Thus, we posed the following research questions:

1. How is TA associated with reported academic self-efficacy?
2. How is TA associated with reported study habits and study effectiveness?
3. How is TA associated with reported procrastination?
4. How is TA associated with reported test-wiseness?

METHOD

Meta-analysis, the empirical summary of domains of scientific literature, has been a viable tool for evaluating the theoretical merit of accounts for persuasion (Allen & Preiss, 1998) and interpersonal processes (Allen, Preiss, Gayle, & Burrell, 2002). We initiated an extensive search of the TA literature by following standard meta-analytic procedures. The search employed the terms test anxiety, academic anxiety, worry, emotionality, academic performance, and achievement anxiety. The resulting citations were narrowed by searching for study habits, study skills, procrastination, test preparation skills, self-efficacy, and note-taking skills. Textbooks were consulted and references and footnotes were extracted and examined. Computer searches of databases (PsychINFO, Dissertation Abstracts, ERIC, ComIndex, and CommSearch95) were performed and hand searches of convention programs were conducted. The reference sections of captured studies were consulted and relevant citations were located. These search procedures yielded a set of published articles and unpublished dissertations involving TA, academic self-efficacy, and study skills. We found five meta-analyses on TA (three on treatment effectiveness, one comprehensive review, and one on the stability of TA performance studies). We did not find any existing meta-analyses on TA and study behaviors (although Hembree [1988] briefly deals with this topic).

Inclusion Criteria

In the 50 years of TA research, many instruments and procedures have been used to explore study behaviors. We included any study that employed a commonly used measure of TA and any instrument measuring study behavior or academic motivation. We also encountered the decisions meta-analysts often must make when processing enduring bodies of literature. Manuscripts varied in the level to which they reported results and described procedures and methods. Manuscripts were excluded if they failed to report summary statistics allowing aggregation, employed methods inappropriate for aggregation, or reported findings from one sample in more than one manuscript.

Statistical Procedures

Consistent with accepted meta-analytic methods, procedures by Hunter, Schmidt, and Jackson (1982) were employed. Summary statistics were converted into standardized effect estimates. Effects were weighted to correct for differences in sample size. The estimates were converted to correlations and summed. Effects were coded for year of publication or presentation, type of academic motivation, category of study behavior, and course and sample characteristics.

RESULTS

A total of 18 separate reports met the inclusion criteria. Summary statistics for these effects are displayed in Table 7.1. There were a sufficient number of effects to allow for a test of moderator variables in the relationships between academic motivation, TA, and study behaviors.

In an effort to understand the effects reported in the primary investigations, we aggregated studies related to TA and academic self-efficacy. Also,

TABLE 7.1
Effect Sizes Associated With Test Anxiety and Study Behaviors

Author	Year	n	TA Scale	Study Behavior	Effect Size
Bagoon	1988	131	TAS	Test-taking skills knowledge (QHTT)	−.170
Birenbaum & Pinku	1997	179	RTT	Ability to organize material	−.300
Blankstein et al.	1992	125	RTT	Problem-solving confidence	−.350
				Personal control over academic problems	−.420
Cassady & Johnson	2002	168	CTAS	Test Procrastination scale	+.230
Desiderato & Koskinen	1969	94	AAT	SSHA	−.690
Hodapp & Henneberger	1983	105	TAI-G	Study task involvement prior to three exams	−.146
Howell & Swanson	1989	57	TAS	Academic self-concept	−.683
				EST–Study skills	+.125
				EST–Test-taking skills	−.219
Kalechstein et al.	1989	70	RTT	Test Procrastination Questionnaire	+.305
Kirkland & Hollandsworth	1979	305	TAS	Study effectiveness (EST)	−.260
Kleijn et al.	1994	129	TAI	Perceived academic competence	−.255
				Perceived test competence	−.525
				Time management	−.290
Milgram et al.	1992	112	TAI	Procrastination	+.260
Mueller et al.	1989	259	TAI	SHQ–Study alone	+.230
				SHQ–Cram studying	+.080
				SHQ–Study routine	+.320
Paulman & Kennelly	1984	205	TAS	Exam Behavior scale (test-taking skills)	−.280
Rickard	1991	105	MARS	Procrastination (PASS–R)	+.450
Rothblum et al.	1986	379	TAS	Procrastination (PASS)	+.240
Smith et al.	1990	178	AAT	Study behaviors (SSHA–Total)	−.470
				Study skills self-efficacy (Smith et al., 1990)	−.410

Author	Year	n	TA Scale	Study Behavior	Effect Size
Waltman1	1997	63	TAI	Study effectiveness (EST)	−.080
Waltman2	1997	47	TAI	Study effectiveness (EST)	−.190

Note. TA = Test Anxiety; TAS = Test Anxiety Scale; QHTT = Questionnaire of How You Take Tests; RTT = Reactions to Tests; CTAS = Cognitive Test Anxiety Scale; ATT = Achievement Anxiety Test; SSHA = Survey of Study Habits and Attitudes; TAI–G = Test Anxiety Inventory–German; EST = Effective Study Test; TAI = Test Anxiety Inventory; SHQ = Study Habits Questionnaire; MARS = Mathematics Anxiety Rating Scale; PASS–R = Procrastination Assessment Scale–Students–Revised.

we examined the TA–study behavior relationship, the TA–test-wiseness relationship, and the TA–procrastination relationship. Table 7.2 displays the effects associated with TA and measures of academic self-efficacy. The average effect size is uniform in direction and substantial in magnitude. Based on the results of five effects involving 489 participants, the average effect is −.42. This effect would be classified as medium using Cohen's (1977) system. This leads us to believe that the answer to Question 1 is that TA is negatively and meaningfully associated with academic motivation.

Question 2 was directed at the TA–study habit relationship. The effects reported in this area reflect a variety of instruments, including commonly used diagnostic questionnaires and single-item questions asking for time estimates. With one exception, effects are consistent in direction. The magnitudes of the effects, however, vary substantially. Table 7.3 displays the effects associated with TA and measures of study habits. Based on the results of nine effects involving 1,044 participants, the average effect is −.261. This would be classified as small using Cohen's (1977) system. This leads us to be-

TABLE 7.2
Test Anxiety and Academic Self-Efficacy

Author	Year	n	TA Scale	Self-Efficacy Measure	Effect Size
Blankstein et al.	1992	125	RTT	Problem-solving confidence	−.350
				Personal control over academic problems	−.420
Howell & Swanson	1989	57	TAS	Academic self-concept	−.683
Kleijn et al.	1994	129	TAI	Perceived academic competence	−.255
Smith et al.	1990	178	AAT	Study skills self-efficacy	−.410

Note. TA = Test Anxiety; RTT = Reactions to Tests; TAS = Test Anxiety Scale; TAI = Test Anxiety Inventory; AAT = Achievement Anxiety Test.

TABLE 7.3
Test Anxiety and Study Habits

Author	Year	n	TA Scale	Study Behavior Measure	Effect Size
Desiderato & Koskinen	1969	94	AAT	SSHA	−.690
Hodapp & Hennenberger	1971	105	TAI–G	Study task involvement prior to three exams	−.146
Howell & Swanson	1989	57	TAS	EST–Study skills	+.125
Kirkland & Hollondsworth	1979	305	TAS	Study effectiveness (EST)	−.260
Kleijn et al.	1994	129	TAI	Time management	−.290
Musch & Broder	1999	66	TAI–G	Study habit items regarding use of time, readiness to work on difficult tasks, tendency to study regularly, and so on	−.200
Smith et al.	1990	178	AAT	Study behaviors (SSHA–Total)	−.470
				Study skills self-efficacy	−.410
Waltman1	1997	63	TAI	Study effectiveness (EST)	−.080
Waltman2	1997	47	TAI	Study effectiveness (EST)	−.190

Note. TA = Test Anxiety; AAT = Achievement Anxiety Test; SSHA = Survey of Study Habits and Attitudes; TAI–G = Test Anxiety Inventory–German; TAS = Test Anxiety Scale; EST = Effective Study Test; TAI = Test Anxiety Inventory.

lieve that the answer to Question 2 is that TA is negatively associated with academic study skills.

The third question addressed the relationship between TA and procrastination. The logic here is that procrastination may result in poor preparedness for tests, which results in TA. It may also be possible that fear of the testing situation results in procrastination. Table 7.4 displays the effects associated with TA and measures of academic self-efficacy. The average effect size is uniform in direction and magnitude. Based on the results of six effects involving 900 participants, the average effect was −.281. This would be classified as small using Cohen's (1977) system. This justifies the answer to Question 3 that TA is negatively associated with academic motivation.

The final question involved the relationship between TA and knowledge about tests, how they are designed, and how to take them. Table 7.5 displays the effects associated with TA and measures of test-wiseness. The average effect size is uniform in direction and somewhat varied in magnitude. Based on the results of five effects involving 701 participants, the average effect was –.300. This would be classified as medium using Cohen's (1977) system. This leads us to believe that the answer to Question 4 is that TA is negatively associated with test-wiseness.

TABLE 7.4
Test Anxiety and Academic Procrastination

Author	Year	n	TA Scale	Procrastination Measure	Effect Size
Cassady & Johnson	2002	168	CTAS	Test Procrastination scale	+.230
Kalechstein et al.	1989	70	RTT	Test Procrastination Questionnaire	+.305
Milgram et al.	1992	112	TAI	Procrastination	+.260
Musch & Broder	1999	66	TAI–G	Readiness to work on difficult tasks, tendency to study regularly, and so on (effect is reversed)	+.200
Rickard	1991	105	MARS	Procrastination (PASS–R)	+.450
Rothblum et al.	1986	379	TAS	Procrastination (PASS)	+.240

Note. TA = Test Anxiety; CTAS = Cognitive Test Anxiety Scale; RTT = Reactions to Tests; TAI = Test Anxiety Inventory; TAI–G = Test Anxiety Inventory–German; MARS = Mathematics Anxiety Rating Scale; PASS–R = Procrastination Assessment Scale–Student–Revised.

TABLE 7.5
Test Anxiety and Test-Wiseness

Author	Year	n	TA scale	Self-Efficacy Measure	Effect Size
Bagoon	1988	131	TAS	Test-taking skills knowledge (QHTT)	–.170
Birenbaum & Pinku	1997	179	RTT	Ability to organize material	–.300
Howell & Swanson	1989	57	TAS	EST–Test-taking skills	–.219
Kleijn et al.	1994	129	TAI	Perceived test competence	–.525
Paulman & Kennelly	1984	205	TAS	Exam Behavior scale (test-taking skills)	–.280

Note. TA = Test Anxiety; TAS = Test Anxiety Scale; QHTT = Questionnaire of How You Take Tests; RTT = Reactions to Tests; TAI = Test Anxiety Inventory.

DISCUSSION

As is often the case for reviewers (narrative and empirical) who attempt to summarize a complex domain of literature, we began with a simple objective. The goal was to assess the evidence for a TA–study habits relationship. We located a body of research on this question, but the complexity of the domain quickly became evident. Related questions regarding self-efficacy, procrastination, and test-wiseness emerged as related issues. In the meta-analysis, we found evidence of motivational, behavioral, and cognitive consequences of TA. The pattern of effects we observed is compatible with Spielberger and Vagg's (1995) transactional process model.

This meta-analysis indicates that the basic reasoning about TA and academic performance is largely consistent with observed effects. Academic self-efficacy, study habits, procrastination, and test-wiseness were negatively associated with TA. Although intuitive, the pattern of findings is internally consistent and points to a rather broad-based system associated with academic evaluation.

Understanding TA is important because testing is at the center (some believe unjustifiably) of the American educational enterprise. On one level, the education system now uses content testing as the benchmark for academic success and curriculum assessment (and school funding). On a conceptual level, most educators use some type of educational outcome as a mechanism to reflect on classroom effectiveness and program assessment. Of course, these outcomes need not be tests, as portfolios, creative projects, research papers, and performances can serve as indexes of academic success. In most cases, however, tests provide efficient sources of information for educators and policymakers.

For these reasons it is understandable that most scholarly activity has been directed at lowering TA and improving performance. This meta-analysis suggests that desensitization, skills training, and hypnosis may miss the roots of the problem. It strikes us as improbable that isolated training sessions or therapies will be able to counteract the transactional nature of TA. It is more likely that measures embedded across the curriculum and at all levels of course work will be required. In light of the self-efficacy, study behavior, procrastination, and test-wiseness effects, these measures should be far reaching.

Specific suggestions can be inferred from the meta-analysis. For example, assignments may be strategically scheduled to minimize opportunities to procrastinate. Tests may be scheduled to punctuate units and connect content to more advanced upcoming material. Teachers may elect to sequence the difficulty of assignments to promote a sense academic self-efficacy. Of course, a basic consideration involves setting clear standards (including conceptual and behavioral objectives) to promote individual initiative and avoid miscues.

These small techniques beg the larger question of academic motivation. Building academic confidence may require a mix of relevant content, skilled instruction, and programmatic curriculum. Educators can make vital contributions in these areas by being student-centered in the design and execution of courses. This approach should employ the transactional process model and stress curricular, cocurricular, and extracurricular routes to effective and efficient learning and assessment.

REFERENCES

References marked with an asterisk indicate studies included in the meta-analysis.

Allen, M., & Preiss, R. (1998). Evaluating the advice offered by the tool users. In M. Allen & R. Preiss (Eds.), *Persuasion: Advances through meta-analysis* (pp. 243–256). Cresskill, NJ: Hampton.

Allen, M., Preiss, R., Gayle, B., & Burrell, N. (Eds.). (2002). *Interpersonal communication research: Advances through meta-analysis.* Mahwah, NJ: Lawrence Erlbaum Associates.

Alpert, R., & Haber, R. N. (1960). Anxiety in academic achievement situations. *Journal of Abnormal and Social Psychology, 61,* 207–215.

*Bagoon, C. (1988). Assessing a conceptual model for the treatment of test anxiety: Contributions of model components to the prediction of test anxiety and test performance (Doctoral dissertation, University of Maryland, 1988). *Dissertation Abstracts International, 50,* DA8827036.

Benjamin, M., McKeachie, W. J., Lin, Y. G., & Holinger, D. P. (1981). Test anxiety: Deficits in information processing. *Journal of Educational Psychology, 73,* 816–824.

Benson, J. (1989). The psychometric and cognitive aspects of test-wiseness: A review of the literature. In A. Fitzpatrick & P. Williams (Eds.), *Test-wiseness: The state of the art. Exemplary Practice Series* (pp. 1–14). Bloomington, IN: Centeron Evaluation and Research, Phi Delta Kappa.

Birenbaum, M., & Nasser, F. (1994). On the relationship between test anxiety and test performance. *Measurement and Evaluation in Counseling and Development, 27,* 293–301.

*Birenbaum, M., & Pinku, P. (1997). Effects of test anxiety, information organization, and testing situation on performance on two test formats. *Contemporary Educational Psychology, 22,* 23–38.

*Blankstein, K. R., Flett, G. L., & Watson, M. S. (1992). Coping and academic problem-solving ability in test anxiety. *Journal of Clinical Psychology, 48,* 37–46.

*Cassady, J. C., & Johnson, R. E. (2002). Cognitive test anxiety and academic performance. *Contemporary Educational Psychology, 27,* 270–295.

Cohen, J. (1977). *Statistical power analysis for the behavioral sciences.* New York: Academic.

Covington, M. V., & Omelich, C. L. (1987). "I knew it cold before the exam": A test on the anxiety-blockage hypothesis. *Journal of Educational Psychology, 79,* 393–400.

Culler, R. E., & Holahan, C. J. (1980). Test anxiety and academic performance: The effects of study-related behaviors. *Journal of Educational Psychology, 72,* 16–20.

*Desiderato, O., & Koskinen, P. (1969). Anxiety, study habits, and academic achievement. *Journal of Counseling Psychology, 16,* 162–165.

Galassi, J. P., Frierson, H. T., Jr., & Sharer, R. (1981a). Behavior of high, moderate, and low test anxious students during an actual test situation. *Journal of Consulting and Clinical Psychology, 49,* 51–62.

Galassi, J. P., Frierson, H. T., Jr., & Sharer, R. (1984). Cognitions, test anxiety, and test performance: A closer look. *Journal of Consulting and Clinical Psychology, 52,* 319–320.

Geen, R. G. (1985). Test anxiety and visual vigilance. *Journal of Personality and Social Psychology, 49,* 963–970.

Geen, R. G. (1987). Test anxiety and behavioral avoidance. *Journal of Research in Personality, 21,* 481-488.

Gonzalez, H. P. (1987). Systematic desensitization, study skills counseling, and anxiety-coping training in the treatment of test anxiety. In I. G. Sarason & P. R. Vagg (Eds.), *Test anxiety: Theory, assessment, and treatments* (pp. 117–132). Hillsdale, NJ: Lawrence Erlbaum Associates.

Grice, G. R. (1955). Discrimination reaction time as a function of anxiety and intelligence. *Journal of Abnormal and Social Psychology, 50,* 71–74.

Hembree, R. (1988). Correlates, causes, effects, and treatments of test anxiety. *Review of Educational Research, 58,* 47–77.

*Hodapp, V., & Henneberger, A. (1983). Test anxiety, study habits, and academic performance. In H. M. van der Ploeg, R. Schawrzer, & E. D. Spielberger (Eds), *Advances in Test Anxiety Research* (pp. 119–127). Hillsdale, NJ: Lawrence Erlbaum Associates.

*Howell, C. C., & Swanson, S. C. (1989). The relative influence of identified components of test anxiety in traditional baccalaureate nursing students. *Journal of Nursing Education, 28*(5), 215–220.

Hunter, F., Schmidt, F., & Jackson, G. (1982). *Meta-analysis.* Newbury Park, CA: Sage.

Janis, I. L. (1955). Anxiety indices related to susceptibility to persuasion. *Journal of Abnormal and Social Psychology, 51,* 663–666.

*Kalechstein, P., Hocevar, D., Zimmer, J. W., & Kalechstein, M. (1989). Procrastination over test preparation and test anxiety. In R. Schwarzer, H. M. van der Ploeg, & C. D. Spielberger (Eds.), *Advances in test anxiety research* (Vol. 6, pp. 63–76). Lisse, The Netherlands: Swets & Zeitlinger.

*Kirkland, K., & Hollandsworth, J. G., Jr. (1979). Test anxiety, study skills, and academic performance. *Journal of College Student Personnel, 20,* 341–436.

Kirkland, K., & Hollandsworth, J. G., Jr. (1980). Effective test taking: Skills acquisition versus anxiety reduction techniques. *Journal of Consulting and Clinical Psychology, 48,* 431–439.

*Kleijn, W. C., van der Ploeg, H. M., & Topman, R. M. (1994). Cognition, study habits, test anxiety, and academic performance. *Psychological Reports, 75,* 1219–1226.

Lazarus, R. S., Deese, J., & Osler, S. F. (1952). The effects of psychological stress upon performance. *Psychological Bulletin, 49,* 293–317.

Liebert, R. M., & Morris, L. W. (1967). Cognitive and emotional components of test anxiety: A distinction and some initial data. *Psychological Reports, 2,* 975–978.

Marsh, H. W. (1993). Academic self-concept: Theory, measurement, and research. In J. Suls (Ed.), *Psychological perspectives on the self* (Vol. 4, pp. 59–98). Hillsdale, NJ: Lawrence Erlbaum Associates.

*Mueller, J. H., Lenhart, K., & Gustavson, K. (1989). Study habits and contextual dependency as a function of test anxiety level. In R. Schwarzer, H. M. van der Ploeg, & C. D. Speilberger (Eds.), *Advances in test anxiety research* (pp. 77–85). Lissel Berugn, PA: Swets and Zeitlinger.

Musch, J., & Broder, A. (1999). Test anxiety versus academic skills: A comparison of two alternative models for predicting performance in a statistics exam. *British Journal of Educational Psychology, 69*, 105–116.

Naveh-Benjamin, M., McKeachie, W. J., & Lin, Y. (1987). Two types of test-anxious students: Support for an information processing model. *Journal of Experimental Psychology, 79*, 131–136.

Nicholson, W. M. (1958). The influence of anxiety upon learning: Interference or drive increment? *Journal of Personality, 26*, 303–319.

Osterhouse, R. A. (1972). Desensitization and study skills training as treatment for two types of test anxious students. *Journal of Counseling Psychology, 19*, 301–307.

*Paulman, R. G., & Kennelly, K. J. (1984). Test anxiety and ineffective test taking: Different names, same construct? *Journal of Educational Psychology, 76*, 279–288.

Pintrich, R. R., & De Groot, E. V. (1990). Motivational and self-regulated learning components of classroom academic performance. *Journal of Educational Psychology, 82*, 33–40.

*Rickard, M. J. (1991). *Procrastination in mathematics: Anxiety, attribution, and persistence correlates*. Unpublished doctoral dissertation, Pacific University, Forest Grove, OR.

*Rothblum, E. D., Solomon, L. J., & Murakami, J. (1986). Affective, cognitive, and behavioral differences between high and low procrastinators. *Journal of Counseling Psychology, 33*, 287–394.

Sapp, M. (1999). *Test anxiety: Applied research, assessment, and treatment interventions*. University Press of America: NY.

Sarason, I. G. (1986). Test anxiety, worry, and cognitive interference. In R. Schwarzer (Ed.), *Self-related cognitions in anxiety and motivation* (pp. 19–33). Hillsdale, NJ: Lawrence Erlbaum Associates.

Sarason, S. B., Mandler, G., & Craighill, P. G. (1952). The effects of differential instructions on anxiety and learning. *Journal of Abnormal and Social Psychology, 47*, 561–565.

Seipp, B. (1991). Anxiety and academic performance: A meta-analysis. *Anxiety Research, 4*, 27–41.

*Smith, R. J., Arnkoff, D. B., & Wright, T. L. (1990). Test anxiety and academic competence: A comparison of alternative models. *Journal of Counseling Psychology, 37*, 313–321.

Solomon, L. J., & Rothblum, E. D. (1984). Academic procrastination: Frequency and cognitive-behavioral correlates. *Journal of Counseling Psychology, 31*, 503–509.

Spence, K. W., Farber, I. E., & McFann, H. H. (1956). The relation of anxiety (drive) level to performance in competitional and non-competitional paired-associates learning. *Journal of Experimental Psychology, 52*, 296–305.

Spielberger, C. D., DeNike, L. D., & Stein, L. S. (1965). Anxiety and verbal conditioning. *Journal of Personality and Social Psychology, 1*, 229–239.

Spielberger, C. D., & Vagg, P. R. (Eds.). (1995). *Test anxiety: Theory, assessment, and treatment*. Washington, DC: Taylor & Francis.

Tobias, S. (1980). Anxiety and instruction. In I. G. Sarason (Ed.), *Test anxiety: Theory, research, and applications* (pp. 289–309). Hillsdale, NJ: Lawrence Erlbaum Associates.

*Waltman, P. A. (1997). Comparison of traditional and non-traditional baccalaureate nursing students on selected components of Meichenbaum and Butler's model of test anxiety. *Journal of Nursing Education, 36*, 171–179.

Westrope. M. R. (1953). Relations among Rorschach indices, manifest anxiety, and performance under stress. *Journal of Abnormal and Social Psychology, 48*, 515–524.

Zimmerman, B. J., & Bandura, A. (1994). Impact of self-regulatory influences on writing course attainment. *American Educational Research Journal, 31*, 845–862.

8

Evaluating Peer Mediation Outcomes in Educational Settings: A Meta-Analytic Review

Nancy A. Burrell
Cindy S. Zirbel
Mike Allen
University of Wisconsin–Milwaukee

The historical context for mediation practices today stems from the mediation movement that grew out of labor disputes in the 1960s, and has grown predominantly into a facilitative or problem-solving approach. Moore (1996) defined this type of mediation as

> the intervention in a negotiation or a conflict of an acceptable third party who has limited or no authoritative decision-making power but who assists the involved parties in voluntarily reaching a mutually acceptable settlement of issues in dispute. In addition to addressing substantive issues, mediation may also establish or strengthen relationships of trust and respect between parties. (p. 15)

Mediation from this perspective is focused on generating agreements acceptable to all parties.

In the problem-solving mediation model, mediators play a dynamic part in the interaction of disputants. The mediator's presence sets the stage for the participants to interact in a new way. Part of the reason the conflict has

not been resolved is because the disputants are unable to interact constructively and resolve the issues on their own. A mediator presents a new dynamic in the communication process to help disputants interact more
effectively. Having a third party present creates a new situation, perhaps a
safer environment, in which to try communicating again. A mediator facilitates a discussion centered on important issues identified by disputants
through a question-asking and reframing process.

This meta-analysis of mediation outcomes in schools reviews existing
studies of mediation practices in elementary and secondary schools employing a problem-solving approach to mediation. The mediation training reported in the studies relies on improving communication skills, developing
mediator competencies, and utilizing effective strategies for conflict resolution. This meta-analysis examines the effectiveness of mediation and related outcomes in educational settings. Once this question is adequately
answered, the necessity for continued measurement of results in school-
based mediation programs becomes less pressing and future research can focus on other outcomes of school mediation programs.

ISSUES IN SCHOOL-BASED MEDIATION PROGRAMS

To review studies evaluating mediation programs in school settings, several components were identified and measured. The broad categories for
outcome measures included behavioral indicators of conflict for students,
mediation outcomes that reflected how many conflicts were resolved and
agreements reached, student and teacher perceptions about conflict and
individual attitudes toward conflict in the school, and personality factors
related to conflict resolution such as student self-concept or self-esteem.
In addition, because the school mediation programs followed a problem-
solving mediation model, much emphasis was placed on the training and
use of communication skills, understanding the dynamics of conflict, and
identifying specific conflict strategies that could be utilized when dealing
with conflict.

Specific research studies looked at various aspects of these broader
components. For behavioral indicators, the types of conflicts among students, the nature or intensity of the disputes, or the frequency of conflict
situations occurring on school property were identified (Bodtker & Jones,
19978; Hart & Gunty, 1997; D. W. Johnson, Johnson & Dudley, 1992; D.
W. Johnson, Johnson, Dudley & Acikgoz, 1994; D. W. Johnson, Johnson,
Mitchell, et al., 1996; Lindsay, 1998; Roush & Hall, 1993; D. W. Johnson,
Johnson, Cotton, Harris, & Louison, 1995; D. W. Johnson, Johnson,
Dudley, Ward, & Magnuson, 1995). The types and frequencies of conflicts
reported may include acts such as physical aggression, insults, playground
issues, or problems with turn-taking (D. W. Johnson, Johnson, Dudley,

Ward, et al., 1995). One study looked at mediation skill transference from the school to the home environment and identified behavioral indicators of conflict within the home and how the student mediators addressed them (Gentry & Benenson, 1993). The suggestion that students who are trained in conflict resolution strategies apply those skills to settings that are external to the school environment in which they were learned (D. W. Johnson et al., 1992) implies that the impact of training students can have longer lasting effects and impact wider audiences such as siblings, families, and the community at large.

The problem-solving model of mediation views conflict as a problem that needs to be fixed, or opportunities to reach an agreement. Many school-based mediation programs follow a formula in which peer mediators (third-party neutrals) work with disputant students to help them through a process to achieve resolution, something that is easily measured by the number of agreements reached for the number of mediations attempted (Araki, 1990; Crary, 1992; Daunic, Smith, Robinson, Landry, & Miller, 2000; Hart & Gunty, 1997; D. W. Johnson, Johnson, Cotton, et al., 1995; D. W. Johnson, Johnson, Mitchell, et al., 1996; Roush & Hall, 1993) Similarly, the satisfaction of participants involved in the mediation process is easily measured and generally results in highly positive satisfaction results (Crary, 1992; Gerber, 1999; Hart & Gunty, 1997; E. A. Johnson, Thomas, & Krochak, 1998).

Because the basic premise of many school-based mediation programs is that conflict resolution strategies can be taught to students, and knowledge about these resolution strategies can then be applied to conflict situations and results effected, it is important to determine the degree to which this training is effective and the ages at which training can occur. Studies differentiate between learning about various conflict strategies and how they might be used in conflict situations (Bodtker & Jones, 1997; D. W. Johnson, Johnson, Dudley, & Magnuson, 1996; D. W. Johnson, Johnson, Dudley, Mitchell, & Fredrickson, 1997; Stevahn, Johnson, Johnson, Laginski, & O'Coin, 1996) and the actual ability to apply appropriate conflict resolution knowledge and strategies in specific situations (Gentry & Benenson, 1993; D. W. Johnson et al., 1992; Stevahn, Johnson, Johnson, Green, & Laginski, 1997), or the presence of both attributes (D. W. Johnson et al., 1994; D. W. Johnson, Johnson, Dudley, & Magnuson, 1995; Johnson, Johnson, Dudley, Ward, et al., 1995; Stevahn, Johnson, Johnson, & Real, 1996).

The idea that conflict resolution strategies and participation in school-based mediation programs potentially affects self-concept and self-esteem in students presents an intriguing concept for expectations of a problem-solving mediation model. Several studies looked at the effects of mediation programs on student self-esteem and teacher perception of changed self-concept, mostly with inconclusive results (Crary, 1992; Gentry & Benenson, 1993; Roush & Hall, 1993; Vanayan, White, Yuen, & Teper,

1996). By combining the results from these individual studies and testing them through the meta-analytic process, a clearer understanding of statistical significance should be determined. However, some of the studies question the selection of student mediators and the potential to recognize the greatest gains in changed self-concept among students who initially had lower self-esteem (Roush & Hall, 1993; Vanayan et al., 1996).

Related to student changes in self-esteem are measurements of conflict orientation and changes in school climate as a result of mediation program interventions. Orientation to conflict refers to student perceptions about the nature of conflict and resulting outcomes. Is conflict viewed as a problem or an opportunity for change? Does the perception of conflict resolution connote win–lose or win–win outcomes? Because conflict represents an inevitable component of student life, being able to positively affect perceptions of conflict and the importance of constructive resolution strategies presents a key to long-term changes in student behavior and the overall impact on school climate. Although some studies cite anecdotal evidence supporting positive changes in conflict orientation and school climate (D. W. Johnson, Johnson, Dudley, & Magnuson, 1995, 1996), only a few report statistical data related to school climate (Bodtker & Jones, 1997; Hart & Gunty, 1997; Lindsay, 1998).

A final area that has been included in the school-based mediation research involves the area of conflict knowledge and influencing positive perceptions of conflict (Stevahn, Johnson, Johnson, Laginski, et al., 1996; Stevahn, Johnson, Johnson, & Real, 1996). Some of the studies specifically measured the improved knowledge about conflict through the effective conflict resolution strategies employed in handling them (D. W. Johnson et al., 1992; D. W. Johnson et al., 1994; D. W. Johnson et al., 1997; Stevahn et al., 1997). When students better understand the dynamics of conflict, they are better equipped to deal constructively with conflict resolution and utilize appropriate skills in handling conflict.

Although there are many supporters of school-based mediation programs, critics have surfaced (Gerber, 1999; Webster, 1993). Research supporting school mediation programs has been criticized as being "primarily anecdotal and supplied by teachers and administrators, who report that peer mediation programs reduce suspension and detention rates" (D. W. Johnson, Johnson, Dudley, Ward, et al., 1995, p. 832). Other critics claim that there is no evidence that mediation programs reduce interpersonal violence, but, rather, the programs provide political cover for politicians and school officials, distracting the public from the structural determinants of youth violence (Webster, 1993). According to Gerber (1999), "Whether or not peer mediation really works may be a moot point in preserving its longevity on the educational scene. Unless it receives convincing empirical support, its demise is predictable" (p. 170). Because there is a body of empirical work evaluating the impact of school-based mediation programs, the next step in examining the outcomes of these programs involves the summary of that research using meta-analysis.

METHODS

Literature Research Description

Manuscript acquisition for this project included a combination of computer searches on various databases (ERIC and PSYCHLIT) as well as reviewing the reference sections in obtained manuscripts. In addition, all of the contents of *Mediation Quarterly* were reviewed and various reviews of the literature were examined for appropriate citations (D. W. Johnson & Johnson, 1996a; Lam, 1989; Powell, Muir-McClain, & Halasyamani, 1995). To be included in the meta-analysis, manuscripts needed to possess the following characteristics:

1. Include students in an educational facility encompassing one or more grade levels between kindergarten and high school seniors as the sample population in the research.
2. Utilize quantitative research methodologies resulting in numerical representation of measurable effects or outcomes.
3. Involve at least one variable relating to mediation training or practices among student peers in which outcomes or effects of the training or actual mediation procedures were measured.

Data from studies that met these criteria were included in the study. Manuscripts were eliminated from the study if they did not meet these criteria or if they relied on research with no quantitative data (Chetkow-Yanoov, 1996; Harris, 1996; Heller, 1996; Hill, 1996; Nor, 1996), evaluated comparative data among training practices without measuring training outcomes, included measures for mediation predictors such as hostile environments or bullying without evaluating mediated interventions (Whitney & Smith, 1993), or relied on sample populations drawn from university students or communities at large (D. W. Johnson, 1967; Leadbeater, Hellner, Allen, & Aber, 1989; Ross, Fischer, Baker, & Buchholz, 1997).

Coding of Program Outcomes

The outcomes implementing mediation programs and training were divided into four general categories consisting of (a) descriptive outcomes, (b) impact on the schools, (c) issues related to conflict resolution, and (d) impact on the mediator.

Descriptive outcomes consisted of two aspects of mediation: (a) percentage of successful mediations or agreements reached, and (b) satisfaction with the overall agreement. In assessing mediation programs, tracking the number of agreements that occurred is important for continued support. In addition, for any program to maintain support, it is paramount that participants are satisfied with the outcomes and overall process.

The second category centered on the overall impact of mediation training and program on the schools. There were three measures in this cluster: (a) students' perceptions of school climate related to conflict; (b) teachers' and administrators' perceptions of the school conflict climate; and (c) behavioral indicators such as fighting, suspensions, expulsions, and other disciplinary actions. This combination of measures indicates the level of conflict, both perceptual and behavioral, from students' and adults' perspectives.

The third category relates to the impact of mediation training on mediators' views about interpersonal conflict. Four measures were included in this cluster: (a) knowledge about conflict, (b) ability to follow procedures during a mediation session, (c) strategies used to resolve conflict, and (d) view of interpersonal conflict. The first measure reflects whether the training increased participants' knowledge about conflict. The second measure indexed trainees' ability to facilitate a mediation session using guidelines established by the program. The third measure indicates the general strategies mediators use to address conflict. The fourth measure in this cluster evaluates whether student mediators view interpersonal conflict positively or negatively.

The last category focuses on the impact of mediation training on trainees. Two measures in this category include: (a) academic achievement and (b) self-esteem. The purpose of these measures is to determine the impact of mediation training on participants. Program evaluators wanted to know if students' grades might improve with mediation training and whether participants might feel better about themselves.

Statistical Procedure

Three stages occurred in this analysis: transformation, averaging, and heterogeneity testing. This meta-analytic review used the variance-centered technique developed by Hunter and Schmidt (1990). Transformation is the process of converting statistical information to a common metric. The correlation coefficient is the metric used in this review. In short, all of the studies' statistical information was transformed into correlation coefficients as outlined by Hunter and Schmidt. The second stage was the averaging process, which computes a weighted average using the sample size of the individual effect as the weight. Finally, testing for homogeneity was the third step in this process. The homogeneity test examines whether the inconsistency in observed effects can be attributed to sampling error. A chi-square test compares the observed variability to the expected variability to sampling error. A nonsignificant chi-square indicates that the sample of correlations can be considered homogenous, whereas a significant chi-square indicates heterogeneity among the effects.

RESULTS

Descriptive Outcomes of Mediation Programs

The first step is to analyze the ability of the program to resolve disagreements. The obvious goal of mediation programs is to give students an opportunity to resolve conflicts with their peers rather than to have an adult solve their problems for them. Eighteen studies report the results of 3,447 mediations with 3,256 reaching agreement, for a 94% success rate. This high percentage of agreements reached indicates the success of mediation programs in the schools.

However, reaching an agreement is not the only index of a successful program. Disputants must also feel satisfied with the process itself. Ten studies report survey data on 4,448 mediations. The results indicate that 3,959 of the disputants in mediation were satisfied with the agreement, for an 89% satisfaction rate. Again, this high percentage indicates not only that agreements have been reached but also that participants were pleased with the outcomes of the mediation process. It may also be the case that students are feeling empowered to resolve their own disputes rather than being told how to solve their problems by an adult.

Impact of Mediation Programs on Schools

The first outcome measure from the perception of students is how they perceive their school climate. Five studies examine the impact of mediation programs on school climate and find that mediation programs have a positive effect on school climates ($r = .441, k = 5, N = 527, p < .05$). These results indicate that students perceive a positive school environment. The test of homogeneity finds the sample of correlations heterogeneous, $\chi^2(4, N = 527) = 20.61, p > .05$. Because of heterogeneity, the average correlation should be interpreted cautiously. An examination was made for outlier studies. One estimate (Bodtker & Jones, 1997) had a correlation entry of .000. This estimate was based on the authors' reporting of a nonsignificant finding and that estimate was the best reasonable estimate of the relationship. The estimate when compared to the average estimate has a z score in excess of 4.00, indicating that the study functions as an outlier. Reestimating the average effect ($r = .441, k = 4, N = 443$, $p < .05$) creates a homogeneous set of correlations $\chi^2(3, N = 443) = 4.86, p < .05$. In short, these findings indicate that school climates improve after the implementation of a mediation program.

A second measure centers on teachers' and administrators' perception of conflict in their respective schools. The results indicate that a mediation program reduces the perception of conflict in a school ($r = -.093, k = 4, N = 379, p < .05$). In other words, both teachers and administrators perceive a reduction in conflict. The test of homogeneity finds the sample of correlations homogeneous, $\chi^2(3, N = 379) = 2.15, p < .05$. The studies consistently find that both teachers and administrators perceive a reduction in conflict. These results indicate that professionals, on a day-to-day basis, attribute less conflict after implementing mediation programs.

A third systemic measure deals with data from school records such as suspensions, expulsions, fighting, and other disciplinary actions. The implication of mediation programs is a drop in disciplinary actions by administrators ($r = -.284, k = 12, N = 4,667, p < .05$). These results indicate that the implementation of a mediation program is related to a drop in administrative suspensions, expulsions, and disciplinary actions. The test of homogeneity finds the sample of correlations heterogeneous, $\chi^2(11, N = 4,667) = 71.36, p > .05$. Because of heterogeneity, the average correlation should be interpreted cautiously. Heterogeneity means that the sample of correlations does not represent a single distribution, but, instead indicates the probability of moderator variables. However, 11 of the 12 effects were positive, indicating that any moderator variable would be indicating differences between small positive and large positive effects. Therefore, the average effect even after considering a moderator variable will always be positive. In short, the data indicate a reduction in disciplinary actions after the implementation of mediation programs.

Issues Related to Conflict

The next set of measures reflects peer mediators' perceptions about conflict. The first measure, knowledge about conflict, reflects what students learned about interpersonal conflict from their mediation training ($r = .530, k = 14$, $N = 1,138, p < .05$). These results indicate students' knowledge and understanding about interpersonal conflict increased from their training. The test of homogeneity finds the sample of correlations heterogeneous, $\chi^2(13, N = 1,138) = 53.84, p > .05$. The range in correlations is $r = .118$ to $r = .960$, which indicates a large variability. The variability in knowledge gained about conflict may reflect differences in mediation training programs, content of the knowledge tests, and different selection processes of mediators among school districts.

A second measure centered on students' ability to follow the steps prescribed in mediating a dispute. Results ($r = .495, k = 9, N = 805, p < .05$) indicate that students are indeed able to follow the steps in mediating interpersonal conflicts. The test of homogeneity finds the sample of correlations heterogeneous, $\chi^2(8, N = 805) = 34.74, p > .05$. Because of heterogeneity, the average correlation should be interpreted cautiously. These findings may index differences in the simplicity or complexity of the mediation training programs.

A third measure centered on the strategies mediators used to resolve interpersonal conflict. Results show that mediation training changes the way mediators address interpersonal conflicts and disputes ($r = .410, k = 14, N = 1,298, p < .05$). The test of homogeneity finds the sample of correlations heterogeneous, $\chi^2(14, N = 1,298) = 61.11, p > .05$. These findings, although heterogeneous, reflect a distribution of all positive effects. Therefore, the average effect demonstrates that mediators' intervention strategies were consistent with the training.

A fourth measure centered on mediators' view of conflict (either positive or negative). Results of mediation training indicate an increased positive view of conflict from peer mediators' perspectives ($r = .341, k = 5, N = 297, p < .05$). The test of homogeneity finds the sample of correlations homogeneous, $\chi^2(4, N = 341) = 3.81, p < .05$. These findings indicate that student mediators' perceptions of conflict were more positive after their training.

Impact of Training and Being a Mediator

These two measures look at the impact of both training and being a peer mediator for a year. The first measure centers on academic achievement of mediators. Results show that peer mediators' grades went up ($r = .404, k = 4, N = 223, p < .05$). The test of homogeneity finds the sample of correlations homogeneous, $\chi^2(3, N = 223) = 0.18, p < .05$. These findings indicate a substantial increase in academic performance after becoming a mediator.

A second measure centered on mediators' self-esteem. Results indicate that peer mediators' sense of self improved over the academic year ($r = .110, k = 4, N = 237, p < .05$). In other words, being a school mediator students' sense of self improved. The test of homogeneity finds the sample of correlations homogeneous, $\chi^2(3, N = 237) = 4.19, p < .05$. Similarly, these findings point to improved self-esteem after becoming a mediator.

DISCUSSION

The results of this meta-analytic review of school-based mediation programs overwhelmingly support the effectiveness of the facilitative or problem-solving mediation model for peer mediators in schools. The study demonstrates that mediation training on understanding conflict situations helps students resolve conflict and can be successfully implemented in elementary and secondary schools. Basically, conflict resolution skills can be taught to students and students can effectively demonstrate the use of these skills in mediating peer conflicts and helping disputants reach agreement. Satisfaction with the peer mediation process is highly positive for students and staff in the schools. This conclusion hopefully will encourage schools without mediation programs to look at the implementation of a problem-solving mediation model in handling student conflict.

This study also suggests additional positive effects related to school-based mediation programs in that trained students utilize their skills outside of the school setting. The transference of conflict resolution skills extends into families and communities, providing unique opportunities for young adults to potentially effect social change in family structures and within neighborhoods. Studies looked specifically at student skills in handling sibling conflict within family structures, but perhaps further monitoring of students would reflect long-term behavioral changes that pervade social networks of peers and neighbors. Learning how to handle conflict provides a powerful resource for young adults to handle many of life's challenges and the successful use of conflict resolution strategies continually reinforces the value and benefit of constructive problem solving. Beyond providing relief for students, these skills can powerfully demonstrate to others involved in their interaction the positive effects of communication and negotiation efforts. This unintended effect of school-based mediation programs fits well with Bush and Folger's (1994) concept of transformative mediation's goal to go beyond the individualistic perspective to more of a relational conception. If mediation skills truly can permeate a student's perspective on conflict beyond the school day, perhaps the problem-solving approach, when used with young people, can help achieve the transformative approach to connect to an "emerging, higher vision of self and society, one based on moral development and interpersonal relations rather than on satisfaction and individual autonomy" (Bush & Folger, 1994, p. 3). Although the transformative approach to mediation focuses on the mediator's capacity to effect change among the disputants involved in mediation, certainly there must be some value to empowering students to gain a sense of their own strength and to realize their increased capacity to learn new strategies in handling life's problems.

Bush and Folger (1994) described the value of transformation as "valuing behavior that integrates the strength of self and compassion for others, behavior that embodies compassionate strength" (p. 230). This implies that the individual uses internal strength to overcome adversity or accomplish great deeds, not for personal well-being and gain, but for the good of others or some greater good. This study does not support the concept of students' utilization of conflict resolution strategies to help create a better society or community, but perhaps it sets the stage for future research on student perspectives that relate to community involvement, volunteerism, and peace initiatives. Do peaceful conflict resolution strategies learned at a young age help to shape the moral development and character of young people to become strong, confident individuals capable of caring for others compassionately?

Another intriguing area for future research involves a question proposed by several researchers in trying to measure changes in student self-esteem and school climate as a result of mediation programs. American schools today, in general, enjoy an all-time low level of school violence. Is there a connection between the introduction of school-based mediation programs and a reduction in school violence? Is there a remarkable difference between schools with and without mediation programs that cannot be attributed to other socioeconomic or demographic factors?

Looking at self-esteem, several studies noted anecdotal data about increased self-esteem among student participants in mediation programs, particularly among those students who themselves had behavior problems and frequent episodes of conflict at school. Because no hard data exist to conclusively determine whether at-risk students benefit more from training on conflict resolution skills, studies that can determine the effectiveness of targeted training interventions can help schools achieve even greater gains in improving school climates and mediation satisfaction, particularly by enriching the lives of at-risk students.

Finally, an entire area of research is open to investigate whether the problem-solving versus transformative mediation model best applies to school settings. The transformative model is relatively new and untested. If this model was effectively applied to student populations, it could have potentially far-reaching societal benefits, beyond the tangential and inadvertent community benefits reaped through the facilitative or problem-solving model currently used in schools. Clearly, the future for peer mediation programs is promising.

REFERENCES

References marked with an asterisk indicate studies included in the meta-analysis.

*Araki, C. T. (1990). Dispute management in the schools. *Mediation Quarterly, 8*, 51–62.

*Bodtker, A. M., & Jones, T. S. (1997, November). *The impact of peer mediation training on conflict competence: Insights from South African students.* Paper presented at the 83rd annual meeting of the National Communication Association, Chicago.

*Bradley, B. (1989). Warwick Valley students learn to mediate. *Journal of the New York State School Boards Association*, 17–18.

Bush, R. A., & Folger, J. P. (1994). *The promise of mediation*. San Francisco: Jossey-Bass.

Chetkow-Yanoov, B. (1996). Conflict resolution skills can be taught. *Peabody Journal of Education, 71*(3), 12–28.

*Crary, D. R. (1992). Community benefits from mediation: A test of the "Peace Virus Hypothesis." *Mediation Quarterly, 9*, 241–252.

*Daunic, A. P., Smith, S. W., Robinson, T. R., Landry, K. L., & Miller, M. D. (2000). School-wide conflict resolution and peer mediation programs: Experiences in three middle schools. *Intervention in School & Clinic, 36*, 94–101.

*Davis, A. M. (1986). Teaching ideas: Dispute resolution at an early age. *Negotiation Journal, 2*, 287–298.

*Gentry, D. B., & Benenson, W. A. (1993). School-age peer mediators transfer knowledge and skills to home setting. *Mediation Quarterly, 10*, 101–109.

*Gerber, S. (1999). Does peer mediation really work? *Professional School Counseling, 2*, 169–172.

Harris, I. (1996). Peace education in an urban school district in the United States. *Peabody Journal of Education, 71*(3), 63–83.

*Hart, J., & Gunty, M. (1997). The impact of a peer mediation program on an elementary school environment. *Peace & Change, 22*, 76–92.

Heller, G. S. (1996). Changing the school to reduce student violence: What works? *NASSP Bulletin, 80*(579), 1–10.

Hill, M. S. (1996). Making students part of the safe schools solution. *NASSP Bulletin, 80*(579), 24–31.

Hunter, J. E., & Schmidt, F. L. (1990). *Methods of meta-analysis: Correcting error and bias in research findings*. Newbury Park, CA: Sage.

Johnson, D. W. (1967). Use of role reversal in intergroup competition. *Journal of Personality and Social Psychology, 7*, 135–141.

*Johnson, D. W., & Johnson, R. T. (1996a). Conflict resolution and peer mediation programs in elementary and secondary schools: A review of the research. *Review of Educational Research, 66*, 459–506.

*Johnson, D. W., & Johnson, R. T. (1996b). Teaching all students how to manage conflicts constructively: The peacemaker's program. *Journal of Negro Education, 65*, 322–334.

*Johnson, D. W., Johnson, R., Cotton, B., Harris, D., & Louison, S. (1995). Using conflict managers in an inner-city elementary school. *Mediation Quarterly, 12*, 379–390.

*Johnson, D. W., Johnson, R., & Dudley, B. (1992). Effects of peer mediation training on elementary school students. *Mediation Quarterly, 10*, 89–99.

*Johnson, D. W., Johnson, R., Dudley, B., & Acikgoz, K. (1994). Effects of conflict resolution training on elementary school students. *Journal of Social Psychology, 134*, 803–817.

*Johnson, D. W., Johnson, R., Dudley, B., & Magnuson, D. (1995). Training elementary schools to manage conflict. *Journal of Social Psychology, 135*, 673–680.

*Johnson, D. W., Johnson, R., Dudley, B., & Magnuson, D. (1996). Training elementary schools to manage conflict. *Journal of Group Psychotherapy, Psychodrama & Sociometry, 49*(1), 24–39.

*Johnson, D. W., Johnson, R., Dudley, B., Mitchell, J., & Fredrickson, J. (1997). The impact of conflict resolution training on middle school students. *Journal of Social Psychology, 137*, 11–22.

*Johnson, D. W., Johnson, R., Dudley, B., Ward, M., & Magnuson, D. (1995). The impact of peer mediation training on the management of school and home conflicts. *American Educational Research Journal, 32*, 829–844.

*Johnson, D. W., Johnson, R., Mitchell, J., Cotton, B., Harris, D., & Louison, S. (1996). Effectiveness of conflict managers in an inner-city elementary school. *Journal of Educational Research, 89*, 280–285.

*Johnson, E. A., Thomas, D., & Krochak, D. (1998). Effects of peer mediation training in junior high school on mediators' conflict resolution attitudes and abilities in high school. *The Alberta Journal of Educational Research, 44*, 339–341.

*Lam, J. A. (1989). *The impact of conflict resolution programs on schools: A review and synthesis of the evidence* (2nd ed.). Amherst: The University of Massachusetts.

Leadbeater, B. J., Hellner, I., Allen, J. P., & Aber, J. L. (1989). Assessment of interpersonal negotiation strategies in youth engaged in problem behaviors. *Developmental Psychology, 25*, 465–472.

*Lindsay, P. (1998). Conflict resolution and peer mediation in public schools: What works? *Mediation Quarterly, 16*, 85–99.

*Maxwell, J. (1989). Mediation in the schools: Self-regulation, self-esteem, and self-discipline. *Mediation Quarterly, 7*, 149–155.

Moore, C. (1996). *The mediation process: Practical strategies for resolving conflict* (2nd ed.). San Francisco: Jossey-Bass.

Nor, L. (1996). Taking a stand against violence: Leadership and responsibility. One school's quest to create a safe harbor. *Schools in the Middle, 5*(4), 14–17.

*Powell, K. E., Muir-McClain, L., & Halasyamani, L. (1995). A review of selected school-based conflict resolution and peer mediation projects. *Journal of School Health, 65*, 426–431.

*Ross, W. H., Jr., Fischer, D., Baker, C., & Buchholz, K. (1997). University residence hall assistants as mediators: An investigation of the effects of disputant and mediator relationships on intervention preferences. *Journal of Applied Social Psychology, 27*, 664–707.

*Roush, G., & Hall, E. (1993). Teaching peaceful conflict resolution. *Mediation Quarterly, 11*, 185–191.

*Sherrod, M. W. (1995). Student peer conflict management in California high schools: A survey of programs and their efficacy as perceived by disciplinarians. *The Peer Facilitator Quarterly, 12*(2), 12–14.

Stevahn, L., Johnson, D. W., Johnson, R., Green, K., & Laginski, A. (1997). Effects of conflict resolution training integrated into English literature on high school students. *Journal of Social Psychology, 137*, 302–315.

*Stevahn, L., Johnson, D. W., Johnson, R., Laginski, A. M., & O'Coin, I. (1996). Effects on high school students of integrating conflict resolution and peer mediation training into an academic unit. *Mediation Quarterly, 14*, 21–36.

*Stevahn, L., Johnson, D. W., Johnson, R., & Real, D. (1996). The impact of a cooperative or individualistic context on the effectiveness of conflict resolution training. *American Educational Research Journal, 33*, 801–823.

*Tolson, E. R., & McDonald, S. (1992). Peer mediation among high school students: A test of effectiveness. *Social Work in Education, 14*(2), 86–93.

*Vanayan, M., White, N., Yuen, P., & Teper, M. (1996). The effects of a school-based mediation program on the attitudes and perceptions of student mediators. *Education Canada, 36*, 38–42.

Webster, D. (1993). The unconvincing case for school-based conflict resolution programs for adolescents. *Health Affairs, 13,* 127–141.

Whitney, L., & Smith, P. (1993). A survey of the nature and extent of bully/victim problems in junior/middle and secondary schools. *Educational Research, 35,* 3–25.

III

Classroom Interactions

III

9

Classroom Interaction
and Educational Outcomes

Jeff Kerssen-Griep
University of Portland

Barbara Mae Gayle
Saint Martin's University

Raymond W. Preiss
University of Puget Sound

Many educators would agree that classroom interaction is an essential aspect of the educational enterprise. Research exploring the complexity of
teacher–student interpersonal behaviors in and out of the classroom has
focused on characteristics of communicative interactions (Garko, Kough,
Pignata, Kimmel, & Eison, 1994; Wubbels, Creton, Levy, & Hooymayers,
1993) and the outcomes of those exchanges (Frymier, 1994a;
Kerssen-Griep, Hess, & Trees, 2003; Tinto, 1987). Both students and teachers appear to recognize that interpersonal communication is a key to building relationships that promote learning (Simonds, Jones, & Bedore, 1994).
Nevertheless, there is a distinct hierarchy that places more responsibility for
establishing and maintaining the relationship on the professor (Shamai,
Ilatov, Hert-Lazarovitz, & Bentsvi-Mayer, 1995). This part of the volume is
focused on the discursive strategies employed by instructors and how these
strategies influence the classroom environment and student performance.
In this review, we summarize research that provides a general context for the
meta-analyses on teacher immediacy, classroom factors such as race and sex,

129

communication apprehension, and conflict mediation. Although hardly exhaustive, the meta-analyses address issues central to achieving educational goals. We consider issues such as interpersonal relationships, affinity between students and teachers, listening behaviors, student motivation, teacher influence, and power. Because this research reflects the nuances of classroom interaction, our remarks are offered as a foundation for the meta-analyses in this part of the volume.

INTERPERSONAL COMMUNICATIVE RELATIONSHIPS

Wubbels, Brekelmans, and Hooymayers (1991) asserted that interpersonal interactions between teachers and students are mutually influenced. In other words, teachers' communicative behaviors determine, and are determined by, students' interpersonal exchanges. Rogoff (1994) explained that teachers' and students' in-class or out-of-class communication likely is structured by the teacher, whose preallocated authority to manage classroom behaviors creates a power imbalance (Shamai et al., 1995). Although the social interactions in the classroom are likely bidirectional (Kovalainen, Kumpulainen, & Vasama, 2001), classroom exchanges are affected by the instructor's attitude toward students' fulfillment of their school roles (Shamai et al., 1995) and the instructor's propensity to be social, managerial, instructional, or evaluative (Ilatov, Shamai, Hertz-Larzarovitz, & Mayer-Young, 1998). Research following this logic has focused on the characteristics of the teacher–student interaction, both in and outside the classroom. We consider these two categories before discussing characteristics of teacher interactions.

Interpersonal Communicative Exchanges in the Classroom

A general consensus exists that teacher–student interaction can be a catalyst for learning. Students and instructors appear to agree on a variety of interpersonal behaviors that create and maintain a classroom environment that fosters discovery and insight. Wubbels et al. (1993) found that students' and professors' ideas of effective interpersonal relations involved teachers who are friendly, helpful, and congenial. Effective teachers were thought to empathize with students while maintaining control, setting standards, and allowing students the freedom to assume responsibility and learn. Perhaps it is not surprising that Garko et al. (1994) discovered that students want to be treated equitably and afforded respect and mutuality. Students wanted professors to engage in open discussions and employ some humor in their lectures and conversations. Students valued professors knowing their names and providing personalized attention. This is consistent with Anderson and

Carta-Falsa's (2002) finding that students want to establish interpersonal interactions that create a positive climate for teaching and learning. Students appear to want relationships with professors that are high in rapport and respect as a way to enhance learning. This evidence indicates that students prefer that faculty and students work closely together to create an environment that facilitates the acquisition of content and skills.

Researchers have also discovered that preferred interpersonal communication patterns between students and teachers in the classroom produce other identifiable outcomes. Wubbels et al. (1991) found that supportive communication behaviors enacted by the instructor increased affective learning. They did not detect the same relationship for cognitive learning, however. Ilatov et al. (1998) discovered that teacher–student interactions are somewhat influenced by gender, but the greatest influence on teacher–student in class interactions was the class "personality," which required a repertoire of managerial and social interactions. Individual student personalities, on the other hand, were also associated with Wooten and McCroskey's (1996) findings that high-assertive teachers garnered more trust from assertive students and less trust from those students who were not assertive. The idea that students want to engage in interpersonal classroom conversations was reinforced by Tinto (1987), who observed that more frequent and rewarding teacher interactions enhanced intellectual and social growth while increasing student retention rates. Taken together these studies suggest that positive teacher–student interactions promote teaching and learning and set the tone for the likely out-of-class interactions.

Interpersonal Communication Beyond the Classroom

Research on out-of-class communication is relatively recent compared to the study of communication in the classroom. Researchers investigating out-of-classroom communication (OCC) believe that the extraclass contact has consequences for teaching and learning. This type of communication extends beyond traditional classroom boundaries to a variety of informal settings, including the professor's office. Lamport (1993) argued that conversations between teachers and students occur more easily outside of the classroom if the professor exhibits positive attitudes, warm nonverbal communication, and the tendency to share personal information inside the classroom. Aylor and Oppliger (2003) found that teachers can cultivate more frequent and satisfactory OCC with students by exhibiting a humorous disposition and a responsive manner. Both of these studies affirm that OCC's occurrence and effects often are based on students' judgment of faculty accessibility and communicative competence.

Pascarella (1980) reviewed motives for OCC and research exploring the instructional impact of OCC student–faculty interactions. He concluded that teacher–student interaction outside of the classroom was part of socializing students into the academy, allowing faculty to influence students' perspectives. This line of research involved the idea that students' beliefs, values, and attitudes would likely be influenced by faculty attitudes and intellectual values. His review pointed to positive associations between faculty and student out-of-classroom interactions. Pascarella found that "satisfaction with college, educational aspirations, intellectual and personal development, academic achievement, and freshman to sophomore year persistence in college" (p. 564) all improved with satisfying OCC interactions with the student's professors. He concluded that the extent and quality of informal teacher–student interactions make a unique contribution to the impact of a college education as they extend formal academic training to students' daily lives.

Several subsequent investigations support Pascarella's (1980) conclusions. Kuh (1995) discovered that when OCC functioned well, students reported increased feelings of self-worth. Milem and Berger (1997) found that OCC promoted integration into the academic culture of a university. Also, Pascarella and Terenzini (1991) concluded that increased OCC was associated with higher educational aspirations, and Terenzini, Pascarella, and Blimling (1991) found that the more satisfying the OCC, the greater the students' academic and cognitive development. It appears that OCC functions to enhance student learning and socialization.

The educational consequences of out-of-class interaction are further supported by Jaasma and Koper's (1999) investigation. They found that OCC was valuable for students' educational development and university retention rates. Tinto's (1987) work also suggests that the amount and quality of OCC interaction plays a significant role in student retention and academic adjustment. It appears that even one office visit can increase perceptions of affective learning and student satisfaction with the learning process (Clark, Keith, & Walker, 2001). OCC does not occur as frequently as might be expected. Nadler and Nadler (2000) found that OCC contact was relatively infrequent and short in duration. Not surprising, Fusani (1994) reported that students desire more personalized attention than they feel they are receiving.

Interestingly, the quality and quantity of OCC also affects student perceptions of faculty members' effectiveness. Nadler and Nadler (2001) found that OCC was related to student perceptions of teacher credibility and the instructors' empathy rating. Similarly, Cooper, Stewart, and Gudykunst (1982) reported that the best predictor of a student's evaluation of the professor was her or his relationship with that teacher. Jaasma and Koper (2002) found that students perceive OCC to be more satisfying from female professors, whereas Nadler and Nadler (2001) discovered that male students engaged in significantly more OCC.

The research on the practice of OCC suggests the importance of this factor in learning. These studies suggest that faculty serve as a powerful socializing force in a student's college experience. To varying degrees, faculty can improve student learning and enhance classroom climate by paying close attention to their in-class and out-of-class interpersonal communication. Establishing interpersonal classroom expectations and reinforcing those expectations with office visits and other types of extra class communication can improve the teaching and learning process. The remainder of this chapter is devoted to classroom interaction issues that apply to both in-class and out-of-class learning.

TEACHER– STUDENT AFFINITY

One strategy teachers and students employ to enhance interpersonal relationships both in class and out of class involves affinity seeking, "the active social-communicative process by which individuals attempt to get others to like and to feel positive toward them" (Bell & Daly, 1984, p. 91). Several studies have explored teachers' use of affinity-seeking strategies (Dolin, 1995; McCroskey & McCroskey, 1986; Myers, 1995) and one published study investigated the strategies students use to enhance the likelihood that their teachers will engage in interpersonal relationships (Wanzer, 1998). Evidence supports the effectiveness of the techniques in producing positive educational outcomes.

Researchers have devised a taxonomy of 25 affinity-seeking strategies, and investigations confirm that teachers or students routinely employ more than half of these strategies. Wanzer (1998) reported that both teachers and students agree on the most frequently used affinity-seeking strategies that students employ in the classroom. Sixty-five percent of the student responses indicated the use of the categories conversational rule keeping (being friendly, polite, and courteous), nonverbal immediacy (signaling interest and liking through nonverbal cues), elicit disclosure (encourages questions and reinforces other for talking), requirements (attends class, turns in assignments on time), and self-inclusion (sets up frequent encounters). Although McCroskey and McCroskey (1986) found that teachers' affinity-seeking strategies with students did not differ greatly from strategies used by college students, other researchers found less overlap (Frymier, 1994b; Frymier & Thomas, 1992; Gorham, Kelley, & McCroskey, 1989; Myers, 1995).

Research about teachers' self-reported use of affinity-seeking strategies in their classrooms is somewhat uneven. Teachers report enhancing student–teacher interpersonal relationships by increasing the students' positive regard for the teacher. Examples of strategies for increasing regard include creating the impression of being comfortable (relaxed, casual, at ease), eliciting disclosure from others, conveying personal autonomy (presenting the self as independent and forward thinking), conversational rule keeping, assuming equality (presenting the self as an equal), conveying trustworthiness, and facilitating enjoyment (making time together enjoyable; Frymier, 1994b; Frymier & Thomas, 1992; Gorham et al., 1989; Myers, 1995).

Affinity-seeking strategies have been associated with student motivation (Frymier & Thomas, 1992), classroom climate (Myers, 1995), teacher character and competence (Frymier & Thomas, 1992), and affect toward the course (Gorham et al., 1989). The results of these studies indicate that teachers may want to have a repertoire of affinity-seeking strategies at their command and match the strategy selected to characteristics of the classroom environment and the personalities of individual students.

LISTENING

An important part of in-class or out-of-class communication involves the development of listening skills, abilities, and attitudes. Coakley and Wolvin (1989) wrote:

> The listeners' motivation to listen and willingness to participate in communication transactions are essential to all listening experiences. Likewise, developing the positive listening attitude that listening is an active—rather than passive—act in which listeners share with speakers the responsibility for successful communication is beneficial to the development of listening skills. (pp. 2–3)

This logic suggests that how students or teachers process, remember, or understand oral messages is fundamental to the educational enterprise. Listening skills and attitudes will affect students' attitudes about in-class or out-of-class communicative interactions and interpersonal relationships. Researchers have investigated both internal and external factors of listening—the characteristics of listeners, the outcomes of listening, and student involvement in the listening process.

It is noteworthy that conceptualizations of listening are ambiguous and researchers have developed diverse schemes to capture the complexities of listener characteristics. For example, Watson, Barker, and Weaver (1995) suggested that individuals engage in four different orientations toward listening. Individuals may be people-oriented, action-oriented, content- oriented, or time-oriented. People-oriented listeners are thought to be concerned with the other person's feelings and emotions. Time-oriented listeners are very explicit about the limited amount of time they can devote to listening. Action-oriented listeners prefer very concise and accurate messages, whereas the content-oriented listener enjoys receiving complex or challenging information. Watson et al. (1995) also found that female respondents reported more people-oriented listening due to its emphasis on interpersonal relationships. Male respondents tended to prefer a high-task, action-oriented listening style. Another conceptualization by McKenzie and Clark (1995) offers a reflexive model of listening that accounts for the biological or cognitive aspects of listening behaviors as well as the contextual and behavioral factors.

Another way listening has been studied is to determine its impact on classroom learning. The findings in this area are diverse and suggest that both teachers and students are consciously or unconsciously involved in the listening process. One line of research has been devoted to determining ways to improve listening. Canfield (1961) found that well-presented material with well-thought-out content could improve overall listening as measured by comprehensive questions. Bostrom and Bryant (1980) found that phrases delivered at a slower rate were easier to retain. Other researchers in this area focused on the ability to listen while engaging in normal classroom activities. Di Vesta and Gray (1973) suggested a relationship between listening and taking notes. They found that students recalled more material when they took notes. However, Aiken, Thomas, and Shennum (1975) found that students who intersperse note taking with listening remembered more than students who took notes while listening and more than those students who took no notes at all. Beatty and Payne (1984) reported that listening to instructional materials alone produced better comprehension than did listening in groups of students. This overall line of research emphasizes the role of cognitive processing in listening competence.

A third line of investigation has focused on listener involvement in the dyadic exchange process. These researchers have explored the rationale for listening and involvement in the process of listening. Petrie and Carrel (1976), Coakley and Wolvin (1989), and McKenzie and Clark (1995) suggested that motivation is a key factor in getting students to engage in attentive listening behaviors. Glenn, Emmert, and Emmert (1995) reported that nonverbal cues, perceived speaker attitude, and presentational characteristics combined to motivate listener involvement. They recommended increased discussion about listening as a route to increased attentiveness and comprehension. They believed that involvement with the content and issue presentation play a role in promoting listener involvement. Taking that rationale a step further, Smeltzer and Watson (1984) believed that teachers should use incentives to encourage student listening effectiveness. The evidence on this position is equivocal, as Gayle (2002) found that incentives, even the use of grades as an incentive, failed to engage listeners (as opposed to speakers) during presentations of a controversial topic. Overall, listener involvement appears to be contingent on the speaker, the nature of the material, and the motivation of the listener.

Taken together, the research on listening as an integral part of classroom interactions is not well developed. We are only beginning to understand the complexity of listening variables in the classroom or out of class. Disjointed conceptualizations of the listening construct and the failure to integrate the educational context into accounts for listening effectiveness limit the confidence in the generalizations about listening behaviors.

MOTIVATIONAL INSTRUCTION

Much of the research investigating student motivation to learn is linked to the teacher's interpersonal behaviors. Defined as a commitment to initiate and maintain involvement in the learning process and learning activities (Ames, 1990), motivation has been studied largely as a facilitator of learning outcomes (Christophel, 1990; Rodríguez, Plax, & Kearney, 1996). Some studies have linked motivation to teacher enthusiasm (Patrick, Hisley, & Kempler, 2000), teacher effectiveness in using student-centered behaviors (Gorham & Christophel, 1992), teacher communication of high standards (Gorham & Millette, 1997), and perceived teacher immediacy (Christensen & Menzel, 1998; Witt & Wheeless, 2001).

Crafting the myriad of interlocking classroom conditions that foster involvement in the learning process has been challenging and the problem has been approached from many directions. Educational research on this topic has been driven primarily by theories of attribution processes (Weiner, 1985), self-efficacy (Bandura, 1997), goal orientation (Ames, 1992), and intention (Nicholls, 1989). Communication research regarding motivation focused mainly on theories of immediacy (Mehrabian, 1966), integrated systems (Watzlawick, Beavin, & Jackson, 1967), and facework (Brown & Levinson, 1987; Cupach & Imahori, 1993; Goffman, 1967). Investigations using these approaches have documented several ways to influence students' learning. We summarize this literature in the next sections.

Structural, Pedagogical, and Environmental Strategies

Intentional (Nicholls, 1989) and goal orientation theorists (Ames, 1992) have found that students' cognitive orientations toward schooling interact with classroom goal structures to produce motivation. They identify avoidance, ego, and task orientations toward school success, showing that students aim to avoid work, outperform classmates, and/or master learning tasks, depending on which goal structures are salient in the educational context. For example, goal structures that rank students, limit autonomy, or link performance with ability rather than effort tend to encourage an ego (competitive) goal orientation (Nicholls, 1989). Ego-oriented students generally do not exert effort, are less optimistic when confronted with difficulty, and implement fewer independent learning strategies (Ames, 1990). On the other hand, students in classrooms with task-mastery-oriented goal structures tend to attribute their performance to effort, to use more and better learning strategies, to be more positive about their classes, and to be more open to challenging tasks (Ames & Archer, 1988).

Other task-focused research has explored specific instructional tactics that help students attribute their performance to effort (rather than to ability, luck, or chance), and thus become more active, reflective, resourceful, and perseverant learners. Based on social learning theory, Bandura (1997) and others have shown that teachers can model these self-efficacious attributes for their students and provide rewarding opportunities to hone these attributes and skills. For example, Oppenheimer (2001) found that establishing personal goals for learning enhanced student motivation. Other instructional tactics have been found to motivate learning by introducing elements of student interest (Shiefele, 1991), risk (Clifford, 1991), "constructive controversy" (Johnson, Johnson, & Smith, 2000), relevance (Frymier & Shulman, 1995), or collaboration (Slavin, 1985). These tactics can add to students' engagement in learning activities.

Another approach stresses classroom social environments that foster students' motivation and engagement (Butler, 2002; Meyer & Turner, 2002). According to self-determination theorists, for example, students maintain intrinsic learning motivation (Ryan & Deci, 2000) when they feel self-initiating and self-regulating of their own actions (autonomous), understand and feel efficacious about performing learning activities (competent), and develop secure and satisfying connections with others (related). Classroom social environments nurture those needs when they offer optimal challenge, interpersonal involvement, informational feedback, acknowledgment of feelings, and choice-making opportunities (Deci, Ryan, & Williams, 1996). Mastery-oriented, "nonthreatening" feedback, and opportunities to evaluate their own and others' learning can enhance motivation (Perry, VandeKamp, Mercer, & Nordby, 2002). Social environments that provide an opportunity for self-regulated learning foster motivation (Pintrich & DeGroot, 1990) better than climates that lack those features. In fact, Corno and Mandinach (1983) found that the academic self-efficacy of students has a strong positive influence on their willingness to engage in complicated or difficult tasks. These authors suggest that motivation will increase if the instructor can move students toward taking responsibility for their learning.

Interactional Strategies

Instructional communication research about motivation generally has explored how teacher–student interactions maintain or inhibit learning relationships and social climates. For example, Myers (2002) discovered that professors who were high in argumentativeness and low in verbal aggressiveness promoted student motivation, favorable instructor evaluations, cognitive learning, satisfaction with the learning experience, and positive attitudes toward the course. On the other hand, Frymier (1993) found that students with communication apprehension were less motivated unless their professors revealed high immediacy behaviors during in-class interactions.

Educational communication researchers have devoted considerable attention to perceived teacher immediacy (Frymier, 1994a), confirmation (Ellis, 2000), and affinity-seeking behaviors (Frymier, 1994b; Richmond, 1990) as vehicles for stimulating student motivation. Numerous studies have reported positive associations between students' perceptions of these friendly, responsive teacher behaviors and students' perceptions that they are empowered (Frymier, Shulman, & Houser, 1996), have learned (Ellis, 2000; Gorham, 1988), and have been motivated to learn (Christophel, 1990). Other recent research findings have called into question some of the assumptions underlying this line of studies (Comstock, Rowell, & Bowers, 1995; Hess, Smythe, & Communication 451, 2001; Witt & Wheeless, 2001).

Facework

Recent research has investigated the motivational potential of instructional facework as a means to negotiate motivationally productive classroom learning identities, relationships, and environments (Kerssen-Griep, 2001). As noted earlier, self-determination research has established motivational outcomes associated with meeting students' needs to feel and seem autonomous, competent, and related to others (Ryan & Deci, 2000). According to Lim and Bowers (1991) these same three needs are considered universal components of face that are respected or disrespected to some degree in every interaction. *Facework* refers to the strategies people use to present, maintain, or restore their own and others' preferred identities (Goffman, 1967). A recent experiment found that instructional facework during feedback (e.g., teachers' use of tact, approbation, and solidarity) that is seen to respect those identity needs statistically predicted students' intrinsic motivations to gain new knowledge and to accomplish things. Perceived instructional facework also predicted students' greater attentiveness, responsiveness, and tendency to see schooling as a task-mastery-oriented (rather than ego performance or work avoidance) activity (Kerssen-Griep et al., 2003).

In summary, it appears that regardless of the theoretical perspective, motivation to learn is a significant corollary of classroom communication between students and their instructors. Although no specific factor emerges to guarantee that students will be motivated to engage in the learning process, research has isolated instructional communication's capacity to convey motivational respect for important student identity needs and to enhance perceived teacher–student immediacy. Instructors may be able to tailor their own interpersonal communication style and adapt to their students' needs for self-efficacy as a way to maximize motivation to learn in both in-class and out-of-class educational encounters.

INSTRUCTIONAL POWER AND INFLUENCE

Educational researchers have studied how interpersonal and institutional authority, power, and control interact to influence or motivate learners and to influence or control attitudes toward those in power (Kohn, 1993; McNeil, 1988). Interpersonal power dynamics generally are conceived as intricate negotiations involving at least two active participants (Berger, 1994; Giles & Wiemann, 1987; Seibold, Cantrill, & Meyers, 1994). This premise shifts slightly when investigating power in the classroom because the "implicit assumption in this research is that a teacher cannot avoid using power in the classroom, that use of power is an inherent part of the teaching process" (McCroskey & Richmond, 1983, p. 178). Research on power in the classroom traditionally has taken a narrower view of the process, focusing either on the teacher as power figure or on power as a mediating factor in classroom dynamics.

Some studies have focused on teachers' "power bases," including their coercive, reward, legitimate, referent, and expert potentialities (French & Raven, 1968) as being crucial to understanding classroom influence relationships. Cheng's (1994) research confirmed teachers' use of expert, personal, and controlling power on a regular basis. In a study of classroom authority, Richardson, Cook, and Macke (1980) found that rank and sex of the teacher determined his or her use of authority and power. They found that assistant and associate female professors were more likely than male professors to reduce their appearance of authority, whereas male professors of the same rank employed more direct and authoritarian styles. However, they found no differences in the use of authority and control by male and female full professors who employed techniques commensurate with their rank. Although Taylor's (1988) research suggests that teachers most often select softer, controlling strategies, she found instructors used these strategies to downplay their underlying power moves. Taken together, these studies suggest that teachers are implementing a variety of interpersonal power strategies in the classroom.

The primary purpose of most of the power in the classroom research has been to investigate how different communication classroom control strategies affect student perceptions of cognitive learning (Richmond, 1990). Beginning with inductive research about students' perspectives, these studies identified teachers' perceived power bases and specific behavioral influence techniques. These factors were examined in light of students' self-reported motivations, affective learning, and perceived learning (Kearney, Plax, Richmond, & McCroskey, 1984; 1985; McCroskey & Richmond, 1983; McCroskey, Richmond, Plax, & Kearney, 1985; Plax, Kearney, Richmond, & McCroskey, 1986; Richmond, 1990; Richmond & McCroskey, 1984; Richmond, McCroskey, Kearney, & Plax, 1987). In her summary of this research, Richmond (1990) concluded that teachers' "prosocial" (i.e., noncoercive, nonpositional), compliance-gaining strategies outperformed "antisocial" strategies in producing positive student learning outcomes. Kearney, Plax, Sorenson, and Smith (1988) isolated an exception to this generalization. Experienced teachers tended to use more prosocial strategies unless there were active misbehaviors in the classroom. These teachers employed more antisocial strategies to curb misbehaviors. Manke (1990), on the other hand, suggested that power usage is a natural result of communicative interactions. She suggested that instructors mask their use of power strategies because students normally seek ways to act that are not in direct conflict with the teacher.

Power dynamics in the classroom affect a variety of outcomes, including students' compliance with instruction, affect toward teachers and classes, motivation to learn, and self-perceived or observed learning (Butland & Beebe, 1992; Plax et al., 1986; Richmond & McCroskey, 1984). Researchers have begun to focus on the power dynamics that produce environments conducive to learning. For example, Cheng (1994) reported that the perceived qualities of the physical classroom environment as well as the teacher's use of expert, personal, and controlling power were the strongest predictors of student affective learning. Hogelucht and Geist's (1997) research indicated that student misbehavior often serves as a strategy for expressing discontent with the current classroom order. This may also indicate discontent with repeated controlling strategies used by the teacher. Thus, misbehaviors may signal a desire for change in classroom practices. Of course, students' perceptions of, and reaction to, teacher power usage is mediated by teacher immediacy behaviors and student emotions (Butland & Beebe, 1992).

Some instructional communication scholars appear to advocate a bi- or multidirectional approach to studying classroom power. The argument here is that a teacher-stimulus approach to instructional power overplays and insufficiently contextualizes how power negotiations are embedded in teacher–student communication (Sprague, 1990, 1994). Other investigations have questioned the impact of instructors' behaviors relative to environmental forces in learning situations. These researchers see the teacher as not the only—nor perhaps even the primary—influence on students' attitudes and actions (Ames, 1992; Butler, 2002; Christophel & Gorham, 1995; Gorham & Millette, 1997; Sprague, 2002). This approach conceptualizes classroom power as a more complex phenomenon than is currently envisioned. Seen through this wider lens, extant studies of behaviors labeled student resistance (Burroughs, Kearney, & Plax, 1989; Kearney, Plax, Smith, & Sorenson, 1988), for example, may be viewed as a different conceptualization of the learners' active participation in classroom power relations.

Overall, these studies suggest that the classroom environment and interpersonal communication among students and teachers may affect and be affected by interpersonal power dynamics. The different silhouettes of power strategies and relationships suggest that educational power and authority is more a process than a product of teacher behavior.

CONCLUSION

The importance of teacher–student interactions in and out of the classroom should not be underestimated. The research reviewed in this part of the volume indicates that the primary responsibility for productive and positive classroom interactions resides with the teacher. Positive communicative interactions are structured and directed by instructors who consciously engage in behaviors that create a classroom atmosphere conducive to studying and learning.

One way instructors foster interactions that enhance learning may be through the use of immediacy behaviors. Students' perceptions of these behaviors have been associated with various productive classroom outcomes. The Witt, Wheeless, and Allen (chap. 10, this volume) meta-analysis reviews the findings of 81 studies examining the relationship between teachers' verbal and nonverbal behaviors and student learning. Other factors that affect the quality of teacher–student interactions in the classroom and outside of the classroom are also elaborated in this section. Bradford, Cooper, Allen, Stanley and Grimes' (chap. 11, this volume) meta-analysis explores the issue of underrepresented populations and student–teacher relationships. Jones, Dindia and Tye's (chap. 12, this volume) meta-analysis examines the effects of sex equity in the classroom. The importance of teacher–student interactions is illustrated in meta-analyses by Bourhis, Allen, and Bauman's (chap. 13, this volume) work on communication apprehension and Allen, Bourhis, Mabry, Burrell, and Timmerman's (chap. 8, this volume) essay comparing face-to-face instruction with distance education. Finally, Timmerman's chapter explores the interpersonal effects of family-provided rather than day care-provided early instruction.

Taken together, the research reviewed in this part provides a clear indicator of the importance of teacher–student in-class and out-of-class communication in establishing the interpersonal relationships that best enhance the likelihood of student learning. We believe that the research in the area of teacher–student interpersonal communication warrants further investigation. The meta-analyses indicate that specific teacher and student behaviors may increase or decrease the likelihood that students become active partners in the learning process. These meta-analyses provide scaffolding for the next generation of classroom interaction research.

REFERENCES

Aiken, E. G., Thomas, G. S., & Shennum, W. A. (1975). Memory for a lecture: Effects of notes, lecture rate, and informational density. *Journal of Educational Psychology, 67,* 439–444.

Ames, C. (1990). Motivation: What teachers need to know. *Teachers College Record, 91,* 409–421.

Ames, C. (1992). Classrooms: Goals, structures, and student motivation. *Journal of Educational Psychology, 84,* 261–271.

Ames, C., & Archer, J. (1988). Achievement goals in the classroom: Students' learning strategies and motivation processes. *Journal of Educational Psychology, 80,* 260–270.

Anderson, L. E., & Carta-Falsa, J. (2002). Factors that make faculty and student relationships effective. *College Teaching, 50*(4), 134–138.

Aylor, B., & Oppliger, P. (2003). Out-of-class communication and student perceptions of instructor humor orientation and socio-communicative style. *Communication Education, 52,* 122–134.

Bandura, A. (1997). *Self-efficacy: The exercise of control.* New York: Freeman.

Beatty, M. J., & Payne, S. K. (1984). Effects of social facilitation on listening comprehension. *Communication Quarterly, 32*(1), 37–40.

Bell, R. A., & Daly, J. A. (1984). The affinity-seeking function of communication. *Communication Monographs, 51,* 91–115.

Berger, C. R. (1994). Power, dominance, and social interaction. In M. L. Knapp & G. R. Miller (Eds.), *Handbook of interpersonal communication* (2nd ed., pp. 450–507). Thousand Oaks, CA: Sage.

Bostrom, R. N., & Bryant, C. L. (1980). Factors in the retention of information presented orally: The role of short-term listening. *The Western Journal of Speech Communication, 44,* 137–145.

Brown, P., & Levinson, S. C. (1987). *Politeness: Some universals in language use.* Cambridge, UK: Cambridge University Press.

Burroughs, N., Kearney, P., & Plax, T. G. (1989). Compliance-resistance in the college classroom. *Communication Education, 38,* 214–229.

Butland, M. J., & Beebe, S. A. (1992, October). *Teacher immediacy and power in the classroom: The application of implicit communication theory.* Paper presented at the annual meeting of the International Communication Association, Miami, FL. (ERIC Document Reproduction Service No. ED 371 421)

Butler, D. L. (2002). Qualitative approaches to investigating self-regulated learning: Contributions and challenges. *Educational Psychologist, 37*(1), 59–63.

Canfield, G. R. (1961, December). How used are lessons on listening? *The Elementary School Journal, 64,* 146–151.

Cheng, Y. C. (1994). Classroom environment and student affective performance: An effective profile. *Journal of Experimental Education, 62,* 221–240

Christensen, L. J., & Menzel, K. E. (1998). The linear relationship between student reports of teacher immediacy behaviors and perceptions of state motivation, and of cognitive, affective, and behavioral learning. *Communication Education, 47,* 82–90.

Christophel, D. M. (1990). The relationships among teacher immediacy behaviors, student motivation, and learning. *Communication Education, 39,* 323–340.

Christophel, D. M., & Gorham, J. (1995). A test–retest analysis of student motivation, teacher immediacy, and perceived sources of motivation and demotivation in college classes. *Communication Education, 44,* 292–306.

Clark, R. K., Keith, S., & Walker, M. (2001, November). *Experimentally assessing the student impacts of out-of-class communication.* Paper presented at the annual meeting of the National Communication Association, Atlanta, GA.

Clifford, M. M. (1991). Risk taking: Theoretical, empirical, and educational considerations. *Educational Psychologist, 26,* 263–297.

Coakley, C. G., & Wolvin, A. D. (1989). *Experiential listening.* New Orleans, LA: Spectra.

Comstock, J., Rowell, E., & Bowers, J. W. (1995). Food for thought: Teacher nonverbal immediacy, student learning, and curvilinearity. *Communication Education, 44,* 251–266.

Cooper, P. M., Stewart, L. P., & Gudykunst, W. B. (1982). Relationship with instructor and other variables influencing student evaluations of instruction. *Communication Quarterly, 30,* 308–315.

Corno, L., & Mandinach, E. B. (1983). The role of cognitive engagement in classroom learning and motivation. *Educational Psychologist, 18,* 88–108.

Cupach, W. R., & Imahori, T. T. (1993). Identity management theory: Communication competence in intercultural episodes and relationships. In R. L. Wiseman & J. Koester (Eds.), *Intercultural communication competence* (pp. 112–131). Newbury Park, CA: Sage.

Deci, E. L., Ryan, R. M., & Williams, G. C. (1996). Need satisfaction and the self-regulation of learning. *Learning and Individual Differences, 8,* 165–183.

Di Vesta, F. J., & Gray, G. S. (1973). Listening and note taking: II. Immediate and delayed recall as functions of variations in thematic continuity, note taking, and length of listening-review intervals. *Journal of Educational Psychology, 64,* 278–287.

Dolin, D. J. (1995). An alternative form of teacher affinity-seeking measure. *Communication Research Reports, 12,* 220–226.

Ellis, K. (2000). Perceived teacher confirmation: The development and validation of an instrument and two studies of the relationship to cognitive and affective learning. *Human Communication Research, 26,* 264–291.

French, J. R., & Raven, B. (1968). The bases of social power. In D. Cartwright & A. Zander (Eds.), *Group dynamics: Research and theory* (3rd ed., pp. 259–269). New York: Harper & Row.

Frymier, A. B. (1993). The relationship among communication apprehension, immediacy, and motivation to study. *Communication Reports, 6,* 8–17.

Frymier, A. B. (1994a). A model of immediacy in the classroom. *Communication Quarterly, 42,* 133–143.

Frymier, A. B. (1994b). The use of affinity-seeking in producing liking and learning in the classroom. *Journal of Applied Communication Research, 22,* 87–105.

Frymier, A. B., & Shulman, G. M. (1995). "What's in it for me?" Increasing content relevance to enhance students' motivation. *Communication Education, 44,* 40–50.

Frymier, A. B., Shulman, G. M., & Houser, M. (1996). The development of a learner empowered measure. *Communication Education, 45,* 181–199.

Frymier, A. B., & Thomas, C. A. (1992). Perceived teacher affinity-seeking in relation to perceived teacher credibility. *Communication Education, 41,* 388–399.

Fusani, D. S. (1994). "Extra-class" communication: Frequency, immediacy, self disclosure, and satisfaction in student–faculty interaction outside the classroom. *Journal of Applied Communication Research, 22,* 232–255.

Garko, M. G., Kough, C., Pignata, G., Kimmel, E. B., & Eison, J. (1994). Myths about student faculty relationships: What do students really want? *Journal on Excellence in College Teaching, 5*(2), 51–65.

Gayle, B. M. (2002, December). How can we teach students to critically evaluate their own stance and seriously consider divergent views? *National Teaching and Learning Forum, 12*(1), 6–8.

Giles, H., & Wiemann, J. W. (1987). Language, social comparison, and power. In C. R. Berger & S. H. Chaffee (Eds.), *Handbook of communication science* (pp. 350–384). Newbury Park, CA: Sage.

Glenn, E. C., Emmert, P., & Emmert, V. (1995). A scale for measuring listenability: The factors that determine listening ease and difficulty. *International Journal of Listening, 9,* 44–61.

Goffman, E. (1967). Interaction ritual: Essays on face-to-face behavior. New York: Pantheon.

Gorham, J. (1988). The relationship between verbal teacher immediacy behaviors and student learning. *Communication Education, 37,* 40–53.

Gorham, J., & Christophel, D. M. (1992). Students' perception of teacher behaviors as motivating and demotivating factors in college classes. *Communication Quarterly, 40,* 239–252.

Gorham, J., Kelley, D. H., & McCroskey, J. C. (1989). The affinity-seeking of classroom teachers: A second perspective. *Communication Quarterly, 37,* 16–26.

Gorham, J., & Millette, D. M. (1997). A comparative analysis of teacher and student perceptions of sources of motivation and demotivation in college classes. *Communication Education, 46,* 245–261.

Hess, J. A., Smythe, M. J., & Communication 451. (2001). Is teacher immediacy actually related to student cognitive learning? *Communication Studies, 52,* 197–219.

Hogelucht, K. S. B., & Geist, P. (1997). Discipline in the classroom: Communicative strategies for negotiating order. *Western Journal of Communication, 97*(1), 1–35.

Ilatov, Z. Z., Shamai, S., Hertz-Lazarovitz, R., & Mayer-Young, S. (1998). Teacher–student classroom interactions: The influence of gender, academic dominance and teacher communication style. *Adolescence, 33*(1), 269–277.

Jaasma, M. A., & Koper, R. J. (1999). The relationship of student–faculty out-of-class communication to instructor immediacy and trust and to student motivation. *Communication Education, 48,* 41–47.

Jaasma, M. A., & Koper, R. J. (2002). Out-of-class communication between female and male students and faculty: The relationship to student perceptions of instructor immediacy. *Women's Studies in Communication, 25,* 119–137.

Johnson, D. W., Johnson, R., & Smith, K. A. (2000). Constructive controversy: The educative power of intellectual conflict. *Change, 32,* 28–32.

Kearney, P., Plax, T. G., Richmond, V. P., & McCroskey, J. C. (1984). Power in the classroom IV: Teacher communication techniques as alternatives to discipline. In R. Bostrom (Ed.), *Communication yearbook 8* (pp. 724–746). Beverly Hills, CA: Sage.

Kearney, P., Plax, T. G., Richmond, V. P., & McCroskey, J. C. (1985). Power in the classroom III: Teacher communication techniques and messages. *Communication Education, 34,* 19–28.

Kearney, P., Plax, T. G., Smith, V., & Sorenson, G. (1988). Effects of teacher immediacy and strategy type on college student resistance to on-task demands. *Communication Education, 37,* 54–67.

Kearney, P., Plax, T. G., Sorenson, G., & Smith, V. (1988). Experienced and prospective teachers' selections of compliance-gaining messages for "common" student misbehaviors. *Communication Education, 37,* 150–164.

Kerssen-Griep, J. (2001). Teacher communication activities relevant to student motivation: Classroom facework and instructional communication competence. *Communication Education, 50,* 256–273.

Kerssen-Griep, J., Hess, J. A., & Trees, A. R. (2003). Sustaining the desire to learn: Dimensions of perceived instructional facework related to student involvement and motivation to learn. *Western Journal of Communication, 67,* 357–381.

Kohn, A. (1993). *Punished by rewards: The trouble with gold stars, incentive plans, A's, praise, and other bribes.* Boston: Houghton-Mifflin.

Kovalainen, M., Kumpulainen, K., & Vasama, S. (2001). Orchestrating classroom interaction in a community of inquiry: Modes of teacher participation. *Journal of Classroom Interaction, 36*(2), 17–28.

Kuh, G. D. (1995). The other curriculum: Out-of-class experiences associated with student learning and personal development. *Journal of Higher Education, 66,* 123–155.

Lamport, M. A. (1993). Student–faculty informal interaction and the effect on college student outcomes: A review of the literature. *Adolescence, 28,* 971–990.

Lim, T., & Bowers, J. W. (1991). Facework: Solidarity, approbation, and tact. *Human Communication Research, 17,* 415–450.

Manke, M. H. P. (1990). Constructing the power relationship: A study of two elementary school classrooms (Doctoral dissertation, University of Virginia, 1990). *Dissertation Abstracts International, 5,* 3635.

McCroskey, J. C., & McCroskey, L. L. (1986). The affinity-seeking of classroom teachers. *Communication Research Reports, 3,* 158–167.

McCroskey, J. C., & Richmond, V. P. (1983). Power in the classroom I: Teacher and student perceptions. *Communication Education, 32,* 175–184.

McCroskey, J. C., Richmond, V. P., Plax, G. T., & Kearney, P. (1985). Power in the classroom V: Behavior alteration techniques, communication training and learning. *Communication Education, 34,* 214–226.

McKenzie, N. J., & Clark, A. J. (1995). The all in one concept: How much must listening research include? *International Journal of Listening, 9,* 29–43.

McNeil, L. M. (1988). *Contradictions of control.* New York: Routledge.

Mehrabian, A. (1966). Immediacy: An indicator of attitudes in linguistic communication. *Journal of Personality, 34,* 26–34.

Meyer, D. K., & Turner, J. C. (2002). Using instructional discourse analysis to study the scaffolding of student self-regulation. *Educational Psychologist, 37,* 17–25.

Milem, J. F., & Berger, J. B. (1997). A modified model of college student persistence: Exploring the relationship between Astin's theory of involvement and Tinto's theory of student departure. *Journal of College Student Development, 38,* 387–400.

Myers, S. A. (1995). Student perceptions of teacher-affinity-seeking and classroom climate. *Communication Research Reports, 12,* 192–199.

Myers, S. A. (2002). Perceived aggressive instructor communication and student state motivation, learning and satisfaction. *Communication Reports, 15,* 114–121.

Nadler, M. K., & Nadler, L. B. (2000). Out-of-class communication between faculty and students: A faculty perspective. *Communication Studies, 51,* 176–188.

Nadler, M. K., & Nadler, L. B. (2001). The roles of sex, empathy, and credibility in out-of-class communication. *Women's Studies in Communication, 24,* 241–261.

Nicholls, J. G. (1989). *The competitive ethos and democratic education.* Cambridge, MA: Harvard University Press.

Oppenheimer, R. J. (2001). Increasing student motivation and facilitating learning. *College Teaching, 49*(3), 96–98.

Pascarella, E. T. (1980). Student–faculty informal contact and college outcomes. *Review of Educational Research, 50,* 545–595.

Pascarella, E. T., & Terenzini, P. T. (1991). *How college affects students: Findings and insights from twenty years of research.* San Francisco: Jossey-Bass.

Patrick, B. C., Hisley, J., & Kempler, T. (2000). "What's everybody so excited about?": The effect of teacher enthusiasm on student intrinsic motivation and vitality. *The Journal of Experimental Education, 68,* 217–236.

Perry, N. E., VandeKamp, K. O., Mercer, L. K., & Nordby, C. J. (2002). Investigating teacher–student interactions that foster self-regulated learning. *Educational Psychologist, 37,* 5–15.

Petrie, C. R., & Carrel, S. D. (1976). The relationship of motivation, listening capability, initial information and verbal organizational ability to lecture comprehension and retention. *Communication Monographs, 43,* 187–194.

Pintrich, P. R., & DeGroot, E. V. (1990). Motivational and self-regulated learning components of classroom academic performance. *Journal of Educational Psychology, 82,* 33–40.

Plax, T. G., Kearney, P., Richmond, V. P., & McCroskey, J. C. (1986). Power in the classroom VI: Verbal control strategies, nonverbal immediacy and affective learning. *Communication Education, 35,* 43–55.

Richardson, L. W., Cook, J. A., & Macke, A. S. (1980, August). *Classroom authority management of male and female university professors.* Paper presented at the meeting of the American Sociological Association, New York. (ERIC Document Reproduction Service No. ED 199 122)

Richmond, V. P. (1990). Communication in the classroom: Power and motivation. *Communication Education, 39,* 181–195.

Richmond, V. P., & McCroskey, J. C. (1984). Power in the classroom II: Power and learning. *Communication Education, 33,* 125–136.

Richmond, V. P., McCroskey, J. C., Kearney, P., & Plax, T. G. (1987). Power in the classroom VII: Linking behavior alteration techniques to cognitive learning. *Communication Education, 36,* 1–12.

Rodríguez, J. I., Plax, T. G., & Kearney, P. (1996). Clarifying the relationship between teacher nonverbal immediacy and student cognitive learning: Affective learning as the central causal mediator. *Communication Education, 45,* 293–305.

Rogoff, B. (1994). Developing understanding of the idea of community of learners. *Mind, Culture and Activity, 1,* 209–229.

Ryan, R. M., & Deci, E. L. (2000). Self-determination theory and the facilitation of intrinsic motivation, social development, and well-being. *American Psychologist, 55,* 68–78.

Seibold, D. R., Cantrill, J. G., & Meyers, R. A. (1994). Communication and interpersonal influence. In M. L. Knapp & G. R. Miller (Eds.), *Handbook of interpersonal communication* (2nd ed., pp. 542–588). Thousand Oaks, CA: Sage.

Shamai, S., Ilatov, Z., Hertz-Lazarovitz, R., & Bentsvi-Mayer, S. (1995). Developing a model of classroom interactions between teacher and students. *Curriculum and Teaching, 10*(2), 45–55.

Shiefele, U. (1991). Interest, learning, and motivation. *Educational Psychologist, 26,* 299–323.

Simonds, C. J., Jones, R., & Bedore, J. (1994, November). *What happened if: Challenge behavior in the college classroom.* Paper presented at the annual meeting of the Speech Communication Association, New Orleans, LA. (ERIC Document Reproduction Service No. ED 385 877)

Slavin, R. (1985). Team-assisted individualization: Combining cooperative learning and individualized instruction in mathematics. In R. Slavin, S. Sharan, S. Kagan, R. H. Lazarowitz, C. Webb, & R. Schmuck (Eds.), *Learning to cooperate, cooperating to learn* (pp. 177–209). New York: Plenum.

Smeltzer, L. R., & Watson, K. W. (1984). Listening: An empirical comparison of discussion length and level of incentive. *Central States Speech Journal, 35,* 166–170.

Sprague, J. (1990, February). *Problematizing power in the classroom: Applying the critical perspective to a significant issue in instructional communication.* Paper presented at the meeting of the Western States Communication Association, Sacramento, CA.

Sprague, J. (1994). Ontology, politics, and instructional communication research: Why we can't just "agree to disagree" about power. *Communication Education, 43,* 273–290.

Sprague, J. (2002). Communication Education: The spiral continues. *Communication Education, 51,* 337–354.

Taylor, E. N. (1988). Power relationships in the classroom and how they are maintained (Doctoral dissertation, Ohio State University, 1988). *Dissertation Abstracts International, 49,* 2105.

Terenzini, P. T., Pascarella, E. T., & Blimling, G. S. (1991). Students' out-of-class experiences and their influence on learning and cognitive development: A literature review. *Journal of College Student Development, 37,* 149–162.

Tinto, V. (1987). *Learning in college.* Chicago: University of Chicago.

Wanzer, M. B. (1998). An exploratory investigation of student and teacher perceptions of student-generated affinity-seeking behaviors. *Communication Education, 47,* 373–382.

Watson, K. W., Barker, L. L., & Weaver, J. B. (1995). The listening styles profile (LSP-16): Development and validation of an instrument to assess four listening styles. *Journal of International Listening, 9,* 7–13.

Watzlawick, P., Beavin, J. H., & Jackson, D. D. (1967). *Pragmatics of human communication: A study of interaction patterns, pathologies, and paradoxes.* New York: Norton.

Weiner, B. (1985). An attributional theory achievement motivation and emotion. *Psychological Review, 92,* 548–573.

Witt, P. L., & Wheeless, L. R. (2001). An experimental study of teachers' verbal and nonverbal immediacy and students' affective and cognitive learning. *Communication Education, 50,* 327–342.

Wooten, A. G., & McCroskey, J. C. (1996). Student trust of teacher as a function of socio-communicative style of teacher and socio-communication orientation of student. *Communication Research Reports, 13,* 94–100.

Wubbels, T., Brekelmans, M., & Hooymayers, H. (1991). Interpersonal teacher behavior in the classroom. In B. J. Fraser & H. J. Walberg (Eds.), *Educational environments: Evaluation, antecedents, and consequences* (pp. 141–160). New York: Pergamon.

Wubbels, T., Creton, H., Levy, J., & Hooymayers, H. (1993). The model for interpersonal teacher behavior. In T. Wubbels & J. Levy (Eds.), *Do you know what you look like? Interpersonal relationships in education* (pp. 13–28). London: Falmer Press.

10

The Relationship Between Teacher Immediacy and Student Learning: A Meta-Analysis

Paul L. Witt
Texas Christian University

Lawrence R. Wheeless
University of North Texas

Mike Allen
University of Wisconsin–Milwaukee

Social psychologist Albert Mehrabian conceptualized immediacy as communication behaviors that "enhance closeness to and nonverbal interaction with another" (Mehrabian, 1969, p. 213). Grounding the concept in approach–avoidance theory, Mehrabian (1981) suggested that "people approach what they like and avoid what they don't like" (p. 22). The term *immediacy* describes the set of verbal and nonverbal behaviors (Mehrabian, 1969, 1971; Wiener & Mehrabian, 1968) that produce the perception of reduced physical or psychological distance between the communicators. In the first examination of immediacy and learning outcomes, Andersen (1978, 1979) examined the relationship between the nonverbal immediacy behaviors of teachers and learning outcomes of their students. After that work, communication education devoted an enormous research effort to understanding the relationship between instructor immediacy behaviors and the various outcomes. The accumulation of research evidence is controversial as persons provided different interpretations of that relationship. This meta-analysis provides a systematic quantitative summarization of the studies of verbal and nonverbal immediacy of teachers in relation to students' affective, cognitive, and perceived learning outcomes. The issue remains an important instructional consideration because if student learning is improved by increased levels of teacher immediacy, training and advice for instructors is affected. The ability to improve learning by changing communication behavior represents an exciting and intriguing possibility. The empirical question that must be answered is whether increased immediacy behavior is correlated with improved student learning.

Student learning is not a single and universal concept. There exist distinctions among cognitive learning, affective learning, and psychomotor domains of learning (Bloom, 1956). Cognitive learning is usually associated with test scores or grades and considered to measure mastery of some course content or critical skill (for challenges to this view see Richmond, Gorham, & McCroskey, 1987; Richmond & McCroskey, 1992). Affective learning outcomes measure greater liking for the teacher and course, greater likelihood of engaging in the behaviors learned, and greater likelihood of enrolling in another course of the same type (Baker, 2001; Folwell, 1995; Gorham & Christophel, 1990). Another measure of learning developed by Richmond et al. (1987) involves *learning loss*, the difference between students' perceived learning and predicted learning if they had the "ideal" instructor. A necessary question deserving consideration is whether the immediacy of a teacher may influence one learning outcome and not others.

NONVERBAL IMMEDIACY AND STUDENT LEARNING

Teacher immediacy can be generated by various nonverbal behaviors such as eye gaze, smiles, nods, relaxed body posture, forward leans, movement, gestures, and vocal variety. The empirical research considers whether increases in those behaviors that reduce the physical or psychological distance between instructor and student improve student learning. Studies report inconsistent results on cognitive learning with some studies finding an increase (Jordan, 1989; Kelley & Gorham, 1988; McDowell, McDowell, & Hyerdahl, 1980) and other studies no relationship (Andersen, 1978, 1979; Andersen, Norton, & Nussbaum, 1981). A more consistent set of findings indicates a relationship between nonverbal immediacy and affective learning (Andersen & Withrow, 1981; Kearney, Plax, & Wendt-Wasco, 1985; Plax, Kearney, McCroskey, & Richmond, 1986; Sorenson, 1989).

A central consideration for nonverbal behavior should be the context and expectation between behaviors and the normative expectations for those behaviors. Nonverbal behaviors are highly inferential and vary based on culture and context. Therefore, any relationship observed in the United States may not exist when considering other cultural or language groups (Gudykunst & Ting-Toomey, 1988). Researchers have compared immediacy and learning among different cultural, ethnic, and national groups, generally finding a positive relationship between nonverbal teacher immediacy and students' affective and perceived learning (Hinkle, 1998; McCroskey, Fayer, Richmond, Sallinen, & Barraclough, 1996; McCroskey, Sallinen, Fayer, Richmond, & Barraclough, 1996; Mortenson, 1994; Myers, Zhong, & Guan, 1998; Neuliep, 1995, 1997; Roach & Byrne, 2001; Sanders & Wiseman, 1990; Thompson, 1992). The question of whether those effects are consistent and similar in magnitude to permit generalization requires systematic and careful analysis.

Other researchers have examined the effects of nonverbal immediacy in various distributed learning environments (Hackman & Walker, 1990; McAlister, 2001; Peterson, 1994), where "reducing the distance" between teacher and students becomes a primary communication goal. Given the relationship of the style of learning to the effectiveness of various technologies in distance learning, the need for psychological closeness may prove important for some students and not others (M. Allen, Timmerman, Bourhis, Mabry, & Burrell, 2002). The impact of teacher immediacy may not appear initially relevant to the distance learning environment but research indicates that communication features may play as important a role in that environment as well.

VERBAL IMMEDIACY AND STUDENT LEARNING

Mehrabian (1969, 1971, Wiener & Mehrabian, 1968) suggested taxonomies of specific word choices and syntactic structures as expressions of liking or closeness that promote the perception of immediacy. Researchers since 1988 have consistently reported significant relationships between verbal immediacy and various types of learning (e.g., Adkins, 1998; Butland & Beebe, 1992; Christensen & Menzel, 1998; Christophel, 1990; Frymier, 1994; Hackman & Walker, 1990; McDowell & McDowell, 1990; Menzel & Carrell, 1999; Peterson, 1994; Powell & Harville, 1990; Thompson, 1992). Many communication researchers employed Gorham's (1988) verbal immediacy measure in conjunction with nonverbal immediacy measures to examine both types of teacher immediacy. Not surprisingly, a number of studies assessing both types of immediacy found substantial relationships between the verbal immediacy and nonverbal immediacy (e.g., Hess & Smythe, 2001; Jordan, 1989; Peterson, 1994). Some researchers combined the two types of immediacy into a single construct (Farren, 1992; Garard, 1998; McAlister, 2001; Menzel & Carrell, 1999; Neuliep, 1995, 1997;

Sanders & Wiseman, 1990). There is some indication that outcomes of teachers' verbal behaviors are mediated or overridden by teachers' nonverbal behaviors (Kearney, Plax, Smith, & Sorenson, 1988; Plax et al., 1986; Witt & Wheeless, 2001).

The relationship of verbal immediacy to student learning is probably positive. However, the problem of co-occurrence with nonverbal immediacy behaviors means that there is a natural expectation of consistency between verbal and nonverbal behaviors. At a level of measurement, the ability to get separate and independent measurements of each source of immediacy may prove difficult. This means that the estimation of any relationship to student learning may not provide independent estimates.

THEORETICAL EXPLANATIONS

The theoretical challenge of explanation requires providing an account that permits an understanding and prediction of the relationship of immediacy to student learning. Mehrabian (1969, 1981) used the idea of approach–avoidance to explain the impact of nonverbal immediacy. If the stimulus is perceived as rewarding, then the person is motivated to approach. A negative or less positive perception promotes avoidance of the person. The impact of the behavior serves as an incentive or disincentive to continue conversation or even to view the stimulus person as someone interesting or desirable.

Various theoretical perspectives contain elements or expectations that are consistent with Mehrabian's view. Reinforcement theory would view immediacy behavior and the resulting perceptions of physical or psychological closeness as a reward that promotes a positive relationship (Berscheid & Walster, 1978). In the context of student learning the argument would be that students feeling that the instructor is accessible and rewarding would promote communication. Going to the classroom becomes a desirable experience because the communication is affirming and rewarding.

Verbal immediacy may be further explained in terms of speech accommodation theory (Giles, Mulac, Bradac, & Johnson, 1987; Jordan & Wheeless, 1990). People adapt the manner and content of their verbal communication to the perceived preference or style of the receiver and context. Immediacy behaviors, then, serve to enhance interpersonal closeness (Mehrabian, 1981). This is consistent with Tinto's (1975) model of the reasons students drop out of school—the inability to form relationships with others, particularly instructors.

Although most immediacy studies report generally positive relationships between teacher immediacy and student outcomes, there is little agreement about how immediacy works to enhance learning. The following are among the explanations advanced by scholars: (a) Immediacy may attract or arouse students' attention, which is related to cognitive learning

(Comstock, Rowell, & Bowers, 1995; Kelley & Gorham, 1988); (b) Immediacy may serve to increase students' state motivation to learn, which in turn increases their learning (Christophel, 1990; Christophel & Gorham, 1995; Frymier, 1994; Richmond, 1990); (c) Immediacy may enhance affect for the teacher and course content, thereby increasing cognitive learning (Rodriguez, Plax, & Kearney, 1996); (d) Teacher immediacy behaviors may function directly to increase students' learning (e.g., Andersen, 1979); and (e) Teacher immediacy may elicit certain positive emotional responses from students, which in turn increase learning (Butland & Beebe, 1992; Mottet & Beebe, 2001).

Essentially, all the theoretical models provide an account that assumes the behaviors by the instructor increase the motivation of the student to learn. The disagreement is whether the motivation is episodic (for the particular session or class) or provides a longer term change in motivation toward the entire class (or even the entire process of college education in general). The point of agreement is that the response to immediacy behaviors is a more positive emotional state that should translate into improved learning. The disagreement is why that occurs. Although causal modeling has been attempted, results show some fit to theoretical systems, but no account has consistently proven superior across the studies. This meta-analysis simply examines the inconsistency in empirical results and attempts to resolve the fundamental relationship between immediacy behaviors and student learning.

METHOD

Literature Search

The initial search for manuscripts was conducted through electronic databases and search systems including ERIC, Dissertation Abstracts International, Comm Search, ComIndex, Social Science Index, Academic Search Premier, and the Psychology and Behavioral Science Collection in EBSCO. In addition, relevant citations in the obtained reports were searched, as were the reference sections of instructional communication books and reports. Finally, to locate a representative sampling of relevant unpublished studies, hand searches were conducted of recent convention programs of the National Communication Association and the International Communication Association.

Manuscripts were included in the meta-analysis if they met the following criteria: (a) teaching–learning context where instruction was delivered to a learner or learners, (b) quantitative measurement of some type of immediacy and some type of learning, (c) studies reported or published from 1979 through 2001.

Some articles, dissertations, or papers reported results from more than one study, or findings from multiple cultural groupings. Following established meta-analytical practice (Lipsey & Wilson, 2001), the unit of analysis for this meta-analytical review was the individual study or unique cultural group, rather than the published article or dissertation.

After screening more than 250 articles, dissertations, theses, and convention papers, a total of 93 immediacy and learning studies were identified. One study was excluded because of unconventional methodological factors related to a semiliterate participant pool (McGreal, 1989), and 11 studies did not report results in a manner that enabled meta-analytic comparison (J. L. Allen, O'Mara, & Long, 1987; Andersen & Withrow, 1981; Daniel, 2000; Frymier, 1993; Furio, 1987; Orpen, 1994; Sidelinger & McCroskey, 1997; Thomas, 1994; Valencic, 2001; Walker & Hackman, 1991; Wanzer & Frymier, 1999). Thus, 81 studies were included in the meta-analysis. (For a full bibliography, please contact Paul L. Witt.)

Coding of Studies

Statistical Analysis.   The correlation coefficient r was selected as the appropriate effect size statistic, and qualified researchers collaborated in the coding of the manuscripts for individual effect sizes. Following the principles of variance-centered meta-analysis, average correlations were computed in cases of multiple measurement of the same variable (Lipsey & Wilson, 2001). When necessary, appropriate calculations were made to statistically transform reported effects into correlation coefficients (Hunter & Schmidt, 1990). In cases where findings were deemed statistically nonsignificant, actual correlations were computed whenever possible, but a zero effect size was recorded if no details were present. Computing accurate effects proved particularly problematic in one instance (Hackman & Walker, 1990) and may have served to underestimate actual correlations in that one sample.

Before analysis, the average correlation coefficients of each study were adjusted to correct for statistical or design artifacts. In four studies (Comstock et al., 1995; Hess & Smythe, 2001; Menzel & Carrell, 1999; Messman & Jones-Corley, 2001), continuous immediacy data had been grouped by researchers for the purpose of analysis in two-group or three-group research designs. Because the use of a median split or 33.3% split in such cases has been shown to systematically understate the size of the effect (Hunter & Schmidt, 1990), the reported or derived effects for these studies were statistically corrected before analysis.

Similarly, reported effects were systematically understated due to imperfect measurement of both independent and dependent variables. Using the actual or estimated reliability for each instrument, reported effects were adjusted to correct for attenuated measurement (Hunter & Schmidt, 1990).

For one-item or two-item measures, an average reliability of .60 was assumed (Hedges & Olkin, 1985). This adjustment was applied, for example, to effects derived from perceived learning data gathered through the widely used learning loss measure. After these corrections were made, both the average effect and the estimate of variance were slightly larger than originally reported. A complete set of coding and effects for each study is available in an earlier report of the data reported in this chapter (Witt, Wheeless, & Allen, 2004).

Types of Immediacy.   The studies were coded on the basis of the measurement of immediacy into the following categories: (a) nonverbal, (b) verbal, and (c) combined measures. Nonverbal measures of immediacy ask about the behaviors of an instructor related to physical behaviors (e.g., eye contact, gestures, facial behavior like smiling). Nonverbal measures include the Generalized Immediacy Scale (GIS) introduced by Andersen (1979) that uses nine semantic differentials. Another scale often used in conjunction with the GIS is the Behavioral Indicants of Immediacy Scale (Andersen, 1979). The scale was modified by Richmond et. al. (1987) and renamed the Nonverbal Immediacy Behaviors Instrument, and further modified and abbreviated by McCroskey, Fayer, Richmond, Sallinen, and Barraclough (1996).

Verbal measures of immediacy measure particular utterances or content and ask about the content of the communication between student and instructor. Verbal measures of immediacy have usually relied on Gorham's (1988) Verbal Immediacy Behaviors Instrument, a 20-item measure. Jordan (1989; Jordan & Wheeless, 1990) also developed an unpublished measure used in some work.

Combined measures are those instruments that do not separate out the separate elements of verbal and nonverbal but have items that assess each of the elements. When some elements of both are present and cannot be separated, the measure was considered a combined measure.

Learning Outcomes.   Learning outcomes were coded as: (a) cognitive, (b) affective, and (c) perceived learning. Cognitive learning was defined, consistent with the view of Bloom (1956), as recall, comprehension, application, and synthesis of newly acquired information. Typically, measures of this have included exam scores, course grades, and other indicators related to some performance.

Perceived learning was defined as self-reports of learning. This category includes the "learning loss" instrument (Richmond et al., 1987) that measures the gap between what a student learned and what he or she would have learned if the "ideal" instructor had been teaching the course. Because some scholars view these self-reports not as measures of actual learning this was considered a separate category. It should be noted that many of the authors of original data reports would categorize the learning loss measure as a measure of cognitive learning. However, given that the learning measure is a measure of what students believe they have learned versus measures of how much the student actually remembers, the decision was made to separate these instruments.

Affective Learning Measures.   Affective learning measures are those emotional responses to the instructor and the classroom or course that could influence the level of information retained by a student. Andersen (1979) used the Affective Learning Scale, which measures the student attitude about the teacher, the course, the behaviors learned, and attitudes about enrolling in another course of the same type or taking another course from the same instructor. Various forms and versions of this approach exist (Frymier, 1994; Mortenson, 1994; Roach & Byrne, 2001; Sanders & Wiseman, 1990). The key distinction is that the measures consider attitudes about the behaviors of the instructor in the learning environment rather than measure some direct accomplishment of the student. The measures should more directly access the underlying motivational aspects of the student affect rather than the mastery of the course content.

Design Features.   Various characteristics of the design of the investigations were explored as a potential moderator variable: (a) publication status, (b) source of participants, and (c) type of empirical design. The publication status was simply whether the investigation had been published in a journal or book or whether the manuscript was a convention paper or unpublished doctoral dissertation or master's thesis. The argument about the potential for the "file drawer," where nonsignificant studies are not published, and significant studies are published represents a potential source of systematic bias. A comparison of the size of the effect would permit consideration of whether this potential bias may influence the outcome.

The source of the participants simply examines whether studies conducted in the United States generate the same outcome as studies conducted outside the United States. This analysis can assess the degree to which the results may or may not be influenced by cultural differences. Not enough studies existed in any other country or region to permit a more detailed and thorough analysis. The ability to provide a more thorough comparison requires additional data sets.

The design characteristic of the investigation is whether the manuscript reports a survey or uses an experimental design. A survey of some persons indicates a naturalistic design where the participants provide an assessment of immediacy, whereas an experimental design has immediacy levels manipulated. The challenge is always between the desire to have a design that more closely resembles field conditions (survey) versus the desire to control extraneous or other influences so that any comparison has conditions different only on the dimension of interest (experiment). The comparison permits an examination of whether different results are generated by the different designs.

RESULTS

Comparisons in the overall analysis found a positive and substantial relationship between overall teacher immediacy and overall student learning (average $r = .500$, variance $= .037, k = 81, N = 24,474$). Relationships of similar strength were found for teacher nonverbal immediacy and overall learning (average $r = .481$, variance $= .040, k = 68, N = 21,171$) and teacher verbal immediacy and overall learning (average $r = .472$, variance $= .036, k = 29, N = 8,468$). Similar but slightly higher correlations were found among studies that measured teacher immediacy as a single construct consisting of both verbal and nonverbal behaviors combined (average $r = .545$, variance $= .035, k = 12, N = 3,158$). These general results should be interpreted with caution, however, because each of these samples was found to be heterogeneous: (overall $\chi^2(80) = 788.48, k = 81$, $N = 24,474, p < .05$; nonverbal $\chi^2(67) = 716.83, k = 68, N = 21,171$, $p < .05$; verbal $\chi^2(28) = 220.22, k = 29, N = 8,468, p < .05$; combined-only immediacy $\chi^2(11) = 117.46, k = 12, N = 3,158, p < .05$), indicating the possibility of one or more moderator variables.

No significant differences were found in overall teacher immediacy and overall learning between published studies (average $r = .505$, variance $= .041, k = 54, N = 15,619$) and unpublished studies (average $r = .490$, variance $= .030, k = 27, N = 8,855$), or between samples of non-U.S. student groups (average $r = .468$, variance $= .053, k = 14, N = 2,700$) and U.S.-only student groups (average $r = .506$, variance $= .034, k = 67, N = 21,774$). However, a significantly larger effect, $t(79) = 2.906, p = < .01$, was obtained in overall teacher immediacy and overall learning between studies that used survey questionnaires (average $r = .518$, variance $= .034, k = 74$, $N = 22,915$) and studies that used experimental research designs (average $r = .306$, variance $= .032, k = 7, N = 1,559$). Again, persistent heterogeneity among all these samples implied the presence of one or more moderator variables causing greater variance in the samples than would be expected from random sampling error alone.

In search of moderator variables, we examined the associations among each of three types of teacher immediacy (nonverbal, verbal, and combined-only) and each of three types of student learning (perceived, cognitive, and affective). Table 10.1 provides a depiction of these analyses. These results

TABLE 10.1
Average Effects Across Differing Types of Teacher Immediacy
and Types of Student Learning

	Perceived Learning	Cognitive Learning	Affective Learning
Nonverbal immediacy	.510	.166	.490
Average r Variance	.053	.019	.028
k	44	11	55
N	13,313	3,777	17,328
Verbal immediacy	.491	.057	.491
Average r Variance	.037	.014	.036
k	25	4	26
N	8,017	1,437	7,139
Combined-only immediacy	.634	.122	.550
Average r Variance	.030		.019
k	10	1	11
N	2,812	223	2,935

provide a consistent pattern of relationships for nonverbal and verbal immediacy and perceived and affective learning, but markedly lower correlations
for all types of teacher immediacy with cognitive learning. Results among
the studies of combined-only immediacy were generally consistent with
these same patterns although, as mentioned previously, slightly greater effect sizes were obtained among these studies. Despite the detailed examination of these subgroupings, significant chi-squares indicated heterogeneity
among these samples. However, given that almost all studies demonstrate
positive correlations, the impact of a moderator would be to distinguish
between the magnitude of a positive correlation rather than changing
direction of the association.

DISCUSSION

Overall Immediacy and Overall Learning

The synthesized result of the meta-analysis of the entire body of quantitative
findings indicated a meaningful relationship between overall teacher immediacy and overall learning, whether measured by verbal, nonverbal, or combined measurement of immediacy. The combined measurement did
demonstrate a slightly higher correlation, which could reflect the impact of
the improvement in measurement that resulted from combined information

by measuring more of the information related to immediacy. The fact that the correlation is only slightly higher may indicate a large degree of overlap or co-occurrence of verbal and nonverbal indicators of immediacy.

In search of moderators of these overall findings the design characteristics of the investigations provided little difference. Published and unpublished research produced similar results in terms of the magnitude of association between teacher immediacy and overall learning. Likewise, no significant difference in r's and related shared variance was observed for overall immediacy and overall learning between U.S. samples and non-U.S. samples. Lack of significance does not, however, indicate lack of any cultural differences in immediacy and learning across different cultural groupings. Even if the correlations were the same, the functions of those differences may still differ based on culture (M. Allen, Hecht, & Martin, 1996). Differences in the immediacy–learning association were found among specific cultures in the 14 non-U.S. studies and in the 4 studies that compared results across ethnic groups of U.S. students (Mortenson, 1994; Neuliep, 1995; Powell & Harville, 1990; Sanders & Wiseman, 1990). However, no single nationality or cultural grouping reflected a sufficient number of studies for meaningful separate comparison. Although some cultural differences may exist, the pattern of consistent positive correlations between teacher immediacy and affective and perceived learning existed across almost all of the nationalities and cultural groupings examined. However, none of the cross-cultural studies investigated cognitive learning performance as indicated by tests of recall, recognition, exams, or course grades.

In overall learning attributable to overall teacher immediacy, significant differences existed between the results from survey questionnaire research and those of experimental studies. These experiments were constrained by factors such as time of teacher immediacy displayed, specific teachers, content topics of messages, the specific situation, the brevity of the inductions, and so on. These results may be inflated by uncontrolled variables associated with immediate teachers. Given the limitations of both methods, the true estimate of the association between teacher immediacy and student learning, although elusive, may lie between the estimates provided by experiments and surveys. Alternatively, examination of the process of enacting or measuring the behaviors of immediacy may require additional examination or articulation to provide greater understanding of the underlying relationships.

These analyses of overall learning and overall teacher immediacy provided general conclusions that facilitated a broad perspective on the relationship of teacher immediacy to learning. Results from heterogeneous samples may be useful to affirm the direction and relative strength of associations, but we continued our analysis by examining three specific categories of immediacy and three specific categories of learning. This further testing provided more analytic insights and specific conclusions.

Three Types of Immediacy and Three Types of Learning

When the three types of learning were compared across verbal, nonverbal, and combined-only immediacy, meta-analysis revealed significant and meaningful results. The correlations differed only a little across the types of immediacy measurement, but large differences were maintained across the type of learning measurements. Essentially, any interaction between the measure of student learning and type of immediacy measurement should be considered small. The results confirm that the major impact for a moderator variable remains the type of learning. The results show that immediacy is highly correlated with perceived and affective learning and has a small correlation to cognitive learning.

The cognitive learning outcome reflects the smallest learning-type association across types of teacher immediacy. Cognitive learning reflects the fewest number of studies and the largest proportion of experimental designs. Although significant, associations with cognitive learning were less than meaningful when viewed in isolation from other studies. However, many of the studies were experimental or time-bound snapshots that restricted the ability to deal with cognitive learning over time. If affect precedes and motivates cognitive learning (as many researchers in this area believe) over time or long term, the small association provides implications for future research. Nevertheless, given the low associations of types of teacher immediacy with actual cognitive learning, care should be taken when interpreting the magnitudes of associations between immediacy and learning that are sometimes reported as "cognitive" but derived from studies relying on survey questionnaires like the learning loss measure. Students' perceptions of their own learning provide useful data that help us understand the effects of teacher immediacy, but lower order cognitive learning as defined by Bloom (1956) may be more accurately assessed through performance measures such as tests of recall, recognition, and retention of specific course content. Although course grades and exam grades are not flawless measures of cognitive gain, most scholars consider them to be more consistent with Bloom's cognitive taxonomy than are students' opinions about their own learning.

The meta-analyses involving affective learning offered little surprise, and the outcomes were similar to those found for perceived learning. Studies reporting nonverbal immediacy of teachers were almost identical with those reporting verbal immediacy. The comparable association with affect for both verbal and nonverbal immediacy of teachers is not surprising. The vast majority of studies involved survey questionnaire research in which both the nonverbal and verbal assessments were juxtaposed sequentially in the questionnaires. The operational independence of these two assessments in these cases is questionable, given global response tendencies in evaluating a single object of judgment (the teacher) and the nature of the questionnaire. When the verbal and nonverbal measurement was combined into a single assessment report, the association of verbal or nonverbal immediacy to affective learning was slightly greater. Even with these potential difficulties, the results of the meta-analysis confirm the relationship such that, as verbal and nonverbal immediacy increase, affective learning meaningfully increases. Moreover, if one assumes consistency between verbal and nonverbal immediacy behaviors of teachers across levels of immediacy, then the methods used to produce the results are not problematic.

Finally, when comparing the results across the three types of immediacy and three types of learning, one notes the striking similarity between immediacy's effects on perceived learning and affective learning, and the marked difference between these and immediacy's effects on cognitive learning. Students like more highly immediate teachers and think they learn more from their courses, but although actual cognitive learning improves, this improvement is not as dramatic as the other measures of student learning. The unexplored issue is the impact of the potential change in motivation to complete a course or program of study that teacher immediacy may create in a student. The educational objectives are incomplete if a student does not complete a course or degree. The extent to which teacher immediacy is viewed in the context of an entire program of education may prove essential in providing evidence of how teacher immediacy in a classroom (or across a curriculum) serves to reduce attrition and therefore increase learning at a programmatic level.

Limitations of the Study

There were a number of difficulties encountered in conducting a thorough and specific meta-analysis. As noted earlier, some meaningful studies of immediacy and learning were excluded from the analysis because the type or detail of statistical information they reported was not sufficient to estimate an effect. However, the general findings of this group of studies fall within the range of those included in the analysis, so their exclusion probably had little effect on the overall results of the meta-analysis. The combination of verbal and nonverbal immediacy into a single measure in some studies precluded specific analysis of separate immediacy types for those studies. Results involving cognitive learning were relatively few and focused primarily on lower level learning. There were few experimental studies and heavy reliance on survey questionnaires, which minimized causal conclusions. Future studies need to expand the number and scope of measures for both student learning and teacher immediacy.

Averaging obtained effects and correcting for statistical artifacts and research design were the methods utilized to compute equivalent effect statistics across the wide variety of reporting styles and research designs. However, the resulting r's used in the analyses served only as a best estimate of actual correlations. The most troublesome aspect of this meta-analysis pertained to the persistent finding of heterogeneity within the samples, even in the 3 (type of student learning) × 3 (type of immediacy measurement) analysis. Post hoc analyses were conducted after removing the most extreme cases as outliers, and variance was, of course, reduced. However, consistent homogeneity within the samples remained elusive. This indicates that undetected moderator variables may still be present in these studies, a matter to be pursued in future research.

Our categorization of cognitive learning was generally restricted in an attempt to more closely match instances in Bloom's (1956) cognitive learning category. All of the included studies that measured cognitive learning performance assessed recall, recognition, test grades, or course grades. Although test or course grades may reflect some types of higher order learning, levels of learning involving analysis, synthesis, and problem solving were not identified or directly measured in this body of research. Only two of the included studies took measures of delayed recall (Comstock et al., 1995; Titsworth, 2001), with mixed and inconclusive results. Due to the small number of delayed recall studies and the lack of statistical independence with other cognitive learning data, these findings were not included in the meta-analysis. The issue of retention of information requires the use of more longitudinal designs than those appearing in current investigations. An important question is the degree to which the emotional or motivational impact of teacher immediacy is immediate and to what extent any attitudinal change is more permanent.

The affective learning category displayed some general consistency in use of recognized affective measures derived from Scott and Wheeless (1975) and modified by others (e.g., Gorham & Christophel, 1990; Hackman & Walker, 1990; McCroskey, 1994). Identical or similar semantic differential-type formats for assessing attitudes toward instructors, courses, content, and so on reoccurred frequently. Measures of behavioral intent (intent to enroll in another course, intent to engage in certain behaviors, etc.) were classified as affective learning. Consistent with attitude theory (Inskso, 1967; Triandis, 1971; Zimbardo & Ebbesen, 1969) and original measurement (Scott & Wheeless, 1975), intent was viewed as a predisposition to behave in a certain way to a specified class of objects. As a predisposition, this type of measurement is attitudinal (thus, affective), and is, indeed, measured in sequence with the same type of format and items as the recognized affective measures. There were, in fact, only three studies (Allen & Shaw, 1990; Comstock et al., 1995; Shaw, 1988) that measured actual behavioral learning, an insufficient number for meaningful analysis. These studies did report, however, that behavioral learning was slightly correlated with nonverbal immediacy. This provides a fruitful avenue for future research by considering more behavioral learning outcomes. If teacher immediacy behaviors impact on motivational states of the student then the impact on subsequent outcomes related to course enrollment should be accessible.

One of the largely unanswered issues is the long-term implications of any exposure to an instructor over the course of a degree program. To what extent does the teacher providing high levels of immediacy motivate students to complete the course of study? Does the presence of high levels of immediacy behavior by an instructor in an introductory course result in changed majors, enrollment in more courses in a particular department, or increased satisfaction with the entire process of education? Although the results for immediacy may be disappointing for cognitive learning outcomes, educational practices expect that degree completion will generate a variety of outcomes in addition to cognitive learning.

CONCLUSION

As with many meta-analyses or reviews of the literature, the call is for more research in the area. We hope, however, that the understanding of the literature is advanced by the review so that additional research can use this summary as a basis for more targeted and precise future research. Rather than viewing the low association between teacher immediacy and cognitive learning as disappointing, we view this as intriguing. There is a need for many more baseline data using a wider variety of designs and measures to confirm and extend this finding. However, the theoretical arguments about the importance of immediacy in terms of the impact on the process of education may be reinforced by the finding rather than challenged by the association.

Understanding of student motivation to learn, complete a program of study, and conversely to drop out, remains important. The size of the association between teacher immediacy and perceived learning and affective learning (around $r = .50$) is large. The challenge becomes an exploration of why the association exists and setting the association in the context of the entire process of educational practices. The call should be to expand the vision beyond the single student and teacher in one course to a more programmatic view of a degree program across 4 years of education in college (which occurs after at least 12 years of primary and secondary education). Expanding the view to consider motivation in that context makes the association potentially extremely important to understanding what motivates students to persevere to complete a program or why a particular program is chosen in the first place. Set in that context, the results are vital and deserve future attention from many scholars.

REFERENCES

Adkins, R. M. (1998). *The differences in students' perception of learning between extended learning program students and on-campus students at Southern Christian University*. Unpublished doctoral dissertation, Auburn University, Auburn, AL.

Allen, J. L, & Shaw, D. H. (1990). Teachers' communication behaviors and supervisors' evaluation of instruction in elementary and secondary classrooms. *Communication Education, 39*, 308–322.

Allen, J. L., O'Mara, J., & Long, K. M. (1987, November). *The effects of communication avoidance, learning styles, and gender upon classroom achievement*. Paper presented at the annual meeting of the Speech Communication Association, Boston.

Allen, M., Hecht, M., & Martin, J. (1996). Examining the impact of culture social scientifically: Some suggestions from examining Martin, Hecht, and Larkey. *World Communication, 25*(2), 69–78.

Allen, M., Timmerman, C., Bourhis, J., Mabry, E., & Burrell, N. (2002, November). *Distance education: A meta-analysis examining how learning style influences outcomes*. Paper presented at the annual meeting of the National Communication Association, New Orleans, LA.

Andersen, J. F. (1978). *The relationship between teacher immediacy and teaching effectiveness*. Unpublished doctoral dissertation, West Virginia University, Morgantown, WV.

Andersen, J. F. (1979). Teacher immediacy as a predictor of teaching effectiveness. In D. Nimmo (Ed.), *Communication yearbook 3* (pp. 543–559). New Brunswick, NJ: Transaction.

Andersen, J. F., Norton, R. W., & Nussbaum, J. F. (1981). Three investigations exploring relationships between perceived teacher communication behaviors and student learning. *Communication Education, 30*, 377–392.

Andersen, J. F., & Withrow, J. G. (1981). The impact of lecturers' nonverbal expressiveness on improving mediated instruction. *Communication Education, 30*, 342–353.

Baker, J. D. (2001). *The effects of instructor immediacy and student cohesiveness on affective and cognitive learning in the online classroom*. Unpublished doctoral dissertation, Regent University, Virginia Beach, VA.

Berscheid, E., & Walster, E. H. (1978). *Interpersonal attraction* (2nd ed.). Reading, MA: Addison-Wesley.

Bloom, B. S. (1956). *A taxonomy of educational objectives*. New York: Longmans, Green.

Butland, M. J., & Beebe, S. A. (1992, May). *A study of the application of implicit communication theory to teacher immediacy and student learning*. Paper presented at the annual meeting of the International Communication Association, Miami, FL.

Christensen, L. J., & Menzel, K. E. (1998). The linear relationship between student reports of teacher immediacy behaviors and perceptions of state motivation, and of cognitive, affective, and behavioral learning. *Communication Education, 47*, 82–90.

Christophel, D. M. (1990). The relationships among teacher immediacy behaviors, student motivation and learning. *Communication Education, 39*, 323–340.

Christophel, D. M., & Gorham, J. (1995). A test-retest analysis of student motivation, teacher immediacy, and perceived sources of motivation and demotivation in college classes. *Communication Education, 44*, 292–305.

Comstock, J., Rowell, E., & Bowers, J. W. (1995). Food for thought: Teacher nonverbal immediacy, student learning, and curvilinearity. *Communication Education, 44*, 251–266.

Daniel, T. R. (2000). *Determining the impact of nonverbal immediacy on cognitive learning and affective perceptions in a post-secondary technical learning environment.* Unpublished doctoral dissertation, Oklahoma State University, Stillwater, OK.

Farren, P. (1992). *Nonverbal teacher immediacy training in the classroom and its effects on learning.* Unpublished master's thesis, San Diego State University, San Diego, CA.

Folwell, A. L. (1995, November). *A comparison of professors' and students' perceptions of nonverbal immediacy behaviors.* Paper presented at the annual meeting of the Speech Communication Association, San Antonio, TX.

Frymier, A. B. (1993). The impact of teacher immediacy on students' motivation: Is it the same for all students? *Communication Quarterly, 41,* 454–464.

Frymier, A. B. (1994). A model of immediacy in the classroom. *Communication Quarterly, 42,* 133–144.

Furio, B. J. (1987, January). *The relationship between instructor behaviors and student perceptions of control in the classroom.* Unpublished research report, West Virginia University, Morgantown, WV.

Garard, D. L. (1998). *The relationship between teacher immediacy and cognitive style: An exploratory investigation.* Unpublished doctoral dissertation, Southern Illinois University, Carbondale, IL.

Giles, H., Mulac, A., Bradac, J. J., & Johnson, P. (1987). Speech accommodation theory: The first decade and beyond. In M. L. McLaughlin (Ed.), *Communication yearbook 10* (pp. 13–48). Newbury Park, CA: Sage.

Gorham, J. (1988). The relationship between verbal teacher immediacy and student learning. *Communication Education, 37,* 40–53.

Gorham, J., & Christophel, D. M. (1990). The relationship of teachers' use of humor in the classroom to immediacy and student learning. *Communication Education, 30,* 46–62.

Gudykunst, W. G., & Ting-Toomey, S. (1988). *Culture and interpersonal communication.* Newbury Park, CA: Sage.

Hackman, M. Z., & Walker, K. B. (1990). Instructional communication in the televised classroom: The effects of system design and teacher immediacy on student learning and satisfaction. *Communication Education, 39,* 196–206.

Hedges, L., & Olkin, I. (1985). *Statistical methods for meta-analysis.* Orlando, FL: Academic.

Hess, J. A., & Smythe, M. J. (2001). Is teacher immediacy actually related to student cognitive learning? *Communication Studies, 52,* 197–219.

Hinkle, L. J. (1998). Teacher nonverbal immediacy behaviors and student-perceived cognitive learning in Japan. *Communication Research Reports, 15,* 45–56.

Hunter, J., & Schmidt, F. (1990). *Methods of meta-analysis: Correcting for error and bias in research results.* Beverly Hills, CA: Sage.

Inskso, C. A. (1967). *Theories of attitude change.* New York: Appleton-Century-Crofts.

Jordan, F. F. (1989). *An examination of the relationship between perceived verbal and paralinguistic immediacy and accommodation to perceived cognitive learning.* Unpublished doctoral dissertation, West Virginia University, Morgantown, WV.

Jordan, F. F., & Wheeless, L. R. (1990, November). *An investigation of the relationships among teachers' verbal immediacy, paralinguistic immediacy, and speech accommodation in diverse classrooms.* Paper presented at the annual meeting of the Speech Communication Association, Chicago.

Kearney, P., Plax, T. G., Smith, V. R., & Sorenson, G. (1988). Effects of teacher immediacy and strategy type on college student resistance to on-task demands. *Communication Education, 37,* 54–67.

Kearney, P., Plax, T. G., & Wendt-Wasco, N. J. (1985). Teacher immediacy for affective learning in divergent college classes. *Communication Quarterly, 33,* 61–71.

Kelley, D. H., & Gorham, J. (1988). Effects of immediacy on recall of information. *Communication Education, 37,* 198–207.

Lipsey, M. W., & Wilson, D. B. (2001). *Practical meta-analysis* (Applied Social Research Methods Series, Vol. 49). Thousand Oaks, CA: Sage.

McAlister, G. (2001). *Computer-mediated immediacy: A new construct in teacher–student communication for computer-mediated distance education.* Unpublished doctoral dissertation, Regent University, Virginia Beach, VA.

McCroskey, J. C. (1994). Assessment of affect toward communication and affect toward instruction in communication. In S. Morreale & M. Brooks (Eds.), *1994 SCA Summer Conference proceedings and prepared remarks* (pp. 55–69). Annandale, VA: Speech Communication Association.

McCroskey, J. C., Fayer, J. M., Richmond, V. P., Sallinen, A., & Barraclough, R. A. (1996). A multi-cultural examination of the relationship between nonverbal immediacy and affective learning. *Communication Quarterly, 44,* 297–307.

McCroskey, J. C., Sallinen, A., Fayer, J. M., Richmond, V. P., & Barraclough, R. A. (1996). Nonverbal immediacy and cognitive learning: A cross-cultural investigation. *Communication Education, 45,* 200–211.

McDowell, E. E., & McDowell, C. E. (1990, May). *An investigation of verbal and nonverbal teacher immediacy behaviors, homophily, interpersonal solidarity, student attentiveness and student learning at the senior high school level.* Paper presented at the annual meeting of the International Communication Association, Dublin, Ireland.

McDowell, E. E., McDowell, C. E., & Hyerdahl. J. (1980, November). *A multivariate study of teacher immediacy, teaching effectiveness, and student attentiveness at the junior high and senior high levels.* Paper presented at the annual meeting of the Speech Communication Association, New York.

McGreal, E. A. (1989). *The relationship of immediacy and communicator style to learning in adult literacy programs.* Unpublished doctoral dissertation, West Virginia University, Morgantown, WV.

Mehrabian, A. (1969). Some referents and measures of nonverbal behavior. *Behavioral Research Methods and Instrumentation, 1,* 213–217.

Mehrabian, A. (1971). *Silent messages.* Belmont, CA: Wadsworth.

Mehrabian, A. (1981). *Silent messages* (2nd ed.). Belmont, CA: Wadsworth.

Menzel, K. E., & Carrell, L. J. (1999). The impact of gender and immediacy on willingness to talk and perceived learning. *Communication Education, 48,* 31–40.

Messman, S. J., & Jones-Corley, J. (2001). Effects of communication environment, immediacy, and communication apprehension on cognitive and affective learning. *Communication Monographs, 68,* 184–200.

Mortenson, S. T. (1994). *Configural and linear communication, teacher nonverbal immediacy, and affective learning in the multicultural classroom.* Unpublished master's thesis, California State University, Long Beach, CA.

Mottet, T. P., & Beebe, S. A. (2001, November). *Relationships between teacher nonverbal immediacy, student emotional response, and perceived student learning.* Paper presented at the annual meeting of the National Communication Association, Atlanta, GA.

Myers, S. A., Zhong, M., & Guan, S. (1998). Instructor immediacy in the Chinese college classroom. *Communication Studies, 49,* 240–254.

Neuliep, J. W. (1995). A comparison of teacher immediacy in African-American and Euro-American classrooms. *Communication Education, 44,* 267–277.

Neuliep, J. W. (1997). A cross-cultural comparison of teacher immediacy in American and Japanese college classrooms. *Communication Research, 24*, 431–452.

Orpen, C. (1994). Academic motivation as a moderator of the effects of teacher immediacy on student cognitive and affective learning. *Education, 115*, 137–139.

Peterson, S. J. (1994). *Interactive television: Continuing education participant satisfaction.* Unpublished doctoral dissertation, University of Missouri, Columbia, MO.

Plax, T. G., Kearney, P., McCroskey, J. C., & Richmond, V. P. (1986). Power in the classroom VI: Verbal control strategies, nonverbal immediacy and affective learning. *Communication Education, 35*, 43–55.

Powell, R., & Harville, B. (1990). The effects of teacher immediacy and clarity on instructional outcomes: An intercultural assessment. *Communication Education, 39*, 369–379.

Richmond, V. P. (1990). Communication in the classroom: Power and motivation. *Communication Education, 39*, 181–195.

Richmond, V. P., Gorham, J. S., & McCroskey, J. C. (1987). The relationship between selected immediacy behaviors and cognitive learning. In M. L. McLaughlin (Ed.), *Communication yearbook 10* (pp. 574–590). Newbury Park, CA: Sage.

Richmond, V. P., & McCroskey, J. C. (1992). *Power in the classroom: Communication, control, and concern.* Hillsdale, NJ: Lawrence Erlbaum Associates.

Roach, K. D., & Byrne, P. R. (2001). A cross-cultural comparison of instructor communication in American and German classrooms. *Communication Education, 50*, 1–14.

Rodriguez, J. I., Plax, T. G., & Kearney, P. (1996). Clarifying the relationship between teacher nonverbal immediacy and student cognitive learning: Affective learning as the central causal mediator. *Communication Education, 45*, 293–305.

Sanders, J. A., & Wiseman, R. L. (1990). The effects of verbal and nonverbal teacher immediacy on perceived cognitive, affective, and behavioral learning in the multicultural classroom. *Communication Education, 39*, 341–353.

Scott, M. D., & Wheeless, L. R. (1975). Communication apprehension, student attitudes, and levels of satisfaction. *Western Journal of Speech Communication, 41*, 188–198.

Shaw, D. H. (1988). *Behaviors and the evaluation of teacher effectiveness, career satisfaction, and student learning.* Unpublished doctoral dissertation, University of Bridgeport, Bridgeport, CT.

Sidelinger, R. J., & McCroskey, J. C. (1997). Communication correlates of teacher clarity in the college classroom. *Communication Research Reports, 14*, 1–10.

Sorenson, G. A. (1989). The relationships among teachers' self-disclosive statements, students' perceptions, and affective learning. *Communication Education, 38*, 259–276.

Thomas, C. E. (1994). *An analysis of teacher socio-communicative style as a predictor of classroom communication behaviors, student liking, motivation, and learning.* Unpublished doctoral dissertation, West Virginia University, Morgantown, WV.

Thompson, C. A. C. (1992). *The relationships among teachers' immediacy behaviors, credibility, and social style and students' motivation and learning: Comparisons among cultures.* Unpublished doctoral dissertation, West Virginia University, Morgantown, WV.

Tinto, V. (1975). Dropout from higher education: A theoretical synthesis of recent research. *Review of Education Research, 45*, 89–125.

Titsworth, S. B. (2001). The effects of teacher immediacy, use of organizational lecture cues, and students' notetaking on cognitive learning. *Communication Education, 50*, 283–297.

Triandis, H. C. (1971). *Attitude and attitude change.* New York: Wiley.

Valencic, K. M. (2001). *An investigation of teachers' temperament and students' perceptions of teachers: Communication behavior and students' attitudes toward teachers.* Unpublished doctoral dissertation, West Virginia University, Morgantown, WV.

Walker, K. B., & Hackman, M. Z. (1991, November). *Information transfer and nonverbal immediacy as primary predictors of learning and satisfaction in the televised course.* Paper presented at the annual meeting of the Speech Communication Association, Atlanta, GA.

Wanzer, M. B., & Frymier, A. B. (1999). The relationship between student perceptions of instructor humor and students' reports of learning. *Communication Education, 48,* 48–62.

Wiener, M., & Mehrabian, A. (1968). *Language within language: Immediacy, a channel in verbal communication.* New York: Appleton-Century-Crofts.

Witt, P. L., & Wheeless, L. R. (2001). An experimental study of teachers' verbal and nonverbal immediacy and students' affective and cognitive learning. *Communication Education, 50,* 327–342.

Witt, P. L., Wheeless, L. R., & Allen, M. (2004). A meta-analytical review of the relationship between teacher immediacy and student learning. *Communication Monographs, 71,* 184–207.

Zimbardo, P., & Ebbesen, E. B. (1969). *Influencing attitudes and changing behavior.* Menlo Park, CA: Addison-Wesley.

11

Race and the Classroom: Interaction and Image

Lisa Bradford
Erica Cooper
Mike Allen
Jennifer Stanley
Denis Grimes
University of Wisconsin–Milwaukee

The issue of race in the U.S. educational system remains divisive and fraught with a number of perils and implications for educators. This chapter considers various issues dealing with how the view of race is manifest inside the educational system in both attitude and behavior. The issues of ethnicity in the classroom play an important role in issues like affirmative action for college admission, distribution of resources to support schools, and the inclusion or exclusion of materials in a curriculum. The focus of this chapter is on two considerations: (a) equity in interaction between instructors and students considering race of the student, and (b) how a positive view of one's own racial group contributes to personal development, social success and educational success. The implications for the development of classrooms with a greater sense of equality could provide improved effectiveness for educational outcomes sought by the system.

A consideration of the impact of how educational formats reflect values and student orientations generates a serious interest when considering curricular reform. A central tenet of Afrocentric education involves the necessity for educational goals to address the needs of African American students. These concerns raised by African American students are mirrored by other groups of students (Latinos, Native Americans, Asian Americans, Arab Americans, etc.) seeking the development of a curriculum that reflects the realities and contributions of various groups.

A critical question is whether educators' attempts to improve self-image impact the outcomes sought by the educational system (better academic preparation). The fundamental issue in education is what the particular structure of the environment (both in terms of teachers and the focus on particular material) provides or implies to the students that are taught within that structure. This view requires a critical self-examination and reflection on how the educational practices interact with how students view themselves as individuals as well as persons placed within a system (Allen, Howard, & Grimes, 1997).

ISSUES OF SELF AND RACIAL CONCEPT

Issues of self-concept or self-esteem have played an important role in the educational system. A person's identity is derived partially from the social system's view of his or her culture or race. Society's reactions can confirm, disconfirm, deny, value, reinforce, or lampoon the view of self as part of a social group. Tajfel (1978) described a second part of identity as, "that part of an individual self concept which derives from knowledge of his (her) membership of social groups together with the value and social significance attached to that membership" (p. 63). This aspect of group membership reflects the desire on the part of a person to affiliate with persons that reflect shared values and orientations. The definition of culture is often that of a community that shares the use of symbols. A culture can be considered a form of language community whose members share particular referents, shared (or assumed shared) values, and history. The shared history, values, and language create a sense of belonging and unity that makes membership in the community something unique and distinguishes members from those not in the community.

Racial identity is quite complicated to represent because of a relationship to biology as well as the need to consider social and cultural issues. Race represents a different category than biological gender (where a meta-analysis demonstrates no generalized difference in self-esteem, Sahlstein & Allen, 2002), because racial identity, although tied to biology, is not determined by biology. Cross (1991) pointed out that Black identity (as is true of any identity) really constitutes a panorama of diverse views. The concept refers to a broad group of diverse people among whom, in fact, there exist a great number of subgroups and the corresponding development of various subcultures.

Evaluation by the individual of the group membership reflects the perception of the group's accomplishment or success and becomes a source of pride. Phrases such as "Black power" or "Black is beautiful" are efforts to create a positive view of the racial group of which one is a part (Hraba & Grant, 1970). Focusing on the positive aspects of identity provides the person a sense of value that comes from belonging to that particular group.

On the other hand, accepting a social judgment that your group is worthless results in a negative self-image (Griffin, 1991). The phrases "self-loathing Jew" and "born losers" reflect the identification of an individual with a group with a negative image. Various motorcycle gangs or political groups may find affiliation in rejection, a shared experience of alienation that is confirmed by membership.

A negative social image is communicated by the lack of inclusion of that group within the educational environment; expressed either overtly or simply by a lack of demonstrated inclusion in the material. Another aspect goes beyond the curriculum and considers the management of the classroom and whether practices within the classroom constitute a form of behavioral discrimination.

Academic Success

This section summarizes the report of an existing meta-analysis (Allen et al., 1997). The central question in this meta-analysis was the relationship between views of one's own racial group and the degree of success in educational settings. Bowman (1994) argued that the lack of endorsement of diversity or affirmation of identity means that the longer that children are in school, the greater the discrepancy between minority students and White students on measures of performance. Bowman argued that rather than an educational system working to close or diminish gaps between groups, the difference in treatment or opportunity actually works to increase the relative advantage of the majority groups.

Gay (1994) noted that although teachers try to treat all children equitably, "A person's humanity cannot be isolated or divorced from his or her culture or ethnicity. One cannot be human without culture and ethnicity, and one cannot have culture and ethnicity without being human" (p. 6). Failure to understand cultural influences or incorporate them may negatively influence educators' ability to teach and could have negative ramifications for their students' attitude toward education, diminishing their sense of self-worth. For example, the failure of teachers to understand some African American or other cultural communication and relational styles may contribute to an erroneous perspective on the critical thinking and reasoning skills of the students (Gay, 1994).

The results of a meta-analysis (Allen et al., 1999) indicate a positive relationship between racial group orientation and academic achievement (average $r = .160, k = 9, N = 2,661$, variance $= .0027$). The average correlation, however, is based on a heterogeneous set of correlations, $\chi^2 \neq (8, N = 2,661) = 16.51$. This indicates that as a person has a positive view of the racial group, there is a demonstrable improvement in the level of academic success.

The finding indicates that a person with a positive view of group membership is likely to perform better in school. A central consideration becomes whether educational institutions can incorporate processes that improve the view of the child. Cultural issues can be incorporated into the curriculum in various ways to improve the value of the education and reinforce existing or emerging senses of value or worth. Jones (1993) reported a simple intervention in education requiring African American and Latino junior high students to make auto-photo histories of their families demonstrated a significant increase in self-image ($r = .257$). This relatively simple intervention indicates that a project focused on the identity of the person can generate significant improvements in self-esteem. Given the expectation of a relationship of self-esteem to success, the importance of finding methods of generating academic exercises that provide multiple outcomes becomes essential in providing more meaningful and useful educational outcomes.

Social Success

The impact of a positive view of one's own racial group has implications for various outcomes: (a) delinquency, (b) mental adjustment, and (c) sociability. Table 11.1 provides data for this report. The identification of a person with a particular culture creates a sense of commitment to values and often actions consistent with that identity. Bradford, Allen, Casey, and Emmers-Sommer (2002) pointed out that issues like acculturation for Latinos (measured by the use of English) represents a factor in identification and HIV risk. The change in identification made by Latinos coming to the United States and transferring national identity is associated with various behavioral changes. Cultural identification represents a process of accepting various values (and the actions implied by consistency with those values). Latinos arriving in the United States are challenged by sexual mores and practices inconsistent with the traditions of the home country. Public messages and educational efforts point to the need for sexually active persons to practice safer sex methods (e.g., use condoms, reduce number of partners, etc.). For most Latinos, the open discussion of sexuality and sexual behaviors is contrary to the original culture. As Latinos acculturate the level of knowledge about HIV increases (average $r = .151, k = 5, N = 1,850$); however, so does participation in sexual activities as well as use of safer sexual practices (average $r = .210, k = 6, N = 6,913$). The new identity as an American carries both the increased risk of HIV infection from changing

TABLE 11.1
Effects Examining Racial Identification and Academic Success
and Social Outcomes

Study	Year	Outcome Measure	Sample Size	Correlation
Bowler et al.	1986	Mental adjustment	552	+.150
Brown & Simons	1999	Academic achievement	94	+.147
Clark	1979	Academic achievement	210	+.025
Dulan	1975	Mental adjustment	1,000	+.312
		Sociability (adults)	1,000	+.183
		Delinquency	1,000	−.097
		Academic achievement	1,000	+.193
		Sociability (peer)	1,000	+.117
Grossman	1981	Academic achievement	410	+.073
		Mental adjustment	410	+.021
Hernandez	1984	Academic achievement	63	+.040
		Mental adjustment	63	+.150
Meyers	1966	Academic achievement	45	+.087
Mobley	1973	Delinquency	163	+.252
Rasheed	1981	Academic achievement	15	−.200
Schmults	1975	Mental adjustment	44	+.373
Spencer	1981	Academic achievement	371	+.217
Verkuyten	1990	Academic achievement	237	+.170
White	1988	Mental adjustment	310	+.170
		Academic achievement	310	+.050

sexual practices and the benefits of safer sex education, so the process of acculturation changes a variety of social beliefs and actions.

Sociability

Children, particularly minority children (the primary focus of this summary), may develop their racial group identities when they are very young. Porter's (1971) research on children in New England found that Black children as young as 3 and White children as young as 4 years old had already determined that White was the socially preferred racial identity. Minority children may also be prone to developing negative racial group orientations. Rosenberg's (1975) research found that when children are racially, religiously, socially, or nationally different from the majority of other children in their environments, their level of self-esteem is negatively affected. This may be particularly the case when they are taught that their race or culture is inferior through the prejudiced attitudes and acts of others (Wilson, 1978). However, negative racial group orientations may be mediated if adults with whom the minority children have salient relationships reject the negative images of the dominant society (Paul & Fischer, 1980). The issue seems to be to what extent the adult feels a positive part of the social system.

Griffin (1991) described the effect of racism on African Americans in particular, using a humiliation dynamic: "The criminal justice system and the news media play very active parts in the every day humiliations with the accompanying pain, anguish, and the sense of oppression experienced repeatedly by members of the African-American community as they watch such biased newscasts" (p. 153). Educators and counselors have operated to some extent assuming that the negative racial group orientation can contribute to diminished sociability.

Two studies (reported in Allen et al., 1999) exist that support this finding (average $r = .150, k = 2, N = 2,000$). The two studies illustrate that positive racial group image is associated with improved scores on sociability scales. The finding indicates that the more positive people feel about the racial group of which they consider themselves a part, the better the feeling of fitting into the social structure.

Mental Adjustment

Mental adjustment refers to the ability of an individual to not experience unwarranted anxieties, depression, suicidal thoughts, as well as to a general sense of well-being. The statistics suggest that African Americans and Hispanics have higher rates of several mental disorders when compared to Whites. These higher rates for mental disorders among minorities are generally attributed to lower socioeconomic status, creating a concentration of the poor in more hazardous urban environments. Combined with the sense of discrimination, the feelings of rejection, inferiority, frustration, and fear may have negative mental health consequences for some minority group members. A central challenge for researchers is developing and testing an explanation for the observed association.

Conversely, a positive view of one's own racial group may serve as a buffer or a method of reducing the consequences of the particular environment. The positive view of self that comes from an endorsement and acceptance of the racial group of which one is a part could serve to reduce anxieties, depression, and uncertainty about the nature of identity (Cross, 1991). The development of a positive view may reduce the effects of an adverse environment and create the conditions that promote success in education and employment that can change the socioeconomic status of a person.

The six studies in this pool demonstrate a positive association between racial group orientation and mental adjustment (average $r = .203, k = 6$, $N = 2,379$, variance $= .0098$). The set of studies was heterogeneous, $\chi^2(5, N = 2,379) = 31.32$. The results of this meta-analysis of six studies support a connection between racial group orientation and the development of a positive sense of mental adjustment. More negative views of one's own racial group are associated with lower levels of mental adjustment (depression, social anxiety, etc.).

Delinquency

Griffin (1991) argued that the effects of racism contribute to the development of negative group orientations among racial and ethnic minorities. These negative group orientations are frequently then acted out in the form of self-abusive behaviors (drug and alcohol use, violence, teenage parenting), particularly among young men. Minorities with negative racial group orientation may engage in violent behaviors that victimize members of the dominant group out of anger and frustration, and to get revenge for injustices and feelings of inferiority (Allport, 1979). Acting out criminal behaviors gives minority group members at least a temporary sense of control or power.

Ironically, violent behaviors and other criminal activities are more frequently directed toward members of one's own minority group. Allport (1979) contended that aggression toward one's own group may be a result of self-hate or one's negative feelings toward one's group members because they possess the characteristics of the ostracized minority group. Aggression toward other members of one's own group may be motivated by perceptions that these individuals are attempting to assimilate into the dominant culture (trying to avoid identification with the minority group), or because they have adopted a different set of tactics for dealing with racism. The terms *apple, coconut, oreo,* and *banana* have been applied by minorities to persons of the same group that are said to have rejected the values of the minority group and instead assimilated by accepting White values and actions. These terms all illustrate that the person's skin color indicates a minority group but the underlying values (inside the person) are in fact White.

Delinquency indicates behavior for adolescents that would not typically be considered illegal for adults. Delinquency is often associated with truancy as well as alcohol and tobacco use. Whereas more Whites are users of hard drugs, minority group youth have more problems related to alcohol use. However, when other risk factors are considered in examining substance use, no causal relationship between race and substance use is found (Fuhrmann, 1990). However, racism has been identified as a correlate of addiction, as have feelings of powerlessness and alienation (Belcher & Shinitzky, 1998).

Two studies examined the connection between racial group orientation and delinquency. The studies indicate a negative relationship ($r = -.119$, $k = 2, N = 1,163$). The summary indicates that as a person has a positive racial group orientation, the level of delinquency diminishes. The studies are consistent with the expectation that a positive racial image would diminish the emotions associated with negative social outcomes.

INTERACTION IN THE CLASSROOM

Students interact with both teachers and peers in the classroom. A central concern of classroom communication has been the consideration of whether students are treated differently by instructors on the basis of some identifiable characteristic. Jones, Dindia, and Tye (chap. 12, this volume) address the issue of gender, and this chapter considers race as a basis of differential treatment. The source of the potential bias (either an overt or unconscious bias on the part of the instructor) remains the same in this chapter and the concern for various outcomes is identical. Does such behavior impact negatively on the ability of students to perform or the development of negative identities? Do instructors treat students the same or differently based on identifiable (often visible) markers of the individual?

The importance of student–teacher interaction should not be underestimated. Teachers are the source of reward, punishment, blame, and recognition, and they impart a strong sense of value to the student. The use of criticism or praise, the regulation of behavior among students, and the simple act of recognition or of ignoring a student all indicate a value that the instructor is imparting to the pupil.

Research indicates a relationship between teacher expectation and interaction (Friedman, 1978; Jeter, 1972), although no meta-analysis existed. The importance of an instructor's expectations and interaction with a student has been labeled the *Pygmalion Effect* (Rosenthal & Jacobson, 1968). This argument that teachers create expectations for students that become used as a basis for evaluation constitutes a serious issue. The same remark or action by a student may be interpreted by the instructor differently based on the general view that the instructor has of the student prior to the action. Rubovits and Maehr (1973) referred to the racial issues of the Pygmalion of Black and White. They argued that teachers will create a variety of expectations related to the race of the individual. The results of such expectations are differences in treatment that over time may generate a large number of differential outcomes.

Expectations of instructors about students is one set of issues, but expectations of students about how instructors should treat them is another set of interaction expectations. Students viewing themselves as less desirable, less worthy of praise, outcasts, and misfits may come to expect more negative interaction and less positive interaction. A student who has accepted the label of "stupid" does not expect to receive praise from the instructor. In fact, praise or reward from the instructor might be viewed suspiciously or treated with disdain or contempt as the motivations for such behavior as well as the competence of the instructor are questioned.

The data for this summary come from the Cooper and Allen (1998) meta-analysis. The coding was done such that ethnic minority students (African American, Latino/Hispanic American, Native American) were compared to White students on the various dependent variables. The term *minority* refers to the numerical status of the students on a national basis; locally, in various school districts, particular groups may constitute the majority. All the studies had to have a direct comparison between the two groups, which meant the classrooms were desegregated or integrated with students of identifiable and diverse ethnic groups.

The coding of interaction in the classroom was diverse, depending on the particular type of interaction system used. To combine across the coding systems, various categories were recategorized into a system of three basic types of interaction measures: (a) positive, (b) negative, and (c) amount. Positive represents those categories in which the instructor is providing some positive feedback to the student, like praise or other rewards. A positive interaction provides a recognition to the student and a reinforcement of an answer, action, or behavior that the instructor wishes to continue.

The negative category might involve blame or issues of behavioral alteration where the student needs to act differently. The negative interaction involves an instructor correcting, admonishing, or asking for change on the part of a minority student. The negative comments may stem from incorrect answers, unacceptable behavior displayed by the student, or the need to have the student focus on what is relevant and appropriate.

The amount of behavior is simply the sum of all interactions with the student, positive, negative, or neutral. The level of interaction is the average interaction per student, so the totals comparing the two groups take into consideration the relative size of each of the groups in the classroom. Almost all studies used intact naturally occurring classrooms that were coded by trained observers, either live or on videotape. The key was that the information should not be self-reports either by the students or the teachers, but instead should reflect some actual behavioral measure of interaction.

The results demonstrate that minority students receive, on average, less interaction with teachers when compared to White students ($r = -.061$). The results do not consider the type of interaction (positive, negative, etc.) but deal only with the outcomes related to quantity. The findings suggest that teachers simply interact less with minority students than majority students.

The type of interaction (positive, negative, and amount) and the differences associated with the level of interaction based on race were separately examined. The studies demonstrate that minority students receive significantly ($t = 2.28, p = .02$) more negative statements ($r = .060$) than White students. This difference indicates that in a classroom, the minority students, although receiving less overall interaction, receive proportionately more of the negative statements from an instructor. The implication of this finding is that the interaction between minority students and instructors becomes more negative and represents a less friendly environment than that for majority students.

The analysis of positive statements finds that minority students receive significantly ($t = 3.15, p < .05$) fewer positive statements (average $r = -.078$) than White students. The research illustrates that instructors provide minority students fewer positive statements in the classroom. Less praise, and less reward for participation or work are provided to minority students. The implication of this finding is found in the often heard statement that you have to be twice as good to make it if you are a minority. That perception is validated by the finding of inequities in the level of praise or positive interaction with instructors in the classroom.

The overall interaction measures indicate that minority students receive less overall interaction (average $r = -.076$). The last measure would include interaction that could be considered neither positive nor negative (question asking, responding to questions, neutral statements, back-channeling, etc.). This indicates that the minority student is involved in less communication with the instructor. The student is receiving less acknowledgment, less concern about the need for assistance, fewer answers to questions, and fewer explanations about the work. The result is that the potential for the student to benefit as a result of the interaction with the instructor is reduced when compared to that for White students.

One limitation of the studies is the limited amount of interaction observed. Most studies coded the interaction of a few hours of classroom time for use in the analysis. The real issue is what the consequences are of the relatively small observed effect across the life span of a student in grades K–12. The impact of even a small effect may in fact generate important consequences if the impact of the association can be considered ultimately to be cumulative. The interaction in a classroom is not a single event, but a series of interactions that span over a decade of a person's academic life. The cumulative impact of these hours is what should be of major import, so a small finding for a few hours may translate into much larger consequences when considered against the backdrop of an entire school career.

Abelson (1985) pointed out that interpreting the influence of what may appear as small effects can be very deceptive if the effect is cumulative across a number of repetitions. The example Abelson used in his article is that of a baseball game and the difference in the ninth inning of replacing a batter with a .200 average (200 hits on average out of 1,000 attempts) with a .300

average batter (300 hits on average out of 1,000 attempts). Most persons would replace the lower probability batter with the higher probability batter and find a rise in the probability of producing a more desirable outcome. The replacement gives the team a 50% increase in the probability of the batter getting a hit (well, 50% across 1,000 attempts). However, when the replacement is made, the concern is for not the 1,000 attempts; rather the concern is for the one-time replacement. Abelson estimated the effect for the one-time replacement at .00317 (using omega squared). Most scientists with that effect size in an experimental or survey investigation would conclude that the effect was trivial and insignificant. Although the single incident demonstrates only a marginal difference, imagine that replacement taking place across a 162 game schedule or across 10 years of 162-game schedules. The difference, hardly important to the single case, has enormous consequences or implications when considered across a large number of accumulated cases or efforts. See Table 11.2 for examination of the impact of findings of this report.

Considering the impact of the effects in this meta-analysis, the results indicate some significant and important differences. One issue, the potential impact of the interaction of student race with teacher race, could not be considered in the data. Unfortunately, not enough data exist to take into account that interaction (as well as the combination of gender, male or female, and race matches). Evidence does exist for issues dealing with communica-

TABLE 11.2
Binomial Effect Size Display of Average Effects

| | Racial Group Orientation | | |
	High	Low	Percentage Increase
Academic success			
High	58%	42%	
Low	42%	58%	38%
Positive mental adjustment			
High	60%	40%	
Low	40%	60%	50%
Diminished delinquency			
High	56%	44%	
Low	44%	56%	27%
Sociability			
High	57.5%	42.5%	
Low	42.5%	57.5%	35%

tion between African Americans and Whites (Allen, Hecht, & Martin, 1996; Martin, Hecht, & Larkey, 1994) that suggests differences based on expectations about interaction. The next stage should be a consideration of the impact of various combinations of features and the impact of those on classroom interaction.

FUTURE RESEARCH

Research on race in the classroom has essentially disappeared from the academic community. A central problem in this area of investigation has been the dearth of study since the early 1980s. Most of the research was conducted prior to the 1980s and few research investigations have examined the impact of various interventions and changes in pedagogical awareness since that time. The increase in diversity training and attempts at raising sensitivity to racial issues may or may not have changed the dynamics found in this investigation. Many of the investigations that we assembled dealt with the description of curriculum or antedoctal evidence of effectiveness or qualitative reflections of various participants.

The problem with such a dearth of research is that any attempt to remediate or to increase sensitivity or raise awareness of bias should have the effectiveness of such programs documented. The documentation of such programs requires an entire body of behavioral research focused on that particular set of issues. The data suggest that minority students in U.S. schools face potentially serious problems. The evidence, however, does not point to the potential mechanisms for success or the current programs that are successful. In other words, are there interventions or procedures that schools or instructors could utilize to correct the imbalance? The current literature does not provide a thorough and systematic examination of these issues in a manner that permits careful consideration and amelioration of the problem.

Future meta-analyses are required to examine the nature of the links involved in this report. Although there are some assumptions about causality, the evidence in this report only starts the process of establishing the nature of potential cause-and-effect relationships. To put it another way, the findings are necessary for causality, but the evidence does not provide sufficient evidence for such claims. The evidence in the meta-analyses does indicate that the basis for concern about an educational system failing not only to educate about the content of material, but failing to contribute to the positive development of the person, may be warranted.

Research in communication education has been examining the issues of behavioral alteration techniques (BATs) used by instructors. The findings of this meta-analysis suggest a reexamination of those data (Kearney & Plax, 1987, 1997; Plax, Kearney, & Tucker, 1986) for potential issues of bias on the part of instructors and potential methods of reducing any behavioral bias. The use of BATs reflects the need for instructors to retain control over the interaction of the classroom and the need to focus on tasks and regulate the appropriateness of behavior. The basis of the use of BATs stems from the instructor using a cultural norm, shared by students in theory, about the nature of appropriate interaction and the requirements for conformity. The potential exists that the use of a BAT may not be viewed as appropriate or used judiciously depending on the particular cultural background or self-image of the student.

The issues raised in this chapter will only grow in significance and importance over the next few decades. The changing demography of the United States indicates that the number of non-White students at all levels of the educational system is going to increase. The question is whether methods of classroom interaction instruction can be developed to ensure fairness and equity.

DISCUSSION

Pride in one's self probably represents an important determinant of academic success. Academic success, after all, is the mark of accomplishment and should represent the mastery of basic skills (reading, writing, arithmetic, etc.) as well as the processing of basic information (history, literature, etc.). However, during that process of accomplishment the student should develop a sense of value and worth that serves to guide him or her into future endeavors. If the experience with the educational system is negative it feeds a sense of failure and cynicism that could develop into anger and antisocial outcomes. The outcomes suggested by this meta-analysis suggest the importance of including racial image as a basis for evaluation of the success of educational programs.

Classroom interaction that is controlled and directed by teachers could exert a profound influence on the development of the identity of an individual. The issues of control are reflected in various writings that consider the need to find alternatives to the traditional methods used in the classroom. The reliance on qualitative statements of self-reflection may or may not correspond to the actual behavior that is enacted. The perception of a behavior may reflect the more extreme values that are perceived rather than the more subtle differences that accumulate on a day-to-day basis (Allen, 1998). Differences that might be unnoticed or lack importance in a single encounter may create large differences when accumulated across a lifetime of such experiences. The issues of discrimination and racism for minority students may not appear understandable or interpretable to most Whites because the bias may exist in such small proportions on any given day or week and therefore be imperceptible.

The cumulated impact of such differences however, may be reflected in the data dealing with racial self-image and various social and personal outcomes. Rather than viewing various outcomes as traceable to a single event or some type of underlying conscious or systematic influence, the difference in interaction patterns may reflect a large number of mutual influences. For example, the minority student's self-concept is lower and the rebellion or lack of conformity to expected behavior results in additional negative comments from an instructor. The negative comments simply serve to confirm the perception and reduce the expectations for success further. The emphasis of this chapter is on a more holistic view of the educational experience and the issues of communication in schools. The conclusions affirm the need to incorporate a diverse curriculum that includes a wider variety of views that provide inspiration and reaffirmation to all students.

REFERENCES

References marked with an asterisk indicate studies included in the meta-analysis.

Abelson, R. (1985). A variance explanation paradox: When a little is a lot. *Psychological Bulletin, 97*, 129–133.

Allen, M. (1998). Methodological considerations when examining a gendered world. In D. Canary & K. Dindia (Eds.), *Handbook of sex differences and similarities in communication: Critical essays and empirical investigations of sex and gender in interaction* (pp. 427–444). Mahwah, NJ: Lawrence Erlbaum Associates.

Allen, M., Bradford, L., Grimes, D., Cooper, E., Howard, L., & Howard, U. (1999, November). *Racial group orientation and social outcomes: Summarizing relationships using meta-analysis.* Paper presented at the National Communication Association Convention, Chicago. (ERIC Document Reproduction Service No. 439 451)

Allen, M., Hecht, M., & Martin, J. (1996). Examining the impact of culture social scientifically: Some suggestions from examining Martin, Hecht, and Larkey. *World Communication, 25*, 69–78.

Allen, M., Howard, L., & Grimes, D. (1997). Racial group orientation and self-concept: Examining the relationship using meta-analysis. *Howard Journal of Communications, 8*, 371–386.

Allport, G. (1979). *The nature of prejudice.* Menlo Park, CA: Addison-Wesley.

Belcher, H., & Shinitzky, H. (1998). Substance abuse in children: Prediction, protection, and prevention. *Archives of Pediatrics and Adolescent Medicine, 152*, 952–960.

*Bowler, R., Rauch, S., & Schwarzer, R. (1986). Self-esteem and interracial attitudes in Black high school students: A comparison with five other ethnic groups. *Urban Education, 21*, 3–10.

Bowman, B. (1994). *Cultural diversity and academic achievement* (Urban Education, Monograph Series). NCREL's Urban Education Program. Washington, DC. Retrieved January 10, 2000 from http://www.ousd.k12.ca.us/netday/links/partnerships/le0bow.htm

Bradford, L., Allen, M., Casey, M., & Emmers-Sommer, T. (2002). A meta-analysis examining the relationship between Latino Acculturation levels and HIV/AIDS risk behaviors, condom use, and HIV/AIDS knowledge. *Journal of Intercultural Communication Research, 31,* 167–180.

*Brown, W., & Simons, R. (1999). *Ethnic identity and attitudes toward school: Sources of variation in the educational achievement of African-American high school students.* Retrieved February 3, 2001 from http://www.udel.edu/psych/rsimons/brwnabst.htm

*Clark, M. (1979). *Race concepts and self-esteem in Black children.* Unpublished doctoral dissertation, University of Illinois, Urbana-Champaign, IL.

Cooper, E., & Allen, M. (1998). A meta-analytic examination of the impact of student race on classroom interaction. *Communication Research Reports, 15,* 151–161.

Cross, W. (1991). *Shades of black: Diversity in African-American identity.* Philadelphia: Temple University Press.

*Dulan, C. (1975). *Ethnic identification and stereotyping by Black children in desegregated elementary schools.* Unpublished doctoral dissertation, University of California at Riverside, Riverside, CA.

Friedman, P. (1978). Comparisons of teacher reinforcement schedules for students with different social class backgrounds. *Journal of Educational Psychology, 68,* 286–292.

Fuhrmann, B. (1990). *Adolescence, adolescents* (2nd ed.). Glenview, IL: Scott, Foresman/Little, Brown.

Gay, G. (1994). *A synthesis of scholarship in multicultural education* (Urban Education Monograph Series). NCREL's Urban Education Program. Retrieved January 10, 2000 from http://www.ncre.org/sdrs/areas/issues/educatrs/leadrshp/le0gay.htm

Griffin, J. (1991). Racism and humiliation of the African-American community. *The Journal of Primary Prevention, 12,* 149–171.

*Grossman, B. (1981). *Ethnic identity and self-esteem: A study of Anglo, Chicano, and Black adolescents in Texas.* Unpublished doctoral dissertation, New School for Social Research, New York.

*Hernandez, M. (1984). *A study of children's racial attitudes and self-esteem.* Unpublished doctoral dissertation, New York University, New York.

Hraba, J., & Grant, J. (1970). Black is beautiful: A reexamination of racial preference and identification. *Journal of Personality and Social Psychology, 16,* 398–402.

Jeter, J. (1972). *Elementary social studies teachers' differential classroom interaction with children as a function of differential expectations of pupil achievement.* Unpublished doctoral dissertation, University of Texas at Austin, Austin, TX.

Jones, M. (1993, November). *The differential effect participation in the Neighborhood Academic Initiative Program has on the auto-photographic self-concepts of inner-city adolescents.* Paper presented at the annual meeting of the National Communication Association, Atlanta, GA.

Kearney, P., & Plax, T. (1987). Situational and individual determinants of teachers' reported use of behavior alteration techniques. *Human Communication Research, 14,* 145–166.

Kearney, P., & Plax, T. (1997). Item desirability bias and the BAT checklist: A reply to Waltman and Burleson. *Communication Education, 46,* 95–99.

Martin, J., Hecht, M., & Larkey, L. (1994). Conversational improvement strategies for interethnic communication: African American and European American perspectives. *Communication Monographs, 61,* 236–255.

*Meyers, E. (1966). *Self-concept, family structure, and school achievement: A study of disadvantaged Negro boys.* Unpublished doctoral dissertation, Columbia University, New York.

*Mobley, B. (1973). *Self-concept and conceptualization of ethnic identity: The Black experience.* Unpublished doctoral dissertation, Purdue University, West Lafayette, IN.

Paul, M., & Fischer, J. (1980). Correlates of self-concept among Black early adolescents. *Journal of Youth and Adolescence, 9,* 163–173.

Plax, T., Kearney, P., & Tucker, L. (1986). Prospective teachers' use of behavior alteration techniques: Reaction to common student misbehaviors. *Communication Education, 35,* 32–42.

Porter, J. (1971). *Black child, White child: The development of racial attitudes.* Cambridge, MA: Harvard University Press.

*Rasheed, S. (1981). *Self-esteem and ethnic identity in African-American third grade children.* Unpublished doctoral dissertation, University of Michigan, Ann Arbor, MI.

Rosenberg, M. (1975). The dissonant context and the adolescent self-concept. In S. Dragastin & G. Elder (Eds.), *Adolescence in the life cycle: Psychological change and social context* (pp. 211–251). New York: Wiley.

Rosenthal, R., & Jacobson, L. (1968). *Pygmalion in the classroom.* New York: Holt, Rinehart, & Winston.

Rubovits, P., & Maehr, M. (1973). Pygmalion black and white. *Journal of Personality and Social Psychology, 21,* 210–218.

Sahlstein, E., & Allen, M. (2002). Sex differences in self-esteem: A meta-analytic assessment. In M. Allen, R. Preiss, B. Gayle, & N. Burrell (Eds.), *Interpersonal communication research: Advances through meta-analysis* (pp. 59–72). Mahwah, NJ: Lawrence Erlbaum Associates.

*Schmults, T. (1975). *The relationship of Black identity to field dependence and adjustment.* Unpublished doctoral dissertation, University of Rhode Island, Kingston, RI.

*Spencer, M. (1981). Race dissonance research on Black children: Stable life course phenomenon or fluid indicator of intraindividual plasticity and unique cohort effect. In J. McAdoo, H. McAdoo, & W. Cross (Eds.), *5th conference on empirical research in Black psychology* (pp. 24–49). Washington, DC: National Institute of Mental Health.

Tajfel, H. (1978). Social categorization, social identity, and social comparison. In H. Tajfel (Ed.), *Differentiation between social groups* (pp. 61–76). London: Academic.

*Verkuyten, M. (1990). Self-esteem and the evaluation of ethnic identity among Turkish and Dutch adolescents in the Netherlands. *Journal of Social Psychology, 130,* 285–297.

*White, C. (1988). Ethnic identity and academic performance among Black and White college students: An interactionist approach. *Urban Education, 23,* 219–240.

Wilson, A. (1978). *The development psychology of the Black child.* New York: Africana Research Publications.

12

Sex Equity in the Classroom: Do Female Students Lose the Battle for Teacher Attention?

Susanne M. Jones
University of Minnesota, Twin Cities

Kathryn Dindia
Stacy Tye
University of Wisconsin–Milwaukee

Achieving sex equity in U.S. classrooms means equally recognizing and rewarding the achievement of both male and female students. It also means providing both male and female students with equal opportunities to pursue training and career paths, including training in traditionally female occupations for males (e.g., elementary school teacher, nurse) or traditionally male occupations for females (e.g., construction, business management; Bailey, 1993). Federal regulatory acts, such as Title VII of the Civil Rights Act of 1964 and Title IX of the Education Amendments of 1972 have aimed at establishing gender equity in the United States and have led to a redefinition of sex discrimination in the classroom. Title IX in particular states that no person shall be discriminated against on the basis of sex in any educational program receiving federal funds. Since its enactment, Title IX has been a powerful source in initiating school reforms in the United States, particularly with respect to sex discrimination in the classroom.

Teacher–student interaction in the classroom is crucial to the learning process of male and female students (Sadker & Sadker, 1982). Impassioned researchers and administrators have frequently claimed that male and female students are not taught equally in American classrooms (Hall & Sandler, 1982). The earliest studies (Ayres, 1909) examined the negative performance of boys in elementary schools, whereas studies conducted after 1970 assert that girls are disadvantaged in America's classrooms (for reviews see Arliss & Borisoff, 2001; Brophy & Good, 1974; Wilkinson & Marrett, 1985). Hall and Sandler's (1982) famous study of the "chilly climate" in the classroom examined the oral participation of male and female students in fourth, sixth, and eighth grades and found that teachers call on male students more frequently than female students, interrupt female students more frequently than male students, and allow fewer female students to respond to questions. Subsequent reports (Hall & Sandler, 1984; Sandler & Hall, 1986) supported these claims and set in motion a series of empirical studies to investigate the causes and related factors of this chilly climate. This meta-analysis examines whether there has been a pattern of sex differences in teacher–student interactions. Although extensive research examines factors that influence student evaluations of effective and ineffective teachers, this chapter focuses most squarely on teacher interactions with students based on student sex. Next is a review of research that has examined sex differences in teacher–student interactions, followed by the report of a meta-analysis of 35 empirical studies on sex differences in student–teacher interactions.

DO TEACHERS INTERACT DIFFERENTLY WITH STUDENTS BASED ON STUDENT SEX?

Rosenthal and Jacobson's (1968) Pygmalion in the Classroom has often been cited as a theoretical explanation for the causes of sex inequity in the classroom. Reminiscent of Eliza Doolittle's amazing transformation due to Professor Higgins in George Bernhard Shaw's play My Fair Lady, the Pygmalion effect in the classroom suggests that teachers form expectations of students who then behave in ways that confirm those initial expectations. Expectations are cognitive schemes or inferences that contain behavioral scripts of how we would like people to behave in various situations (Brophy & Good, 1974; Sadker & Sadker, 1994). Expectations usually result from observed performance and help us form logical decisions in everyday situations. However, if expectations are rigid and inflexible, they cause behavior and act as self-fulfilling prophecies, a term first coined by Merton (1948).

In their now famous experiment at an "Oak Elementary School," Rosenthal and Jacobson (1968) tested self-fulfilling prophecies in the classroom and found that teacher expectations for the achievement for students who were labeled as late bloomers influenced the academic performance of these students. Specifically, late bloomers exhibited improved schoolwork and showed significantly higher gains on their IQ scores than those in a control group. Follow-up studies demonstrated that teacher expectations influenced their interactions with these late bloomers, primarily because teachers interacted more frequently and paid more attention to these students. Although Rosenthal and Jacobson's findings suggest positive consequences for students, the negative repercussions of teacher expectations toward students are all too obvious. If teachers expect certain students to perform poorly because of certain demographic or psychographic student characteristics (e.g., race, sex, intelligence, economic status), then, in line with Rosenthal and Jacobson, these students will indeed perform poorly, because teachers will interact less and possibly more harshly with those students. Brophy and Good (1974) aptly described this dynamic:

> If continued indefinitely, such treatment constitutes a pressure on the student to begin to conform to the teacher's expectations by behaving in the ways that the teacher expects the student to behave. This, in turn, reinforces the teacher's expectations all the more, and a self-regenerating vicious circle is established. If the situation persists, a true expectation effect is likely to occur. (p. 39)

Teachers' interactions with students can therefore be affected by teachers' expectations for student performance, as well as teachers' attitudes toward individual students. Teachers who perceive and expect certain students to be low (or high) achievers and who view such students as unchangeable in their performance will vary their interaction toward students, thereby impeding or inducing student learning and ultimately student success. Note that expectations need not be inaccurate; indeed, teachers can have accurate expectations about the performances of certain students. What matters is the degree to which the teacher is flexible to change his or her expectations for the student. The crucial question relevant for this study is whether teachers form expectations based on student sex. In other words, does student sex trigger a certain set of teacher expectations and behavior toward male and female students?

Observation Systems

Researchers have developed several coding systems to observe and subsequently record teacher–student interactions in the classroom. The Brophy–Good Dyadic Child Interaction System developed by Brophy and Good (1974) is one of the most comprehensive and frequently used observation systems of classroom interaction. It contains about 40 categories to yield a comprehensive record of quantitative and qualitative teacher–student interactions. Initially developed for use in elementary schools, the system allows observers to code classroom interactions into three categories. The first category is the most complex and involves academic response opportunities, including the following subcategories:

1. Teacher-initiated questions.
    a. Direct questions.
        i. Process questions (student outlines a process).
        ii. Product questions (student reports one specific fact from memory).
    b. Call-outs (student provides spontaneous answer to teacher question).
    c. Open questions (teacher asks class a question and waits until students raise hands).
2. Teacher-initiated feedback.
    a. Criticism (negative statement).
    b. Praise (positive statement).
    c. Neutral.

The second category allows for coding of nonacademic teacher-initiated interactions and involves statements about classroom management. Nonacademic teacher-initiated interactions can be coded into four subcategories (i.e., negative or neutral behavioral or procedural statements). For instance, a statement directed at a student, such as "Are you listening?" would be coded as a neutral behavioral nonacademic interaction, whereas "You should be ashamed of yourself" would be a negative behavioral statement.

The final category involves coding of student-initiated interactions, including student volunteering, spontaneous statements, questions, and other student-initiated interactions (for a complete descriptions see Sikes, 1971; Good & Brophy, 1973). Further distinctions are made between teacher–student public and private interactions.

Researchers rarely use all 40 categories to code for classroom interactions and often use a modified version to adapt the observation system to the specifics of their empirical study. Observational data have been analyzed by combining several categories to generate a more manageable set of dependent measures (e.g., Good, Cooper, & Blakey, 1980). In addition, researchers who have examined sex differences in the classroom frequently generate a standardized score that reflects the proportion of an individual response category made by a male or female student relative to all students in a given classroom. The formula most frequently used is this:

$$\frac{\text{Total number of interactions for variable } x \text{ in a student sex category (i.e., male or female)}}{\text{Total number of interactions for variable } x} \times \frac{\text{Total number of students in classroom}}{\text{Total number of students in sex category (i.e., male or female)}}$$

The result is a standardized score that is based on observed frequency counts of interactions that are commonly analyzed using chi-square statistics, and thus allow for the application of inferential statistical analyses. Interestingly, the standardized score, based on frequency counts of categorical measures, has sometimes been treated as a continuous dependent measure in some studies. For instance, Good, Cooper, and Blakey (1980) generated five continuous clusters (appropriateness, academic instruction, nonacademic interaction, absolute feedback, residual feedback) with student sex, time of year, and teacher expectations as independent measures.

The second most frequently used observational coding system is the Interactions for Sex Equity in Classroom Teaching (INTERSECT) system developed by Sadker, Sadker, Bauchner, and Hardekopf (1984). The system allows coding for teacher–student interactions by:

1. Initiation (teacher or student).
2. Receiver (student, teacher, class, group).
3. Gender of teacher and student.
4. Method (hand up, move toward, call out, private).
5. Evaluative type.
   a. Praise (positive reaction to student's comment or work).
   b. Acceptance (e.g., "Uh-huh," "Okay").
   c. Remediation (helping student to correct comment or work).
   d. Criticism (explicit statement that an answer is incorrect).
6. Evaluative content (intellectual, content, appearance, other).

Researchers have most frequently coded interactions for the evaluative type of teacher-initiated feedback (for a summary see Sadker et al., 1984). The system also allows for recording observed student-initiated interactions. Again, data consist of frequency counts that are frequently analyzed with chi-square statistics (see Duffy, Warren, & Walsh, 2001).

Numerous additional observational coding systems have been developed (e.g., Weshner Observation Scale; Weshner, 1975). The observational technique for college classroom interaction (OTCCI; Brady & Eisler, 1999), for instance, is a more recent observational coding system that relies on a time sampling recording system designed to measure teacher–student interactions using discontinuous intervals. This sampling method does not provide frequencies or durations. Rather, it allows the researcher or observer to infer these measurements, allowing for simultaneous recordings of multiple behaviors.

The OTCCI, the Brophy–Good, the INTERSECT, and other systems are largely similar in their categories and subcategories of observed behavior, although qualitative differences exist. For instance, not all systems differentiate between evaluative content and quantity of teacher–student interactions. Furthermore, some systems are more comprehensive than others. Although systems are not alike, the most severe incongruencies across studies emerge in the treatment, statistical analysis, and subsequent report of the observed teacher–student interaction variables. Consequently, conclusions drawn from observed interaction studies examining sex differences in the classroom have to be investigated with great care.

Summary of Findings for Observed Teacher–Student Interactions in the Classroom

Numerous studies suggest that male students tend to have more interactions of all kinds with their teachers than do female students. Male students are more frequently responded to, are allowed to call out more frequently, and are called on more frequently than female students (Hillman & Davenport, 1978; Hutchinson & Beadle, 1992; Karp & Yoels, 1976; Sternglanz & Lyberger-Ficek, 1977). Teachers also tend to be more accepting of male dominance in the classroom, and these differences persist across teacher sex (Sadker & Sadker, 1985). Sadker and Sadker's (1982) frequently cited observational study of teacher–student interactions in 100 fourth-, sixth-, and eighth-grade classrooms of diverse populations showed that male students consistently outtalked and outparticipated female students. Becker (1981) also found that teachers initiated more conversation with male students than with female students. These findings also reflect those of She (2000), who found that male students make up the majority of teacher-initiated interactions. In a study using the Brophy–Good Dyadic Child Interaction System She found that of 355 teacher-initiated questions, boys responded to 78.7% of the questions, given a 50:50 sex distribution in the class. Altermatt, Jovanovic, and Perry (1998) also found that teachers ask more questions of boys than of girls (60.7% and 39.3%, respectively). Likewise, Becker (1981), as well as Good, Sikes, and Brophy (1973), found that teachers asked boys significantly more open and process questions than girls.

According to Hall and Sandler (1982) approximately 50% of all teacher-initiated feedback consists of acceptance comments (e.g., "okay," "uh-huh"), and the rest consists of more precise feedback in the form of praise, criticism, and remediation. Once more, findings suggest that male students receive the majority of teacher feedback (Morse & Handley, 1985; Sadker & Sadker, 1982). Whether boys receive more praise or more criticism is debatable. For instance, Morse and Handley (1985) found that boys received 61% of the criticism, whereas girls received only 32% in junior high school. Becker (1981), as well as Jones and Wheatley (1990), found that teachers praised boys more than girls (62%), whereas criticisms was equally distributed between boys and girls.

The differential teacher-initiated interaction patterns seem to hold across the educational life span. Becker (1981), for instance found that boys received 63% of contact from teachers, even in secondary classrooms. Likewise, Sikes (1971) found that male students are asked more direct, process, and open questions than female students.

For college classrooms, Krupnick (1985) as well as Hutchinson and Beadle (1992) found that regardless of demographic information, female students never spoke as long as male students. Likewise, Irvine (1985, 1986) found that female students received less feedback than male students. Hall and Sandler (1982) claimed that the gender disparity continues through graduate school. Indeed, in their qualitative study based on 10 interviews with graduate students, Holmstrom and Holmstrom (1974) found that female students report having the impression that faculties often do not take female graduate students seriously. In addition, Schroeder and Mynatt (1999) found that male professors met more frequently with male students, and female students made a greater amount of negative psychosocial comments about male professors than female professors.

However, for every study that detected patterns of sex inequity in U.S. classrooms largely favoring male students, there is at least one study that did not find such patterns. Cornbleth and Korth (1978), as well as Brady and Eisler (1999), found no sex differences in call outs, and adequate and inadequate responses. Sex difference disappeared in Altermatt et al.'s (1998) study once student volunteering was taken into account. Leder (1987) also found no support for sex differences in teacher-initiated question-asking behavior (e.g., product questions, process questions). Likewise, Brooks (1982) found no significant differences in the number of times or the amount of interactions in a social works master's class. Constantinople, Cornelius, and Gray (1988) set out to test the chilly climate in the classroom and examined the interaction effects of teacher sex, student sex, course type, and time in semester in 48 college courses over the course of one semester and found that although male students are generally more active in female-taught arts classes than in male-taught arts classes, there were no teacher sex effects on teacher-initiated behaviors, such as expanding on comments, asking questions, calling on students, and acknowledging students. Student sex had comparatively little impact, such that the researchers only found marginal differences in rates of participation between males and females (see also Hillman & Davenport, 1978).

Given the confusing set of results, Canada and Pringle (1995) suggested that the social context of the classroom might influence the extent to which male and female students interact with teachers. Indeed, their observational study found that interaction by male and female students varied as a result of the gender ratio in the classroom, although not in predictable ways. Indeed, Brophy and Good (1974) provided an insightful explanation.

It is unlikely that particular student attributes have simple universal effects in triggering specific teacher attitudes. Although it is likely that the great majority of teachers will react to a given student attribute positively or negatively, there is much room for interaction between particular teachers' personality traits and particular students' personality traits ... a given teacher's attitude toward a given student will depend greatly upon the particulars of the relationship between that student and that teacher. (p. 149)

It seems clear that teachers treat male students differently than female students. However, given the diverging results of empirical studies, the causes for such patterns might not be solely attributable to student sex. As Brophy and Good (1974) pointed out, there might be several teacher- and student-relevant factors that shape the relationship between teacher-initiated behavior and student sex. It seems therefore reasonable to explore various contextual and psychological factors that potentially shape this relationship. What follows is a brief summary of several moderating factors that shape teacher expectations and attitudes, and consequently their behaviors toward male and female students.

Factors That Shape Teacher–Student Interactions

Teacher Sex. The most obvious factor that seems to shape sex equity in the classroom is teacher sex. Several studies suggest a Teacher Sex × Student Sex interaction (Hutchinson & Beadle, 1992; Karp & Yoels, 1976; Pearson & West, 1991; Sternglanz & Lyberger-Ficek, 1977). Sternglanz and Lyberger-Ficek (1977) recorded numbers and types of teacher-initiated behaviors, such as asking questions and responding, and student-initiated behaviors, such as call outs and hand raising, in 60 college classes, and found that male students were disproportionately more likely than female students to respond to and initiate interaction in male-taught classes. No differences in interactions were detected in female-taught classes. Karp and Yoels (1976) reported similar results after having observed 10 classes and found that in female-taught classes, women accounted for 42% of the interaction, whereas in male-taught classes females accounted for only 24%.

Likewise, Boersma, Gay, Jones, Morrison, and Remick (1981) studied interactions between college instructors and students of 50 different classes and found no gender differences in number and type of interactions for male and female students, except for female-taught classes, where male students tended to interact more with instructors than female students. In addition, Hutchinson and Beadle (1992) found that women and men made equal numbers of contributions in a female-taught class, whereas men took longer and more frequent speaking turns in male-taught classes. Finally, Jones and Wheatley (1990) found that female professors reprimand male students more than female students, whereas male professors equally reprimand male and female students. These studies suggest that teacher sex, indeed, might be a factor that influences teacher–student interactions.

Individual Teacher and Student Factors.   Additional factors that might shape teacher–student interactions in the classroom are individual teacher factors, such as a teacher's sex role, and individual student factors, such as student classroom behavior, student achievement, and student race. Admittedly, individual factors are broad and have not been fully examined. Therefore, we focus our discussion on those factors that have been most frequently empirically investigated.

Often ignored in the literature of sex differences in the classroom is the role students themselves may play in influencing the quantity and quality of interactions they receive from their teachers (Altermatt et al., 1998; Bank, Biddle, & Good, 1980). Differential behavior of boys and girls in elementary school might set the tone for teacher-initiated behavior toward students. Interestingly, research suggests that a minority of male students dominate the majority of male-focused teacher–student interactions (see Brophy & Good, 1974). For instance, Hall and Sandler (1982) found that more than 30% of the students do generally not interact at all, and less than 10% made up the "star students," typically male, whose talk received three times the share of the instructor's attention.

Furthermore, boys might receive the majority of teacher attention because boys misbehave more frequently than girls, particularly in elementary school. Because boys seem to be more in the "perceptual field" of the teacher, they are more frequently reprimanded and called on for instruction (Brophy & Good, 1974; French & French, 1984; Simpson & Erickson, 1983; Stake & Katz, 1982). In addition, Dweck, Davidson, Nelson, and Enna (1978) found that boys largely receive criticism for failure to obey rules, whereas girls receive criticism for intellectual performances. Likewise, Croll (1985) found that the largest amount of interaction goes to boys who have learning disabilities and these students only make up a small percentage. This might contribute to findings that girls outperform boys on the elementary school level, and boys show lower reading achievement and require more remedial reading help and assistance with learning disabilities in elementary school (Brophy & Good, 1974).

Because boys misbehave more frequently than girls, teacher attitudes and expectations might be more negative toward boys than toward girls (Chesterfield & Enge, 1998). The results of this dynamic might explain the interaction patterns favoring boys: If boys misbehave more frequently in class, they might also receive more attention, not only in the form of teacher criticism and reprimand, but also in the form of praise as a pedagogical tool to help them better integrate into the classroom environment. Support for this dynamic comes from Simpson and Erickson (1983), who recorded the verbal and nonverbal behaviors of elementary pupils and found that boys received more verbal and nonverbal praise as well as criticism. Once more however, Martin (1972) found that the high rate of teacher-initiated behaviors with boys is characteristic only for a small percentage of boys in the class, namely those who have been identified as problem-behavior boys.

A second individual student factor that seems to influence teacher–student interaction and that has been explored most extensively is student achievement (see Brophy & Good, 1974). Although Heller and Parsons (1981) found no effects for student achievement, several studies suggest that teachers interact more frequently and favorably with high achievers than with low achievers, offer more criticism to low achievers, wait less time for low achievers, do not stay with low achievers in failure situations, reward inappropriate behavior for low achievers, and pay less attention to low achievers (Good et al., 1980; Good et al., 1973; Jeter & Davis, 1982; Rosenthal, 1974; for a review see Brophy & Good, 1974).

Related to student achievement is teachers' expectation of student achievement. The achievement and intelligence of girls seems to be largely overestimated, and teachers often have lower expectations for boys than for girls of equal ability. Jeter and Davis (1982), as well as Good et al. (1980), found no confirmation for the Pygmalion effect with respect to student sex, but found that teachers initiated more interaction with students who were expected to perform well in class. Good et al. (1973) found that low-achieving boys, relative to other students, received the poorest contact patterns with both male and female teachers. This result seems to reflect teacher expectations that consist of negative attitudes toward boys and toward low achievers. Given that boys have been found to frequently misbehave, particularly in elementary school, and given that boys require more assistance in learning than girls, it might be that boys are labeled more frequently as low achievers than girls. Although this reasoning might explain why boys receive more overall classroom attention as well as reprimands and critiques, it does not explain why boys have been found to also receive more praise.

A final student factor that has been frequently explored is student race, although statistical information for the Student Sex × Student Race interactions for teacher-initiated contact has frequently not been reported (e.g., Brown, Cervero, & Johnson-Bailey, 2000; Ehrenberg, Goldhaber, & Brewer, 1995; Hillman & Davenport, 1978; Irvine, 1985, 1986; Simpson & Erickson, 1983). Once more, findings are inconclusive. For instance, Hillman and Davenport (1978) and Simpson and Erickson (1983) found no Race × Student Sex interaction effect and reported that Black and male students received the majority of teacher attention, which contradicts the findings of Irvine (1985, 1986), who found that White students received more classroom attention than Black students. Interestingly however, Simpson and Erickson, as well as Hillman and Davenport, detected a Teacher Race × Student Sex interaction, suggesting that White teachers interacted more differentially toward male and female students than did Black teachers.

Individual teacher factors, other than teacher sex, have been less frequently explored; however, one such factor that has been examined to some degree is the teacher's sex role. Whereas sex reflects a categorical distinction based on biological characteristics of males and females, gender role orientations are socially constructed, continuous concepts ranging from masculine to feminine orientations with androgynous orientations denoting an equal balance between masculine and feminine behaviors. Undifferentiated behavior denotes complete nonexistence of gendered behaviors and attitudes (Bem, 1981). The Bem Sex-Role Inventory and the Personal Attributes Questionnaire (Spence, Helmreich, & Stapp, 1973) are two self-report measures that have frequently been used to assess the gender role orientation of individuals, including teachers and students, and to develop gender-typed hypothetical teacher descriptions (e.g., Freeman, 1994).

Whenever specific behaviors, abilities, interests, and values are attributed to one sex, then sex-role typing is taking place. Stereotypical male behavior conjures up images of strength, assertiveness, independence, and minimal emotional expression. Overly emotional expression, dependent behavior, and nonaggressive behavior are often considered female. Whenever sex stereotyping leads to specific behaviors, we refer to this as sex bias. For instance, a teacher who believes that female students are not as capable in math as boys might provide female students with less challenging math assignments. Biased behavior can significantly influence students' self-images, expectations, and attitudes toward their own and the other sex.

University teaching has commonly been portrayed as a masculine occupation, not the least because the majority of professors are male. Elementary school teaching, on the other hand, has been viewed as a feminine domain. Harris (1976) examined whether college students rated teachers differently based on gender across nursery school, elementary school, high school, and college. She found that masculine traits were given more positive evaluations on all levels, but the difference between these ratings was smallest at the nursery school level and increased as the grade level increased. Thus, a teacher's sex-role behavior might be a factor that influences teacher–student interactions. Bledsoe (1983) explored the relationship of teacher self-reported sex role and approval and disapproval behaviors in 44 junior high school courses. He found that masculine female and male teachers are more approving of boys' behavior than of girls' behavior, whereas feminine female and male teachers are more approving of girls' behavior than boys' behavior.

One contextual factor, the school subject, seems to also influence the relationship between student sex and teacher-initiated interaction. Empirical research exploring the performance of male and female students in science (e.g., mathematics, physics, biology) and nonscience courses (e.g., humanities, reading, arts) is vast. For instance, Leinhardt, Seewald, and Engel (1979) found that teachers expect boys to outperform girls in elementary school math, whereas a reversal of the sexes in terms of achievement expectations holds for reading ability. They found that teachers spend more time with girls in reading than with boys, and spend more time with boys in math than with girls. Indeed, end-of-year achievement differed markedly, such that girls outperformed boys. Likewise, Whyte (1984) examined female underachievement in science courses in a British junior high school and found that boys take the lion's share of teacher's attention, and girls remained largely silent during class.

Summary

We have identified one contextual factor (school subject), as well as several student factors (student behavior, achievement, race) and teacher factors (teacher sex, teacher sex role) that have been found to moderate the relationship between teacher–student interaction and student sex. Undoubtedly, the list of moderating factors influencing sex differences in teacher–student interactions is not exhaustive, but the review suggests that the relationship between student sex and teacher–student interactions might not be as clear cut as some empirical research suggests.

Previous meta-analyses have attempted to corroborate the patterns of sex differences in the classroom. However, even the results of these meta-analyses remain inconclusive. For instance, Kelly (1988) conducted a meta-analysis of gender differences in teacher–student interactions with 81 studies.[1] She coded 17 different interaction categories (e.g., total teacher–student interaction, total teacher-initiated interaction, total student-initiated interaction, teacher praise, teacher complaint). No study yielded data points for more than 12 categories, with the highest number of data points (45 studies) in the total teacher–student interaction category and the lowest number of data points in the praise category (7 studies). Kelly's unit of analysis was the observed interaction, and her studies were weighted in proportion of the number of observations. Kelly concluded that teachers consistently interact more with boys than with girls. For instance, girls participate in 44% of total teacher–student interactions. However, her gen-

---

[1] Kelly was able to include 81 studies because her sample included theses, dissertations, and conference papers. Furthermore, Kelly chose to treat six studies as multiple studies because they contained more than one age group. A list of studies entered in the meta-analysis could not be generated from the author.

eralizations have to be examined with caution, because Kelly relied on descriptive statistics, such as box plots and average percentages of student sex distributions, for each interaction category and did not perform tests of statistical significance. Given her descriptive data analysis, a second meta-analysis seems warranted, particularly to include empirical studies conducted in the past 20 years.

METHOD

Literature Search and Sample

Articles were obtained through an electronic search of ERIC and PsycINFO databases, as well as a manual search of reference lists. Keywords used to generate the sample included all relevant combinations of *classroom interaction, classroom communication, student–teacher interaction, teacher–student interaction,* as well as *gender differences, sex differences, teacher sex,* and *student sex.* Once a potential article was identified, its reference list was examined for additional relevant sources. A total of 127 articles were identified as relevant for the meta-analysis and were subsequently screened for final inclusion. The following restrictions were applied to assure consistent coding of the empirical studies. All articles had to (a) be published in scholarly, peer-reviewed journals or books after 1970, (b) contain quantitative data, (c) examine, at least partially, message production behavior as opposed to message evaluations, (d) use a systematic observation coding system, (e) record demographic information of student sex, and (f) occur within the context of a pedagogical setting, beginning with elementary school (preschool studies were excluded). Empirical studies examining multiple independent measures were included as long as quantitative information for teacher-initiated interactions for male and female students was reported.

A number of articles were not included because they relied on nonquantitative assessments (Brown et al., 2000; Condravy, Skirboll, & Taylor, 1998; Goodwin & Stevens, 1993; Heller & Parsons, 1981; Illatov & Shamai, 1998; Krupnick, 1985; Schroeder & Mynatt, 1999), did not rely on observations (Ehrenberg, Goldhaber, & Brewer, 1995; Hopf & Hatzichristou, 1999; Peterson & Fennema, 1985; Worrall & Tsarna, 1987), did not use a systematic observational coding system (Chesterfield & Enge, 1998; Hechtman & Rosenthal, 1991; Rickards & Fisher, 1996), did not occur in at least elementary school (Fagot, 1984; Hall, Braunwald, & Mroz, 1982), or did not provide sufficient statistical information (Canada & Pringle, 1995; Cornelius, Gray, & Constantinople, 1990; Heller & Parsons, 1981; Merrett & Wheldall, 1992; Morgan, 2001; Smith, 1989, 1991, 1992).

Coding Procedures

A total of 35 studies were coded for school level, school subject (science or nonscience), student sample size and sex distribution, teacher sample size and sex distribution, and type of observational coding system used in the empirical study.

Coding Teacher-Initiated Teacher–Student Interactions. Given the plethora of observational coding systems, an attempt was made to code observed interactions into general categories. All studies were coded for frequencies or proportions of positive, negative, and total interactions (see Cooper & Allen, 1998). Negative interactions include teacher interactions in the form of verbal and nonverbal criticisms, reprimands, behavioral warnings, and other ways of providing nonsupportive feedback. Interactions involving incorrect student answers were not included. Positive interactions include teacher interactions in the form of verbal and nonverbal praise, acceptance, affirmations, approval, and other positive reinforcement behaviors. For instance, affirming a student answer or a student question constitutes positive teacher-initiated interaction. Coding for the number of total interactions involved, in some instances, the sum of positive and negative interactions (e.g., the sum of INTERSECT coding categories of praise, acceptance, remediation, and criticism), and in other instances, the sum of neutral observational coding categories, such as asking questions (direct or open questions). In some cases, where coding was unclear, student-initiated teacher interactions were coded. Coding procedures for each study are available from the authors.

Procedures for the Meta-Analysis

Once coded for positive, negative, and total interactions, patterns of teacher–student interactions were analyzed with three meta-analyses. Kenny's (1999) META-ANALYSIS: Easy to Answer was used to enter and analyze the data. Effect sizes for each study were calculated using d. A positive average effect size indicates that males receive more interaction, whereas a negative average effect size would indicate that females receive more interaction. The majority of the studies relied on the number of students, rather than the number of teachers or the number of interactions, as the sample size in conducting tests of statistical significance. Therefore, the sample sizes entered into META were based on the student sample. In some cases, where the student sample size was not reported, the teacher sample size multiplied by two was entered as the sample size (it was assumed that each teacher had at least one male and one female student). Furthermore, in the few cases where the sex distribution of the teacher or the student samples was not reported, the groups were assumed to be equal. Finally, because the student sample sizes varied greatly, the effect size for each study was weighted by the sample size.

Given the nature of the observed interactional data, the type of statistic that was most frequently recorded for each study consisted of proportions (and sometimes a chi-square statistic of the proportions), as well as the means and standard deviations for male and female students. Proportions, means, and standard deviations were converted to d. There were a few studies that reported nonsignificant results. In cases where studies reported nonsignificant results and provided information regarding the direction of the relationship, the effect size was calculated as one half of the effect size for the minimal significant value using the appropriate degrees of freedom. In cases where studies reported nonsignificant results but did not provide information about the direction of the relationship, the effect size was coded as zero.

RESULTS

Total Observed Teacher-Initiated Interactions

Twenty-nine studies reported results for total teacher-initiated interactions. The meta-analysis revealed that teachers interacted more with male students than with female students ($d = .171, k = 29, N = 8,612$).[2] However, although the average effect size was significantly different from zero, $t(28) = 4.52, p < .01$, the sample was heterogeneous, $\chi^2(28) = 120.555$, $p < .001$, which suggests that moderating factors other than sampling error influenced the sampling distribution. Thus, we searched for possible correlates or moderators of the effect size.

Two moderating factors were tested to examine whether they influenced the effect size for teacher–student interactions. First, reviews of the empirical results concerning sex differences in teacher-initiated interactions suggested that teacher sex might potentially influence observed teacher–student interactions. A total of 14 studies provided sufficient statistical information (i.e., cell proportions or cell means and standard deviations for male and female teachers to male and female students) and were coded for observed total teacher interactions. The effect size for male teachers is larger than for female teachers ($d = .58$ and $.34$, respectively). However, the difference between

---

[2]One study (Sternglanz & Lyberger-Ficek, 1977) was identified as an outlier (the d for this study for total interaction was $d = 7.497$, weight = 2,284). This study reported extremely large t values for a number of its statistical tests, which suggests inconsistencies in the study's methodology or data collection and subsequent analysis. In particular, we wondered if it was analyzing the data using N of students as the unit of analysis but reporting the results using N of teachers as the unit of analysis. Therefore, this study was eliminated from all analyses.

these effect sizes was nonsignificant, $t(12) = 1.03, p = .32$. Thus, we cannot conclude that the difference in treatment of male and female students is greater for male teachers than for female teachers. A possible reason for this nonsignificant outcome could be a lack of sufficient power.

Although previous research suggests no significant differences for school level, we nevertheless tested for possible influences. Although our sample sizes were small for each category, we entered four school levels into the analysis (elementary, middle, high schools, and college). Table 12.1 confirms the past research findings that school level does not significantly influence sex differences in teacher–student interactions, $F(3, 21) = .54, p = .66$.

Positive Teacher-Initiated Interactions

With respect to positive teacher-initiated interactions, such as praises and acceptances, our meta-analysis generated a homogeneous effect size ($d = .055, k = 12, N = 4,034$), $\chi^2(11) = 15.67$, ns. However, the average effect size was not significantly different from zero, $t(11) = 1.41$, ns. This result suggests that teachers do not praise male students more than female students. However, it should be noted that the power to detect an effect size that is significantly different from zero is low ($k = 12$).

Negative Teacher-Initiated Interactions

With respect to negative teacher-initiated interactions, 11 studies contained sufficient statistical information for analysis. The meta-analysis generated an average effect size of $d = .35$, indicating that teachers reprimand and critique male students more than female students ($k = 11, N = 1,871$). Although the average effect size was significantly different from zero, $t(10) = 3.22, p < .01$, the effect size was heterogeneous, $\chi^2(10) = 36.93, p < .001$, which suggests that moderating factors other than sampling error influence

TABLE 12.1
School Level as a Moderating Factor for Observed Teacher–Student Interactions

School Level	k	N	d	t	χ^2	df
Elementary	7	1,398	.18	2.5	7.28	6
Middle	9	1,730	.17	2.03	51.97*	8
High School	3	992	.24	1.76	0.35	2
College	6	3,623	.10	1.36	54.51*	5

*$p < .001$.

the sampling distribution. Unfortunately, no exploration for moderating factors, such as teacher sex, school level, or educational content, was conducted because 11 studies in the meta-analysis did not provide sufficient statistical information for testing.

DISCUSSION

The results of this meta-analysis suggest that teachers initiate more overall interactions and more negative interactions, but not more positive interactions with male students than with female students. However, these results have to be evaluated with caution.

With respect to total teacher–student interactions, our results suggest that the effect size is significantly different from zero but heterogeneous. This finding suggests that there are other moderating factors that influence this interaction pattern. We tested whether teacher sex moderated this relationship and did not find that it moderated the effect of student sex on teacher–student interaction. However, the power to detect a significantly different effect size for male and female teachers was low due to the small number of studies that provided sufficient information to calculate separate effect sizes for male and female teachers. Similarly, the school level (elementary, middle, high school, or college) did not moderate sex differences in teacher–student interactions. Because of the heterogeneous findings for total teacher–student interaction, the results remain inconclusive. Although the average effect size is greater than zero and favors total teacher–student interactions with male students, the variability of the effect sizes across studies indicates that something moderates the relationship between total teacher–student interaction and student sex.

The findings for positive teacher–student interaction were homogenous but they were not significantly different from zero, which suggests that although the overall average effect size favors males receiving more positive teacher–student interaction than females, this difference is not statistically significant. Thus, the results of the meta-analysis indicate that male students do not receive more positive teacher–student interaction than do female students. However, the lack of significant results may be due to the sample size. Only 12 studies examined whether teachers provide more positive interaction with male students than female students. Consequently, the power to detect a significant effect size was low.

Findings for negative teacher–student interaction were significantly different from zero ($d = .35$), suggesting that teachers provide more negative feedback to male than to female students. Once more, however, the results were heterogeneous, indicating that the effect size across studies varies more than one would expect due to chance. Although we could not test for moderators, it is likely that sex differences in negative teacher–student interactions are moderated by several factors. Taken together, our findings are in line with the empirical results that attempted to examine whether, why, and to what extent sex equity exists in the classroom. Although male and female students are treated differently, sex might be only one of many factors that define this differential treatment.

Theoretical Issues

It is important to understand the advantages and limitations of theoretical approaches that have been used to explain sex equity in the classroom, because theoretical approaches ultimately offer insight and solutions to this phenomenon. Two theoretical approaches have been used to explain sex inequity in the classroom. The first and most frequently used theoretical model is a cognitive process model or expectancy confirmation model that proposes that perceivers communicate expectations through behavior, which subsequently changes the behavior of the receiver. This approach advocates that teachers can learn to become aware of their sex-inequitable expectations to moderate their behavior toward male and female students and to create an optimal learning environment. Sadker and Sadker's (1982), *Sex Equity Handbook for Schools* not only offers exercises that help teachers become aware of sexist teaching practices, but also offers useful guidelines, as well as teaching lessons for nonsexist teaching practices. Although this approach helps us understand the cognitive processes that shape sex inequity in the classroom, this approach also advocates a somewhat static view of the social interaction process, because it fails to take into account the active, participatory role of the receiver (see Darley & Fazio, 1980). Of course, elementary school children do not possess the comprehensive cognitive abilities to actively shape others' perceptions of them through their behavior. Nevertheless, elementary school children certainly have the cognitive ability to grasp sex-specific behaviors and attitudes (Bem, 1984).

The powerful force of sex typing is further highlighted in the second theoretical approach, the developmental approach, which examines the ways children adopt behaviors and roles that identify them as men or women. Two developmental approaches, social learning theories and cognitive developmental theories, are frequently used to explain how people learn to identify with one sex. Social learning theories suggest that children behave in sex-typical ways for the simplest of possible reasons: They are rewarded if they do so and punished if they do not (see Mischel, 1970). In general, children learn what they are supposed to do as boys and girls by imitating parents, peers, and teachers. Whereas social learning theories emphasize what boys and girls must do to fit their roles as men and women, cognitive developmental theories of sex typing focus on children's understanding of sex roles (Kohlberg, 1966). In line with the cognitive developmental approach, children learn over the course of the first 6 years to adopt what has commonly been referred to as *sex constancy*—the recognition that being male or female is irrevocable (Gleitman, 1991; Maccoby, 1966). What we learn from this approach is that teachers, and particularly elementary school teachers, have a significant influence on substantiating the sex constancy of a child. Teachers can seize the opportunity to help children through the confusion of adopting a specific sex role.

Whereas the cognitive process approach emphasizes that people impose sex-typed schemas on human behavior and assert that sex differences lie in the eye of the beholder, the two developmental approaches focus on the acquisition of sex roles. A third theoretical model, the interactive model, integrates these approaches and is particularly useful for the investigation of communicative processes, because it focuses on the display of sex-typed behavior, rather than its perception and acquisition (Deaux & Major, 1987). Deaux and Major's (1987) interactive model of gender differences acknowledges the importance of biological, cognitive, and cultural influences on sex roles and suggests that more immediate factors, such as expectations and situational pressures, shape sex-typed behavior. Indeed, these factors are responsible for the diverse empirical research findings on sex equity in the classroom, including the results of our meta-analysis. In the center of this approach stand the perceiver and the receiver, who enter the interaction with their own gender-related schemas. Social interaction occurs in an environment that makes sex-related issues more or less salient, and is relevant for teacher–student interactions, because it highlights the importance of social interaction among the perceiver (the teacher) and the receiver (the student), and envisions interaction as process oriented and ongoing. In line with this interactive model, sex-related behavior becomes more flexible and situationally fluid.

This model also suggests that sex inequity might not be readily captured with categorical counts of observational coding systems, which seem to simplify the dynamics of social interaction. To code and subsequently analyze interaction, events have to be punctuated. However, this method ignores the dyadic process of the teacher–student interaction and does not examine its overall discursive nature. Examining student-initiated behavior is, of course, equally important, but to assume sex equity in the classroom based on frequency counts of interaction categories such as question asking and evaluative feedback seems to eradicate the interactive dynamic between teacher and student in the classroom.

There are also numerous methodological issues that contribute to the plethora of diverging research results. Cornelius et al. (1990) argued that studies examining teacher–student interactions have largely relied on different methodology and they suggested that inconsistencies in results concerning sex differences most commonly occur when methodological dissimilarities exist across studies. Furthermore, numerous confounding factors influence the analysis of observational data. The number of times a single class was observed, the overall number of classes that were observed, whether coders were trained, whether interactions were coded from a videotape, as well as volunteer bias of teachers who agree to be observed are all factors that influence the outcome of an empirical study. In addition, statistical decisions have not been consistent across studies. For instance, several studies computed relevant statistics using student sample size to calculate the degrees of freedom (e.g., Cornbleth & Korth, 1978), whereas others used teacher sample size. These issues might contribute to the diverse results of empirical studies on sex equity in the classroom.

In addition, there has been a considerable debate concerning the qualitative and quantitative magnitude of these gender differences. Cohen (1969) offered the following guidelines for interpreting average effect sizes: $d = .20$ reflects small effect sizes, whereas $d = .50$ and $d = .80$ reflect medium and large effect sizes, respectively. Following Cohen's guidelines, the average effect size for total interaction was small ($d = .17$), a result that is also reflected in many sex difference studies, including the meta-analysis conducted by Friedman (1989). For negative interaction, the effect size was small to moderate ($d = .35$). For positive interaction, the effect size was extremely small ($d = .05$) and was not significantly different from zero. Several researchers point to the shortcomings of quantitative research and its inability to examine the real-life dynamics of male and female interaction. Certainly, it can be argued that what men and women record on a self-reported survey or how men and women interact in the laboratory does not fully reflect real-life behavior. If this is the case, however, the studies used in this meta-analysis should have generated larger effect sizes, because the studies record real-life interactions that were coded by trained observers.

CONCLUSION

One of our core stereotypes is that women and men are different. Popular press articles further sustain this belief. The study of sex differences has been pervasive and has generated thousands of empirical studies and popular best-selling books, most of which exaggerate the differences between men and women. No doubt, empirical research on sex differences will continue. This review suggests that sex differences in teacher–student interactions are small to moderate and are moderated by numerous factors. Although we found that male students are the main recipients of total and negative interactions, this finding should not be exaggerated. Rather, our study supports empirical studies such as those by Cornelius et al. (1990), who suggested that the social context of the classroom as well as a slew of additional factors, such as the teacher's sex and race, and student behaviors, shape teacher–student interactions. Finally, a theoretical model, such as the interactive model forwarded by Deaux and Major (1987), can advance fruitful hypotheses to explore the richness of the social interactive process between teachers and students in U.S. classrooms.

REFERENCES

Altermatt, E. R., Jovanovic, J., & Perry, M. (1998). Bias or responsivity? Achievement-level effects on teachers' classroom questioning practices. *Journal of Educational Psychology, 90,* 516–527.

Arliss, L. P., & Borisoff, D. J. (2001). *Women and men communicating.* Prospect Heights, IL: Waveland.

Ayres, L. (1909). *Laggards in our schools.* New York: Russell Sage.

Bailey, S. M. (1993). The current status of gender equity research in American schools. *Educational Psychologist, 28,* 321–339.

Bank, B., Biddle, B., & Good, T. (1980). Sex roles, classroom instruction and reading achievement. *Journal of Educational Psychology, 72,* 119–132.

Becker, J. R. (1981). Differential treatment of females and males in mathematics classes. *Journal of Research in Mathematics Education, 12,* 40–53.

Bem, S. L. (1981). Gender schema theory: A cognitive account of sex typing. *Psychological Review, 88,* 354–364.

Bem, S. L. (1984). Androgyny and gender schema theory: A conceptual and empirical integration. In T. B. Sondregger (Ed.), *Nebraska Symposium on Motivation* (pp. 179–226). Lincoln: University of Nebraska Press.

Bledsoe, J. C. (1983). Sex differences in female teachers' approval and disapproval as related to their self-definition of sex role type. *Psychological Reports, 53,* 711–714.

Boersma. P. D., Gay, D., Jones, R. A., Morrison, L., & Remick, H. (1981). Sex differences in college student–teacher interactions: Fact or fantasy? *Sex Roles, 7,* 775–784.

Brady, K. L., & Eisler, R. M. (1999). Sex and gender in the college classroom: A quantitative analysis of faculty–student interactions and perceptions. *Journal of Educational Psychology, 91,* 127–145.

Brooks, V. R. (1982). Sex differences in student dominance behavior in female and male professors' classrooms. *Sex Roles, 8,* 683–690.

Brophy, J., & Good, T. (1974). *Teacher–student relationships: Causes and consequences.* New York: Holt, Rinehart, Winston.

Brown, A. H., Cervero, R. M., & Johnson-Bailey, J. (2000). Making the invisible visible: Race, gender, and teaching in adult education. *Adult Education Quarterly, 50,* 273–288.

Canada, K., & Pringle, R. (1995). The role of gender in college classroom interactions: A social context approach. *Sociology of Education, 68,* 161–186.

Chesterfield, R., & Enge, K. (1998). Gender, cognitive categorization, and classroom interaction patterns of Guatemalan teachers. *Human Organization, 57,* 108–116.

Cohen, J. (1969). *Statistical power analysis for the behavioral sciences.* New York: Academic.

Condravy, J., Skirboll, E., & Taylor, R. (1998). Faculty perceptions of classroom gender dynamics. *Women & Language, 21,* 18–27.

Constantinople, A., Cornelius, R., & Gray, J. (1988). The chilly climate: Fact or artifact? *Journal of Higher Education, 59,* 527–550.

Cooper, E., & Allen, M. (1998). A meta-analytic examination on the impact of student race on classroom interaction. *Communication Research Reports, 15,* 151–161.

Cornbleth, C., & Korth, W. (1978). Teacher perceptions and teacher–student interaction in integrated classrooms. *Journal of Experimental Education, 48,* 259–263.

Cornelius, R. R., Gray, J. M., & Constantinople, A. P. (1990). Student–faculty interaction in the college classroom. *Journal of Research and Development in Education, 23,* 189–197.

Croll, P. (1985). Teacher interaction with individual male and female pupils in junior-age classrooms. *Educational Research, 27,* 220–223.

Darley, J. M., & Fazio, R. H. (1980). Expectancy confirmation processes arising in the social interaction sequence. *American Psychologist, 35,* 867–881.

Deaux, K., & Major, B. (1987). Putting gender into context: An interactive model of gender-related behavior. *Psychological Review, 94,* 369–389.

Duffy, J., Warren, K., & Walsh, M. (2001). Classroom interactions: Gender of teacher, gender of student and classroom subject. *Sex Roles, 45,* 579–593.

Dweck, C., Davidson, W., Nelson, S., & Enna, B. (1978). Sex differences in learned helplessness: II. The contingencies of evaluative feedback in the classroom III: An experimental analysis. *Developmental Psychology, 14,* 268–276.

Ehrenberg, R. G., Goldhaber, D. D., & Brewer, D. J. (1995). Do teachers' race, gender, and ethnicity matter? Evidence from the National Educational Longitudinal Study of 1988. *Industrial and Labor Relations Review, 48,* 547–561.

Fagot, B. I. (1984). Teacher and peer reactions to boys' and girls' play styles. *Sex Roles, 11,* 691–702.

Freeman, H. R. (1994). Student evaluations of college instructors: Effects of type of course taught, instructor gender and gender role, and student gender. *Journal of Educational Psychology, 86,* 627–630.

French, J., & French P. (1984). Gender imbalances in the primary classroom. *Educational Research, 26,* 127–136.

Friedman, L. (1989). Mathematics and the gender gap: A meta-analysis of recent studies on sex differences in mathematical tasks. *Review of Educational Research, 2,* 19–42.

Gleitman, H. (1991). *Psychology* (3rd ed.). New York: Norton.

Good, T. L., Cooper, H. M., & Blakey, S. L. (1980). Classroom interaction as a function of teacher expectations, student sex, and time of year. *Journal of Educational Psychology, 72,* 378–385.

Good, T., Sikes, J., & Brophy, J. (1973). Effects of teacher sex and student sex on classroom interaction. *Journal of Educational Psychology, 65,* 74–87.

Goodwin, L. D., & Stevens, E. A. (1993). The influence of gender on university faculty members' perceptions of "good" teaching. *Journal of Higher Education, 64,* 166–185.

Hall, J. A., Braunwald, K. G., & Mroz, B. J. (1982). Gender, affect and influence in a teaching situation. *Journal of Personality and Social Psychology, 43,* 270–280.

Hall, R. M., & Sandler, B. R. (1982). *The classroom climate: A chilly one for women?* Project on the status and education of women. Washington, DC: Association of American Colleges.

Hall, R. M., & Sandler, B. R. (1984). *Out of the classroom: A chilly campus climate for women?* Washington, DC: Association of American Colleges.

Harris, M. B. (1976). The effects of sex, sex-stereotyped descriptions, and institutions on evaluations of teachers. *Sex Roles, 2,* 15–21.

Hechtman, S. B., & Rosenthal, R. (1991). Teacher gender and nonverbal behavior in the teaching of gender-stereotyped materials. *Journal of Applied Social Psychology, 21,* 446–459.

Heller, K. A., & Parsons, J. E. (1981). Sex differences in teachers' evaluative feedback and students' expectancies for success in mathematics. *Child Development, 52,* 1015–1019.

Hillman, S. B., & Davenport, G. G. (1978). Teacher–student interactions in desegregated schools. *Journal of Educational Psychology, 70,* 545–553.

Holmstrom, E. I., & Holmstrom, R. W. (1974). The plight of the woman doctoral student. *American Educational Research Journal, 11,* 1–17.

Hopf, D., & Hatzichristou, C. (1999). Teacher gender-related influences in Greek schools. *Educational Psychology, 69,* 1–18.

Hutchinson, L., & Beadle, M. (1992). Professors' communication styles: How they influence male and female seminar participants. *Teaching & Teacher Education, 8,* 405–418.

Illatov, Z. Z., & Shamai, S. (1998). Teacher–student classroom interactions: The influence of gender, academic dominance and teacher communication style. *Adolescence, 33,* 269–278.

Irvine, J. J. (1985). Teacher communication patterns as related to the race and sex of the student. *Journal of Educational Research, 6,* 338–345.

Irvine, J. J. (1986). Teacher–student interactions: Effects of student, race, sex, and grade level. *Journal of Educational Psychology, 78,* 14–21.

Jeter, J. T., & Davis, O. L. (1982). Differential classroom interaction in social studies as a function of differential expectations of pupil achievements. *Journal of Social Studies Research, 6,* 1–7.

Jones, M. G., & Wheatley, J. (1990). Gender differences in student–teacher interactions. *Journal of Research in Science Teaching, 27,* 861–874.

Karp, D. A., & Yoels, W. C. (1976). The college classroom: Some observations on the meanings of student participation. *Sociology and Social Research, 60,* 421–439.

Kelly, A. (1988). Sex stereotypes and school science: A three-year follow-up. *Educational Studies, 14,* 151–163.

Kenny, D. (1999). META: Meta-analysis easy to answer (Version II). Retrieved June 1, 2003 from http://users.rcn.com/dakenny/meta.htm

Kohlberg, L. (1966). A cognitive developmental analysis of children's sex-role concepts and attitudes. In E. E. Maccoby (Ed.), *The development of sex differences* (pp. 82–171). Stanford, CA; Stanford University Press.

Krupnick, C. G. (1985). Women and men in the classroom: Inequality and its remedies. *On Teaching and Learning, 1,* 18–25.

Leder, G. (1987). Teacher student interaction: A case study. *Educational Studies in Mathematics, 18,* 255–271.

Leinhardt, G., Seewald, A. M., & Engel, M. (1979). Learning what's taught: Sex differences in instruction. *Journal of Educational Psychology, 71,* 432–439.

Maccoby, E. E. (Ed.). (1966). *The development of sex differences.* Stanford, CA: Stanford University Press.

Martin, R. (1972). Student sex and behavior as determinants of the type and frequency of teacher–student contacts. *Journal of School Psychology, 10,* 339–346.

Merrett, F., & Wheldall, K. (1992). Teachers' use of praise and reprimands to boys and girls. *Educational Review, 44,* 73–79.

Merton, R. K. (1948). The self-fulfilling prophecy. *Antioch Review, 8,* 193–210.

Mischel, W. (1970). Sex-typing and socialization. In P. H. Mussen (Ed.), *Carmichael's manual of child development* (Vol. 1, pp. 3–72). New York: Wiley.

Morgan, C. (2001). The effects of negative managerial feedback on student motivation: implications for gender differences in teacher–student interactions. *Sex Roles, 44,* 513–535.

Morse, L. W., & Handley, H. M. (1985). Listening to adolescents: Gender differences in science classroom interaction. In L. C. Wilkinson & C. B. Marrett (Eds.), *Gender influences in classroom interaction* (pp. 37–54). Orlando, FL: Academic.

Pearson, J. C., & West, R. (1991). An initial investigation of the effects of gender on student questions in the classroom: Developing a descriptive base. *Communication Education, 40,* 22–32.

Peterson, P. L., & Fennema, E. (1985). Effective teaching, student engagement in classroom activities, and sex-related differences in learning mathematics. *American Educational Research Journal, 22,* 309–335.

Rickards, T., & Fisher, D. (1996). Associations between teacher–student interpersonal behavior, gender, cultural background and achievement. In *Proceedings of the Western Australian Institute for Educational Research Forum 1996.* Retrieved July 21, 2005 from http://education.curtin.edu.au/waier/forums/1996/rickards.html.

Rosenthal, R. (1974). *On the social psychology of the self-fulfilling prophecy: Further evidence for Pygmalion effects and their mediating mechanisms.* New York: Mss Modular.

Rosenthal, R., & Jacobson, L. (1968). *Pygmalion in the classroom.* New York: Holt, Rinehart & Winston.

Sadker, M., & Sadker, D. (1982). *Sex equity handbook for schools.* New York: Longman.

Sadker, M., & Sadker, D. (1985). Between teacher and student: Overcoming sex bias in classroom interaction. In M. Sadker & D. Sadker (Eds.), *Sex equity handbook for schools* (2nd ed., pp. 96-132). New York: Longman.

Sadker, M., & Sadker, D. (1994). *Failing at fairness: How America's schools cheat girls.* New York: Scribner.

Sadker, M., Sadker, D., Bauchner, J., & Hardekopf, C. (1984). *Observer's manual for IN-TERSECT: Post-secondary form interactions for sex equity in classroom teaching.* Unpublished manuscript, American University, Washington, DC.

Sandler, B. R., & Hall, R. (1986). *The campus climate revisited: Chilly for women faculty, administrators, and graduate students.* Washington, DC: Association of American Colleges.

Schroeder, D. S., & Mynatt, C. R. (1999). Graduate students' relationship with their male and female major professors. *Sex Roles, 40,* 393–420.

She, H. C. (2000). The interplay of a biology teacher's beliefs, teaching practices and gender-based student–teacher interaction. *Educational Research, 42,* 100–111.

Sikes, J. N. (1971). *Differential behavior of male and female teachers with male and female students.* Unpublished doctoral dissertation, University of Texas, Austin, TX.

Simpson, A. W., & Erickson, M. T. (1983). Teachers' verbal and nonverbal communication patterns as a function of teacher race, student gender, and student race. *American Educational Research Journal, 20,* 183–198.

Smith, D. C. (1989). Gender disparity in vocational education. *Southern Journal of Occupational Education, 3,* 23–33.

Smith, D. C. (1991). Classroom interaction and gender disparity in secondary vocational instruction. *Journal of Vocational Education Research, 16,* 35–48.

Smith, D. C. (1992). A description of classroom interaction and gender disparity in secondary business education instruction. *The Delta Pi Epsilon Journal, 4,* 183–193.

Spence, J. T., Helmreich, R. I., & Stapp, J. (1975). Ratings of self and peers on sex-role attributes and their relations to self-esteem and conceptions of masculinity and femininity. *Journal of Personality and Social Psychology, 32,* 29–39.

Stake, J. E., & Katz, J. F. (1982). Teacher–pupil relationships in the elementary school classroom: Teacher-gender and pupil gender differences. *American Educational Research Journal, 19,* 465–471.

Sternglanz, S. H., & Lyberger-Ficek, S. (1977). Sex-differences in student–teacher interactions in the college classroom. *Sex Roles, 3,* 345–352.

Weshner, M. C. (1975). *An investigation of teacher–student interaction contingencies through development of an observation instrument.* Unpublished doctoral dissertation, University of Georgia, Athens, GA.

Whyte, J. (1984). Observing sex stereotypes and interactions in the school lab and workshop. *Educational Review, 36,* 75–86.

Wilkinson, L. C., & Marrett, C. (Eds.). (1985). *Gender influences in classroom interaction.* Orlando, FL: Academic.

Worrall, N., & Tsarna, H. (1987). Teachers' reported practices toward girls and boys in science and languages. *British Journal of Educational Psychology, 57,* 300–312.

13

Communication Apprehension: Issues to Consider in the Classroom

John Bourhis
Missouri State University

Mike Allen
University of Wisconsin–Milwaukee

Isabelle Bauman
Missouri State University

Communication apprehension (CA) provides one reference to the anxiety or fear about communication, constituting a fundamental challenge for all classrooms. Scholars (Dwyer, 1998; McCroskey, 1977) feel that the level of CA felt by a student has implications for numerous educational issues. This chapter considers a number of meta-analyses examining the impact, implication, and various methods of remediation for CA. The term CA crops up in a multitude of ways when considering the various manifestations of the fear about communication. In theater, the fear of performance or evaluation is referred to as stage fright. Musical instructors refer to the fear of performance or "performance anxiety" as that emotional reaction that interferes with recitals. Athletes call the feeling having butterflies in the stomach before a competition. Interpersonal communication scholars often refer to the issues of CA by calling it shyness or reticence. Clinical psychologists label the experience a phobia or social anxiety and PsychINFO uses the heading

"Fear of Public Speaking," as a keyword to index published information. Whatever the context or genesis, the issue of a person feeling anxiety about the act of communication appears universal and crosses culture and context. For the purposes of this chapter, CA is used to denote the family of terms represented by that general fear. The issues of CA are probably among the oldest issues to which social scientific research was applied in the discipline (Knower, 1937). The fear about communication and the conquering of that anxiety represents one of the fundamental goals or objectives for any skill-based communication course, but the implications of this anxiety extend to many other arenas across the curriculum.

Fears about the act of communicating in the classroom are not unwarranted. Communication in the classroom is often associated with fulfilling an assignment (proofs in geometry, book reports, speeches, reciting a passage aloud during reading instruction) subject to evaluation at both a social and academic level. Not only is communication an expected and common part of the classroom, communication is often the basis for the evaluations an instructor makes about a student. Anxiety about such communication events, both to protect a grade and not to appear to the teacher or other students as "stupid," makes communicating in a classroom an anxiety-producing event. The emotional reaction to the communication episode or event reflects an underlying fear about the possibility of failure or negative labeling that may result from a lack of adequate performance.

A central consideration of instruction should be how to include or assist those students who, for whatever reason, will not seek assistance or participation in the educational setting. This chapter argues that CA is associated with general academic success, as well as success in communication performance courses. Given the negative feelings associated with anxiety and the demonstration of negative consequences for that feeling, communication scholars need to be at the forefront of finding effective means of remediation. A central goal of communication scholarship should involve the identification, development, and application of methods of reducing the levels of CA experienced by persons. This process must begin early, because the meta-analyses on educational success find relationships as early as the first grade. Considering the possibility that such effects are cumulative across the educational life span, the need for remediation to reduce levels of anxiety felt about communicating may require consideration at a very early stage of educational development.

MEASUREMENT ISSUES RELATING
TO COMMUNICATION APPREHENSION

State and Trait

One serious consideration is whether CA is a trait or state. A *trait* is an enduring personality characteristic that goes across situations and tends to be stable (Hewes & Haight, 1980). A *state* is a feeling that is more situational and lacks the level of cross-situational consistency of a trait, and the feeling or reaction is far less permanent and much more episodic (McCroskey, 1982). Although several types of communication situations exist, data indicate a high correlation across situations for the level of anxiety that a person experiences (Levine & McCroskey, 1990). However, this consistency occurs across a multitude of situations that, although related, are independent and identifiable. The argument that there exists a set of underlying parameters with regards to a potential facet structure (or Guttmann simplex; for arguments about this, see Bell, 1986) does not receive support in the Levine and McCroskey (1990) analysis. What that analysis indicates is that the various situations (dyadic, group, interpersonal, and public), although correlated, represent separate but related anxieties, viewed from a trait perspective.

A state, by contrast to a trait, is a feature that is specific to a situation and changes over time, which may or may not reoccur depending on the particular context involved. A central issue is whether the feelings of anxiety are simply a function of a particular circumstance and a combination of unique characteristics or whether the feeling of anxiety is something that goes across situations and extends longitudinally. The difference between a state or trait characterization has implications for the expectation of whether the anxiety is permanent or not and whether the expectation should be that the fear extends across situations. A state focuses more on the identification of specific cues that vary and the relationship of those cues to the anxious feelings.

A meta-analysis that examines the correlation between state and trait measures of CA was conducted by Booth-Butterfield (1989). The results of the comparison demonstrate a high correlation between state and trait measures of CA (average $r = .70$); indicating that there exists a high correlation in terms of measuring the existence of the anxiety. Essentially, the type of self-report measurement device employed did not differentiate much between state or trait measures. The finding becomes problematic for those arguing for a trait or state approach as a fundamental conceptualization to CA. The high correlation indicates a great deal of consistency in the measurement. The problem is that state measures should not generate that high level of consistency. The argument may be for acceptance of the trait measures because a high correlation across situations would indicate consistency with that approach. However, as demonstrated later, this trait is subject to change or modification on the basis of remediation techniques. Fundamental to trait theories is the assumption of permanence. If a trait can be changed and modified with a few hours of intervention, the expectation of permanence is challenged.

One alternative to the state and trait approach to handling CA is to treat CA as a phobia. Essentially, a phobia is some type of fear that a person has about some stimulus. The fear is generally considered "unreasoned" in the sense that the fear is something that can be conquered or reduced as a result of appropriate intervention and is not something that is beyond control. The level of ingratiation of the fear is such that the type of approach necessary to reduce the fear is not particularly large (when compared to other conditions like depression, schizophrenia, or other much more severe psychological conditions). A fear can be generalized across a variety of circumstances (fear of heights can apply to a ladder, high window, steep stairway, etc.) as well as to a limited set of circumstances. The genesis or origin of the fear could be a variety of sources; intervention techniques reduce the connection between the event and the anxiety that the person feels. The next section considers the operationalization of particular measures and the relationship to the belief in the origin and manifestation of the fear.

Physiological and Psychological Issues

Principally, three methods of assessing CA exist: (a) self-report, (b) observer report, and (c) physiological measures. Each measurement approach examines a particular aspect of the issues dealing with the anxiety felt by an individual. The assumption of anxiety is that a person is self-aware of the anxiety and the cause (necessary for self-report), that the anxiety manifests itself in behavioral routines (observable actions), and that, finally, the anxiety will create various measurable physiological reactions that can be assessed using some type of device (changes in heart rate, blood pressure, galvanic skin response, etc.). The examination is to what degree the various measures are in agreement when considering the levels of anxiety due to communication situations. The question is whether the three types of measurement are consistent, because if there is fundamental disagreement among types of devices, the results of any meta-analysis may simply reflect an artifact of the particular measurement device and not necessarily the underlying construct.

Self-report measures ask a person to provide a response to some type of verbal measure. A person essentially indicates the level of fear associated with communication episodes (McCroskey, 1984). The range of self-report measures covers the simple set of measures that include only a single item like a fear thermometer (Hayes & Marshall, 1984) to more inclusive and extensive measurement devices like the Personal Report of Communication Apprehension (O'Leary, 1988). Allen, Hunter, and Donohue (1989) listed 28 different self-report measures associated with the measurement of the family of CA issues just dealing with treatment. Broader and more extensive measurement reviews generate a wide range of self-report measures (Daly, 1978; McCroskey, 1977, 1984; O'Leary, 1988). The construct continues to expand with new measures being developed to measure different aspects of the issues or situations: (a) apprehension in employment interviews (Ayres, Ayres, & Sharp, 1993), (b) compulsion to talk—talkaholism (McCroskey &

Richmond, 1993), (c) intercultural and interethnic CA (Neuliep & McCroskey, 1997), (d) intercultural willingness to communicate scale (Kassing, 1997), and (e) fear of talking with a physician (Richmond, Heisel, Smith, & McCroskey, 1998).

Observer measures assume that the outcome of the anxiety or fear presents a number of observable outcomes. CA should manifest a number of observable behaviors, including a quaking voice, shaking hands, uncertainty in the voice, and questioning about the effectiveness and comfort with delivering the message (grooming behaviors, scratching, rubbing of the legs, pacing back and forth). The physical and vocal manifestations of the fear are such that most observers can readily identify the person's level of anxiety. Mulac and Wiemann (1984) outlined a variety of measures associated with the use of observers to document and verify the existence of the level of CA. The two most frequently used measures are usually some form of behavioral checklist or anxiety scale (Allen, 1989). The behavioral checklist has a list of behaviors for which the observer rates the degree of presence; the sum of the scores is used to indicate the level of anxiety felt by the individual. The anxiety scale is a more holistic assessment of the issues of behavior and has the observer rate the overall level of anxiety manifested. The move to use observer-based measures stems from issues about the accuracy of self-report data (Wilson & Nisbett, 1978).

Physiological measures involve the use of machines to record and evaluate changes in bodily functions as a result of the anxiety (Beatty, 1984). Anxiety is presumed to create various physiological changes, such as elevated blood pressure, increased respiration, increased heart rate, and more palmar sweat. The results of anxiety are related to physiological changes as the emotional state of the individual changes in response to the stimulus. An argument has been made to move CA beyond the social to the biological (Beatty, McCroskey, & Heisel, 1998). The current meta-analytic evidence (Beatty, Heisel, Hall, Levine, & LaFrance, 2002) on the study of twins does demonstrate a heritability for social anxiety (effect size = .65). The current findings indicate the need to consider the issues of biology as part of the construct of CA.

The only meta-analysis considering measurement issues across all three techniques considers the issues dealing with treatment for CA (Allen, 1989). The analysis finds no interaction effects across the three different measures of CA. Essentially, although the mean level of change was different based on the particulars of the measurement device, the rank order of the particular instruments in terms of measuring the effectiveness of treatments remained the same. This means that the relative importance of the various treatments in reducing the level of anxiety felt by the speakers did not differ based on the particular type of measurement device employed in the investigation. One interpretation of this issue of treatment (Beatty et al.,

2002) is that the need to expand biological explanations may be required because the therapies assume too much of a social learning model (this aspect receives much attention later).

The Broad Appeal of the Construct

The construct has very broad and nearly universal appeal. Most communication courses that deal with skills will involve some reference to the potential family of conceptual terms that are related to the issues in the desire of persons to avoid communication situations. Whether one is examining interpersonal (shyness, reticence, dating anxiety) or more public settings (fear of public speaking, stage fright), the construct appears in virtually every part of the communication literature. The need is to determine whether the fundamental issues of CA are such that the setting of the anxiety simply reflects a particular manifestation of the underlying construct or the settings represent separate fears. The evidence is contradictory on that issue. The Booth-Butterfield (1989) meta-analysis indicates consistency, whereas the Levine and McCroskey (1990) measurement study indicates the need for separation. Given that the Levine and McCroskey study involved approximately 25,000 participants, the single study is so large that it provides a relatively firm foundation on which to build. Future research must determine methods and theoretical means to aggregate the apparent inconsistency to create a more fruitful course to understand the methodological issues.

EFFECTS OF COMMUNICATION APPREHENSION

A central consideration is what effects a high level of CA has on an individual. CA represents an anxiety felt by a person about a communication event. The question is what behavioral or other outcomes occur because the individual feels anxiety about the act of communication. The consequences of CA justify the need for remediation and the attention of the discipline as well as the categorization of CA as a barrier or a problem for persons trying to communicate to others.

Behavioral

The behavioral implications of high levels of CA involve what happens to the quality and duration of communication. The available meta-analysis demonstrates that high levels of CA are consistent with perception of a lower quality of communication as well as a diminished quantity of communication (Allen & Bourhis, 1996). The importance of this finding is the demonstration of a connection between the anxiety, largely a psychological evaluation, and the manifestation of that anxiety on observable behaviors.

The justification for the remediation techniques stems from the belief that the anxiety produces demonstrable (and negative) changes in behavior.

Not surprisingly, the Allen and Bourhis (1996) meta-analysis finds that persons with higher levels of CA are likely not to communicate as long as persons lower in levels of CA ($r = -.286$). A smaller effect exists for nonverbal behavior ($r = -.057$). The importance of nonverbal behavior to communication should not be underestimated; a meta-analysis of this factor finds that 33% of meaning is attributed on the basis of nonverbal behavior (Philpott, 1983). However, the issue of quantity does not address the quality of communication. For example, a body movement could be distracting and not enhance the quality of the message, so the overall quantity may be reduced but a larger effect could be observed for a reduction in nonverbal communication quality.

If a person feels anxious about the process or act of communicating, the desire not to communicate would reduce the amount or duration of communication. In a classroom context, when assignments have an oral component or requirement, the student may likely be communicating less in duration. Clearly, the desire to avoid communication is evident in the reduction of the oral behavior. The qualitative diminishment in the perception of the behavior was evident as well. In the classroom, performance assignments generated less positive evaluations when the person was high in CA ($r = -.146$). This was not as negative as trained observers viewing communication behavior in other settings ($r = -.319$). The reduction in size may indicate that the course was partially successful in improving communication quality. Many performance courses seek to evaluate standardized behaviors and provide practice and training to improve achievement. Part of coping with anxiety is finding methods to overcome and improve, and the introduction of structures, either by using directions or through some type of psychological orientation, may improve the student's skills (Ayres & Hopf, 1993; Booth-Butterfield & Butterfield, 1986).

Cognitive

The cognitive impact of high levels of CA is the diminished effectiveness of the educational environment. Our assumption is that a child with a high level of CA will find educational processes less effective. Most educational techniques require or expect active participation on the part of the student. To a large degree, it is the interaction of a student with a teacher that permits the student to summon assistance or demonstrate competence.

Consider the manner in which such subjects as reading and mathematics are taught. Reading is often taught as a process where a passage or story is read and each student is assigned a portion to read aloud. Essentially, the pedagogy is establishing a public performance event that is highly stressful because the performance will be evaluated by the professional (instructor) as well as one's peers. The teaching of math is often associated with a person going to the board to solve or demonstrate the solution to a problem in a public presentation (often geometry and other advanced courses assign proofs for a kind of formal presentation). What on the surface may appear to be content matter unrelated to communication issues becomes teaching affected by the manner in which the material is communicated in the classroom. The impact of CA in the classroom should be the need for increased reflection about the process of communication in the classroom. Essentially, a student with a high level of anxiety about communication is placed in an environment where communication is an assumed skill necessary to complete the task. Given that persons with high levels of anxiety manifest behavior that is less in duration and evaluated as poorer in quality, the outcome in this educational setting is not positive.

The impact or association of CA with academic performance has been demonstrated in a meta-analysis (Bourhis & Allen, 1992). The overall correlation demonstrates a significant negative association between level of CA and cognitive performance ($r = -.118$). This correlation indicates that as CA levels increase, the performance of the student diminishes. Importantly, the meta-analysis found an average correlation indicating a negative association with measures of intelligence ($r = -.131$), overall grade point average and CA ($r = -.101$), grades in the particular course ($r = -.147$) ,and grades in assignments ($r = -.123$). The content of the course demonstrated the same level of consistency of the negative association: (a) math, $r = -072$; (b) English, $r = -.107$; and (c) reading, $r = -.160$. Overall, the battery of various measures demonstrates a consistent and negative correlation between cognitive performance and CA.

The findings indicate that the child with high levels of CA will have lower grades and simply develop less as a result of the anxiety. One important part of the Bourhis and Allen (1992) meta-analysis was the examination of elementary school children. Elementary school children show the same negative association ($r = -.142$) as other age groups. The impact of CA can be demonstrated at the very earliest ages in the educational system.

The findings overall suggest that CA has consequences across the curriculum and for all age groups. The impact of CA is particularly subtle because the effect would probably be cumulative across the life span of a K–12 student. The student who does not ask a question, participate in an exercise, present an argument, or read correctly may not only be labeled by the instructor, but may internalize feelings of inadequacy. The results may be a student who avoids various educational activities and opportunities due to the anxiety about communicating.

Intercultural Comparisons

An essential question is whether cultural factors change the level or expectation of CA felt by individuals. This question becomes important in a variety of contexts, particularly in diverse multicultural classrooms or when international students are attending a university (Bolls & Tan, 1996; Huett, Ayres, & Manvi, 1999). There is much research on issues of CA and the manifestation of that anxiety in a particular culture (Klopf & Cambra, 1979, 1980; Klopf, Ishii, & Cambra, 1979).

A comparison of the outcomes associated with various cultures begins to help us understand how the culture constructs social relations and the requirements of successful communication competence within that culture. Communication patterns differ from culture to culture in terms of the expected behaviors and manifestations of particular behaviors. Even within the same culture, groups may manifest different expectations when encountering members of a different group (Allen, Hecht, & Martin, 1996; Martin, Hecht, & Larkey, 1994). The learning of appropriate behaviors for a particular culture is a method of gaining competence (Bradford, Allen, & Beisser, 2000). The improvement of competence is one way of reducing the potential of anxiety by learning culturally appropriate methods of communication.

A summary of the existing research dealing with various cultures does exist (Bourhis, Tkachuk, & Allen, 1993). The comparison of various cultural groups provides a framework to discuss the issues of how the various anxieties manifest themselves across cultures. The question is how the various cultures array themselves on the feelings of CA. The meta-analysis demonstrates that, not surprisingly, many Asian cultures (Polynesian, Korean, Philippines, and Japanese) view themselves as most apprehensive about communication events. This is not surprising because a loss of face in a communication setting (involving events in front of other people) would create stress from the fear of the evaluation. U.S. participants test in the midrange of CA, but not as low as participants from cultures such as Australia, Norway, or Puerto Rico. Apparently, the fear of CA is viewed as less serious in those cultures.

The argument inherent in this approach is that the conceptualization of CA is universal. The particular manifestation of the anxiety, however, will differ from culture to culture. Culture, in our view, represents a system of shared symbols and conventions, the construction of appropriate communication norms (and the anxiety attached or associated with that norm) for the conduct of communication. One measure of cultural differences should be how CA manifests itself across the panoply of communication situations. The data analyses were not able to separate out the various situations (group, public, dyadic) and levels of communication to present a more complete explanation. Given the concerns expressed by Levine and McCroskey

(1990) about using only the overall scale, the need to address potential situational differences remains for future research and summary.

The findings indicate that cultures view themselves differently on the basis of the level of CA expressed. Whether these differences simply express the frequency or the importance of the behavior is unclear. Cultures simply may have fewer instances of particular communication events or view the importance of such events differently. The problem is that although the meta-analysis provides some interesting insight into the feelings of members of the culture about communication, the findings provide little descriptive understanding of why those feelings exist. Understanding the genesis of the feelings and what exists to reinforce or ameliorate those feelings requires further attention.

Interpersonal Issues

One consideration is whether CA, referred to as dating anxiety, is related to various problems associated with interpersonal communication and the ability to develop a relationship. The impact of such an association requires the potential for the schools to consider that students with high levels of dating anxiety (another type of CA) could be considered at risk and subject to remediation (Allen, Bourhis, Emmers-Sommer, & Sahlstein, 1998). The potential exists for a variety of additional considerations beyond the immediate classroom application.

The importance of CA is that it may interfere with the development of a male to form relationships with members of the opposite sex. The felt inhibition may mean that the man is unable to approach women and is afraid to be alone with a woman. Dating anxiety is usually treated by some form of skills training, where literally the man is taught how to go out and interact with a woman in a dyadic setting (Allen et al., 1998).

Indirectly, a meta-analysis of men convicted of sex crimes demonstrates a lower level of communicative competence than among normal males ($r = -.321$; Emmers-Sommer et al., 2004). A meta-analysis of the predictors of sexual coercion finds a path model that involves a number of issues of communication competence (Emmers-Sommer & Allen, 1999). The argument from this is that peoples unable to form functional relationships may turn to alternatives like pornography, which feed an unrealistic and antisocial view of the world. A meta-analysis of criminal sexual offenders indicates increased levels of sexual arousal matched to the crime ($r = .476$). When considering that convicted sexual offenders are more likely to use sexual materials prior to engaging in sex ($r = .234$), the evidence for a link between media consumption and action becomes more probable.

This analysis potentially indicates that the lack of social skills for heterosexual dating skills may create a potential risk. The result of the skills deficit may be a contributing factor in the development of dysfunctional and anti-social behavioral patterns. Early intervention and remediation of this communication skills deficit provides the potential to reduce a number of social outcomes.

CURES FOR COMMUNICATION APPREHENSION

CA represents a fundamental issue or barrier to the effectiveness of any classroom technique or procedure. Education often requires the active and willing participation of students to be effective. CA represents a fundamental barrier to the effectiveness of virtually any pedagogy by diminishing the willingness of the student to participate in the educational process. Anxiety about participation can be felt in any subject matter. Given that education carries with it a fear of evaluation, not only are the performance anxieties manifested in education, but the additional burdens of anxieties related to evaluation become relevant.

There exist three broad classes of techniques used to reduce the level of CA (Allen et al., 1989) felt by an individual: (a) skills training, (b) systematic desensitization, and (c) cognitive modification. Skills training refers to those techniques that believe that the anxiety felt about communication is the product of a person not being able to perform adequately due to a lack of knowledge and experience that would permit success (Kelly, 1984). Most public speaking classes would constitute efforts at skills training because the courses teach skills like research, outlining, organization, introductions, conclusions, gesture, use of voice, and so on. For example, practicing the speech would reduce the level of anxiety (Ayres, Schliesman, & Sonandré, 1998).

Systematic desensitization represents the process of an emotional connection or association between a stimulus and some type of reaction. The problem is that the stimulus, in this case a public speaking or other communication context, generates a negative emotional reaction on the part of the individual. The reaction often carries with it a great deal of physiological response related to dealing with fear or anxiety. The assumption of a curative comes from finding a method of generating an alternative emotional response to the situation (Paul, 1966). The term *systematic desensitization* simply describes the process of finding some method of creating a way to desensitize the person to the stimulus causing the fear.

Cognitive modification approaches view the problem of CA as one stemming from bad beliefs about the situation. A person who believes in failure will create and react in a manner that is consistent with failure. The cognitive modification approach essentially finds a way to take what are erroneous or bad beliefs and replace them with good beliefs (Ayres & Hopf, 1993). Many times cognitive modification techniques involve elements of visualization. Visualization is the process of having a person visualize desirable outcomes. By concentrating on making those outcomes a reality, the person visualizes and therefore believes in success. The result is the replacement of beliefs associated with failure with a new set of beliefs that provide the basis for the person to believe that he or she will be successful.

The resulting meta-analysis verifies that all three techniques successfully reduce the level of CA felt by an individual (Allen et al., 1989). This indicates that regardless of the method, the person participating in some form of CA reduction can expect to find an improvement. The effect does indicate that systematic desensitization and cognitive modification are more effective than skills training, but that employing skills training is effective.

The model that best describes the outcome is one of an additive effect. Taking the results of each technique, skills training ($r = .16$), systematic desensitization ($r = .27$), and cognitive modification ($r = .29$) will be most effective when all three techniques are added together, for a triple combination of therapy ($r = .55$). That means the effectiveness of each technique can be added to the effectiveness of another technique to reach increased levels of effectiveness. The effect is that a program can be implemented that will maximize effectiveness by combining all three methods. In fact, one suggestion might have a person self-select a treatment as appropriate (Dwyer, 2000).

Subsequent to the meta-analysis, Ayres, Hopf, and their associates spent a great deal of effort analyzing the impact of sequencing of the techniques and the relative effectiveness of the various approaches, particularly visualization as well as improving the procedure (e.g., Ayres, Heuett, & Sonandré, 1998; Ayres & Hopf, 1989, 1990, 1991, 1992). Eventually, these data, when summarized within a next-generation meta-analysis, offer the possibility of creating new insights and improving the effectiveness of existing approaches to CA reduction. The research program by Ayres represents the next step, going beyond demonstrating that a technique is effective to an examination of whether various forms or structures can be used to increase the effectiveness of the method.

The reticence approach that was pioneered at Pennsylvania State University was a part of the assessment (Phillips, 1968, 1977). The reticence program was effective in reducing the anxiety felt by the students in the public speaking program. The meta-analysis, by including data from the Penn State reticence program, provides validation for the validity and utility of using that program to reduce levels of anxiety. Similarly, subsequent to the meta-analysis, more research was conducted to expand the understanding of the method (Keaton, Kelly, & Finch, 2000; Kelly & Keaton, 1992; Kelly, Phillips, & Keaton, 1995).

As provided for earlier, the consistency among the various measures of CA indicates that the reduction techniques and the function of the model remain largely consistent across type of measurement (self-report, observer, or physiological; see the Allen, 1989, meta-analysis for the full report). Equally important, the particular self-report scale used to measure the impact of the improvement did little to alter the fundamental nature of the findings; which indicate that the improvements seem to be invariant with regard to the particular nature of the measurement employed to measure the change.

Various legal issues do exist for those persons implementing CA reduction as part of a course (Allen & Hunt, 1993; Booth-Butterfield & Cottone, 1991). We recommend that any program implementation be reviewed for possible legal issues and ramifications. However, these ramifications generally do not apply to classroom procedures and are more likely to apply to persons seeking to reduce CA as part of a consulting practice. Generally, the expectation should be that the remediation of CA would involve few, if any, legal complications. However, appropriate levels of awareness and professional caution should be exercised. In fact, it might be argued that failure to engage in some method of reduction is academically irresponsible given the known magnitude of the consequences and the relatively easy ability to effect improvement.

CONCLUSIONS

The impact of CA within the educational environment constitutes a factor that deserves continued attention, particularly for the basic course in college (Bourhis & Allen, 1993). The pedagogical practices in many educational settings expect and require a student to communicate both in interpersonal and public contexts. The conduct of most classrooms generates interaction at interpersonal, group, and public levels (this may not be a requirement in the future, as computer-assisted instruction and distance learning change the requirements of the classroom).

One consideration in the classroom is whether the use of videotapes, quite routine in the public speaking course, has any impact on the anxiety felt by the student. A meta-analytic summary (Bourhis & Allen, 1998) indicates that the use of videotapes has little impact ($r = -.006$) on the anxiety felt by the students in a classroom. The issues of giving a public speech probably dwarf the issues associated with the use of a camera and the videotaping of a speech. This information provides instructors with the ability to videotape students without having to be concerned with how the use of such technology is impacting on the performance of the student. The impact of being "camera shy" simply is not as large or as relevant as the fears associated with communication in general. This points out that although CA has a variety of influences on classroom issues, CA does not necessarily impact every pedagogical decision that an instructor makes.

The summary of the available research indicates that CA is associated with significant classroom impacts that require attention on the part of educators. The question is how the educational system can begin to handle an understanding of an individual's reaction to the most necessary and subtle aspect of the educational environment, the need to communicate. The pattern of classroom interaction may be changing with the introduction of technology and the potential reduction in student participation in pedagogy requiring public communication. This may permit students with more individual and less social learning styles a greater opportunity to develop and participate in the educational practices, consistent with the manner in which they learn.

Reducing the level of public communication required may provide one set of options, but another set of options would simply approach the issues as a need for remediation. Remediation, or implementing methods of reducing the level of anxiety experienced by a student, would provide a means of improvement that does not require fundamentally altering or enlarging the set of educational practices. Restructuring the learning environment may help the student in the classroom but handicap that person later when the requirements for communication skills become more important, as in employment.

The pervasiveness and impact of CA goes farther and is more encompassing than most persons probably realize. CA becomes a factor in virtually any course design as well as a possible barrier to effective instruction. The responsibility for the examination and remediation of this problem, in our view, should primarily lie with those interested in communication. Given the significant and demonstrable impact of this issue across the curriculum, culture, and over the course of a life span, CA represents one of the few communication issues that the discipline can and should take responsibility for in terms of research and application.

REFERENCES

Allen, M. (1989). A comparison of self-report, observer, and physiological assessments of public speaking anxiety reduction techniques using meta-analysis. *Communication Studies, 40,* 127–139.

Allen, M., & Bourhis, J. (1996). The relationship of communication apprehension to communication behavior: A meta-analysis. *Communication Quarterly, 44,* 214–226.

Allen, M., Bourhis, J., Emmers-Sommer, T., & Sahlstein, E. (1998). Reducing dating anxiety: A meta-analysis. *Communication Reports, 11,* 49–55.

Allen, M., D'Alessio, D., & Emmers-Sommer, T. (1999). Reactions of criminal sexual offenders to pornography: A meta-analytic summary. In M. Roloff (Ed.), *Communication yearbook 22* (pp. 139–169). Thousand Oaks, CA: Sage.

Allen, M., Hecht, M., & Martin, J. (1996). Examining the impact of culture social scientifically: Some suggestions from examining Martin, Hecht, and Larkey. *World Communication, 25,* 69–78.

Allen, M., & Hunt, S. (1993). Legal issues in the treatment of communication apprehension. *Journal of Applied Communication Research, 21,* 385–390.

Allen, M., Hunter, J., & Donohue, W. (1989). Meta-analysis of self-report data on the effectiveness of public speaking anxiety treatment techniques. *Communication Education, 38,* 54–76.

Ayres, J., Ayres, D., & Sharp, D. (1993). A progress report on the development of an instrument to measure communication apprehension in employment interviews. *Communication Research Reports, 10,* 87–92.

Ayres, J., Heuett, B., & Sonandré, D. (1998). Testing a refinement in an intervention for communication apprehension. *Communication Reports, 11,* 73–86.

Ayres, J., & Hopf, T. (1989). Visualization: Is it more than extra attention? *Communication Education, 38,* 1–5.

Ayres, J., & Hopf, T. (1990). The long-term effect of visualization in the classroom: A brief research report. *Communication Education, 39,* 75–87.

Ayres, J., & Hopf, T. (1991). Visualization: The next generation. *Communication Research Reports, 8,* 133–140.

Ayres, J., & Hopf, T. (1992). Visualization: Reducing speech anxiety and enhancing performance. *Communication Reports, 5,* 1–10.

Ayres, J., & Hopf, T. (1993). *Coping with speech anxiety.* Norwood, NJ: Ablex.

Ayres, J., Schliesman, T., & Sonandré, D. (1998). Practice makes perfect but does it help reduce communication apprehension? *Communication Research Reports, 15,* 170–179.

Beatty, M. (1984). Physiological assessment. In J. Daly & J. McCroskey (Eds.), *Avoiding communication: Shyness, reticence, and communication apprehension* (pp. 95–106). Beverly Hills, CA: Sage.

Beatty, M., Heisel, A., Hall, A., Levine, T., & LaFrance, B. (2002). What can we learn from the study of twins about genetic and environmental influences on interpersonal affiliation, aggressiveness, and social anxiety?: A meta-analytic study. *Communication Monographs, 69,* 1–18.

Beatty, M., McCroskey, J., & Heisel, A. (1998). Communication apprehension as temperamental expression: A communibiological paradigm. *Communication Monographs, 65,* 197–219.

Bell, R. (1986). The multivariate structure of communication avoidance. *Communication Monographs, 53,* 365–375.

Bolls, P., & Tan, A. (1996). Communication anxiety and teacher communication competence among Native American and Caucasian students. *Communication Research Reports, 13,* 205–213.

Booth-Butterfield, S. (1989). The relationship between state and trait communication anxiety. *Communication Research Reports, 6,* 19–25.

Booth-Butterfield, S., & Cottone, R. (1991). Ethical issues in the treatment of communication apprehension. *Communication Education, 40,* 172–179.

Bourhis, J., & Allen, M. (1992). Meta-analysis of the relationship between communication apprehension and cognitive performance. *Communication Education, 41,* 68–76.

Bourhis, J., & Allen, M. (1993). The needs of the apprehensive student. In L. Hugenberg, P. Gray, & D. Trank (Eds.), *Teaching and directing the basic communication course* (pp. 71–76). Dubuque, IA: Kendall/Hunt.

Bourhis, J., & Allen, M. (1998). The role of videotaped feedback in the instruction of public speaking: A quantitative synthesis of published empirical literature. *Communication Research Reports, 15,* 256–261.

Bourhis, J., Tkachuk, T., & Allen, M. (1993). *A comparison of and commentary on cross-cultural communication apprehension research: A preliminary assessment.* Paper presented at the annual meeting of the Speech Communication Association, Chicago.

Bradford, L., Allen, M., & Beisser, K. (2000). Meta-analysis of intercultural communication competence research. *World Communication, 29,* 28–51.

Daly, J. (1978). The assessment of social-communicative anxiety via self-reports: A comparison of measures. *Communication Monographs, 45,* 204–218.

Dwyer, K. (1998). *Conquer your speechfright: Learn how to overcome the nervousness of public speaking.* Fort Worth, TX: Harcourt Brace.

Dwyer, K. (2000). The multidimensional model: Teaching students to self-manage high communication apprehension by self-selecting treatments. *Communication Education, 49,* 72–81.

Emmers-Sommer, T., & Allen, M. (1999). Variables related to sexual coercion: A path model. *Journal of Social and Personal Relationships, 16,* 659–678.

Emmers-Sommer, T., Allen, M., Bourhis, J., Sahlstein, E., Laskowski, K., Falato, W., et al. (2004). A meta-analysis of the relationship between social skills and sexual offenders. *Communication Reports.*

Hayes, B., & Marshall, W. (1984). Generalization of treatment effect in training public speakers. *Behavioral Research Therapy, 22,* 519–533.

Hewes, D., & Haight, L. (1980). Multiple-act criteria in the validation of communication traits. *Human Communication Research, 6,* 352–366.

Huett, B., Ayres, J., & Manvi, M. (1999). Imagery and public speaking apprehension in India. *Communication Research Reports, 16,* 131–137.

Kassing, J. (1997). Development of the intercultural willingness to communicate scale. *Communication Research Reports, 14,* 399–407.

Keaton, J., Kelly, L., & Finch, C. (2000). Effectiveness of the Penn State program in changing beliefs associated with reticence. *Communication Education, 49,* 134–145.

Kelly, L. (1984). Social skills training as a mode of treatment for social communication problems. In J. Daly & J. McCroskey (Eds.), *Avoiding communication* (pp. 189–208). Beverly Hills, CA: Sage.

Kelly, L., & Keaton, J. (1992). A test of the effectiveness of the Reticence Program at the Pennsylvania State University. *Communication Education, 41,* 361–374.

Kelly, L., Phillips, G., & Keaton, J. (1995). *Teaching people to speak well: Training and remediation of communication reticence.* Cresskill, NJ: Hampton.

Klopf, D., & Cambra, R. (1979). Communication apprehension among college students in America, Australia, Japan, and Korea. *Journal of Psychology, 102,* 27–31.

Klopf, D., & Cambra, R. (1980). Apprehension about speaking among college students in the Philippines. *Perceptual and Motor Skills, 80,* 51–58.

Klopf, D., Ishii, S., & Cambra, R. (1979). The fear of speaking and the fear of writing among Japanese college students. *Speech Education, 27,* 55–59.

Knower, F. (1937). A study of speech attitudes and adjustments. *Quarterly Journal of Speech, 23,* 130–203.

Levine, T., & McCroskey, J. (1990). Measuring trait communication apprehension: A test of rival measurement models of the PRCA-24. *Communication Monographs, 57,* 62–71.

Martin, J., Hecht, M., & Larkey, L. (1994). Conversational improvement strategies for interethnic communication: African American and European American perspectives. *Communication Monographs, 61,* 236–255.

McCroskey, J. (1977). Oral communication apprehension: A review of recent theory and research. *Human Communication Research, 4,* 78–96.

McCroskey, J. (1982). Oral communication apprehension: A reconceptualization. In M. Burgoon (Ed.), *Communication yearbook 6* (pp. 136–170). Beverly Hills, CA: Sage.

McCroskey, J. (1984). Self-report assessment. In J. Daly & J. McCroskey (Eds.), *Avoiding communication* (pp. 189–208). Beverly Hills, CA: Sage.

McCroskey, J., & Richmond, V. (1993). Identifying compulsive communicators: The talkaholic scale. *Communication Research Reports, 10,* 107–114.

Mulac, A., & Wiemann, J. (1984). Observer-perceived communication anxiety. In J. Daly & J. McCroskey (Eds.), *Avoiding communication* (pp. 107–124). Beverly Hills, CA: Sage.

Neuliep, J., & McCroskey, J. (1997). The development of intercultural and interethnic communication apprehension scales. *Communication Research Reports, 14,* 145–156.

O'Leary, M. (1988). Socially-based anxiety: A review of measures. In C. Tardy (Ed.), *A handbook for the study of human communication: Methods and instruments for observing, measuring, and assessing communication practices* (pp. 365–384). Norwood, NJ: Ablex.

Paul, G. (1966). *Insight versus desensitization in psychotherapy.* Stanford, CA: Stanford University Press.

Phillips, G. (1968). Reticence: Pathology of the normal speaker. *Speech Monographs, 35,* 39–49.

Phillips, G. (1977). Rhetoritherapy versus the medical model: Dealing with reticence. *Communication Education, 26,* 34–43.

Philpott, J. (1983). *The relative contribution of meaning of verbal and nonverbal channels of communication: A meta-analysis.* Unpublished master's thesis, University of Nebraska, Lincoln, NE.

Richmond, V., Heisel, A., Smith, R., & McCroskey, J. (1998). The impact of communication apprehension and fear of talking with a physician and perceived medical outcomes. *Communication Research, 15,* 344–353.

Wilson, T., & Nisbett, R. (1978). The accuracy of verbal reports about the effects of stimuli on evaluations and behavior. *Social Psychology, 41,* 118–131.

14

Comparing Distance Education to Face-to-Face Methods of Education

Mike Allen
University of Wisconsin–Milwaukee

John Bourhis
Missouri State University

Edward Mabry
Nancy A. Burrell
C. Erik Timmerman
University of Wisconsin–Milwaukee

The increased use of technology to substitute for traditional face-to-face in-struction continues to impact on higher education in the United States and throughout the world. This chapter considers three comparisons of face-to-face (traditional or F2F) education pedagogy versus distance learning (DL). We define DL techniques as those learning techniques where no expectation that the learner and teacher will be physically copresent exists during the instruction. The comparison made in the chapter of DL is to F2F where the expectation is that the learner and teacher meet simultaneously in the same location. This chapter does not consider the issues of use of technology in the classroom or computer-assisted instruction (that comparison occurs in Timmerman, chap. 6, this volume). This comparison does not involve the addition of computers or other online instructional methods, but rather the substitution or replacement of one educational practice with another. The guiding question is the ability of DL techniques to attain the same outcomes as F2F techniques of learning. Critics of moves toward an inclusion of DL into the curriculum have often voiced concern over the ability of the practice to achieve the same outcomes. This chapter does not include courses that blend a combination of F2F and DL approaches; these comparisons only consider environments solely administered in either a DL or F2F format.

This chapter examines three comparisons in that context: (a) whether performance changes when comparing the techniques, (b) whether student satisfaction with the education changes, and (c) whether a particular learning style is associated with a particular outcome for either method of instruction. Each outcome considers a potential issue facing educational practice. Performance, usually measured through tests, papers, or other graded or evaluated outcomes, examines whether classes perform differently based on the structure. Satisfaction considers how students evaluate the practice and the level of professionalism and value. Learning styles considers whether the particular approach a student brings to learning differentiates outcomes associated with DL or F2F practices.

A central question that considers the impact of the various outcomes of distance education is very important. The appropriateness of moves to include technology in a classroom provides an important question. However, DL offers the substitution of the traditional F2F co-present classroom with a pedagogical structure that requires both technological equipment as well as changes in the manner in which a course is constructed and taught. A reoccurring question is the degree to which the interaction in the classroom, for example, can be replicated in an online environment (Althaus, 1997).

The profound impact that technological innovations are having in all facets of education focuses attention on assessing changing modes and practices of instruction and the effects on learning and students. Understanding technologically driven differences between traditional classrooms and DL contexts is clearly appropriate (Althaus, 1997; Greene & Meek, 1998; McHenry & Bozik, 1995; Verduin & Clark, 1991; Whittington, 1987). Phipps and Merisotis (1999) concluded that current research, although rapidly accumulating, generally lacks systematic comparisons of factors that can differentiate traditional classroom and DL outcomes. This sentiment is also present in calls for more research on the consequences of using mediated communication technologies in instructional settings (Institute for Higher Education Policy, 2000; Kuehn, 1994).

DL represents a change in the fundamental orientation of the learning environment. Traditional classrooms and pedagogical practices involve physically copresent, F2F, instructor–learner relationships. Physically and socially immediate instructional contexts become transformed in DL through the technological intermediation of communication between teacher and students (Berge & Collins, 1995; Hiltz, 1986, 1994; Kuehn, 1994). Distance education is not a one-dimensional construct. DL refers to a wide range of pedagogical choices and instructional tools (Berge, 2001; Greene & Meek, 1998; Harasim, 1990). The diversity of possible DL formats is large even considering the fact that instructor and students will never be physically together (Benbunan-Fich & Hiltz, 1999; Hiltz, 1994). Therefore, any comparison of a DL environment to F2F instruction should consider the nature of the DL course and how various elements are either present or absent.

DL can be conducted using asynchronous (or time-independent) communication formats like postal mail correspondence, electronic mail (e-mail), and taped or digitally compressed video recordings. A second category of formats is labeled synchronous (or time-dependent) communication, like radio, television, telephone, closed-circuit television (CCTV), satellite broadcast television, and interactive video. When describing a distance education course, it is often necessary to provide a detailed explanation of the types of technology involved with its delivery and the procedural processes involved in applying technology to learning goals.

The value of distance education is still a controversial issue among educators. Hiltz (1986) demonstrated computer-mediated communication (CMC) technologies supporting online courses (a common form of DL) were perceived as an effective mode of instruction. However, Mottet's (2000) assessment of interactive television instruction indicated teachers' preexisting positive attitudes and experiences produced positive impressions of distance teaching, but teachers still perceived distance instruction negatively (even among generally approving teachers) because of the diminished contact with students and a loss of control over the classroom environment caused by technological intrusiveness.

Satisfaction With New Communication Technologies

Besides the issue of instructor satisfaction, an equally pressing question of whether students are relatively satisfied with the experiences in distance education exists (Whittington, 1987). In an observation of an interactive television distance education class, McHenry and Bozik (1995) noted substantial variability in classroom climates that evolved at different instructional sites. However, the variability did not appear to undermine students' relatively positive orientation toward the class. Thus, we must delve more deeply into the question of how students perceive the experience of distance education.

Early research dealing with user impressions of rudimentary audio and video teleconferencing technologies did not show strong user satisfaction compared with F2F communication (Fowler & Wackerbarth, 1980; Ryan, 1976; Williams, 1978). Yet, there were clear differences among these three modes of communication. Williams (1978), for example, noted that nearly 50% of the F2F meetings could be substituted for by using an audio or video conference with little negative reaction from participants. Ryan (1976) found that both videoconferencing and F2F communication modes were perceived as more aesthetically positive than audio conferencing. Both mediums, video and audio conferencing, were perceived as more "potent" communication channels than F2F communication. It is likely that the mediated channels in Ryan's (1976) study evoked a greater sense of social distance and formality (very common reactions to communication technology) even though they represented a somewhat narrower signal (or stimulus) bandwidth than F2F communication.

In addition to the perceptions of technologies, various human factors (e.g., personality, attitudes, skill) emerge to influence user reactions to communication technologies in distance education. Early research on CMC conferencing systems showed that user attitudes toward the technology, prior use experience, and skill positively affected user satisfaction with participating in computer conferencing (Kerr & Hiltz, 1982). Application of similar technologies to the university classroom (creating the so-called virtual classroom), with more experienced and extensively oriented students, produced strong relationships between evaluation attributes about the experience and learning outcomes (Hiltz, 1986). User experience played a similar role in Althaus's (1997) study of students involved in online electronic mail discussion groups used in supporting traditional classroom instruction. Students with more computer experience were more likely to use the online discussion groups and perceive them as beneficial. Cody, Dunn, Hoppin, and Wendt (1999) reported a similar connection between the extent of mentoring experiences used in training and subsequent use of the Internet in a group of elderly adult learners. Scott and Rockwell (1997) noted opposite trends for self-reported likelihood of use of new communication technologies and both computer apprehension and communication-bound apprehension. Higher scores on the anxiety measures were negatively correlated with technology usage preferences.

Clearly, both user and technological efficacy are involved in the success of new communication technologies when they are applied in learning contexts. A critical question is whether DL opportunities can provide a consistent level of satisfaction for students. One theoretical approach to the issues surrounding the diverse set of communication channels that comprise new communication technologies (e.g., e-mail, telephone/audio, interactive video) is the perceived message *richness* (complexity of message stimuli) contained in a mode of communication that delivers an intact message. This is the goal of media richness theory (Fulk, Steinfield, Schmitz, & Power, 1987). Media richness theory has been valuable in explaining the interplay between mediated messages and distance education effects.

Distance Learning and Instructional Effectiveness

There is evidence that communication technologies involved in DL have active effects on the learning process. Hackman and Walker (1990) noted that communication technology influences learning outcomes. Students participating in interactive television classes believed the classes were effective when technology worked well and did not impede the message channel. Human factors also influence the effectiveness of communication technologies used in distance education. Hiltz (1986) found experience and extensive orientations to class technologies among students participating in her virtual classroom produced strong correlations with learning outcomes. Althaus's (1997) study of students involved in his e-mail discussion groups also showed a connection between experience and participation. Students with more computer experience were more likely to use the groups and perceive them as beneficial to mastering course material.

The critical question is whether DL produces results equal to or better than traditional learning environments (Meriostis & Phipps, 1999). Benbunan-Fich and Hiltz (1999) concluded that CMC systems generally produced either moderate positive effects or no significant differences on learning outcomes compared to traditional modes of instruction. Their review included research not specifically designed to embrace distance learners but it is enlightening and suggestive. Specifically, with respect to the delivery of distance education, the nature of the communication context constructed to support a DL environment is critically important for understanding comparative outcomes either between traditional and DL instruction or between DL methods.

Distance Learning and Learning Style

The types and properties of communication channels elected for distance instruction comprise the most accessible variables for study. Communication channels incorporate one or more of three modes of expression: (a) audio, (b) video, or (c) written text. Communication channels create connectivity between sender and receiver, or teacher and learner. However, the connective properties of communication channels may be further defined by their *interactivity*, the capability of the channel to function similarly between sender and receiver. Thus, for example, receiving a televised lecture broadcast over a public television channel is roughly equivalent to hearing a radio broadcast of the same material delivered over public radio. Neither channel permits the receiver to employ it as a means of communicatively reacting to the sender. This constraint on interactivity can be contrasted with the interactivity of asynchronous e-mail, synchronous "chat" connections for exchanging textual messages in real-time interaction, or using a telephone connection. These and similar channels provide connectivity that allows a two-way flow of messages between sender and receiver.

Accounting for the communication context created by channel type and channel interactivity choices is indispensable in understanding how DL is accomplished. It is particularly important for understanding how learners adapt to the DL environment.

METHODS

This series of meta-analyses is an updated compilation of four existing meta-analyses (Allen, Bourhis et al., 2002; Allen et al., 2004; Allen, Timmermann, Bourhis, Mabry, & Burrell, 2002; Machtmes & Asher, 2000). The meta-analyses consider the issues of student satisfaction compared with traditional F2F instruction, student performance comparing DL to F2F instruction, and finally the relationship of learning styles of a student to the reported level of satisfaction with DL as well as course performance. Due to space and other limitations details of all analyses and methods are not presented. For additional analyses and details the reader is encouraged to obtain the original reports. Various compilations of existing literature served as a place to collect information for these reports (Russell, 1999; Stickell, 1963).

RESULTS

Performance

Performance refers to the outcomes associated in education with learning operationalized as grades or tests. A better reference might call these measures educational achievement rather than learning. The term *performance* indicates whether F2F or DL students differ on measures of outcomes associated with learning. A central question for DL is whether the performance of students changes depending on the pedagogical structure.

The overall effect illustrates only a small difference in performance between the two groups (see Table 14.1). The F2F group and the DL groups exhibit about the same level of performance (average $r = -.047$, $k = 54$, $N = 74,275$). The positive effect indicates a slight favoring of DL performance over F2F-type classes. The studies in this meta-analysis had to compare a traditional F2F version of a course with a DL version of the course. The performance measures reflect test scores or grades for the course.

TABLE 14.1
Outcomes Dealing With Student Performance

	Average r	k	N	χ^2
Overall	−.047	54	74,275	170.31*
Interaction				
Present	−.064	31	7,069	156.20*
Not present	−.042	21	3,641	37.96*
Course content				
Foreign language	−.218	3	2,238	1.08
Social science	−.085	15	1,417	34.58*
Natural science	.012	9	1,075	36.08*
Military	.183	3	210	4.01
Education	.002	18	2,475	12.25*
Across curriculum	−.036	3	2,377	7.06*

*$p < .05$.

One question about performance was whether it was impacted by the access to direct student-/teacher interaction. Interaction was defined as the ability of the students to simultaneously interact with an instructor in the DL environment. The presence of interaction did not change the average effect (average $r = -.064$) compared to studies in which interaction was not part of the design (average $r = -.042$). This indicates that the level of performance did not differ when comparing DL courses to F2F courses on the basis of interaction.

A central consideration is whether the content of the course moderates the observed effect. A mathematics course, it could be argued, is fundamentally different from a course in sociology, and therefore the expectations for how content is learned could be different. The findings were grouped according to the type of course content to examine whether differences in performance are related to the type of course or its content.

The examination of course content reveals some differences but the effects are mixed when considering the size of the available data pool. Instruction in foreign language found the most positive effect for DL courses (average $r = -.218$). However, the format of the DL courses in this investigation involved students in the United States interacting with foreign nationals whose native language was the one that they were learning. This impact of the advantage of DL indicates the positive contribution that technology can make to a particular form or content of instruction.

Social science courses (communication, political science, sociology, psychology, etc) demonstrate some positive effect for DL format (average $r = -.085$), as do the examinations that run across the curriculum (average $r = -.036$). The comparison involving education was essentially zero (average $r = .002$) as were the courses in the natural sciences, which included mathematics (average $r = .012$).

The only areas demonstrating a favoring of the F2F course learning was the military or Reserve Officer Training Course courses (average $r = .183$). Several of us are familiar with military educational issues and one of the outcomes sought, requiring F2F interaction, is the development of trust. One reason for military training that brings in officers from around the world and different branches of military service is to permit them to build interpersonal relationships that develop trust over the longer term. The issue of quality performance in the military goes beyond simply the score on a test to also involve the issues dealing with the need for participants to trust each other in settings requiring cooperation and a high level of personal risk. It remains to be seen whether that kind of relationship can develop using DL structures.

Satisfaction

The overall analysis (see Table 14.2) demonstrates that students have only a slight preference for live courses when compared to DL environments ($r = .031, k = 25, N = 4,702$). However, after removal of outliers, the difference in favor of live classrooms does become larger ($r = .090, k = 22, N = 3,866$) and the effect is homogenous. The reason that the original effect was much smaller was due to one study (Köymen, 1992) in which the effect favoring DL was large ($r = -.239$). An examination of the manuscript finds that the author reported that the university had a room that was overcrowded with poor lighting and inadequate heating and cooling. The students preferred DL because the quality of the distance education was viewed as a superior experience compared to the live overcrowded and unpleasant classroom. This study illustrates that although students do indicate a preference for the live classroom, that preference can be mitigated or even reversed if the live environment is less than optimal. The findings should therefore not be interpreted as a blanket statement of preference for one setting over another; instead, the findings should indicate a general sense of preference that is subject to changes in technology or in the live setting.

One consideration in pedagogical design is whether the structure of the course offering in terms of the channels of communication available (video, audio, and written) is used. The assumption is that video would include audio and written communication and that audio would include written communication. However, there were not enough studies using strictly audio communication to form a separate group. This comparison was restricted to

TABLE 14.2
Comparisons Involving Student Satisfaction

	Average r	k	N	χ^2
Overall	.031	25	4,702	138.29*
Removing outliers	.090	22	3,866	27.21
Channel of distance learning				
Video	−.006	23	4,277	89.81*
Print	.247	4	255	0.83
Interaction				
Audiovisual	.078	12	2,476	16.72
Limited	.049	3	421	2.00
None	.029	5	674	7.41

*$p < .05$.

written versus video. A comparison of F2F and DL courses using video illustrates a small correlation favoring the DL course (average $r = −.006, k = 23$, $N = 4,277$). The results indicate no difference between video DL and F2F courses in terms of student satisfaction. When considering the courses conducted entirely on the basis of written work, the F2F course demonstrates slightly higher levels of satisfaction (average $r = .247, k = 4, N = 255$). Not surprisingly, the addition of sensory information slightly increases the level of satisfaction reported. Students demonstrate a preference for video DL courses versus written courses compared to an F2F version of the same course. This finding provides support for those arguing that the level of sensory input is related to the level of student satisfaction with a particular course format.

One feature of DL courses is the degree to which there is interaction possible with the instructor. Interaction is defined as simultaneous message transmission. Examples include a live broadcast, a two-way audiovisual signal, or telephone or other audio or written interactive (often e-mail) system. This requires that the course be live to the student and not either entirely online or in some video format. One question is whether employing and incorporating such feedback improves the satisfaction with the course expressed by the student (Fulford & Zhang, 1993). The key to interaction is whether the inclusion of some form of interaction provides a social as opposed to a physical presence that creates a better relationship between student and instructor (Gunawardena & Zittle, 1997). Obviously, the requirement of simultaneous communication reduces the potential flexibility of a DL format when compared with something like a video, correspondence, or online format for instruction. There were only enough studies to conduct this examination using the courses that used a combination of video and audio. The studies were placed into three groups: (a) full and live interaction, where the students and instructor could communicate immediately and simultaneously; (b) limited interaction, where students and instructors could communicate either by a restricted means (telephone or computer) or were limited to a few times; and (c) where no direct interaction was provided for the course. The expectation would be that the most satisfying experience would be the full interaction, followed by the limited interaction and then the no interaction condition.

Contrary to the expectations there is a slight trend that indicates a greater difference between F2F and DL courses based on the level of channel and availability of information. The fully interactive audiovisual demonstrates the largest effect favoring F2F (average $r = .078, k = 12, N = 2,476$), followed by the limited interaction group (average $r = .049, k = 3, N = 421$) and then the no interaction group (average $r = .029, k = 5, N = 674$). The trend of effects indicates that the addition of information led to scores more favorable for the F2F version of the course.

Learning Styles

Learning styles refer to an individual difference model of education in which students have preferences and procedures for how material is acquired. The concern is that a change from an F2F class to a DL environment may make the environment less friendly to those whose learning styles require more direct social or personal interaction. At the same time, a move toward a DL environment permits students whose learning style is more technologically oriented or with a higher locus of internal control to maximize the advantage. The consideration of learning styles and the association with performance and satisfaction indicates that the outcomes of instruction can be maximized if the pedagogical structure of the course is matched to the individual learning style of the student. This finding would indicate the need for a greater sensitivity and diversity in educational format to maximize the positive impact of any educational program.

A person-centered or social educational style, where a person likes to work with individuals either one on one or in groups, reflects a preference for a more social or interactive learning environment. The F2F setting would work better and be preferred by this student because the learning process requires a great deal of social interaction. Literally, this student wants to see ideas bounced off people, and the relationship to verbal and nonverbal immediacy might be more direct or important for this student to learn. The result of the meta-analysis supports this conclusion (see Table 14.3). The relationship of social styles of learning to performance (average $r = .371$,

TABLE 14.3

Comparisons of Outcomes When Considering Learning Style of the Student

	Average r	k	N
Learning Styles		.	
Person centered	−.173	11	1,116
Locus of control	.148	9	1,475
Motivation	.367	9	806
Technological orientation	.221	5	872

$k = 3$, $N = 143$) indicates that F2F is the preferred outcome. The same finding, although the relationship is smaller, is replicated when student satisfaction scores are considered (average $r = .148$, $k = 6$, $N = 1,166$). The findings support an underlying relationship between outcomes of performance and satisfaction related to the pedagogical structure of the course.

The person with a high internal locus of control finds that DL is a preferable method of instruction. The person with a high internal locus of control prefers an environment that he or she can manipulate and possesses a high sense of internal drive. The person does not like to depend on others or want an environment where success is measured by some type of collaborative or interactive method. DL as a method should be preferred because the person can structure time and assignments to fit within a time table and framework that favors or re-creates the manner in which he or she learns best. Similarly, an F2F learning situation would minimize the sense of control that the person has over the situation. The findings are consistent with that expectation. Internal locus of control is associated with higher levels of satisfaction and performance (average $r = .148$, $k = 9$, $N = 1,475$). No difference was found between the satisfaction and performance measures, so the approaches were combined. The outcome indicates that DL approaches work better when the locus of control is related to features of the individual rather than relying on external cues or sources of motivation.

The technologically oriented person finds DL environments a better method of instruction than the F2F educational environment. The use of technological aids provides an incentive or attraction to the entire process of learning. DL, in most manifestations, requires the mastery of technology, particularly if some platform like Blackboard or Peoplesoft is used that requires the student to become proficient at the use of the technology as well as the material content of the course.

The general measure of motivation considered how the structure of the course (whether DL or F2F) was related to the felt level of motivation by the individual. The results indicate that persons with higher motivation perform better and are more satisfied with DL (average $r = .367, k = 9, N = 806$). Essentially, the explanation for much of the finding in this assessment of learning styles may be related to the underlying motivation that a student feels when participating in a course.

The final set of measures considers how the technological orientation of the individual is related to outcomes in the course. The issues of technological orientation consider the desire of the student to use technology as a means for learning and the anxiety felt about using technology as part of education. The results demonstrate that students with more positive orientations towards technology demonstrate higher levels of performance and are more satisfied with DL (average $r = .221, k = 5, N = 872$). The findings indicate that the orientation toward technology plays an important role in the ability of DL to generate positive outcomes. The findings also suggest that the anxiety a student has toward technology and equipment (computers for online classes specifically) should be a consideration. Attempts to reduce the anxiety felt about the use of technology should receive consideration and attention. Such efforts may make the experience and desirability of a DL experience more profitable for both the student and the institution.

Essentially, the success or performance as well as the satisfaction with the particular pedagogical structure should be reflected by the degree to which it "matches" the learning style. Persons who do better in a DL environment have individual learning styles, an internal locus of control, are motivated, and have a desire to use technology (as well as little anxiety about the use of machines). Conversely, the F2F context is better for a person with a social learning style, an external locus of control, and fear of or a desire to avoid the use of technology. The results indicate that rather than talking about the superiority of one setting for instruction over another, the focus should be on examining the individual learner and determining which learning environment is better suited in maximizing the outcomes sought through instruction.

CONCLUSIONS

The essential conclusions of the current meta-analyses demonstrate that there exists little difference in outcome when one considers the level of student satisfaction or performance between either courses taught in traditional F2F formats or by DL procedures. The outcomes of these two meta-analyses demonstrate that the expectation that DL is somehow different from traditional education appears unwarranted.

The most interesting finding comes to the issues of dealing with learning styles and the association with the particular method of instruction. There does exist a relationship between the learning style of the student and the satisfaction and performance in the course. Not surprisingly, the results indicate that students report higher levels of satisfaction when the particular learning style that they prefer matches the pedagogical structure used. The same finding is true for measurements involving issues of performance as well: Students perform better in educational environments where the structure of the instruction matches their learning style. This finding not only impacts the issues of DL, but F2F education as well. The finding indicates that either environment may need to make some modifications to provide a structure that is more effective as well as inclusive.

The findings indicate that rather than a broad argument in favor of or against distance education, the issue is the relationship of how the student learns to the particular structure of the educational material. Essentially, the conclusion would argue for a kind of match such that the learning style of the student should be matched to the appropriate educational format to maximize both student satisfaction and performance.

A central consideration is not simply the immediate outcomes, but the long-term implications of DL education. Do students stay in the program or have higher levels of attrition in this structure (Fjortoft, 1995, 1996)? Most educational programs are not simply a single course, but require the completion of an entire degree program to be considered fully successful. The issues of attrition and dropout rates require comparison, and attention should be given to ways of reducing the level of student dropout.

The arguments about a generalized difference on the basis of educational format appear unrealized. The findings of this connection also offer an explanation for issues in the use of Microsoft PowerPoint, chalkboards, overheads, self-paced, and other forms of instruction. Some students may be increased in learning effectiveness because the addition of some information is made in a format that is more readily accessible or consistent with how they learn. Some people may learn better in a more cooperative and visual environment, but that environment may diminish the learning of other students whose style is more individual and introspective.

One consideration is the attitude of faculty toward the inclusion or substitution of DL. In most institutions faculty governance and participation is required for the success of any program. The attitudes of faculty who participate, as well as those who do not participate, in DL require monitoring and consideration (Clark, 1993). The potential of research to demonstrate the comparability or even desirability of DL formats for students should play a role in the establishment of the need and value for such programs. Any educational innovation, particularly DL, that must go across the curriculum requires much participation and acceptance by many faculty.

DL offers a challenge to educational formats and thinking. The fundamental challenge is determining how best to incorporate this tool into the educational system. The problem of relying on a "one size fits all" format for instruction may not be maximizing the potential of individual students. Instead, the need may exist for some diagnosis and matching of pedagogical format to the ability of a student to achieve maximum success. This approach provides not only the ability for DL approaches to work in fulfilling educational missions. The admonition is that effective educational practice is going to require a combination of both F2F and DL approaches to maximize the potential of every student in higher education.

REFERENCES

Allen, M., Bourhis, J., Burrell, N., Mabry, E., Emmers-Sommer, T., Titsworth, S., et al. (2002). Comparing student satisfaction with distance education to traditional classrooms in higher education: A meta-analysis. *American Journal of Distance Education,* 16(2), 83–97.

Allen, M., Mabry, E., Mattrey, M., Bourhis, J., Titsworth, S., & Burrell, N. (2004). Evaluating the effectiveness of distance learning: A comparison using meta-analysis. *Journal of Communication,* 54, 402–420.

Allen, M., Timmermann, E., Bourhis, J., Mabry, E., & Burrell, N. (2002, November). *Distance education: A meta-analysis of how learning styles influence outcomes.* Paper presented at the annual meeting of the National Communication Association, New Orleans, LA.

Althaus, S. L. (1997). Computer-mediated communication in the university classroom: An experiment with on-line discussion. *Communication Education,* 46, 158–174.

Benbunan-Fich, R., & Hiltz, S. R. (1999). Educational applications of CMCS: Solving case studies through asynchronous learning networks. *Journal of Computer-Mediated Communication,* 4(3). Retrieved from http://www.ascusc.org/jcmc/vol4/issue3/benbunan-fich.html

Berge, Z. L. (Ed.). (2001). *Sustaining distance training: Integrating learning technologies into the fabric of the enterprise.* San Francisco: Jossey-Bass.

Berge, Z. L., & Collins, M. (Eds.). (1995). *Computer mediated communication and the online classroom.* Cresskill, NJ: Hampton.

Clark, T. (1993). Attitudes of higher education faculty toward distance education: A national survey. *American Journal of Distance Education,* 7, 19–33.

Cody, M. J., Dunn, D., Hoppin, S., & Wendt, P. (1999). Silver surfers: Training and evaluating Internet use among older adult learners. *Communication Education,* 48, 269–286.

Fjortoft, N. (1995, October). *Predicting persistence in distance learning programs.* Paper presented at the Mid-Western Educational Research Meeting, Chicago. (ERIC Document Reproduction Service No. ED 387 620)

Fjortoft, N. (1996). Persistence in a distance learning program: A case in pharmaceutical education. *American Journal of Distance Education,* 10, 39–48.

Fowler, G. D., & Wackerbarth, M. E. (1980). Audio teleconferencing versus face-to-face conferencing: A synthesis of the literature. *Western Journal of Speech Communication,* 44, 236–252.

Fulford, C., & Zhang, S. (1993). Perceptions of interaction: The critical predictor in distance education. *American Journal of Distance Education,* 7(3), 8–21.

Fulk, J., Steinfield, C., Schmitz, J., & Power, J. (1987). A social information processing model of media use in organizations. *Communication Research,* 14, 529–552.

Greene, B., & Meek, A. (1998). *Distance education in higher education institutions: Incidence, audiences, and plans to expand* (Rep. No. NCES–98–132). Washington, DC: U.S. Government Printing Office.

Gunawardena, C., & Zittle, F. (1997). Social presence as a predictor of satisfaction within a computer-mediated conferencing environment. *American Journal of Distance Education, 11*(3), 8–26.

Hackman, M. Z., & Walker, K. B. (1990). Instructional communication in the televised classroom: The effects of system design and teacher immediacy on student learning and satisfaction. *Communication Education, 39,* 196–206.

Harasim, L. (Ed.). (1990). *On-line education: Perspectives on a new medium.* New York: Praeger/Greenwood.

Hiltz, S. R. (1986). The "virtual classroom": Using computer-mediated communication for university teaching. *Journal of Communication, 36,* 95–104.

Hiltz, S. R. (1994). *The virtual classroom: Learning without limits via computer networks.* Norwood, NJ: Ablex.

Institute for Higher Education Policy. (2000). *Quality on the line: Benchmarks for success in Internet-based distance education.* Washington, DC: Institute for Higher Education Policy and National Education Association.

Kerr, E. B., & Hiltz, S. R. (1982). *Computer-mediated communication systems.* New York: Academic.

Köymen, U. (1992). Comparisons of learning and study strategies of traditional and open-learning-system students in Turkey. *Distance Education, 13,* 108–117.

Kuehn, S. A. (1994). Computer-mediated communication in instructional settings: A research agenda. *Communication Education, 43,* 171–183.

Machtmes, K., & Asher, J. (2000). A meta-analysis of the effectiveness of telecourses in distance education. *American Journal of Distance Education, 14*(1), 27–46.

McHenry, L., & Bozik, M. (1995). Communicating at a distance: A study of interaction in a distance education classroom. *Communication Education, 44,* 362–371.

Merisotis, J., & Phipps, R. (1999, May–June). What's the difference? Outcomes of distance vs. traditional classroom-based learning. *Change, 12,* 13–20.

Mottet, T. P. (2000). Interactive television instructors' perceptions of students' nonverbal responsiveness and their influence on distance education. *Communication Education, 49,* 146–164.

Phipps, R. A., & Merisotis, J. P. (1999). *What's the difference? A review of contemporary research on the effectiveness of distance learning in higher education.* Washington, DC: American Federation of Teachers and National Education Association.

Russell, T. (1999). *The no significant difference phenomenon.* Raleigh: Instructional Telecommunications, North Carolina State University.

Ryan, M. G. (1976). The influence of teleconferencing medium and status on participants' perception of the aestheticism, evaluation, privacy, potency, and activity of the medium. *Human Communication Research, 2,* 255–261.

Scott, C. R., & Rockwell, S. C. (1997). The effects of communication, writing, and technology apprehension on likelihood to use new communication technologies. *Communication Education, 46,* 44–62.

Stickell, D. (1963). *A critical review of the methodology and research comparing televised and face-to-face instruction.* Unpublished doctoral dissertation, Pennsylvania State University, State College, PA.

Verduin, J. R., & Clark, T. A. (1991). *Distance education: The foundations of effective practice.* San Francisco: Jossey-Bass.

Whittington, N. (1987). Is instructional television educationally effective? A research review. *American Journal of Distance Education, 1,* 47–57.

Williams, E. (1978). Teleconferencing: Social and psychological factors. *Journal of Communication, 28,* 125–131.

15

Family Care Versus Day Care: Effects On Children

Lindsay M. Timmerman
University of Wisconsin–Milwaukee

As mothers of young children increasingly are employed in the workforce and infants and toddlers are spending more time in nonfamilial care, research has increasingly focused on whether and how nonparental care affects the development of children. Currently, over 60% of mothers with children less than 3 years of age are either employed outside the home or looking for work (U.S. Department of Labor Women's Bureau, 2002). Of the mothers with children between 3 and 5 years of age, 70% are employed or looking for work. More than half of those children are being cared for on a regular basis by someone who is not a parent or grandparent (Coleman & Ganong, 2003).

Because infants and toddlers develop cognitive, emotional, and social skills so rapidly, they are considered rather vulnerable at their early age. Further, select studies have garnered sufficient public attention to raise questions about whether day care might compromise children's development (Cryer & Harms, 2000). Recently, the popular and scholarly press have intensified their focus on whether children who receive nonparental care are at risk for later attachment, cognitive, social, and emotional developmental problems (Barnett, 1995; Belsky, 1988; Clarke-Stewart, 1988; Colwell, Pettit, Meece, Bates, & Dodge, 2001; Gore Schiff, 2002; Lamb, 1996; Phillips, McCartney, & Scarr, 1987). Interestingly, the research is somewhat inconclusive about the effects of nonparental care on the development of children.

Many scholars have argued that day care is detrimental to children's development (Bates et al., 1994; Belsky, 1988; Karmaniola, Pierrehumbert, & Ramstein, 1994; Vandell & Corasaniti, 1990b), whereas others have found no effects or positive effects of extensive day care on the same variables (Broberg, Wessels, Lamb, & Hwang, 1997; Burchinal, Lee, & Ramey, 1989; Christian, Morrison, & Bryant, 1998; Field, 1991; Hegland & Rix, 1990; Macrae & Herbert-Jackson, 1976). The inconsistencies of previous research justify a quantitative review of the literature to answer the questions about the effects of nonparental care. The purpose of this chapter is to determine what effect nonparental care has on children's maternal attachment, as well as their social, cognitive, and emotional development.

Forms of Child Care

In this study, two forms of child care are compared. The first is referred to as *family care*, which is typically defined in the literature as care of a child by one or both of the parents, a relative, or a close friend. The care takes place in the child's home or the home of the friend or family member. This form of child care is typically unpaid.

Conversely, *day care* is typically defined as care of a child by a paid provider, such as a day care center employee, a nanny, a neighbor, or a relative. The care may take place in a home setting (the family's own home, or perhaps the caregiver's), or in a day care center. The child may receive care on his or her own, with one other child, or with many children. Day care facilities may be run by a church, a community organization, a school district, the government, or an individual entrepreneur. Further, day care may adhere to a curriculum that stresses education, social skills, play, or some combination of these.

Extensive care outside of the home is becoming commonplace for infants and toddlers in many countries (Cryer & Harms, 2000). By way of example, consider the National Institute of Child Health and Human Development (NICHD) Study of Early Child Care, a multisite longitudinal study comparing the effects of day care launched in 1991. By the time the 1,364 infants in the study were 4 months old, approximately three fourths of them were in some type of nonmaternal care (Caldwell, 1997). Approximately one third of children in day care attend at least 35 hours per week (Clarke-Stewart, Gruber, & Fitzgerald, 1994). As the rates of maternal employment and single motherhood continue to rise, it seems likely that the effects of day care, specifically with regard to various aspects of children's development, will remain a prevalent concern.

Maternal Attachment

Research on the relationship between child care and attachment is extensive and has generated a great deal of controversy, due to contradictory results (Blehar, 1974; Moskowitz, Schwarz, & Corsini, 1977; NICHD, 1997; Ragozin, 1980). Of particular interest to many scholars and mothers alike is the effect of separation from the mother on the attachment bond. According to attachment theory, separation from the primary caregiver (typically the mother) is profoundly and enduringly stressful to a child, and may disrupt the establishment of secure relationships, even in adulthood (Zeifman & Hazan, 1997). Results from studies in this area range widely, from reports that day care does not disrupt secure attachment (Burchinal, Bryant, Lee, & Ramey, 1992; Doyle, 1975; Howes, Rodning, Galluzzo, & Myers, 1988; NICHD, 1998), to evidence that children in day care are more likely to form insecure attachments with their mothers than will children in family care (Egeland & Hiester, 1995; Schwartz, 1983). A meta-analysis may resolve whether day care has a beneficial or detrimental effect on children's maternal attachment.

Social Development

In their first 3 years, children become "experts" in social interaction and relationship formation (Howes, 2000). They learn to role play, understand symbolic meaning, and create and maintain relationships with family members, peers, and teachers. Studies have shown that children in day care are more cooperative (Johnson, 1979), responsive and playful (Edwards, Logue, Loehr, & Roth, 1986; Rubenstein & Howes, 1979), exhibit more positive social behavior (Field, 1991; Hegland & Rix, 1990), and exhibit less social withdrawal (Egeland & Hiester, 1995) than children in family care. Other studies, however, have shown that time spent in day care is positively related to fussing, crying, and negative verbal interaction (Field, Masi, Goldstein, Perry, & Parl, 1988; Honig & Park, 1995). A third research team found no differences in play behavior when comparing children in family care and those in day care (Roopnarine & Lamb, 1980b).

The differences between children's social experiences at home versus day care may be especially marked for children who are in center-based care, because centers have more children, fewer caregivers per child, and more educational equipment and activities than are typical of family care arrangements. There are a tremendous number of social developmental variables that have been examined in day care research. Aside from those already mentioned, scholars also have explored differences in assertiveness, compliance, attention seeking, avoidance, interaction, touching behavior, information giving, and so on. Unfortunately, the results are inconclusive and a meta-analysis is needed to determine whether day care is beneficial or detrimental to children's social development.

Cognitive Development

Newborns begin their lives with rather humble intellect; however, in the first 2 years of life they develop an astonishing amount of knowledge about the world around them (DeLoache, 2000). Although there is an overwhelming amount of evidence indicating that the environment in which a child spends his or her prekindergarten years has an effect on learning and acquisition of language, among other intellectual skills, there is a great deal of discrepancy about whether family care or day care has a more positive effect on children's cognitive development. Some research indicates that family care positively impacts children's later cognitive performance (Vandell & Corasaniti, 1990a; Winett, Fuchs, Moffatt, & Nerviano, 1977). Other scholars have found the opposite, that day care enhances child learning as evidenced via performance later in school (Caughy, DiPietro, & Strobino, 1994; Chin-Quee & Scarr, 1994; Davies & Brember, 1997; Medcalf-Davenport, 1993; Robinson & Robinson, 1971). Still others have found virtually no difference in cognitive development between children in family care and those in day care (Broberg, Hwang, & Chace, 1993; Scarr & Thompson, 1994). Again, the findings in this area are difficult to interpret.

Emotional Development

The expression of emotion begins early in a child's life. By about the third year of life, children recognize common facial expressions, understand their meaning, and can identify what types of emotions may encompass the preceding event. In addition, they are learning how to regulate their emotions and aggressive behavior (Howes, 2000). Research on the effects of day care on a child's emotional development, however, yields inconsistent findings.

Whereas some studies have found that children in day care exhibit more aggressive behavior and more aggression (Field et al., 1988; NICHD, 2001), as well as more anxiety (Field et al., 1988), others have shown the opposite trend. Some scholars have found that children in family care were more aggressive (Hagekull & Bohlin, 1995) and hyperactive (Schwarz, 1983). Still others found no differences in emotional development between children in family care and those in day care (Burchinal, Ramey, Reid, & Jaccard, 1995; Thornburg, Pearl, Crompton, & Ispa, 1990).

After reviewing a portion of the relevant literature comparing effects of family care and day care on children's development, it is apparent that there is a substantial body of research from which to draw. Unfortunately, results are inconclusive and further analysis must be done to determine which is more beneficial: family care or day care. To that end, a meta-analysis was performed examining the effects of day care on maternal attachment, as well as on social, cognitive, and emotional development.

METHOD

Sample

A thorough search of the literature on the effects of day care was conducted. The relevant literature was obtained through a search of journals in communication, social psychology, sociology, psychiatry, and linguistics, as well as an examination of social science indexes, including ERIC (1967–December 2002) and PsycINFO (1967–December 2002). The keywords used for the search included *day care effects, child care effects, day care comparison, child care comparison*, and variations on these themes.

Five criteria were developed to determine whether a study would be included in the final analysis. Each study had to: (a) contain data from an original study, (b) define day care and family care in a manner consistent with the operational definitions given earlier, (c) examine one (or more) of the four dependent variables outlined earlier, (d) contain recoverable data, and (e) include one of the following study designs: day care versus family care, partial day care versus full day care, or a design that compared length of time in day care. Finally, it should be noted that data were not included from samples of "high-risk" children (i.e., children with a high risk of cognitive disability).

One hundred and twenty-three articles were located for this meta-analysis. Of these, 47 studies (45 published and 2 unpublished), ranging between the years of 1971 and 2001, were included in the data analysis. The remaining 76 articles were not included because they did not meet the criteria for inclusion. A total of 7,800 participants were included in the 47 studies. The mean age of the participants at the time of the study was 55.07 months ($SD = 33.77$ months). A list of these studies, along with their overall effect sizes and dependent variables, is provided in Table 15.1.

Coding the Studies

All studies were coded for one or more of the following dependent variables: maternal attachment, social development, cognitive development, and emotional development. In addition, three potential moderator variables were coded: type of day care (e.g., public vs. private), type of study (cross-sectional vs. longitudinal), and cultural context (i.e., was the study conducted inside or outside of the United States?).

Meta-Analysis Procedures

The procedure employed in this study involved transforming available summary statistics (i.e., means, standard deviations, correlations, t statistics, F

TABLE 15.1
Summary of Studies Included in the Analysis

Author(s)	Year	N	Overall Effect	Variables
Andersson	1992	105	−.469	cognitive
Bates et al.	1994	574	+.128	social
Blanchard & Main	1979	21	−.495	attachment, emotional
Blehar	1974	40	+.219	attachment
Broberg, Hwang, & Chace	1993	128	.000	cognitive
Broberg et al.	1997	69	−.269	cognitive
Burchinal et al.	1992	45	−.318	attachment
Burchinal, Lee, & Ramey	1989	60	−.264	cognitive
Burchinal et al.	1995	333	−.031	cognitive, emotional
Caughy, DiPietro, & Strobino	1994	789	−.092	cognitive
Chin-Quee & Scarr	1994	74	−.045	cognitive, social
Christian, Morrison, & Bryant	1998	424	−.247	cognitive
Clarke-Stewart, Gruber, & Fitzgerald	1994	150	−.213	cognitive, social
Colwell et al.	2001	438	−.010	emotional
Davies & Brember	1997	291	−.286	cognitive
Doyle	1975	24	−.034	cognitive, social, attachment
Edwards et al.	1986	38	−.228	social
Egeland & Hiester	1995	60	−.022	social, attachment, emotional
Fein, Gariboldi, & Boni	1993	46	−.255	social, emotional
Field	1991	56	−.178	cognitive, social, emotional
Field et al.	1988	71	+.068	cognitive, social, emotional
Hagekull & Bohlin	1995	123	−.230	emotional
Hegland & Rix	1990	32	−.126	social, emotional
Honig & Park	1995	105	+.193	social
Howes et al.	1988	88	−.045	attachment
Johnson	1979	30	+.048	social
Karmaniola, Pierrehumbert, & Ramstein	1994	55	+.275	cognitive

Author(s)	Year	N	Overall Effect	Variables
Lamb et al.	1988	84	−.020	social
Macrae & Herbert-Jackson	1976	16	−.728	cognitive, social
Medcalf-Davenport	1993	60	−.122	cognitive
Moskowitz, Schwarz, & Corsini	1977	24	−.067	attachment
NICHD	1997	520	+.002	attachment
NICHD	1998	294	.000	cognitive, social, attachment, emotional
NICHD	2001	534	−.009	social, emotional
Ragozin	1980	28	+.079	attachment
Robinson & Robinson	1971	11	−.078	cognitive
Roopnarine & Lamb	1980a	23	+.240	attachment, emotional
Roopnarine & Lamb	1980b	45	−.098	social, attachment
Rubenstein & Howes	1979	30	−.243	social
Scarr & Thompson	1994	427	.000	cognitive
Schwartz	1983	50	+.070	attachment
Schwarz	1983	53	+.068	cognitive, social, emotional
Schwarz, Krolick, & Strickland	1973	32	−.500	social, emotional
Thornburg et al.	1990	740	−.012	cognitive, social, emotional
Vandell & Corasaniti	1990a	236	+.044	cognitive, social, emotional
Vandell & Corasaniti	1990b	236	+.094	cognitive, social, emotional
Winett et al.	1977	88	+.035	cognitive

statistics) into correlations. A positive correlation (a randomly assigned designation) indicated that family care was more beneficial than day care. The correlations were weighted for sample size and averaged.

A chi-square test for homogeneity was then performed on the summary data. If the chi-square test was nonsignificant, the average correlation was considered to be an accurate true score estimate. If, however, the chi-square test was significant, alternative methods of determining the average correlation were performed.

RESULTS

Overall Effect

The average weighted effect size for the main overall effect of family care versus day care was $r = -.048$ ($k = 47, N = 7,800$). The negative effect size indicates that day care was slightly more beneficial than family care. The results of the homogeneity test were significant, $\chi^2(46, N = 7,800) = 139.85$, $p < .05$, indicating that the variation of effect sizes was not solely due to sampling error. After four outliers were removed (Andersson, 1992; Blanchard & Main, 1979; Macrae & Herbert-Jackson, 1976; Schwarz, Krolick, & Strickland, 1973), the average effect size was slightly smaller, $r = -.038$ ($k = 43, N = 7,626$), although the chi-square was still significant, $\chi^2(42, N = 7,626) = 105.46, p < .05$, indicating the likelihood of moderating variables. To assess the effect of family care versus day care on various aspects of children's development, separate analyses were performed on the aforementioned dependent variables: attachment to the mother, social development, cognitive development, and emotional development. Table 15.2 reports the summary statistics for overall effect size, as well as for each of the dependent variables.

Dependent Variables

Attachment to the Mother. Attachment was included in 13 studies, employing a total of 1,262 participants. The effect was $r = -.009$, and the vari-

TABLE 15.2
Summary of Results

Effect	k	N	r	χ^2
Overall	47	7,800	−.048	139.85*
Outliers removed	43	7,626	−.038	105.46*
Attachment	13	1,262	−.009	12.25
Social Development	23	3,560	+.026	73.54*
Outliers removed	20	3,428	+.023	35.05*
Cognitive development	24	4,790	−.088	86.49*
Outlier removed	23	4,774	−.086	81.99*
Emotional development	17	3,328	−.023	35.92*
Outliers removed	13	3,206	−.010	11.18

*$p < .05$.

ance was found to be trivial, $\chi^2(12, N = 1{,}262) = 12.25, p > .05$. The negative effect size indicates slightly more benefits to day care than family care for maternal attachment.

Social Development.   The average effect size for the effect of family care versus day care on social development was $r = +.026$ ($k = 23, N = 3{,}560$), indicating that family care has a slightly more beneficial effect than day care on social development. The results of the homogeneity test were significant, $\chi^2(22, N = 3{,}560) = 73.54, p < .05$. After removing three outliers (Lamb, Hwang, Broberg, & Bookstein, 1988; Macrae & Herbert-Jackson, 1976; Schwarz et al., 1973), the effect size was slightly smaller, $r = +.023$ ($k = 20$, $N = 3{,}428$), but the chi-square was still significant, $\chi^2(19, N = 3{,}428) = 35.05, p < .05$.

Cognitive Development.   There were 24 studies in the data set that examined cognitive development, including a total of 4,790 participants. The effect was $r = -.088$, $\chi^2(23, N = 4{,}790) = 86.49, p < .05$, indicating a significant amount of variance. One outlier was identified (Macrae & Herbert-Jackson, 1976), and without it the effect was $r = -.086$ ($k = 23, N = 4{,}774$). The results of the test for homogeneity were still significant, $\chi^2(22, N = 4{,}774) = 81.99, p < .05$. The results indicate that day care was slightly more beneficial for cognitive development than family care.

Emotional Development.   The effect for emotional development was $r = -$ ($k = 17, N = 3{,}328$). The results of the homogeneity test were significant, $\chi^2(16, N = 3{,}328) = 35.92, p < .05$. After removing four outliers (Blanchard & Main, 1979; Fein, Gariboldi, & Boni, 1993; Roopnarine & Lamb, 1980a; Schwarz et al., 1973), the effect size was slightly smaller, $r = -.010$ ($k = 13, N = 3{,}206$). Without the outliers, the sample was homogeneous, $\chi^2(12, N = 3{,}206) = 11.18, p > .05$. The negative effect size indicates that day care was slightly more beneficial than family care with respect to emotional development.

Moderator Variables

The significant results on several of the homogeneity tests already reported suggest that there are additional moderators to consider. As such, the moderating influences of the type of day care, type of study, and cultural context on the effect of family care versus day care were examined. Results are reported for each potential moderator next, as well as in Table 15.3.

Type of Day Care.   It is possible that different day care settings affect children's development in different ways. To determine whether the type

TABLE 15.3
Summary of Results for Potential Moderators

Effect	k	N	r	χ^2
College day care	4	122	−.177	2.64
Private day care	4	399	−.184	12.91*
Public federal day care	10	1,260	−.127	15.19
Cross-sectional studies	37	6,003	−.043	101.94*
Outliers removed	34	5,934	−.037	85.89*
Longitudinal studies	10	1,797	−.067	37.16*
Conducted within United States	36	6,712	−.029	86.97*
Outliers removed	33	6,643	−.023	70.05*
Conducted outside United States	11	1,088	−.170	34.19*

*$p < .05$.

of day care moderated the effect of family care versus day care on children's development, the effect sizes were calculated for college day care, private day care, and public federal-funded day care. The effect sizes for all three types of care were negative, indicating that each of these types of day care were more beneficial than home care. Private day care yielded the largest effect size, $r = -.184$ ($k = 4$, $N = 399$), and although the variance was found to be significant, $\chi^2(3, N = 399) = 12.91$, $p < .05$, there were no outliers identified. The effect for college day care was $r = -.177$ ($k = 4$, $N = 122$), and the variance was found to be trivial, $\chi^2(3, N = 122) = 2.64$, $p > .05$. The effect for public federal-funded day care was $r = -.127$ ($k = 10$, $N = 1,260$), and the variance was found to be trivial, $\chi^2(9, N = 1,260) = 15.19$, $p > .05$.

Type of Study. The importance of longitudinal research on day care effects has long been touted in the literature. To that end, cross-sectional studies were evaluated separately from longitudinal studies to determine whether the type of study moderated the effect of family care versus day care. The effect for cross-sectional studies was $r = -.043$ ($k = 37$, $N = 6,003$). The results of the homogeneity test were significant, $\chi^2(36, N = 6,003) = 101.94$, $p < .05$. After removing three outliers (Blanchard & Main, 1979; Macrae & Herbert-Jackson, 1976; Schwarz et al., 1973), the effect size was slightly smaller, $r = -.037$ ($k = 34$, $N = 5,934$), but the chi-square was still significant, $\chi^2(33, N = 5,934) = 85.89$, $p < .05$. The effect for longitudinal studies was $r = -.067$ ($k = 10$, $N = 1,797$), and although the variance was found to be significant, $\chi^2(9, N = 1,797) = 37.16$, $p < .05$, there were no outliers identified. The negative effect sizes indicate that in both types of studies, day care was more beneficial than home care.

Cultural Context.   It is possible that day care arrangements outside of the United States are different enough in nature and focus that they might affect children's development in different ways. To determine whether the cultural context moderated the effect of family care versus day care on children's development, the effect sizes were calculated for studies conducted within the United States and those conducted outside of the United States. The effect for the U.S. studies was $r = -.029$ ($k = 36, N = 6,712$), but the chi-square revealed a significant amount of variance, $\chi^2(35, N = 6,712) = 86.97$, $p < .05$. Three outliers were identified (Blanchard & Main, 1979; Macrae & Herbert-Jackson, 1976; Schwarz et al., 1973), and without them the effect was $r = -.023$ ($k = 33, N = 6,643$). The results of the test for homogeneity were still significant, $\chi^2(32, N = 6,643) = 70.05, p < .05$. The effect for non-U.S. studies was $r = -.170$ ($k = 11, N = 1,088$), and although the variance was found to be significant, $\chi^2(10, N = 1,088) = 34.19, p < .05$, there were no outliers identified. The negative effect sizes indicate that day care was more beneficial than home care in both U.S. and non-U.S. contexts.

DISCUSSION

Extant literature regarding the effects of family care versus day care on various aspects of children's development has produced conflicting results. In this investigation, results from 47 studies ($N = 7,800$) examining the effects of day care were subjected to meta-analysis. Overall, results indicated that day care was more beneficial than family care, although the effect size was extremely small. When looking at the dependent variables separately, day care was more beneficial than family care with respect to maternal attachment, cognitive development, and emotional development, whereas family care was more beneficial with respect to social development. Again, however, it should be noted that the individual effect sizes for these variables were very small.

When considering the possible moderators, including type of day care, type of study, and cultural context, day care was found to be more beneficial across the board. When examining college, private, and public federal day care settings, taking into account both cross-sectional and longitudinal designs, and whether inside or outside the United States, day care had a favorable effect on children's development. In no instance, however, did the effect size meet or exceed $\pm.20$, which indicates that the "favorable" results should be interpreted with extreme caution. Further, the prevalence of significant tests for homogeneity suggests that there are additional moderators left to uncover. Finally, in some cases the effect sizes were computed based on very small sample sizes (e.g., college day care, $k = 4, N = 122$), in which case the validity of the effect size is somewhat more questionable. Further analysis in this area is warranted.

Future Research

Although not examined in this chapter, quality of care is fast becoming a topic of interest in the day care literature. Quality was not coded for in this data set because too few studies addressed it, but more recent investigations show an increasing focus on variables related to quality of care (Burchinal et al., 2000; Kwan & Sylva, 2001; Lamb, 1996; Peisner- Feinberg et al., 2001; Sundell, 2000). As such, there are compelling reasons to conduct a meta-analysis on the effect of quality of care on children's development. It has been noted, specifically with respect to the NICHD Study of Early Child Care, that when child care factors are found to be significant, the ones most likely to be associated with child outcomes are those related to quality (Caldwell, 1997).

Quality of care is typically indexed via either structural or dynamic measures (Lamb, 1996). Structural measures comprise variables in the child care setting that might facilitate warm, enriching interaction. Examples of structural variables include caregiver-to-child ratios, group size, quality of the physical setting, level of caregiver education and training, and amount of caregiver experience. Dynamic measures are meant to assess the quality of the experiences provided for the child, such as the affective quality of interactions, level of caregiver sensitivity, and developmental appropriateness of activities. Although there are many instruments available to assess quality of care, there appears to be ample consensus about what constitutes high-quality care (Lamb, 1996). Future meta-analyses addressing quality of care may help to illuminate the effects of day care on children's development.

CONCLUSION

It is quite possible that family care and day care are more similar (with regard to these particular variables) than most scholars would have us believe. Each time a new study is published, the media relays the results to "family care parents" and "day care parents" everywhere. Because results are so often contradictory, these parents alternately feel guilty, then validated. In this investigation, very small effect sizes were uncovered, indicating that there are not substantial differences (likely not even noticeable differences) between day care and family care with respect to children's development. These results indicate that family care and day care have similar advantages and disadvantages; that both types of care are approximately equal in benefits. The findings of this investigation suggest that it is time to stop perpetuating the myth that day care is harmful for a child's development.

REFERENCES

References marked with an asterisk indicate studies included in the meta-analysis.

*Andersson, B.-E. (1992). Effects of day-care on cognitive and socioemotional competence of thirten-year-old Swedish schoolchildren. *Child Development, 63,* 20–36.

Barnett, W. S. (1995). Long-term effects of early childhood programs on cognitive and school outcomes. *The Future of Children, 5,* 25–50.

*Bates, J. E., Marvinney, D., Kelly, T., Dodge, K. A., Bennett, D. S., & Pettit, G. S. (1994). Child-care history and kindergarten adjustment. *Developmental Psychology, 30,* 690–700.

Belsky, J. (1988). The "effects" of infant day care reconsidered. *Early Childhood Research Quarterly, 3,* 235–272.

*Blanchard, M., & Main, M. (1979). Avoidance of the attachment figure and social-emotional adjustment in day-care infants. *Developmental Psychology, 15,* 445–446.

*Blehar, M. C. (1974). Anxious attachment and defensive reactions associated with day care. *Child Development, 45,* 683–692.

*Broberg, A. G., Hwang, C. P., & Chace, S. V. (1993, March). *Effects of day care on elementary school performance and adjustment.* Paper presented at the 60th anniversary meeting of the Society for Research in Child Development, New Orleans, LA. (ERIC Document Reproduction Service No. 360 052)

*Broberg, A. G., Wessels, H., Lamb, M. E., & Hwang, C. P. (1997). Effects of day care on the development of cognitive abilities in 8-year-olds: A longitudinal study. *Developmental Psychology, 33,* 62–69.

*Burchinal, M. R., Bryant, D. M., Lee, M. W., & Ramey, C. T. (1992). Early day care, infant–mother attachment, and maternal responsiveness in the infant's first year. *Early Childhood Research Quarterly, 7,* 383–396.

*Burchinal, M. R., Lee, M., & Ramey, C. (1989). Type of day-care and preschool intellectual development in disadvantaged children. *Child Development, 60,* 128–137.

Burchinal, M. R., Ramey, S. L., Reid, M. K., & Jaccard, J. (1995). Early child care experiences and their association with family and child characteristics during middle childhood. *Early Childhood Research Quarterly, 10,* 33–61.

Burchinal, M. R., Roberts, J. E., Riggins, R., Jr., Zeisel, S. A., Neebe, E., & Bryant, D. (2000). Relating quality of center-based child care to early cognitive and language development longitudinally. *Child Development, 71,* 339–357.

Caldwell, B. (1997). Child care research comes of age: The NICHD study of early child care. *Child Care Information Exchange, 118,* 35–39.

*Caughy, M. O., DiPietro, J. A., & Strobino, D. M. (1994). Day-care participation as a protective factor in the cognitive development of low-income children. *Child Development, 65,* 457–471.

*Chin-Quee, D. S., & Scarr, S. (1994). Lack of early child care effects on school-age children's social competence and academic achievement. *Early Development and Parenting, 3,* 103–112.

*Christian, K., Morrison, F. J., & Bryant, F. B. (1998). Predicting kindergarten academic skills: Interactions among child care, maternal education, and family literacy environments. *Early Childhood Research Quarterly, 13,* 501–521.

Clarke-Stewart, K. A. (1988). "The 'effects' of infant day care reconsidered" reconsidered: Risks for parents, children, and researchers. *Early Childhood Research Quarterly, 3,* 293–318.

*Clarke-Stewart, K. A., Gruber, C. P., & Fitzgerald, L. M. (1994). *Children at home and in day care.* Hillsdale, NJ: Lawrence Erlbaum Associates.

Coleman, M., & Ganong, L. (Eds.). (2003). *Points and counterpoints: Controversial relationship and family issues in the 21st century: An anthology.* Los Angeles: Roxbury.

*Colwell, M. J., Pettit, G. S., Meece, D., Bates, J. E., & Dodge, K. A. (2001). Cumulative risk and continuity in nonparental care from infancy to early adolescence. *Merrill-Palmer Quarterly, 47,* 207–234.

Cryer, D., & Harms, T. (Eds.). (2000). *Infants and toddlers in out-of-home care.* Baltimore: Brookes.

*Davies, J., & Brember, I. (1997). The effects of pre-school experience on reading attainment: A four year cross-sectional study. *Educational Psychology, 17,* 255–266.

DeLoache, J. S. (2000). Cognitive development in infants: Looking, listening, and learning. In D. Cryer & T. Harms (Eds.), *Infants and toddlers in out-of-home care* (pp. 7–47). Baltimore: Brookes.

*Doyle, A. B. (1975). Infant development in child care. *Developmental Psychology, 11,* 655–656.

*Edwards, C. P., Logue, M. E., Loehr, S., & Roth, S. (1986). The influence of model infant–toddler group care on parent–child interaction at home. *Early Childhood Research Quarterly, 1,* 317–322.

*Egeland, B., & Hiester, M. (1995). The long-term consequences of infant day-care and mother–infant attachment. *Child Development, 66,* 474–485.

*Fein, G. G., Gariboldi, A., & Boni, R. (1993). The adjustment of infants and toddlers to group care: The first 6 months. *Early Childhood Research Quarterly, 8,* 1–14.

*Field, T. (1991). Quality infant day-care and grade school behavior and performance. *Child Development, 62,* 863–870.

*Field, T., Masi, W., Goldstein, S., Perry, S., & Parl, S. (1988). Infant day care facilitates preschool social behavior. *Early Childhood Research Quarterly, 3,* 341–359.

Gore Schiff, K. (2002, November). Where are America's "family values?" *Glamour, 172,* 174.

*Hagekull, B., & Bohlin, G. (1995). Day care quality, family and child characteristics and soioemotional development. *Early Childhood Research Quarterly, 10,* 505–526.

*Hegland, S. M., & Rix, M. K. (1990). Aggression and assertiveness in kindergarten children differing in day care experiences. *Early Childhood Research Quarterly, 5,* 105–116.

*Honig, A. S., & Park, K. J. (1995). Infant/toddler nonparental care: Differential effects on boys/girls? *Montessori Life, 7,* 25–27.

Howes, C. (2000). Social development, family, and attachment relationships of infants and toddlers. In D. Cryer & T. Harms (Eds.), *Infants and toddlers in out-of-home care* (pp. 87–113). Baltimore: Brookes.

*Howes, C., Rodning, C., Galluzzo, D. C., & Myers, L. (1988). Attachment and child care: Relationships with mother and caregiver. *Early Childhood Research Quarterly, 3,* 403–416.

*Johnson, R. L. (1979). Social behavior of 3-year-old children in day care and home settings. *Child Study Journal, 9,* 109–122.

*Karmaniola, A., Pierrehumbert, B., & Ramstein, T. (1994). The effects of non-parental care and the quality of the child care setting on the young child's development: A Swiss study. European *Early Childhood Education Research Journal, 2,* 43–50.

Kwan, C., & Sylva, K. (2001). Observations of child behaviours as indicators of child care quality in Singapore. *Canadian Journal of Research in Early Childhood Education, 8,* 23–37.

Lamb, M. E. (1996). Effects of nonparental child care on child development: An update. *Canadian Journal of Psychiatry, 41,* 330–342.

*Lamb, M. E., Hwang, C. P., Broberg, A., & Bookstein, F. L. (1988). The effects of out-of-home care on the development of social competence in Sweden: A longitudinal study. *Early Childhood Research Quarterly, 3,* 379–402.

*Macrae, J. W., & Herbert-Jackson, E. (1976). Are behavioral effects of infant day care program specific? *Developmental Psychology, 12,* 269–270.

*Medcalf-Davenport, N. A. (1993). A comparative study of the general world knowledge and language development of pre-kindergarten children from either day care or in-home care. *Early Child Development and Care, 93,* 1–14.

*Moskowitz, D. S., Schwarz, J. C., & Corsini, D. A. (1977). Initiating day care at three years of age: Effects on attachment. *Child Development, 48,* 1271–1276.

*NICHD. (1997). The effects of infant child care on infant–mother attachment security: Results of the NICHD study of early child care. *Child Development, 68,* 860–879.

*NICHD. (1998). Relations between family predictors and child outcomes: Are they weaker for children in child care? *Developmental Psychology, 34,* 1119–1128.

*NICHD. (2001). Child care and children's peer interaction and 24 and 36 months: The NICHD study of early child care. *Child Development, 72,* 1478–1500.

Peisner-Feinberg, E. S., Burchinal, M. R., Clifford, R. M., Culkin, M. L., Howes, C., Kagan, S. L., et al. (2001). The relation of preschool child-care quality to children's cognitive and social developmental trajectories through second grade. *Child Development, 72,* 1534–1553.

Phillips, D., McCartney, K., & Scarr, S. (1987). Child care quality and children's social development. *Developmental Psychology, 23,* 537–543.

*Ragozin, A. S. (1980). Attachment behavior of day-care children: Naturalistic and laboratory observations. *Child Development, 51,* 409–415.

*Robinson, H. B., & Robinson, N. M. (1971). Longitudinal development of very young children in a comprehensive day care program: The first two years. *Child Development, 42,* 1673–1683.

*Roopnarine, J. L., & Lamb, M. E. (1980a). The effects of day care on attachment and exploratory behavior in a strange situation. *Merrill-Palmer Quarterly, 24,* 81–95.

*Roopnarine, J. L., & Lamb, M. E. (1980b). Peer and parent–child interaction before and after enrollment in nursery school. *Journal of Applied Developmental Psychology, 1,* 77–81.

*Rubenstein, J. L., & Howes, C. (1979). Caregiving and infant behavior in day care and in homes. *Developmental Psychology, 15,* 1–24.

*Scarr, S., & Thompson, W. W. (1994). The effects of maternal employment and non-maternal infant care on development at two and four years. *Early Development and Parenting, 3,* 113–123.

*Schwartz, P. (1983). Length of day-care attendance and attachment behavior in eighteen-month-old infants. *Child Development, 54,* 1073–1078.

*Schwarz, J. C. (1983, April). *Infant day care: Effects at 2, 4, and 8 years.* Paper presented at the biennial meeting of the Society for Research in Child Development, Detroit, MI. (ERIC Document Reproduction Service No. 233 806)

*Schwarz, J. C., Krolick, G., & Strickland, R. G. (1973). Effects of early day care experience on adjustment to a new environment. *American Journal of Orthopsychiatry, 43,* 340–346.

Sundell, K. (2000). Examining Swedish profit and nonprofit child care: The relationships between adult-to-child ratio, age composition in child care classes, teaching and children's social and cognitive achievements. *Early Childhood Research Quarterly, 15,* 91–114.

*Thornburg, K. R., Pearl, P., Crompton, D., & Ispa, J. M. (1990). Development of kindergarten children based on child care arrangements. *Early Childhood Research Quarterly, 5,* 27–42.

U.S. Department of Labor Women's Bureau. (2002). *Women in the labor force: A databook* (Rep. No. 973). Washington, DC: Author.

*Vandell, D. L., & Corasaniti, M. A. (1990a). Child care and the family: Complex contributors to child development. *New Directions for Child Development, 49,* 23–37.

*Vandell, D. L., & Corasaniti, M. A. (1990b). Variations in early child care: Do they predict subsequent social, emotional, and cognitive differences? *Early Childhood Research Quarterly, 5,* 555–572.

*Winett, R. A., Fuchs, W. L., Moffatt, S. A., & Nerviano, V. J. (1977). A cross-sectional study of children and their families in different child care environments: Some data and conclusions. *Journal of Community Psychology, 5,* 149–159.

Zeifman, D., & Hazan, C. (1997). A process model of adult attachment. In S. Duck (Ed.), *Handbook of personal relationships: Theory, research, and interventions* (2nd ed., pp. 179–195). New York: Wiley.

IV

Teacher Effectiveness and Communicative and Instructional Processes

16

An Overview of Teacher Effectiveness Research: Components and Processes

Derek Cortez
University of Texas at Austin

Barbara Mae Gayle
Saint Martin's University

Raymond W. Preiss
University of Puget Sound

We approached communication and instructional processes in the classroom using three general perspectives as the framework for this book. The first section emphasized pedagogical issues underlying classroom techniques, and the second focused on classroom interaction practices. In this section, we examine the empirical literature focusing on teacher effectiveness as a central issue in instructional communication. In this section, our goal is to summarize the techniques and characteristics associated with classroom learning.

In an effort to conceptualize the construct of teacher effectiveness, researchers have explored a variety of instructor behaviors and predispositions. Some scholars have explored teacher effectiveness in terms of the instructor's ability to create and maintain environments that foster deep understanding of the concepts being taught. Other researchers investigated aspects of teacher efficacy, competency, credibility, or pedagogical activities.

In this overview, we present a conceptual picture of teacher effectiveness, summarize some of the recent contributions in this area, and offer connections to the meta-analyses in this section.

THE THEORETICAL APPROACH
TO TEACHER EFFECTIVENESS

There are three major paradigms or ways of thinking about teacher effectiveness that Doyle (1975) and later MacAulay (1990) used to capture what happens, or can happen, to facilitate the effectiveness of classroom teaching. The first paradigm, called by some the process–product paradigm, illustrates the most common approach to the teaching and learning relationship. The basic idea here is that teacher behaviors in the classroom precede student learning and achievement. Thus, the process–product approach views the teacher as being primarily responsible for the success of the endeavor. According to the process–product paradigm, the frequency with which the instructor enacts certain behaviors such as clarity or enthusiasm determines student performance. From this perspective, the teacher is the overt agent of change and students become expert audience members observing teachers perform. The idea is that if faculty design and implement strategic, polished courses, then students will learn.

A void in the process–product paradigm involves student responsibilities in the learning process. To fill this gap, researchers moved to a student mediating paradigm in an attempt to shift the sole responsibility for learning from the teacher to student engagement in specific learning behaviors (Doyle, 1975). The underlying assumption here is based on what students bring to the learning process—their abilities, their willingness to be diligent in completing course work, their willingness to grapple with new ideas, and their ability to acquire new skills. Researchers have explored how students' traits or characteristics mediate their ability to learn more than the educational environment would normally allow. The idea is if students do not assume their responsibility to learn (to regularly study, complete assignments, and engage the reading), any instructional technique could fail to enhance student understanding and learning. Thus, student motivation mediates teacher effectiveness, and students are responsible to sustain behaviors that help them learn.

The third paradigm called culture-of-the-school by some (Doyle, 1975) assesses the contribution of the context in which the teaching and learning takes place. It is frequently acknowledged that the school environment has an effect on the ability to engage in the learning process (MacAulay, 1990). The thesis here is that each institution defines the boundaries or basic parameters of student learning as administrators and teachers structure the environment and promote ways of thinking about the learning process. This paradigm endorses the idea that students interact with other students and with their instructors in ways that affect the learning process. The classroom culture established by individual faculty members is usually intertwined with institutional norms and it affects the student's ability to understand course material. This explanation also recognizes that disciplinary norms—ways of thinking and knowing—impact the learning environment and a student's capacity to understand a particular subject. Supporters of this paradigm maintain that the complexity of the teaching and learning process can be altered or designed in such a way to encourage or inhibit successful student performance.

All three of these paradigms, however, fail to capture the student–faculty interaction that occurs both inside and outside of class. The focus here is on each of the partners in the ideal teaching and learning paradigm having obligations and responsibilities. We consider this to be a fourth approach, the interaction paradigm. Gayle (2004) took this view when she described three relational aspects of the interaction paradigm that affect the teaching and learning relationship: dialogue, community building, and growth through collegiality. Gayle viewed teaching effectiveness as one aspect of an outward manifestation of the relationship between the teacher and the student. This approach is a more complex process than is captured by exploring the context in which that relationship resides or each partner in the learning process separately. The assumption is that teacher effectiveness is enhanced by discourse processes that lay the foundation for critical inquiry. Thus, classroom environments should encourage both teachers and students to interact and form a community of inquiry as a context for learning. Students must willingly engage in the learning process and faculty must validate the capacity of learners to know and inspire and affirm the students' role in the learning process through face-to-face interaction. The strength of this paradigm is its ability to simultaneously embrace the relationship between teachers and students and the classroom context.

Taken together, each of these paradigms suggests a particular lens to explain why effective teaching enhances student learning. Researchers using these frames have investigated the components of teacher effectiveness to illuminate the traits and characteristics that promote deep understanding and positive student learning outcomes. We summarize these findings in the following sections.

Teacher Effectiveness Through the Process–Product Paradigm

The overriding concern addressed by the process–product paradigm involved identifying the stable behaviors used by teachers to increase student performance. Teacher effectiveness viewed through this lens is narrowly researched to determine which teaching behaviors affect student understanding or broadly explored to identify actual increases in student learning (Arthur, Tubre, Paul, & Edens, 2003). Campbell, Kriakides, Maijs, and Robinson (2003) maintained that teaching effectiveness focuses on how a teacher's work directly impacts students' ability to learn. There is support for this thesis. Some research emerging from the process–product paradigm is rooted in the assumption that the teacher's actual ability to engage students in the learning process is an essential foundation for student learning (Patrick & Smart, 1998). Other researchers in this tradition have focused on teacher competency in terms of expectations of self and students (Yin & Kwok, 1998).

The rubric of teacher effectiveness implies the existence of a taxonomy of teaching characteristics that promote effectiveness. MacAulay (1990), Campbell et al. (2003), and Mottet (1997) attributed success to the personality traits of individual teachers. These authors found that being able to motivate students through high expectations is one teacher characteristic that correlates with effectiveness. According to Gordon (2001) and Herman (2000) the most effective teacher is one who is likely to assert that she or he has the ability to directly influence student learning. In other words, effective teachers are capable of being reflective about their teaching behaviors (Giovannelli, 2003) and employing behaviors that motivate student performance.

Some researchers exploring teacher effectiveness have focused on displayed teacher behaviors. Overall, it appears that positive teacher behaviors in the classroom enhance student learning behaviors (Patrick & Smart, 1998). Research reveals that being emotionally calm, affectionate, generous, tolerant yet enthusiastic, or passionate about one's subject matter creates a benevolent disposition toward students that appears to encourage student performance (Campbell et al., 2003; Gordon, 2001; Kyriades, Campbell, & Christofidore, 2002; MacAulay, 1990; Walls, Norde, von Mider, & Hoffman, 2002; Wheeler & McLeod, 2002). The basic idea is that a teacher's personality impacts the students' perception of their effectiveness (Murray, Rushton, & Paunonen, 1990).

Other researchers have addressed teacher effectiveness by focusing on the teacher's higher order cognitive abilities. In these studies, what teachers knew about pedagogical efficiency influenced the successful performance of their students (Giovannelli, 2003; Rosenshine, 1971). Being goal-directed, structuring cooperative learning environments, sharing responsibility for classroom management with students, and organizing the classroom to support the establishment of respect, trust, support, and friendship were all factors found to enhance the perceptions of teacher effectiveness (Giovannelli, 2003; Johnson & Johnson, 1983; MacAulay, 1990; Walls et al., 2002). However, Kyriades et al. (2002) argued teacher effectiveness is not just classroom behaviors or cognitive reflections. These authors appear to believe that teacher effectiveness is the result of collaboration with other teachers and a fundamental love of students.

One measure of whether the teacher is perceived as effective focuses on the overall rating of the teacher as being perceived as credible or competent (Buck & Tiene, 2001; Frymier & Thompson, 1992; Patton, 1999; White, 2000). Frymier and Thompson (1992) reasoned that teachers can establish competency because they have regular contact with students. Over a period of time, teachers may dramatically increase their credibility and maintain perceptions of competency by repeatedly employing affinity-seeking behaviors. McGlone and Anderson (1973) found that students are "more certain about their conceptualizations of a credible teacher at the very beginning and the very end of a course than during any intermediate stage" (p. 199). This suggests that teacher credibility is the result of weighing perceptions of teacher verbal and nonverbal behaviors and attributing those perceptions to mental representations of what it means to be an "excellent" teacher.

Nonverbal communication has been studied as a source of cues marking effective teachers. Gazes, smiles, vocal warmth, and facial expressions have been identified as enhancing perceptions of teacher credibility in the classroom (Guerrero & Miller, 1998; White, 2000). Woolfolk and Woolfolk (1974) reported that when a teacher displayed an extremely positive attitude, she or he was perceived as being more credible. The teacher's ability to organize the social climate of the classroom and her or his skill at structuring the environment to maximize learning was linked to positive student outcomes. Guerrero and Miller (1998) examined "the associations between nonverbal behavior and initial judgments of instructor competence (i.e., as likeable, trustworthy and sensitive) and course content (i.e., as interesting, enjoyable, and valuable)" (p. 31). They concluded that "even in non-interactive environments, the more warm and involved a student perceives an instructor to be, the more likely the student is to perceive the instructor as competent and likable and to see the course content as valuable and enjoyable" (p. 38). However, Guerrero and Miller (1998) found that if instructors appear to be too polished, students may see them as insincere or phony. In some studies, vocal cues affected students' perceptions of teacher credibility. Beatty and Behnke (1980) noticed that "during student–teacher interactions" vocal cues were likely to "convey empathy and interpersonal sensitivity, thereby elevating perceptions of confidence" (p. 59).

Other researchers have explored teacher credibility in terms of dress and appearance. Studies conducted by Gorham, Cohen, and Morris (1999) and Morris, Gorham, Stanley, and Huffman (1996) reported that the style of dress for the teacher (e.g., formal or casual) is not necessarily a predictor of a student's perceptions related to teacher credibility. Gorham et al. (1999) proposed that "students' judgments of such attributes are influenced far more by how teachers behave than by what they wear" (p. 295). In another study on appearance, Buck and Tiene (2001) concluded that an instructor's teaching style is a more significant factor determining perceived competence than is the instructor's physical attractiveness. This provides some evidence that teacher credibility may be more easily granted if the teacher's mannerisms and behaviors are perceived as being appropriate and caring, rather than being based on tangible items such as clothing or appearance.

In a related line of investigation, some researchers have explored whether a faculty member's gender or ethnicity affected her or his perceived effectiveness or credibility. Patton (1999) found that "ethnicity was related to credibility, with the African American instructors seen as more credible than the European American instructors" (p. 131). He suggested that "the significant relationship of ethnicity to credibility in this study may be attributed to a number of possibilities, including immediacy, novelty, presensitization and social correctness" (p. 132). Finally, Patton concluded that female instructors were somewhat more credible than male instructors. Buck and Tiene's (1989) study supported this notion. The authors found that attractive female professors were rated as being more competent than authoritarian professors. Taken together, it appears that teacher effectiveness involves gender and ethnic expectations, as well as expectations associated with the teacher's status and role in the classroom.

Teacher clarity is another construct embedded in the concept of teacher effectiveness. Clarity is described as the ability of teachers to unambiguously explain ideas and directions and the ability to discern student understanding of the material presented. In a meta-analysis of two studies, Laut (1995) found that teacher clarity moderately improved student achievement. Fendick (1990), Toale (2001), Murray (1991), Hines, Cruickshank, and Kennedy (1985), Smith (1985), and Civikly (1992) independently reported that teacher clarity led to more effective and positive student learning outcomes. Thus, it appears that clarity is one of a set of identifiable behaviors associated with teacher effectiveness.

Obviously, a great deal of research has been devoted to establishing the role that teachers play in creating effective learning environments. Whether or not they are perceived as competent and credible, researchers using this lens believe that teachers can engage in certain behaviors that are more or less likely to enhance student learning outcomes. Basically, this line of research subordinates the student's role in promoting specific learning objectives. Researchers adopting the process–product paradigm measure and theorize about teacher effectiveness based on characteristics or personality traits, as well as a teacher's pedagogical performance in the classroom.

Teacher Effectiveness Through the Student Mediating Process Paradigm

The student mediating process paradigm focuses on whether student responses to teacher behavior are the real catalyst in determining learning outcomes. The idea here is that students influence the selection of effective teacher behaviors and that these student behaviors and characteristics affect student learning. The concern that researchers using this lens address is whether student responses play an important or modest role in determining teaching effectiveness.

Research in this area has focused on student characteristics and student learning behaviors. For example, Campbell et al. (2003) suggested that a student's background and personal characteristics play a substantial role in judgments regarding teacher effectiveness. The authors claim that learning may differ "according to the pupils' personal characteristics such as their personality, cognitive learning style, and extent of motivation and self esteem" (Campbell et al., 2003, p. 355). Yin and Kwok's (1998) and Johnson and Johnson's (1983) investigations also support this view. Similarly, Herman (2000) found that teaching effectiveness was related to student self-efficacy beliefs about course mastery. Some findings dispute the magnitude of this relationship, as Arthur et al. (2003) found a small relationship between student evaluations of teacher effectiveness and students' actual pretest–posttest achievement scores.

It is noteworthy that a few studies in this area investigate teacher effectiveness as student preferences for engaging in classroom activities. MacAulay (1990) maintained that students prefer positive classroom climates and they are willing to cooperate and engage in behaviors that foster individual accountability. When these climates occur, students attribute their accountability to teacher effectiveness. Walls et al. (2002) claimed that student achievement and teacher effectiveness perceptions are rooted in behaviors that mark productive classroom climates.

Overall, there is less research grounded in the student mediating paradigm than is found for other approaches to the teacher effectiveness literature. However, studies in this area indicate that, at the very least, teacher effectiveness is cocreated. It is the result of both student predispositions and student-elicited teacher behaviors. However, this explanation does not specifically acknowledge the idea that cultural norms at individual schools or embedded in different subject materials may also affect student learning outcomes. This possibility is discussed in the next section.

Teacher Effectiveness Through the Culture-of-the-School Paradigm

The culture-of-the-school paradigm emphasizes the institutional structure and elements that organize teaching and learning. Institutional factors may define the possible teaching behaviors and student responses that can occur in the classroom (Doyle, 1975). The idea here is that the structure of an organization or institution can affect teaching behaviors and student performance. The cultures that evolve in these structures may enhance or inhibit productive learning environments. Thus, this paradigm suggests that institutional standards and values become mediating factors in aiding or preventing positive student performance outcomes.

Researchers using this approach discovered that some structures that inhibit or promote learning are teacher designed and others are institutionally sanctioned. For example, Lippert-Martin (1992) argued that the classroom effectiveness is dependent on the institutional climate, and Anderson (1999) reasoned that students who enter the classroom are influenced primarily by the dominant campus culture and structure. Supporting this paradigm's premise, Campbell et al. (2003) reported that urban schools create a totally different atmosphere than nonurban schools. Thus, different strategies are needed to effectively increase student learning in urban environments and cultures. The authors also indicated that disciplinary norms mediated the pedagogical practices necessary to promote student learning.

Other researchers have explored how the institutional or classroom structure enhanced or impeded student learning. Dowaliby and Schumer (1973) discerned that anxiety can occur as a function of classroom structure, whereas MacAulay (1990) observed that teacher effectiveness may operate as a function of class size and seating assignments. MacAulay found that smaller classes and sitting in rows was associated with greater student performance. Also, Yin and Kwok (1998) found that a team teaching structure enhanced student learning. Thus, it is not altogether surprising that Walls et al.'s (2002) participants reported that their most effective teachers took control and structured their classrooms to encourage student academic achievement. Lage, Platt, and Treglia (2000) argued that inverting the classroom structure so that the learning that traditionally took place in the classroom also occurred outside the classroom increased understanding of the course materials.

The culture-of-the-school paradigm is concerned less with formal structure and more with perceptions of the learning environment. This approach to conceptualizing teacher effectiveness focuses on the creation of a productive classroom structure through enhancing the classroom climate. The assumption here is that educational goals are highly dependent on establishing an interesting, engaging classroom climate. Some researchers maintain that the structure, as well as the behavior of students and teachers, create an effective learning environment. As Dijkstra (1998) claimed, "it is difficult to predict how the classroom climate will develop" (p. 105). Nevertheless, research on classroom climate continues to be a robust line of investigation regarding teacher effectiveness.

Kelly (2002) reported that creating equitable classroom climates serves all students' learning needs. She argued that preservice teachers who create democratic social values have a better chance in enhancing student performance. DeYoung (1977) reported that the social climate in a classroom contributes to independent learning and increases the motivation to learn. Furman (1998), on the other hand, found that a creative classroom climate encouraged creative and innovative thinking. He concluded that student performance was enhanced when students felt free to inquire and ask questions. Furman maintained that a creative classroom climate led students to expect that teachers would structure working conditions. This relationship appears to hold for male and female students. Salter (2003) found that, overall, gender did not influence a preference for a particular classroom climate. Women whose learning style was described as "feeling" preferred a more emotionally tuned classroom atmosphere. She also discovered that both males and females with a learning style classified as "feeling" felt less comfortable in cognitive-based classrooms.

There is disagreement on the magnitude of outcomes associated with equitable classroom climates. For example, Phillips (1997) questioned the idea of establishing a warm and affirming classroom climate. She concluded that "shared values and activities, positive adult social relationships, [and] positive teacher–student relations" (p. 633) were less related to strong academic performance in mathematics than were the teacher's high expectations. Hearn and Moos (1978) extended the high expectation research. These authors found that a warm social climate can lead to high expectations and produce a cohesive group. On the other hand, Shapiro's (1993) research suggested that developing activities that shape the social climate in the classroom provided an opportunity for students and teachers to become a more focused and cohesive learning group. Her investigation, and Ghaith's (2003) research, indicates that a positive classroom atmosphere maximizes student performance. Ghaith reported that a collaborative atmosphere rather than an individualist or competitive atmosphere encourages maximum student performance. Haines and McKeachie (1967) supported the idea that a cooperative classroom climate enhances student learning more than a competitive classroom climate. Lippert-Martin (1992) and Wenzel (2003) suggested strategies for building classroom climate that are more inclusive of female students to enhance classroom climate and teacher effectiveness. Waite-Stupiansky and Stupiansky (1998) observed that an effective classroom climate encourages student problemsolving.

Overall, it appears that institutional and classroom structures may nurture or inhibit a student's academic performance. Although cooperative climates are preferred, teacher expectations play a key role in facilitating learning. However, this paradigm does not investigate or account for the communication that often structures interactions within any classroom. The interactional paradigm attempts to fills this void.

Teacher Effectiveness Through the Interactional Paradigm

The interactional paradigm considers the discourse necessity for relationship building. The idea is that both students and faculty lay the foundation for critical inquiry through their discourse, and a quality teaching and learning relationship requires some form of collegiality achieved through dialogue. This interaction involves a learning process that validates the capacity of learners to know and inspires confidence in the ability of the teacher and learner to simultaneously engage in the learning process.

Several researchers have examined this approach to teacher effectiveness. Kyriades et al. (2002) believed that the teacher's relationship with her or his students is associated with their perceptions of teacher effectiveness. Superstein (1994) maintained that positive engagement between faculty and students and the teacher–student relationship promotes active participation in the learning process. Campbell et al.'s (2003) proposed model of teacher effectiveness refers to teacher activity both in and out of the classroom. These authors seem to suggest that some form of teacher interaction enhances teacher effectiveness.

Several researchers have linked interaction patterns to classroom climates. Wildman (1989) discussed expanding the "boundaries of permissible discourse" (p. 334) to enhance a safe classroom environment that will enhance difficult dialogues. To maximize the effectiveness of the classroom, Anderson (1999) stressed the importance of harnessing student diversity to produce a coercive-free, safe environment. In this environment, students and faculty are charged with creating an atmosphere that allows all students' needs to be met. In this way, interactions among students do not become the catalyst for inequality and dissent. Lippert-Martin (1992) and Wenzel (2003) discerned that supportive communication behaviors can positively impact classroom climate for female students and negate the negative impact of male students.

Other researchers have explored the types of interactions that enhanced perceptions of teacher effectiveness or credibility. Mottet (1997) discovered that teachers who try to establish relationships through playful behavior that includes using humor and light profanity are more effective in the classroom. Kher, Molstad, and Donahue (1999) found that humor creates a positive learning environment and creates the interactions necessary to enhance student performance. Similarly, Walls et al.'s (2002) participants described the emotional environment created by effective teachers as "friendly, warm and caring" (p. 45), Dijkstra (1998) reported that friendly teacher–student interactions produced a positive classroom climate. Also, Thibodeaux and Siltanen (1985) concluded that teacher openness and "dramatic" interaction enhances student success. This is consistent with Wubbels, Creton, and Holvast's (1988) finding that stable teacher–student interactions set the tone for learning activities. Haleta (1996) made a link between language use and these interactions. She discovered that the use of certain types of language not only affects student–teacher relationships, but alters perceptions of teacher competence and credibility. She found that "students assigned more favorable ratings to teachers who used a concise, direct style of language than teachers who used a language style that contained multiple hesitations" (p. 24). Using the categories of powerful and powerless ("speech characterized by hedges, intensifiers, deictic phrases and hesitation forms"), Haleta found that students may view teachers using powerless language as lacking control and being less competent and those using powerful speech as being more expert and professional.

Taken together, these studies indicate that building community and strengthening dialogue and discourse are means of enhancing the teaching and learning relationship. In this paradigm, the premise that face-to-face communication develops a strong teaching and learning relationship seems reasonable. It is apparent that discourse extends the idea of ownership and responsibility for establishing teacher effectiveness.

CONCLUSION

Clearly, teacher effectiveness involves a variety of different components and processes. The lens with which we view the relationship between teacher effectiveness and positive student learning outcomes focuses our attention on specific aspects of a complex process. It appears that the interaction among the various elements has not been captured, nor has research in this area identified a prescriptive model. The factors ensuring teacher effectiveness in enhancing student learning have remained somewhat elusive and other related constructs continue to be investigated.

The meta-analyses chosen for this part of the volume illuminate the four paradigms used to account for teacher effectiveness and its outcomes. Gayle, Preiss, and Allen (chap. 17, this volume) explore the role of oral questions in promoting student learning by examining whether the level of oral question can be structured to enhance students' ability to remember and apply course material. Preiss and Gayle (chap. 20, this volume) investigate where oral advanced organizers provide the architecture or scaffolding to support the integration and understanding of subsequent information on complex concepts. They isolated oral advanced organizers used in a variety of disciplines to test their effectiveness in enhancing student learning outcomes. In another meta-analysis selected for this section, Preiss and Gayle (chap. 19, this volume) sought to identify the rate of speech that maintained student comprehension levels without allowing students' minds to wander. These authors investigated how effective teachers are in compressing speech to enhance student performance. Additionally, Martin, Preiss, Gayle, and Allen (chap. 18, this volume) investigate the role of humor in facilitating understanding and learning. These authors looked at whether humor usage increased perceptions of teacher effectiveness. Finally, Allen's (chap. 21, this volume) meta-analysis provides information on the relationship between teaching effectiveness and research productivity. He explored student evaluations of the faculty's teaching effectiveness and the number of published works by the faculty member to produce a complementary skill set. Theses metas help begin the process of explicating various components of teacher effectiveness.

REFERENCES

Anderson, J. A. (1999). Faculty responsibility for promoting conflict-free college classrooms. *New Directions for Teaching and Learning, 77,* 69–76.

Arthur, W., Tubre, T., Paul, D. S., & Edens, P. S. (2003). Teaching effectiveness: The relationship between reaction and learning evaluation criteria. *Educational Psychology, 23,* 275–285.

Beatty, M. J., & Behnke, R. R. (1980). Teacher credibility as a function of verbal content and paralinguistic cues. *Communication Quarterly, 28,* 55–59.

Buck, S., & Tiene, D. (1989). The impact of physical attractiveness, gender, and teaching philosophy on teacher evaluations. *Journal of Educational Research, 82,* 172–177.

Campbell, R. J., Kyriades, I., Murijs, R. D., & Robinson, W. (2003). Differential teacher effectiveness: Towards a model for research and appraisal. *Oxford Education Review, 29,* 347–362.

Civikly, J. (1992). Clarity: Teachers and students making sense of instruction. *Communication Education, 41,* 138–152.

DeYoung, A. J. (1977). Classroom climate and class success: A case study at the university level. *Journal of Educational Research, 70,* 252–257.

Dijkstra, S. (1998). The many variables that influence classroom teaching. *Issues in Education, 4*(1), 105–111.

Dowaliby, F. J., & Schumer, H. (1973). Teacher-centered versus student-centered mode of college classroom instruction as related to manifest anxiety. *Journal of Educational Psychology, 64,* 125–132.

Doyle, W. (1975, April). *Paradigms in teacher effectiveness research.* Paper presented at the annual meeting of the American Educational Research Association, Washington, DC.

Fendick, F. (1990). The correlation between teacher clarity of communication and student achievement gain: A meta-analysis (Doctoral dissertation, University of Florida, 1990). *Dissertation Abstracts International, 52,* 01A.

Frymier, A. B., & Thompson, C. A. (1992). Perceived teacher affinity-seeking in relation to perceived teacher credibility. *Communication Education, 41*, 388–399.

Furman, A. (1998). Teacher and pupil characteristics in the perception of the creativity of classroom climate. *Journal of Creative Behavior, 32*, 258–277.

Gayle, B. M. (2004, April). *The ideal relationship: The teaching and learning partnership.* Keynote address given at the Northwest Communication Association Conference, Couer d'Alene, ID.

Ghaith, G. (2003). The relationship between forms of instruction, achievement and perceptions of classroom climate. *Educational Research, 45*(1), 83–93.

Giovannelli, M. (2003). Relationship between reflective disposition toward teaching and effective teaching. *Journal of Educational Research, 96*, 293–310.

Gordon, L. M. (2001, October). *High teacher efficacy as a marker of teacher effectiveness in the domain of classroom management.* Paper presented at the annual meeting of the California Council on Teacher Education, San Francisco.

Gorham, J., Cohen, S., & Morris, T. (1999). Fashion in the classroom III: Effects of instructor attire and immediacy in natural classroom interactions. *Communication Quarterly, 47*, 281–299.

Guerrero, L. K., & Miller, T. A. (1998). Associations between nonverbal behaviors and initial impressions of instructor competence and course content in videotaped distance education courses. *Communication Education, 47*, 30–42.

Haines, D. B., & McKeachie, W. J. (1967). Cooperative versus competitive discussion methods in teaching introductory psychology. *Journal of Educational Psychology, 58*, 386–390.

Haleta, L. L. (1996). Student perceptions of teachers' use of language: The effects of powerful and powerless language on impression formation and uncertainty. *Communication Education, 45*, 16–28.

Hearn, J. C., & Moos, R. H. (1978). Subject matter and classroom climate: A test of Holland's environmental propositions. *American Educational Research Journal, 15*(1), 111–124.

Herman, P. (2000). *Teacher experience and teacher efficacy: Relationship to student motivation and achievement.* Unpublished doctoral dissertation, University of North Carolina, Chapel Hill, NC.

Hines, C. V., Cruickshank, D. R., & Kennedy, J. J. (1985). Teacher clarity and its relationship to student achievement and satisfaction. *American Educational Research Journal, 22*(1), 87–99.

Johnson, D. W., & Johnson, R. T. (1983). Social interdependence and perceived academic and personal support in the classroom. *The Journal of Social Psychology, 120*, 77–82.

Kelly, C. A. (2002). Creating equitable classroom climates: An investigation of classroom strategies in mathematics and science instruction for developing pre-service teachers' use of democratic social values. *Child Study Journal, 32*(1), 39–52.

Kher, N., Molstad, S., & Donahue, R. (1999). Using humor in the college classroom to enhance teaching effectiveness in "dread courses." *College Student Journal, 33*, 400–407.

Kyriades, L., Campbell, R. J., & Christofidore, E. (2002). Generating criteria for measuring teacher effectiveness through self-evaluation approach: A complementary way of measuring teacher effectiveness. *School of Effectiveness and School Improvement, 13*, 291–325.

Lage, M. J., Platt, G. J., & Treglia, M. (2000). Inverting the classroom: A gateway to creating an inclusive learning environment. *Journal of Economic Education, 31*(1), 30–43.

Laut, J. T. (1995). The identification of critical teaching skills and their relationship to student achievement: A quantitative synthesis (Doctoral dissertation, The Ohio State University, 1995). *Dissertation Abstracts International, 56,* 09A.

Lippert-Martin, K. (1992). The classroom climate. *Liberal Education, 78*(2), 41–53.

MacAulay, D. J. (1990). Classroom environment: A literature review. *Educational Psychology, 10,* 239–245.

McGlone, E. L., & Anderson, L. J. (1973). The dimensions of teacher credibility. *Speech Teacher, 22,* 196–200.

Morris, T., Gorham, J., Stanley, H., & Huffman, D. (1996). Fashion in the classroom: Effects of attire on student perceptions of instructors in college classes. *Communication Education, 45,* 135–148.

Mottet, T. P. (1997, November). *A conceptualization and measure of teacher verbal effectiveness.* Paper presented at the annual meeting of the National Communication Association, San Diego, CA.

Murray, H. G. (1991). Effective teaching behaviors in the college classroom. In J. C. Smart (Ed.), *Higher education: Handbook of theory and research* (pp. 135–172). New York: Agathon.

Murray, H. G., Rushton, J. P., & Paunonen, S. V. (1990). Teacher personality traits and student instructional ratings in six types of university courses. *Journal of Educational Psychology, 82,* 250–261.

Patrick, J., & Smart, R. M. (1998). An empirical evaluation of teacher effectiveness: The emergence of three critical factors. *Assessment and Evaluation in Higher Education, 23,* 165–179.

Patton, T. O. (1999). Ethnicity and gender: An examination of its impact on instructor credibility in the university classroom. *The Howard Journal of Communications, 10,* 123–144.

Phillips, M. (1997). What makes schools effective: A comparison of the relationships of communitarian climate and academic climate to mathematics achievement and attendance during middle schools. *American Educational Research Journal, 34,* 633–662.

Rosenshine, B. (1971). *Teaching behaviors and student achievement.* Urbana-Champaign, IL: NFER.

Salter, D. W. (2003). Exploring the "chilly classroom" phenomenon as interactions between psychological and environmental. *Journal of College Student Development, 44*(1), 110–121.

Shapiro, S. (1993). Strategies that create a positive classroom climate. *Clearing House, 67*(2), 91–98.

Smith, B. O. (1985). Research used for teacher education. *Phi Delta Kappan, 66,* 685–690.

Superstein, D. (1994). Adolescents' attitudes toward their schooling: The influence of encouragement and discouragement. *Individual Psychology, 50,* 183–191.

Thibodeaux, T. M., & Siltanen, S. A. (1985, November). *Classroom communication climate: The development and testing of a measure of the nonverbal communication in the classroom.* Paper presented at the annual meeting of the National Communication Association, Denver, CO.

Toale, M. C. (2001). Teacher clarity and teacher misbehaviors: Relationships with students' affective learning and teacher credibility (Doctoral dissertation, West Virginia University, Morgantown). *Dissertation Abstracts International, 62,* 05A.

Waite-Stupiansky, S., & Stupiansky, N. E. (1998). Create a climate for problem-solving instructor primacy. *Instructor Primary, 108*(1), 54–55.

Walls, R. T., Norde, A. H., von Mider, A. M., & Hoffman, N. (2002). The characteristics of effective and ineffective teachers. *Teacher Education Quarterly, 29*(1), 39–48.

Wenzel, T. (2003). Controlling the climate in your classroom. *Analytical Chemistry, 75*(13), 311a–314a.

Wheeler, J. V., & McLeod, P. L. (2002). Expanding our teaching effectiveness: Understanding our response to "in-the-moment" classroom events. *Journal of Management Education, 26,* 693–716.

White, G. W. (2000). Non-verbal communications: Key to improved teacher effectiveness. *The Delta Kappa Gamma Bulletin, 66*(4), 12–16.

Wildman, S. M. (1989). The classroom environment: Encouraging student involvement. *Berkeley Women's Law Journal, 4,* 326–334.

Woolfolk, R. L., & Woolfolk, A. E. (1974). Effects of teacher verbal and nonverbal behaviors on student perceptions and attitudes. *American Educational Research Journal, 11,* 297–303.

Wubbels, T., Creton, H. A., & Holvast, A. (1988). Undesirable classroom situations: A systems communication perspective. *Interchange, 19*(2), 25–40.

Yin, C. C., & Kwok, T. T. (1998). Research on total teacher effectiveness: Conception strategies. *The International Journal of Education, 12*(1), 39–44.

17

How Effective Are Teacher-Initiated Classroom Questions in Enhancing Student Learning?

Barbara Mae Gayle
Saint Martin's University

Raymond W. Preiss
University of Puget Sound

Mike Allen
University of Wisconsin–Milwaukee

Anecdotal and empirical evidence indicates that oral questioning is a fundamental aspect of daily classroom interactions. Written questions are common in handouts, assignments, projections, Web content, and study guides. The pervasive use of educational questions indicates that educators believe that questions are an essential element in increasing student learning. The small body of quantitative and qualitative studies on questions, as well as research on the theory and practice of question asking, reflect the sustained interest in the nature of questioning (e.g., Boeck, 1970; Dantonio & Paradise, 1988; Dillon, 1981; Fincke, 1967; Grow-Maienza, Hahn, & Joo, 2001; Madden, 1991).

Forty years of empirical research has focused on the frequency of questioning (Fagan, Hassler, & Szabo, 1981; Johns, 1968), the type of questions asked (Guszak, 1967; West & Pearson, 1994), the cognitive level of the question (Pressley, McDaniel, Turnure, & Ahmad, 1987; Ryan, 1973), the nature of the response elicited in relationship to the type of question asked (Cole & Williams, 1973; Dillon, 1982b), the time necessary to evoke high-order cognitive responses (Andrews, 1980; Swift & Gooding, 1983), and the long-term efficacy of the question-asking process (Buggey, 1972; Martin & Pressley, 1991). Qualitative studies, on the other hand, focused on explicating teacher questioning practices pedagogically (Nielsen, 1988; Ryan, 1973). Other studies reviewed the overall literature on oral questions both quantitatively (Redfield & Rousseau, 1981; Samson, Strykowski, Weinstein, & Walberg, 1987) and qualitatively (Gall, 1984; Winne, 1979). However, the largest portion of the oral question literature has been devoted to pragmatically advising teachers about the process of designing and implementing questioning strategies in their classrooms (e.g., McCue-Aschner, 1961; Sachen, 1999). Some of these publications focused on the psychology of asking questions (Graesser & Black, 1985); others focused on the aspects of information processing (Lauer, Peacock, & Graesser, 1992).

Overall, the research on oral questioning is not as definitive as might be expected after 40 years of investigation. Additionally, the amount of research tended to subside during the 1990s. The purpose of this study is to review this body of empirical findings both narratively and meta-analytically. Our goal is to assess the relationship of teacher oral questioning procedures and student learning. A narrative examination of the theoretical perspectives driving this line of inquiry is followed by results of a meta-analytic review of the relationship between student achievement and classroom questioning procedures, the cognitive correspondence between teacher questions and student answers, and the influence of thinking or wait time in promoting student learning. These investigations of teacher questioning procedures in the classroom are followed by an interpretation of the findings.

LITERATURE REVIEW

Questions have been conceptualized as inquiries that seek specific information or elicit cognitive elaboration (Graesser, Person, & Huber, 1992). Hunkins (1972) urged educators to use questions to enhance student thought, discussion, and achievement. Lower level cognitive questions "require students to recall previously presented information" (Gall, 1984, p. 40), whereas higher cognitive level questions require the integration of material and going beyond the information presented (Pressley & Forest-Pressley, 1985). Teachers have been advised that increasing the number of higher level questions boosts students' thinking capacity and improves students' overall level of academic achievement (Graesser & Black, 1985). Issues related to the questioning–achievement relationship include the effect of the question level on thinking time requirements and the correspondence between cognitive level of the question asked and the cognitive level of students' responses. These issues are considered in greater detail after we review the most common pedagogical advice regarding question use.

Advice for Effective Questioning Practices

Most of the advice or pedagogical exploration articles written are based on the observation that teachers frequently ask questions in their classrooms. Dillon (1982c) cited a variety of educators while making the case that verbal questions are essential for student learning. He argued that perhaps there is too much emphasis on the assumption that a question functions to stimulate a student's thought processes and not enough research into whether or not the use of questions limits or inhibits the expression of students' thoughts. Our review supports the conclusion that most educators believe that question use promotes learning.

In published advice, authors discuss the scope of possible questions, the ways to incorporate question asking into one's teaching style, and the considerations involved when choosing the right type of question and the right time to use that question (e.g., Brualdi, 1998; Guthrie, 1983; Hollingsworth, 1982; Sachen, 1999). Wilen and Clegg's (1986) analysis is typical in this area. They suggested that phrasing questions clearly, asking questions that are content based, employing both high-level and low-level cognitive questions, encouraging student responses, and allowing sufficient wait time for student responses all promote learning. They also asserted that to be effective, teachers need to balance responses from volunteering and nonvolunteering students, permit called-out answers, assist with incorrect responses, probe for deep-level consideration, and acknowledge correct responses.

Farrar (1983) took a slightly different approach, arguing that the social aspects of questioning practices must also be considered when taking into account how questions function in the classroom. She maintained that mutuality between the question asker and question responder must be established if the threatening, power-laden nature of question asking is overcome. Farrar preferred that teachers use mutuality enhancers such as indirect questions, hints, or an extended chain of questions designed to elicit the desired response to make the questions less threatening for students. Bruadli (1998) discussed a similar notion, which she defined as precipitating a feeling of failure. She maintained that teachers asking vague, trick, or overly abstract questions inhibit student responses and evoke negative feelings toward learning.

Taken together, the authors advocating specific pedagogical techniques make similar question-asking prescriptions for "best practices" in the class-

room. However, these studies vary considerably in the approach to acknowledging and overcoming the power issues associated with classroom
questioning. These conceptual issues are considered in the next sections.

Student Achievement

One major area of study in the efficacy of question-asking research explores
the relationship between teacher questioning practices and student learning. This research examines whether contemplating answers to questions
stimulates critical thinking better than considering factually presented information alone (Martin & Pressley, 1991; Miller & Pressley, 1989; Tyler,
1971), and whether the relationship between the cognitive level of the
question asked and student achievement can be established (Bedwell, 1974;
Kleinman, 1965; Ripley, 1981).

Overall, studies comparing whether question asking improves recall
more than presenting factual information are inconclusive. The majority of
studies reported that question asking improves associative or factual learning better than reading text alone (Fincke, 1967; Martin & Pressley, 1991;
Pressley et al., 1987; Pressley, Symons, McDaniel, Synder, & Turnure, 1988;
Tyler, 1971). For example, Fincke (1967), Martin and Pressley (1991), Tyler
(1971), and Pressley et al. (1988) found that oral questioning practices enhance comprehension more than just reading the material. Pressley et al.
(1987) found that questioned participants recalled more than participants
given base statements or precise elaboration. Most of these authors concluded that questioning has a positive effect on comprehension, although
Martin and Pressley (1991) argued that the type of answer sought in response to a given question is as important in determining recall or
comprehension as is asking a particular type of question.

Unlike the previous studies, Wright and Nuthall (1970) discovered that
the more questions that were asked, the lower the student recall or comprehension. Additionally, Miller and Pressley (1989) found very little difference in recall between participants who were questioned and those who
were not. These authors concluded that questioning depresses recall and
prevents the elaboration necessary to promote comprehension. Thus,
whether questioning activates different aspects of memorization or aids in
cognitive elaboration is equivocal, and it is reasonable to investigate
whether asking oral questions is related to increased student achievement.

Studies exploring the effects of the cognitive level of questions on learning are also inconsistent (see Table 17.1). The majority of this research
found no significant difference in student achievement due to the type of
question asked (Bedwell, 1974; Ghee, 1975; Martikean, 1973; Mathes,
1977; Millett, 1968; Ripley, 1981; Rogers, 1968; Ryan, 1974; Savage, 1972).
However, there are some studies with findings suggesting that lower cogni-

TABLE 17.1

Effect Sizes for Studies Investigating the Relationship Between the Level of Oral Question and Student Achievement

Author	Year	Sample Size	Effect Size
Bedwell	1974	4	−.540
Buggey	1971	108	.921
Clark et al.	1979	386	.343
Gall et al.	1978	371	.592
Ghee	1975	28	.047
Kleinman	1965	766	.117
Ladd & Anderson	1970	40	.724
Martikean	1973	30	−.027
Mathes	1977	122	.222
Ripley	1981	154	.056
Ryan	1973	104	.415
Ryan	1974	105	.462
Tyler	1971	120	.708

tive-level questions enhance student learning (Clark et al., 1979; Wright & Nuthall, 1970) and several other studies that revealed high-level cognitive questions were more effective in enhancing student achievement (Aagard, 1973; Beseda, 1973; Buggey, 1971; Gall et al., 1978; Kleinman, 1965; Ladd & Anderson, 1970; Lucking, 1975). At issue in this aspect of question-asking research is how the cognitive level of the question functions to enhance recall or comprehension.

Winne (1979) narratively reviewed 18 dissertations, paper presentations, and published studies testing the assumption that asking students questions to manipulate information rather than recalling previously presented factual information increased student achievement. He distinguished between teacher training experiments and experimenter-directed questioning skills. By calculating percentages of studies in each category, Winne found that 60% of the studies examined revealed no significant differences in student achievement based on the cognitive level of the question. Fifteen percent of the studies examined supported the hypothesis that higher cognitive-level questions produced greater student achievement than lower-level cognitive questions and 25% of the studies reported that factual questions were more effective in promoting student achievement than higher-order questions.

This box score approach tended to discount the educational benefits of higher order questions.

When Redfield and Rousseau (1981) revisited Winne's (1979) study meta-analytically, they claimed that "gains in achievement can be expected when higher cognitive questions assume a predominate role during classroom instruction" (p. 237). These authors compared 13 of Winne's (1979) original studies and 1 additional unpublished study. Redfield and Rousseau (1981) found a positive overall effect size (difference score in standard deviation units) of .73, indicating that instruction using higher cognitive-level questions can significantly improve student achievement.

Because the effect size calculated by Redfield and Rousseau (1981) was so much larger than other meta-analytic research, Samson et al. (1987) replicated the meta-analysis. These authors, using 14 studies (many of the same ones used by Redfield and Rousseau), calculated a median effect size of .13, suggesting that asking higher-level cognitive questions has a small effect on student learning, not the large effect identified by Redfield and Rousseau (1981). When Samson et al. (1987) compared their results to Winne (1979), they found that 88% (vs. Winne's 60%) of the studies examined revealed no significant differences in student learning based on the cognitive-level of the question asked. They also discovered that 6% rather 15% of the studies examined revealed that higher cognitive-level questions produced greater student learning than lower-level cognitive questions and 6% rather than 25% of the studies reported that factual questions were more effective in promoting student learning than higher-order questions. In comparing their results with Redfield and Rousseau (1981), for Samson et al. (1987) the mean effect size was .26 versus the .73 effect size Redfield and Rousseau calculated.

The difference in findings and the inability of the review studies to reconcile contradictory findings (see Table 17.2) suggests that more research is warranted in this area. Also, new studies have emerged during the 15 years since the last empirical review. Thus, it is reasonable to explore the relationship between the cognitive level of the question asked and the overall increase in student achievement.

Teacher–Student Correspondence

A second area of question-asking research involves the idea that the level of cognitive questions tends to elicit a similar cognitive-level response. To maximize learning, this line of research suggests that teachers must pay equal attention to the type of question asked and the type of response received. Arnold, Atwood, and Rogers (1973, 1974), Cole and Williams (1973), Dantonio and Paradise (1988), and Guszak (1967) found that the level of instructor questioning is generally related to the characteristics of

TABLE 17.2

Effect Sizes for Studies Investigating the Relationship Between Oral Question and Student Learning

Author	Year	Sample Size	Effect Size
Fincke	1967	32	.353
Martin & Pressley	1991	110	.209
Miller & Pressley I	1989	64	.438
II		32	.309
Pressley et al. I	1987	120	.502
II		76	.317
III		76	.318
Pressley et al. I	1988	60	.606
II		60	.673
III		70	.594
IV		70	.417
Tyler	1971	120	.504
Wright & Nuthall	1970	17	.540

student responses. Dantonio and Paradise (1988) found that high-level questions, which require students to process readily available information at a higher level than rote recall, elicited high-level responses and lower cognitive-level questions requiring the recall of factual information elicited lower-level cognitive responses. However, Dantonio and Paradise also discovered that questions requiring inferences in which students were required to process information in excess of available information had varying degrees of corresponding answers.

Several studies have examined the relationship between higher cognitive-level questions and replies. Fagan et al. (1981), Arnold et al. (1973), and Madden (1991) concluded that asking higher-level questions produces higher-level responses. Other researchers disagree, suggesting that only half of the time is there any correspondence between the cognitive level of teachers' questions and students' responses (Dillon, 1982a; Mills, Rice, Berliner, & Rousseau, 1980). One explanation given for the incongruence between the level of teacher questions and student responses is that students may experience confusion in identifying the needed response or in having the mental agility or ability to answer the question (Winne & Marx, 1980). Another issue that may account for the discrepancy in findings could be the operationalization of high- and low-level questions. Regardless of the reason for the lack of congruence, the findings in this area of question-asking re-search are inconsistent (see Table 17.3). Thus, it seems reasonable to inves-tigate whether there is any correspondence between the cognitive level of the questions asked and the answers received.

Wait Time

A relatively new line of question-asking research focuses on the amount of thinking time necessary to enhance the level of student response (see Table 17.4). The idea here is that teachers must provide time after asking a ques-tion to allow students to process the question and conceptualize their an-swer. The problem appears to be that teachers allow only 1 to 3 seconds for answer processing (Atwood et al., 1974; Rowe, 1978). Referred to as wait time or lapse time, the construct is usually operationalized by using a stop-watch to track the amount of time that occurs after the question is asked and before the answer begins.

Some of the research in this area focuses on question complexity and think time. Andrews (1980) and Madden (1991) found that students re-sponding to higher cognitive-level questions do not require more wait time than students responding to lower cognitive-level questions. In fact, Mad-den (1991) discovered that pausing after higher-level questions does not necessarily produce higher-level responses.

On the other hand, Arnold et al. (1974), Fagan et al. (1981), and Gambrell (1983) found a significant difference between the level of ques-tioning and the amount of wait time used. Fagan et al. (1981) revealed a sig-nificant interaction between using higher-level questions and increased

TABLE 17.3

Effect Sizes for Studies Investigating the Relationship Between the Level of Oral Questioning and the Level of Response

Author	Year	Sample Size	Effect Size
Arnold et al.	1973	12	.770
Arnold et al.	1974	11	.734
Cole & Williams	1973	8	.513
Dantonio & Paradise	1988	22	.363
Dillon	1982a	27	.182
Fagan et al.	1981	20	.543
Guszak	1967	12	.760
Madden	1991	12	.435
Mills et al.	1980	54	.260

TABLE 17.4

Effect Sizes for Studies Investigating the Relationship Between the Level
of Oral Questioning and the Amount of Wait Time Required or Given

Author	Year	Sample Size	Effect Size
Andrews	1980	7	.010
Arnold et al.	1973	12	.009
Arnold et al.	1974	11	.271
Fagan et al.	1981	20	.591
Gambrell	1983	9	.083
Madden	1991	5	.000

thinking or wait time and the production of higher level cognitive responses.
Gambrell (1983) discovered that higher-order questions did not require
more think time and that lower level text-based questions required more
think time before eliciting a response. Arnold et al. (1974) found that analysis questions required more think time than knowledge, comprehension, application, synthesis, or evaluation questions. One study discovered that
overall question level was not related to lapse time and neither was lapse
time related to the response level (Arnold et al., 1973). These authors found
that the majority of questions elicited responses at the level of knowledge
and comprehension (low-order responses). The authors concluded that
teachers failed to capitalize on the use of higher-order questions that may
improve educational outcomes. Taken together the wait time studies' results
are divergent, and no specific pattern of wait time differences has emerged in
the literature. It is reasonable to ask how the cognitive level of the question
affects the amount of wait time.

METHODS

To explore the effect of oral questioning procedures, relevant studies were
located using databases such as ERIC, Education Abstracts, Academic Universe, PsychINFO, and Communication Index. The reference section of
each manuscript collected was searched for additional studies not previously identified. To be included in this study, each manuscript had to investigate some aspect of oral question asking used in an instructional context and
provide enough information to allow conversion of results into a common
metric for comparison.

The search procedure addressing whether the level of oral questioning
increases student achievement resulted in the capture of 13 manuscripts.

The search procedure for research studies concentrating on whether oral questions improve student learning overall resulted in the location of seven manuscripts with 14 independent tests relevant to the variables of interest. The search procedure for manuscripts investigating whether there is any correspondence between the cognitive level of the oral question asked and the cognitive level of a student's response resulted in the location of nine studies. The search procedure to locate studies exploring whether the cognitive level of oral questions affects the amount of wait time given or required resulted in the location of six manuscripts.

The summary statistics of each study were converted to correlations so that the magnitude of outcomes attributable to oral question-asking procedures could be quantified. The correlations were weighted for sample size and then averaged. Each average correlation was assessed to determine if the variance in the observed sample correlations was larger than expected by random sample error (Hedges & Olkin, 1985). To detect a moderator variable, the sum of the squared error was tested using a chi-square test. A nonsignificant chi-square indicates that the amount of variability is probably the result of chance, whereas a significant chi-square indicates that the amount of variability is probably the result of some type of moderating variable.

RESULTS

Results assessing whether the level of oral questioning increases student achievement revealed a wide range of effect sizes for the 13 studies (range $= -.54 - .92$). The average effect size of .334 for 2,337 respondents can be classified as moderate. The significant chi-square $\chi^2(12, N = 2,337) = 145.93, p < .05$, suggests the possibility of one or more moderating variables, which were not identifiable.

Results exploring whether oral questioning improves student learning overall revealed mostly moderate effect sizes for the 13 separate experiments with 907 respondents. The average effect size of .437 was moderate, $\chi^2 = 22.65, p < .05$. Removing the Martin study, which appeared as an outlier on the scatter plot increased the average effect size to .471 based on a homogenous set of effects, $\chi^2(12, N = 907) = 10.24, p > .05$.

Results investigating whether there is any correspondence between the cognitive level of the oral question asked and the cognitive level of a student's response revealed overall moderate effect sizes for the nine studies. The average effect size was .413 and involved 178 participants, $\chi^2(8, N = 178) = 7.66, ns$, indicating that the amount of variation is probably due to sampling error.

Results for six studies with 64 respondents that explored whether the cognitive level of oral questions affects the amount of wait time given or required revealed mostly small individual effect sizes and an overall small average effect size of .246, $\chi^2(5, N = 64) = 3.75$, indicating that the amount of variation is probably due to sampling error.

DISCUSSION

Classroom questions appear to affect student learning in several ways. Results from this study suggest that the interaction between teachers and students can be structured to enhance student ability to remember and apply course material at a later date. The findings of this study are discussed next in terms of the implications for current and future classroom practices.

The first analysis summarizes whether the level of oral questioning increases student achievement. The observed average effect of .334 is generally consistent with earlier meta-analyses. The effect sizes varied widely, however, and the likely presence of a moderator variable was indicated. Nevertheless, the moderate, positive effect has classroom implications. Achievement scores tended to increase following exposure to high-order questioning. This finding lends credence to the advice often offered to educators that high-order questions promote learning and critical thinking. Considering the Arnold et al. (1974) observation that teachers miss many opportunities to employ high-order questions, greater attention should be directed at strategically altering patterns of question use.

The notion that question level as a valuable learning device is underscored by our findings regarding whether the use of oral questions improves student learning. The average effect was positive, stable, and approached a large effect. The fact that using questions is associated with learning (.471) provides the context for interpreting the results of studies varying the level of the questions. The results suggest that using high-order questions provides substantial increases (up to .334) over and above the learning resulting from mere question use. Because these studies did not systematically control the types of questions employed, we cannot estimate the additional contribution with precision. If Arnold et al. (1974) are correct, however, most questions were likely low-order in nature. If so, the contribution offered by high-order questions should be meaningful.

This meta-analysis provides a possible vehicle for understanding the question use–learning relationship and the question level–learning relationship. A stable, positive association was detected between level of teacher questioning and level of student response. This indicates that educators can induce high-order responses by strategically posing questions designed to encourage synthesis and integration. Also, it appears that teachers need not belabor wait time to elicit these high-order responses. The small, positive average effect indicates that high-order questions require only slightly more processing time than low-order questions.

Although teachers routinely pose interrogatives to their students, these questions are often employed without consideration of power relationships and without appreciation for the various question forms. This may be short-sighted, as this meta-analysis indicates that skillful questioning is clearly associated with integration and synthesis of conceptual material. Considering the potential benefits, structuring lecture time to include ample questioning opportunities seems to be justified. Also, strategically managing question-answering time appears to be warranted. Finally, from our experiences, the use of questions is a skill not routinely stressed in many graduate programs.

REFERENCES

References marked with an asterisk indicate studies included in the meta-analysis.

Aagard, S. A. (1973). Oral questioning by the teacher: Influence on student achievement in eleventh grade chemistry (Doctoral dissertation, New York University, 1973). *Dissertation Abstracts International, 34,* 631A.

*Andrews, J. D. W. (1980). The verbal structure of teacher questions: Its impact on class discussion. *POD Quarterly, 2*(3–4), 29–163.

*Arnold, D. S., Atwood, R. K., & Rogers, V. M. (1973). An investigation of relationships among question level, response level and lapse time. *School Science and Mathematics, 73,* 591–594.

*Arnold, D. S., Atwood, R. K., & Rogers, V. M. (1974). Question and response levels and lapse time intervals. *Journal of Experiemental Education, 4,* 11–15.

*Bedwell, L. E. (1974). The effects of training teachers in question-asking skills on the achievement and attitudes of elementary pupils (Doctoral dissertation, Indiana University). *Dissertation Abstracts International, 35,* 5980–09A.

Beseda, C. G. (1973). Levels of questioning used by student teachers and its effects on pupil achievement and critical thinking ability. (Doctoral dissertation, North Texas State University, 1972). *Dissertation Abstracts International, 32,* 2543A.

Boeck, M. A. (1970). Experimental analysis of questioning behavior of pre-service secondary school science teachers (Doctoral dissertation, University of Minnesota, 1970). *Dissertation Abstracts International, 32,* 0230–01A.

Brualdi, A. M. (1998). *Classroom questions* (Rep. No. EDO–TM–98–02). College Park, MD: The Catholic University of America, Shriver Laboratory. (ERIC Document Reproduction Service No. ED422407)

*Buggey, L. J. (1971). A study of the relationship of classroom question and social studies achievement of second-grade children (Doctoral dissertation, University of Washington, 1971). *Dissertation Abstracts International, 32,* 2543A.

*Clark, C. M., Gage, N. L., Marx, R. W., Peterson, P. L., Staybrook, N. G., & Winne, P. H. (1979). A factorial experiment on teacher structuring, soliciting, and reacting. *Journal of Educational Psychology, 71,* 534–552.

*Cole, R. A., & Williams, D. M. (1973). Pupil responses to teacher questions: Cognitive level, length and syntax. *Educational Leadership, 31,* 142–145.

*Dantonio, M., & Paradise, L. V. (1988). Teacher question–answer strategy and the cognitive correspondence between teacher questions and learner responses. *Journal of Research and development in Education, 21*(3), 71–75.

Dillon, J. T. (1981). To question and not to question during discussion. *Journal of Teacher Education, 32,* 15–20.

*Dillon, J. T. (1982a). Cognitive correspondence between question/statement and response. *American Educational Research Journal, 19,* 540–551.

Dillon, J. T. (1982b). The effect of questions in education and other enterprises. *Journal of Curriculum Studies, 14,* 127–152.

Dillon, J. T. (1982c). The multidisciplinary study of questioning. *Journal of Educational Psychology, 74*(2), 147–165.

*Fagan, E. R., Hassler, D. M., & Szabo, M. (1981). Evaluation of questioning strategies in language arts instruction. *Research in the Teaching of English, 16,* 267–278.

Farrar, M. T. (1983). Another look at oral questions for comprehension. *The Reading Teacher, 36,* 370–375.

*Fincke, W. M. (1967). The effect of asking questions to develop purposes for reading on the attainment of higher levels of comprehension in a population of third grade children (Doctoral dissertation, Temple University, 1967). *Dissertation Abstracts International, 29,* 1778–06A.

Gall, M. D. (1984). Synthesis of research on teacher's questioning. *Educational Leadership, 40,* 40–47.

*Gall, M. D., Ward, B. A., Berliner, D. C., Cahen, L. S., Winne, P. H., Elashoff, J. D., et al. (1978). Effects of questioning techniques and recitation on student learning. *American Educational Research Journal, 15,* 175–199.

*Gambrell, L. B. (1983). The occurrence of think-time during reading comprehension. *Journal of Educational Research, 77*(2), 77–80.

*Ghee, H. J. (1975). A study of the effects of high level cognitive questions on the levels of response and critical thinking abilities in students of two social problems classes (Doctoral dissertation, University of Virginia, 1975). *Dissertation Abstracts International, 36,* 5187–08A.

Graesser, A. C., & Black, J. B. (1985). *The psychology of questions.* Hillsdale, NJ: Lawrence Erlbaum Associates.

Graesser, A. C., Person, N., & Huber, J. (1992). Mechanisms that generate questions. In T. W. Lauer, E. Peacock, & A. C. Graesser (Eds.), *Questions and information systems* (pp. 167–187), Hillsdale, NJ: Lawrence Erlbaum Associates.

Grow-Maienza, J., Hahn, D. D., & Joo, C. A. (2001). Mathematics instruction in Korean primary schools: Structures, processes, and a linguistic analysis of questioning. *Journal of Educational Psychology, 93,* 363–376.

*Guszak, F. J. (1967). Teacher questioning and reading. *The Reading Teacher, 21,* 227–234.

Guthrie, J. T. (1983). Questions as teaching tools. *Journal of Reading, 26,* 478–479.

Hedges, L. V., & Olkin, I. (1985). *Statistical methods for meta-analysis.* Orlando, FL: Academic.

Hollingsworth, P. M. (1982). Questioning: The heart of teaching. *The Clearinghouse, 55,* 350–252.

Hunkins, F. P. (1972). *Questioning strategies and techniques.* Boston: Allyn & Bacon.

Johns, J. P. (1968). The relationship between teacher behaviors and the incidence of thought-provoking questions by students in secondary schools. *The Journal of Educational Research, 62,* 117–122.

*Kleinman, G. S. (1965). Teachers' questions and student understanding of science. *Journal of Research in Science Teaching, 3,* 307–317.

*Ladd, G. T., & Anderson, H. O. (1970). Determining the level of inquiry in teachers' questions. *Journal of Research in Science Teaching, 7,* 396–400.

Lauer, T. W., Peacock, E., & Graesser, A. C. (1992). *Questions and information systems.* Hillsdale, NJ: Lawrence Erlbaum Associates.

Lucking, R. A. (1975). A study of the effects of a hierarchically-ordered questioning technique on adolescents' responses to short stories (Doctoral dissertation, University of Nebraska, 1975). *Dissertation Abstracts International, 36,* 0138–08A.

*Madden, S. J. (1991, February). *A study of instructor techniques and strategies.* Paper presented at the meeting of the Western States Communication Association, Phoenix, AZ.

*Martikean, A. (1973). *The levels of questioning and their effects upon student performance above the knowledge level of Bloom's taxonomy of educational objectives* (Research Paper No. E585, Division of Education). Gary: Indiana University Northwest. (ERIC Document Reproduction Service No. ED091248)

*Martin, V. L., & Pressley, M. (1991). Elaborative-interrogation effects depend on the nature of the question. *Journal of Educational Psychology, 83,* 113–119.

*Mathes, C. A. (1977). The effects of two different reading comprehension achievement of students at a fourth grade reading level. (Doctoral dissertation, Indiana University Nebraska) *Dissertation Abstracts International, 39,* 7139–40A.

McCue-Aschner, M. J. (1961). Asking questions to trigger thinking. *NEA Journal, 50,* 44–46.

*Miller, G. E., & Pressley, M. (1989). Picture versus question elaboration on young children's learning of sentences containing high and low probability content. *Journal of Experimental Child Psychology, 48,* 431–450.

Millett, G. B. (1968). Comparison of four teacher training procedures in achieving teacher and pupil "translation" behaviors in secondary school social studies (Doctoral dissertation, Stanford University, 1967). *Dissertation Abstracts International, 28,* 4514A.

*Mills, S. R., Rice, C. T., Berliner, D. C., & Rousseau, E. W. (1980). The correspondence between teacher question and student answers in classroom discourse. *Journal of Experimental Education, 48,* 194–204.

Nielsen, R. S. (1988). Improving teacher questioning. *Illinois School Research and Development, 24,* 94–101.

Pressley, M., & Forrest-Pressley, D. (1985). Questions and children's cognitive processing. In A. C. Graesser & J. B. Black (Eds.), *The psychology of questions* (pp. 277–296). Hillsdale, NJ: Lawrence Erlbaum Associates.

*Pressley, M., McDaniel, M. A., Turnure, J. E., & Ahmad, M. (1987). Generation and precision of elaboration: Effects on intentional and incidental learning. *Journal of Experimental Psychology: Learning, Memory and Cognition, 13,* 291–300.

*Pressley, M., Symons, S., McDaniel, M. A., Synder, B. L., & Turnure, J. E. (1988). Elaborative interrogation facilitates acquisition of confusing facts. *Journal of Educational Psychology, 80,* 268–278

Redfield, D. L., & Rousseau, E. W. (1981). A meta-analysis of experimental research on teacher questioning behavior. *Review of Educational Research, 51,* 237–245.

*Ripley, J. P. (1981). The effects of preservice teacher's cognitive questioning level and redirecting on student science achievement. *Journal of Research in Science Teaching, 18,* 303–309.

Rogers, V. M. (1968). Varying the cognitive levels of classroom questions in elementary social studies: An analysis of the use of questions by student-teachers (Doctoral dissertation, University of Texas at Austin). *Dissertation Abstracts International, 30,* 1459–04A.

Rowe, M. B. (1978). Wait-time and rewards as instructional variables, their influence on language, logic, and fate control: Part one—Wait-time. *Journal of Research in Science Teaching, 11,* 81–94.

*Ryan, F. L. (1973). Analyzing the questioning activity of students and teachers. *College Student Journal, 6,* 116–123.

*Ryan, F. L. (1974). The effects of social studies achievement of multiple student responding to different levels of questioning. *Journal of Experimental Education, 42*(4), 71–75.

Sachen, J. B. (1999). Instructing the instructor: Effective questions. *Fire Engineering, 52,* 130–134.

Samson, G. E., Strykowski, B., Weinstein, T., & Walberg, H. J. (1987). The effects of teacher questioning levels on student achievement: A quantitative synthesis. *Journal of Educational Research, 80,* 290–295.

Savage, T. V. (1972). A study of the relationship of classroom questions and social studies achievement of fifth grade children (Doctoral dissertation, University of Washington). *Dissertation Abstracts International, 33,* 2245–05A.

Swift, J. N., & Gooding, C. T. (1983). Interaction of wait time feedback and questioning instruction on middle school science teaching. *Journal of Research in Science Teaching, 20,* 721–730.

*Tyler, J. F. (1971). A study of the relationship of two methods of question presentation, sex, and school location to the social studies achievement of second-grade children (Doctoral dissertation, University of Washington). *Dissertation Abstracts International, 32,* 2561–05A.

West, R., & Pearson, J. C. (1994). Antecedent and consequent conditions of student questioning: An analysis of classroom discourse across the university. *Communication Education, 43,* 299–311.

Wilen, W. W., & Clegg, A. A. (1986). Effective questions and questioning: A research review. *Theory and Research in Social Education, 14,* 153–161.

Winne, P. H. (1979). Experiments relating to teachers' use of higher cognitive questions to student achievement. *Review of Educational Research, 49,* 13–50.

Winne, P. H., & Marx, R. (1980). Matching students cognitive responses to teaching skills. *Journal of Educational Psychology, 78,* 257–264.

*Wright, C. J., & Nuthall, G. (1970). Relationships between teacher behaviors and pupil achievement in three experimental elementary science lessons. *American Educational Research Journal, 7,* 477–491.

18

A Meta-Analytic Assessment of the Effect of Humorous Lectures on Learning

Diane M. Martin
University of Portland

Raymond W. Preiss
University of Puget Sound

Barbara Mae Gayle
Saint Martin's University

Mike Allen
University of Wisconsin–Milwaukee

Educators have often been told that using humor in lectures is likely to improve classroom climate and promote learning. Although some writers appear to hold unrealistically high expectations for the educational benefits of humor (Gilliland & Mauritsen, 1971; Welker, 1977), humor is a common device in many classrooms. The humor–learning relationship has been asserted in diverse disciplines, including advertising (Sternthal & Craig, 1973; Weinberger & Gulas, 1992), biology (Wandersee, 1982), communication studies (Gruner, 1970), English (Donelson, 1973), geology, (Backlawski, 1980), literature (Mitchell, 1981), management (Duncan, Smeltzer, & Leap, 1990), mathematics, (Rosenthal, 1981), statistics (Berk & Nanda,

1998), and physics (Adams, 1972). Although some investigators point to limitations and inconsistencies in the basic relationship, most view humor as a valuable asset for promoting learning.

Considerable disagreement exists regarding why humor might result in greater comprehension and recall. Explanations for the humor–learning relationship include heightened student motivation (Larson, 1982), stress reduction (McMorris, Urbach, & Connor, 1985), favorable classroom climate (Stuart & Rosenfeld, 1994), interest in lecture content (White, 2001), selective exposure (Wakshlag, Day, & Zillmann, 1981), and student–teacher rapport (Neuliep, 1991). Although this list of explanations is not comprehensive, gifted teachers seem to understand the value of classroom humor. Award-winning teachers use humor strategically to clarify and stress relevance (Downs, Javidi, & Nussbaum, 1988; Javidi, Downs, & Nussbaum, 1998) and experienced teachers use humor more frequently than novice teachers (Javidi & Long, 1989). Regardless of the explanation for why humor promotes learning, humor use is a common and accepted practice.

It is paradoxical that humor researchers have largely ignored the humor–learning relationship. When Lynch (2002) offered a narrative account of the functions and outcomes of humor, no mention was made of the educational implications of classroom humor. This gap supports Lynch's conclusion that communication approaches to humor are underdeveloped and that scholars should "identify the space and need in humor theory that a communication-based understanding will fill and satisfy" (p. 423). This chapter explores the role of humor in facilitating understanding and learning by reviewing theoretical accounts for humor, surveying the social scientific evidence, and summarizing the humor–learning literature meta- analytically.

REVIEW OF APPROACHES
TO THE HUMOR CONSTRUCT

Theoretical accounts for humor and responses to humorous messages may provide insight for why humor is thought to enhance learning. We acknowledge the complexity of this endeavor. Theorizing about humor almost certainly means continual development of complementary and contrasting possibilities. Chapman and Foot (1976) believed that "no all-embracing theory of humor and/or laughter has yet gained widespread acceptance," (p. 4), as the variable is incorrectly viewed as a unitary process. Humor plays a myriad of roles and serves a number of different functions. Still, several researchers agree that three primary theories of humor (incongruity, relief, and superiority) each partially illuminates the role of humor in human communication (e.g., Chapman & Foot, 1976; Meyer, 1998, 2000; Morreall, 1983; Raskin, 1985).

Meyer (2000) linked three primary theories of humor (incongruity: deliberate violation of rational language patterns; relief: the release of tension and stress through humor; and superiority: a sense of triumph over another) to social functions of humor. Meyer suggested that the same humor event can serve a variety of rhetorical goals and that humorous events are purposefully ambiguous. This humorous ambiguity provides the opportunity for theoretical variety and meaning, such that the joke or humorous event may be tension release to some and superiority humor to others (Meyer, 2000). It is apparent then, that joking can be risky business, opening one up to misinterpretations and unintended results.

The Incongruity Approach

Incongruity theory suggests that people laugh at what surprises them or is otherwise unexpected (La Fave, Haddad, & Maesen, 1976; McGhee, 1979; Rossel, 1981). Kant is often credited with the origins of incongruity theory, linked to his definition of laughter: "an affectation arising from sudden transformation of a strained expectation into nothing" (as cited in Lynch, 2002, p. 428). Rossel (1981) explained that:

> the punch line in a joke works because it suddenly diverts the stream of thought, pulling it into a climax which points to a paradox of incongruity in the meaning of the words, turns specific ideas or expectations on their head, or switches roles or behavioral expectations. (p. 129)

In other words, the humor initiator relies on the play of words or the surprising phrase to create the paradox of word meanings. In doing this, the initiator violates the expectations with a humorous twist; the punch line is funny only in contrast to the serious meaning of the preceding discourse (e.g., Bolman & Deal, 1991).

With a basis in surprise and quick switching between serious and comic discourse, the successful humor initiator is often the most linguistically dominant individual, one who is "versatile in the combined use of metaphor and humor to tease others about his or her identity without being 'teased out'" (Rossel, 1981, p. 129). Incongruity theory is often exemplified with jokes, where it is the structure of the joke itself that prepares the audience for the humorous punch line. The joke initiator needs both the attention of the audience and the implicit agreement that the attempted discourse is indeed an attempt at humor. If the audience is reticent either to give the initiator its attention or to meet the social demands of the joke structure, the joke may fail.

The Relief Approach

Relief humor theory is based on the idea that humor is used to release tension and stress. Freud (1905/1960) extended humor relief theory with his description of relief humor as both a healing release of pent-up tension and disguised aggression. Morreall (1991) described two strategic uses of humor linked to relief theory: promoting health by reducing stress and acting as a social lubricant. Spencer is generally considered to be the originator of humor relief theory. He compared the release of pent-up laughter to a safety valve on a steam pipe (in Morreall, 1983; Zijderveld, 1983).

McGuffee-Smith and Powell's (1988) empirical investigation shows that self-disparaging humor by an organizational leader acts as a tension reliever and encourages member participation and shared decision making. They noted that "disparaging humor may be affected by the group's role expectations of a leader and the anticipated functions of the leader toward group facilitation" (p. 289). In other words, the funniness of humor is at least partially based on the idea that everyone agrees to the "unreal" (Raskin, 1985) nature of humor. The joke is funny because it is not "true."

The Superiority Approach

Superiority humor theory contends that all humor is created from the longing to feel superior over or to control others (e.g., Duncan, 1985; Duncan et al., 1990; Graham, Papa, & Brooks, 1992; Lundberg, 1969). This theory stems from the work of Hobbes (1840; as cited in Morreall, 1983) published in *Taking Humor Seriously* and has become the generally accepted definition of superiority theory:

> The passion of laughter is nothing else but sudden glory arising from sudden conception of some eminency in ourselves by comparison to the infirmity of others, or with our own formerly: for men laugh at the follies of themselves past, when they come suddenly to remembrance, except they bring with them any present dishonor. (as quoted in Morreall, 1983, p. 20)

Duncan's (1985) empirical work in a hospital setting shows that status differential and superiority in humor creation includes three positional power components: "First, high-status members of a group joke more than low-status members. Second, high-status initiators most often direct jokes toward low-status foci. Third, when other (high-status) members are present, high-status members refrain from self-disparaging humor" (p. 559). Thus, according to superiority theory, humor is used to exert control over others. Specific enactment of superiority humor is often related to an individual's positional power or membership in a more powerful group. Graham et al. (1992) noted that "much of the research that examines humor from a superiority perspective deals with disparagement humor that evaluates a person above the target of humor" (p. 161). Lundberg (1969) also argued that joking reinforces ranking and status as within and between groups. Put succinctly, the superiority theory of humor "views the basis of laughter as the triumph of one person over other people" (Duncan et al., 1985, p. 558). Thus the lens of superiority shades humor research in hues of control and bifurcation.

META-ANALYTIC SUMMARY

A review of the explanations for the humor literature indicates a disconnect between theoretical explanations for humor's educational effects and the opportunities for educational investigations to capitalize on humor theory. Exploring this gap, we recognized that characteristics of the humorous stimuli (incongruity, relief, and superiority) were rarely considered in the instructional literature (one exception is the research on disparaging classroom humor; Darling & Civikly, 1987). A reasonable first step to bridge this void was to empirically summarize the basic humor–learning relationship. We considered all investigations that involved the incongruity, relief, and superiority criteria. This reasoning resulted in the following question: Does exposure to educational messages containing humorous material result in understanding and learning?

METHOD

Meta-analysis, the empirical summary of domains of scientific literature, has been used as a tool for evaluating the theoretical merit of accounts for persuasion (Allen & Preiss, 1998) and interpersonal communication (Allen, Preiss, Gayle, & Burrell, 2002). We initiated an extensive search of the humor and learning literature by following standard meta-analytic procedures. We searched for the terms *humor, mirth, cartoons, funny,* and *jocular.* The resulting references were narrowed by searching for the terms *learning, recall, comprehension, understanding,* and *education.* Educational textbooks and conference papers were consulted and references and footnotes were extracted and examined. Computer searches of databases (PsychINFO, Dissertation Abstracts, ERIC, ComIndex, and CommSearch95) were initiated and hand searches of convention programs were conducted. The reference sections of captured studies were consulted and relevant citations were located. These search procedures yielded a set of published articles, unpublished papers, and unpublished dissertations involving humor and learning. Surprisingly, we did not find any existing meta-analyses on this relationship.

Inclusion Criteria

In the 50 years of humor and learning research, many operationalizations have been used to test the humor–learning hypothesis. In some cases, participants have been asked to read funny or unfunny messages, and in other cases they listened to lectures containing humorous (or serious) inserts. Some participants have read informative articles, others have assessed the wit of their teachers and self-assessed their own learning. Other studies presented recorded educational messages (on audiotape, visual slides, or videotape) and assessed comprehension using examinations. We included a study in the meta-analysis if the study exposed participants to a humorous and serious lecture or asked student raters to assess a teacher's use of humor in a lecture. Studies were included that reported any evaluation of learning (perceived, affective, or objective) from the lecture or stimulus message.

On a second level, we were faced with decisions meta-analysts commonly confront when processing enduring bodies of literature. Manuscripts varied in the reporting of results and description procedures and methods. Manuscripts were excluded if they failed to report summary statistics allowing aggregation, employed methods inappropriate for aggregation, or reported findings from one sample in more than one manuscript. To reduce the danger of capitalizing on chance due to reporting multiple comparisons in a single experiment, the decision rule was established to aggregate only a single effect size associated with any one type of learning from each data set.

Consistent with accepted meta-analytic methods, procedures by Hunter, Schmidt, and Jackson (1982) were employed. Summary statistics were converted into standardized effect estimates. Effects were weighted to correct for differences in sample size. The estimates were converted to correlations and summed. Effects were coded for year of publication or presentation, topic, and type of humor employed.

RESULTS

A total of 20 separate reports met the inclusion criteria. There were 21 independent tests of the humor–learning relationship, a complete set of the coding is available from the first author. The captured studies reflect a variety of participants, humor inductions, and learning assessment methods. Central to this investigation is the humor–learning relationship. Table 18.1 displays the total sample of studies and the three types of learning measured. For the total number of studies, a small average effect of +.20 was observed. This average effect is based on 21 independent experiments involving 4,801 participants. In an effort to locate potential moderator variables, a formal test of homogeneity was initiated. A significant chi-square, $\chi^2 = 132.40, p < .05, (20, N = 4,801)$ indicates that the ob-

TABLE 18.1
Humor–Learning Effect Sizes and Sample Sizes

Author	Year	Sample Size	Type of Learning	Effect Size
Burt	1998	42	Cognitive	
Bryant et al.	1979	70	Perceived	+.236
Bryant et al.	1980	70	Perceived	+.310
Cantor & Venus	1980	117	Cognitive	−.355
Chapman & Compton	1978	30	Cognitive	+.432
Conkell et al.	1999	543	Cognitive	+.033
Desberg et al.	1981	100	Cognitive	+.308
Fisher	1997	495	Cognitive	−.102
Foot et al.	1978	48	Cognitive	−.141
Frymier & Wanzer	1999	314	Affective	+.470
Gorham	1988	387	Perceived	+.390
Gorham & Christophel	1990	206	Perceived	+.080
Gorham & Zakahi	1990	526	Perceived	+.310
			Affective	+.210
Gruner & Freshley	1979	156	Cognitive	.000
Kaplan & Pascoe	1977	508	Cognitive	+.034
Sadowski et al.	1994	41	Cognitive	+.220
Tribble	2001	100	Cognitive	+.030
Vance	1987	32	Cognitive	+.033
Van Giffen	1990	849	Perceived	+.523
Wanzer & Frymier	1999	314	Affective	+.470
Ziv Study 1	1988	161	Cognitive	+.181
Ziv Study 2	1988	132	Cognitive	+.311

Note. A positive correlation indicates that including humor in an educational message increased learning. A negative correlation indicates that including humor decreased learning.

served variance is probably not due to sampling error. This suggests that a moderator variable may be operating.

In an effort to locate potential moderator variables, studies were coded for type of learning measure employed. A study was coded cognitive learning if the learning associated with humor was measured using recall tests or course examinations. Often these tests employed true–false or multiple-choice questions. A study was coded as perceived learning if the learning associated with humor was measured by asking respondents how much they thought they had learned during a lecture or during the course. A study was coded as affective learning if the learning associated with humor was measured by asking respondents how much they enjoyed the course or enjoyed behaviors associated with a course.

Results for studies using cognitive humor–learning assessment are displayed in Table 18.2. A very small average effect of +.020 was observed. This average effect is based on 14 independent experiments involving 2,505 participants. In an effort to locate potential moderator variables, a formal test of homogeneity was initiated. A significant chi-square, $\chi^2 = 66.35, p < .05$, (13, $N = 2,505$) indicates that the observed variance is probably not due to sampling error. This suggests that a moderator variable may be operating.

Results for studies using affective humor–learning assessment are displayed in Table 18.3. A moderate average effect of +.380 was observed. This average effect is based on three independent experiments involving 1,097 participants. In an effort to locate potential moderator variables, a formal test of homogeneity was initiated. A significant chi-square, $\chi^2 = 20.15, p < .05$, (2, $N = 1,097$) indicates that the observed variance is probably not due to sampling error. Again, this suggests that a moderator variable may be operating.

TABLE 18.2
Cognitive Humor–Learning Effect Sizes and Sample Sizes

Author	Year	Sample Size	Type of Learning	Effect Size
Burt	1998	42	Cognitive	+.060
Cantor	1980	117	Cognitive	−.355
Chapman & Crampton	1978	30	Cognitive	+.432
Conkell et al.	1999	543	Cognitive	+.033
Desberg et al.	1981	100	Cognitive	+.308
Fisher	1997	495	Cognitive	−.102
Foot et al.	1978	48	Cognitive	−.141
Gruner & Freshley	1979	156	Cognitive	.000
Kaplan & Pascoe	1977	508	Cognitive	+.034
Sadowski et al.	1994	41	Cognitive	+.220
Tribble	2001	100	Cognitive	+.030
Vance	1987	32	Cognitive	+.038
Ziv Study 1	1988	161	Cognitive	+.181
Ziv Study 2	1988	132	Cognitive	+.311

Note. A positive correlation indicates that including humor in an educational message increased learning. A negative correlation indicates that including humor decreased learning.

TABLE 18.3
Affective Humor–Learning Effect Sizes and Sample Sizes

Author	Year	Sample Size	Type of Learning	Effect Size
Frymier & Wanzer	1999	314	Affective	+.470
Gorham & Zakahi	1990	526	Affective	+.210
Wanzer & Frymier	1999	314	Affective	+.470

Note. A positive correlation indicates that including humor in an educational message increased learning. A negative correlation indicates that including humor decreased learning.

Results for studies using perceived humor–learning assessment are displayed in Table 18.4. A moderate average effect of +.39 was observed. This average effect is based on six independent experiments involving 2,108 participants. In an effort to locate potential moderator variables, a formal test of homogeneity was initiated. A significant chi-square, $\chi^2 = 67.26, p < .05$, (5, $N = 2,108$) indicates that the observed variance is probably not due to sampling error (see Table 18.5). Again, this suggests that a moderator variable may be operating.

Finally, a summary for all learning categories (cognitive or objective, perceived, and affective) is displayed in Table 18.5. The effect sizes are uniformly positive and vary in magnitude.

DISCUSSION

As is often the case for reviewers (narrative and empirical) who attempt to summarize a complex domain of literature, it begins with a simple objective. We developed this basic question: Does exposure to educational mes-

TABLE 18.4
Perceived Humor–Learning Effect Sizes and Sample Sizes

Author	Year	Sample Size	Type of Learning	Effect Size
Bryant et al.	1979	70	Perceived	+.236
Bryant et al.	1980	70	Perceived	+.310
Gorham	1988	387	Perceived	+.390
Gorham & Christophel	1990	206	Perceived	+.080
Gorham & Zakahi	1990	526	Perceived	+.310
Van Giffen	1990	849	Perceived	+.523

Note. A positive correlation indicates that including humor in an educational message increased learning. A negative correlation indicates that including humor decreased learning.

TABLE 18.5
Average Effect Sizes for Learning Conditions

Condition	r	N	K	Chi-square	p Value
Total sample	+.22	5,622	23	277.27	<.05
Objective learning	+.02	2,505	14	66.35	<.05
Perceived learning	+.39	2,108	6	67.26	<.05
Affective learning	+.38	1,097	3	20.15	<.05

Note. A positive correlation means that an increase in the variable is associated with an increase in learning.

sages containing humorous material result in understanding and learning? Our fundamental conclusion is that classroom humor produces some effects on learning, although the basic reasoning about humor and learning may be equivocal. Researchers have assumed that humor reinforces the content of a lecture or illustrates a concept central to a lecture, yet the meta-analysis provides only limited support for this view. Students do report that humorous lectures are enjoyable and that the classroom experience is pleasant. By objective measures, however, the learning associated with humor is unremarkable. In this section, we consider the theoretical and practical implications of the classroom humor literature and examine possible moderating variables.

The fundamental finding is that the outcome of humorous lectures varies by types of learning. Humorous lectures are associated with a very small increase in cognitive or objective learning. Studies included in this category used recall tests and course examinations to measure learning. It is reasonable to assert that objective tests of recall and understanding represent the best test of the relationship, yet the effect size for this category is the smallest. This finding calls into question the chorus of scholars who support Grotjahn's (1957) assertion that "what is learned with laughter is learned well" (p. ix). The effect sizes for perceived learning are moderate and positive. The studies included in this category employed self-assessments of how much the student believed he or she learned during the class or lecture. The effect sizes are uniform, and although a moderator may still be present, the evidence is rather consistent. Using classroom humor tends to increase perceptions of learning. It is noteworthy that the magnitude of this perception is much larger than the average effect size of humor and learning measured by objective tests and recall measures. Students tend to believe that humor is associated with learning, although the evidence for this belief is rather tenuous.

An equally strong humor–learning average effect size involved enjoying the learning process and the behaviors associated with learning. Although the moderate effect size (Cohen, 1977) for affective learning comes from three large investigations, the magnitude of the average effect is impressive. The effect may be associated with the perception and self-assessment that learning has occurred. It is equally likely that humorous lectures are entertaining and engaging. The use of humor may lead students to feel that they are competent learners and may make them feel confident to learn. Still, this meta-analysis indicates that the basic reasoning about humor and learning may be overly optimistic. Although students report enjoying learning and they report that they believe that they have learned course material, objective measurements of the recall associated with humorous lectures are rather minuscule.

Scholars interested in classroom communication may profit from understanding the relationship among objective, perceived, and affective learning. Researchers may find opportunities to increase objective learning while strengthening affective and perceived learning. These opportunities may involve teachers' level of humor orientation, classroom social structure, student–teacher relationships, and teacher sex. Additional research is needed to explore these relationships. At the very least, the findings indicate that course evaluations should be examined cautiously. Classroom techniques can create perceptions of learning that may not be reflected in assignments and examinations.

Potential Moderator Variables

The primary finding on the humor–learning relationship may be affected by moderator variables. Some of these variables were assessed in the studies. Other potential moderator variables pose promising avenues for future research. One issue, humor relevance, was examined in several studies. *Relevance* refers to using humor to strategically enhance instructional effectiveness and achieve instructional objectives. This issue is embedded in the humor–perceived learning studies. For example, Bryant, Comisky, and Zillmann (1979) had raters code if classroom humor "contributes to the educational point" (p. 117). Other studies used humorous material that was designed to support a principle or concept that was part of the recall test. A few studies placed humorous material close to a concept that was on the recall test or far away from the concept. The studies examining this issue (Burt, 1998; Desberg, Henechel, Marshall, & McGhee, 1981) were assessed meta-analytically. A small, positive average effect for humor relevance was observed (average $r = -.020$, $N = 142$). Relevant humor resulted in a very small reduction in objective learning when compared with irrelevant humor. This finding cuts against the notion that humor can be used to emphasize an issue to be recalled later.

An untested potential moderator variable involves teacher characteristics. Booth-Butterfield and Booth-Butterfield (1991), for example, argued that humor is an orientation, a predisposition to enact humorous messages that "elicit laughter, chuckling, and other forms of spontaneous behavior taken to mean pleasure, delight, or surprise in the targeted receiver" (p. 206). Researchers note that humor orientation is a communication strategy (Booth-Butterfield & Booth-Butterfield, 1991; Lefcourt et al., 1995; Martin, 2001; Wanzer, Booth-Butterfield, & Booth-Butterfield, 1995), which works as a social lubricant, having positive benefits also, generating support, approval, and goal attainment (Booth-Butterfield & Booth-Butterfield, 1991). High humor orientation is characterized by attempts to employ diverse humor strategies across a variety of situations, whereas low-humor-orientation people avoid initiating humor attempts and do not try to interact by making others laugh. High-humor-orientation individuals will invoke a wider variety of humor, more often, and in a wider variety of situations. As such, the humor orientation approach suggests that some teachers may be more likely to use humor in their classrooms than others.

Environmental and climate issues may also affect learning. For example, the social structure of the classroom may contribute to students' reactions to humor. Bryant and Zillmann (1989) noted that successful classroom humor depends on the right type of humor, under the right conditions, at the right time, with properly motivated and receptive students. It is not for every teacher, particularly college instructors: "Many if not most of the reports of negative or negligible results using humor in the classroom come from investigations using college students and college teachers in college classrooms of laboratories" (p. 52). They argued that college students paying for their education expect serious results and have heard all the jokes in their previous educational situations.

The relationship between instructor and student may also act as a moderating variable in the humor–learning relationship. Civikly (1986) noted that "humor as an act of communication necessarily involves persons and the relationships that exist among those persons" (p. 62). Darling and Civikly (1987) argued that the development of a relationship between teacher and student is critical to the student's accurate interpretation of the teacher's humor. They noted that without establishment of a relational base, teacher humor is more "defense-arousing than supportive and may be more detrimental than the use of no humor" (Darling & Civikly, 1987, p. 66). Student perceptions of their teacher as a person and as an instructor appear to be contingent on sex-role expectations. Students expect female teachers to act more nurturing and male teachers to act more assertive and domineering (Darling & Civikly, 1987). This may be especially important when it comes to classroom humor.

Early work in humor and gender research reifies familiar sex-role expectations that more men than women tell jokes (Chapman & Gadfield, 1976; Goodchilds, 1972). Not surprisingly, studies show that male college teachers and junior high teachers use more humor than their female peers (Bryant et al., 1979). Generally, humor usage has no impact on either male or female instructors' competency ratings (Bryant, Crane, Comisky, & Zillmann, 1980) or student perceptions of their instructor's intelligence (Tamborini & Zillmann, 1981). However, Bryant et al. (1980) noted that the use of self-disparaging humor by male instructors positively affects their appeal, delivery, and overall performance evaluations. The use of sexual humor by male instructors was also positively associated with student ratings (Tamborini & Zillmann, 1981). Male teachers using untendentious (nonhostile) humor are perceived as being more defensive than supportive by students (Darling & Civikly, 1987). However, conflicting findings suggest that the use of humor may be risky for female instructors. Bryant et al. (1980) noted that female instructors' appeal ratings were enhanced by their use of hostile and sexual humor. In contrast, Darling and Civikly (1987) argued that female teachers using tendentious (hostile) humor are perceived as being more defensive than supportive by students. They argued that "classroom behavior which dramatically contradicts the student's expectations for social structure of the classroom might be expected to create the most defensive and negative classroom environment" (Darling & Civikly, 1987, p. 61). Tamborini and Zillmann (1981) concurred, arguing that the use of sexual humor by female instructors was negatively associated with student ratings. Bryant et al. (1980) added:

> Another and perhaps more convincing explanation for the apparent sex differences in humor use is sex stereotyping by students. Students may expect, accept and even appreciate an occasional joke coming from a male professor. The joking female professor, in contrast may be perceived as a person breaking an unspoken rule of "appropriate" classroom conduct. Loss of appeal and related aspects of teacher evaluation may result in turn, from this perception of unfitting behavior (or "misconduct"). (p. 518)

Generally, both men and women find jokes less humorous when males blunder in female roles than in either "appropriate" male roles, but more humorous when women blunder in male roles than in "appropriate" female roles (Borges, Barrett, & Fox, 1980).

Considering the effects of these moderating variables may partially illuminate the role of humor in learning. However, opportunities to uncover compelling insights in humor–learning relationships are available to researchers and teachers who consider humor theory in their investigations and practices.

Applying the Three Humor Theories

The empirical review of the humorous lecture–learning relationship pointed to a disconnect between theoretical approaches to humor and the investigations assessing humor. It became clear that theoretical approaches to humor are not surfacing in the instructional communication literature. Few studies consider the primary theories of incongruity, relief, and superiority in their discussion of classroom humor and learning. This is unfortunate, as the theories can increase novelty and precision of predictions. Theory development of this sort can help educators move beyond the basic injunction to use humor. For example, the incongruity theory of humor is based on the cognitive-appraisal viewpoint that the discovery of the incongruity in a joke produces an increase in cognitive activity (Duncan et al., 1990). Consider the argument that most formal education trains students for convergent thinking, not divergent thinking (Ziv, 1988). The degree of shift or level of diversion to the unexpected is an important aspect of comprehension and insight. Incongruity humor may be best used when the students need that jolt and unexpected diversion from "real" discourse to an "unreal" or "play frame" (Raskin, 1985). Moving the student from convergent thinking to divergent thinking and insight may result in learning and retention of material. The material may be perceived as humorous because of the violation of expectations (Duncan et al., 1990). The usual juxtaposition of ideas at the heart of incongruity humor provides an opportunity for increased student understanding through an increase in the cognitive activity necessary to understand the humor (Duncan et al., 1990). Finding such a juxtaposition–learning relationship would suggest creative ways to use humor strategically at a predetermined level of incongruity.

On a different level, consideration of relief humor in the classroom provides important insights for praxis. Two strategic uses of humor linked to relief theory are promoting health by reducing stress and acting as a social lubricant. McGuffee-Smith and Powell (1988) noted that self-disparaging humor by an organizational leader acts as a tension reliever and encourages member participation and group facilitation. Although some researchers argue that humor also lowers anxiety and promotes improved test performance (Adams, 1972; Ziv, 1976), conflicting results surround research on humor and student anxiety level. Smith, Ascough, Ettinger, and Nelson (1971) noted that humor facilitated recall among college students with high anxiety, but distracted less anxious students and impaired their concentration. Conversely, humorous test items (Townsend & Mahoney, 1981) and arousal from attention to humor (Ziv, 1976) were highly detrimental to highly anxious college students. In practice, relief humor can break down barriers of status difference between instructors and students. This is particularly useful for instructors who want to develop collaborative learning environments in college classrooms.

Finally, superiority theory contends that all humor is created from the longing to feel superior over or to control others (Duncan, 1985). Consideration of humor as a form of social control underscores some of the opportunities to discover the moderating effects of superiority humor. At first glance the practical application of superiority humor may seem improbable. However, Tamborini and Zillmann (1981) noted that the strategic use of ridicule and sarcasm may be useful to correct behavioral problems, particularly in junior high and high school classrooms.

Clearly the role of humor in learning merits additional investigation. Scholars should investigate the types of humor attempted and effects of teacher sex. Teachers should be aware of the variety of social functions different types of humor can play in their classrooms and the pitfalls of violating students' humor and sex-role expectations. Our review indicates that classroom humor has more complicated effects on student learning than is evident in the current literature. One way to better understand the complicated relationship between humor and learning is to consider humor as a fundamental educational communication event. Employing both humor theory and communication theory in our investigations may result in more sophisticated understanding and application of humor in the classroom.

REFERENCES

References marked with an asterisk indicate studies included in the meta-analysis.

Adams, R. A. (1972). Is physics a laughing matter? *Physics Teacher, 10,* 265–266.

Allen, M., & Preiss, R. W. (Eds.). (1998). Persuasion: Advances through meta-analysis. Cresskill, NJ: Hampton.

Allen, M., Preiss, R. W., Gayle, B. M., & Burrell, N. (Eds.). (2002). *Interpersonal communication research: Advances through meta-analysis.* Mahwah, NJ: Lawrence Erlbaum Associates.

Backlawski, D. (1980). A humorous approach to learning geological vocabulary. *Journal of Geological Education, 28,* 158–160.

Berk, R. A., & Nanda, J. P. (1998). Effects of jocular instructional methods on attitudes, anxiety, and achievement in statistics courses. *Humor, 11,* 383–409.

Bolman, L. G., & Deal, T. E. (1991). *Reframing organizations: Artistry, choice and leadership.* San Francisco: Jossey-Bass.

Booth-Butterfield, S., & Booth-Butterfield, M. (1991). Individual differences in the communication of humorous messages. *Southern Journal of Communication, 56,* 205–218.

Borges, M. A., Barrett, P. A., & Fox, J. L. (1980). Humor ratings of sex-stereotyped jokes as a function of gender of actor and gender of rater. *Psychological Reports, 47,* 1135–1138.

*Bryant, J., Comisky, P., & Zillmann, D. (1979). Teachers' humor in the college classroom. *Communication Education, 28,* 110–118.

*Bryant, J., Crane, J. S., Comisky, P. W., & Zillmann, D. (1980). Relationship between college teachers' use of humor in the classroom and students' evaluations of their teachers. *Journal of Educational Psychology, 72,* 511–519.

Bryant, J., & Zillmann, D. (1989). Using humor to promote learning in the classroom. In P. E. McGhee (Ed.), *Humor and children's development: A guide to practical applications* (pp. 49–78). New York: Hawthorn.

*Burt, B. J. (1998). *Effect of content-related humor on recall of content.* Unpublished master's thesis, Clarkson College, Boston.

Cantor, J. R., & Venus, P. (1980). The effect of humor on recall of a radio advertisement. *Journal of Broadcasting, 24,* 13–22.

*Chapman, A. J., & Crompton, P. (1978). Humorous presentations of material and presentations of humorous material: A review of the humor and memory literature and two experimental studies. In M. Gruneberg, P. Morris, & R. Sykes (Eds.), *Practical aspects of memory* (pp. 84–92). London: Academic.

Chapman, A. J., & Foot, H. C. (1976). *Humour and laughter: Theory, research and applications.* London: Wiley.

Chapman, A. J., & Gadfield, N. J. (1976). Is sexual humor sexist? *Journal of Communication, 26,* 141–153.

Civikly, J. M. (1986). Humor and the enjoyment of teaching. In J. Civikly (Ed.), *Communicating in the college classroom* (pp. 61–70). San Francisco: Jossey-Bass.

Cohen, J. (1977). *Statistical power analysis for the behavioral sciences* (Rev. ed.). New York: Academic.

*Conkell, C. S., Imwold, C., & Ratliffe, T. (1999). The effects of humor on communicating fitness concepts to high school students. *Physical Educator, 56*(1), 8–18.

Darling, A. L., & Civikly, J. M. (1987). The effect of teacher humor on student perceptions of classroom communicative climate. *Journal of Classroom Interaction, 22*(1), 24–30.

*Desberg, P., Henechel, D., Marshall, C., & McGhee, P. (1981, September). *The effect of humor on the retention of lecture materials.* Paper presented at the annual meeting of the American Psychological Association, Montreal, Canada. (ERIC Document Reproduction Service No. ED223118)

Donelson, K. (1973). Humor and satire in the English classroom. *Arizona Teacher Bulletin, 6,* 1–13.

Downs, V. C., Javidi, M. M., & Nussbaum, J. F. (1988). An analysis of teachers' verbal communication within the college classroom: Use of humor, self-disclosure, and narratives. *Communication Education, 37,* 127–141.

Duncan, W. J. (1985). The superiority theory of humor at work. *Small Group Behavior, 16,* 556–564.

Duncan, W. J., Smeltzer, L. R., & Leap, T. L. (1990). Humor and work: Applications of joking behavior to management. *Journal of Management, 16,* 255–278.

*Fisher, M. S. (1997). The effect of humor on learning in a planetarium. *Science Education, 81,* 703–713.

*Foot, H. C., Sweeney, C. A., & Chapman, A. J. (1978). Effects of humor upon children's memory. In M. Gruneberg, P. Morris, & R. Sykes (Eds.), *Practical aspects of memory* (pp. 434–441). London: Academic.

Freud, S. (1960). *Jokes and their relation to the unconscious* (J. Strachey, Trans.). New York: Norton. (Original work published 1905)

*Frymier, A. B., & Wanzer, M. B. (1999, November). *Student perceptions of teacher humor use in relationship to learning and motivation: Examining appropriate and inappropriate* *teacher humor.* Paper presented at the annual meeting of the National Communication Association, Chicago.

Gilliland, H., & Mauritsen, H. (1971). Humor in the classroom. *Reading Teacher, 24,* 753–756.

Goodchilds, J. D. (1972). On being witty: Causes, correlates, and consequences. In J. Goldstein & P. McGhee (Eds.), *The psychology of humor: Theoretical perspectives and empirical issues* (pp. 173–193). New York: Academic.

*Gorham, J. (1988). The relationship between verbal teacher immediacy behaviors and student learning. *Communication Education, 37,* 40–53.

*Gorham, J., & Christophel, D. M. (1990). The relationship of teachers' use of humor in the classroom to immediacy and student learning. *Communication Education, 39,* 46–61.

*Gorham, J., & Zakahi, W. R. (1990). A comparison of teacher and student perceptions of immediacy and learning: Monitoring process and product. *Communication Education, 39,* 354–368.

Graham, E. E., Papa, M. J., & Brooks, G. P. (1992). Functions of humor in conversation: Conceptualization and measurement. *The Western Journal of Communication, 56,* 161–183.

Grotjahn, M. (1957). *Beyond laughter: Humor and the subconscious.* New York: McGraw-Hill.

*Gruner, C. R. (1970). The effects of humor in dull and interesting informative speeches. *Central States Speech Journal, 21,* 160–166.

Gruner, C. R., & Freshley, D. L. (1979, November). *Retention of lecture items reinforced with humorous and non-humorous exemplary material.* Paper presented at the annual meeting of the Speech Communication Association, New York. (ERIC Document Reproduction Service No. ED193725)

Hunter, J. E., Schmidt, F. L., & Jackson, G. B. (1982). *Meta-analysis: Culminating research findings across studies.* Beverly Hills, CA: Sage.

Javidi, M. M., Downs, V. C., & Nussbaum, J. F. (1998). A comparative analysis of teachers' use of dramatic style behaviors at higher and secondary educational levels. *Communication Education, 37,* 278–288.

Javidi, M. N., & Long, L. W. (1989). Teachers' use of humor, self-disclosure, and narrative activity as a function of experience. *Communication Research Reports, 6,* 47–82.

*Kaplan, R. M., & Pascoe, G. C. (1977). Humorous lectures and humorous examples: Some effects upon comprehension and retention. *Journal of Educational Psychology, 69,* 61–65.

La Fave, L., Haddad, J., & Maesen, W. A. (1976). Superiority, enhanced self-esteem, and perceived incongruity humour theory. In A. J. Chapman & H. C. Foot (Eds.), *Humour and laughter: Theory, research and applications* (pp. 63–92). London: Wiley.

Larson, G. (1982). Humorous teaching makes serious learning. *Teaching English in the Two-Year College, 8,* 197–199.

Lefcourt, H. M., Davidson, K., Shepherd, R., Phillips, M., Prkachin, K., & Mills, D. (1995). Perspective-taking humor: Accounting for stress moderation. *Journal of Social and Clinical Psychology, 14,* 373–391.

Lundberg, C. C. (1969). Person-focused joking: Pattern and function. *Human Organization, 28*(1), 22–28.

Lynch, O. H. (2002). Humorous communication: Finding a place for humor in communication research. *Communication Theory, 12,* 423–445.

Martin, D. M. (2001). *Women, work, and humor: Negotiating paradoxes of organizational life.* Unpublished doctoral dissertation, University of Utah, Salt Lake City, UT.

McGhee, P. E. (1979). The role of laughter and humor in growing up female. In C. B. Kopp (Ed.), *Becoming female: Perspectives on development* (pp. 183–206). New York: Plenum.

McGuffee-Smith, C., & Powell, L. (1988). The use of disparaging humor by group leaders. *The Southern Speech Communication Journal, 53,* 279–292.

McMorris, R. F., Urbach, S. L., & Connor, M. C. (1985). Effects of incorporating humor in test items. *Journal of Educational Measurement, 22,* 147–155.

Meyer, J. C. (1998, November). *Humor as political boundary-setter: Warm fuzzies and double edges in political humor.* Paper presented at the annual meeting of the National Communication Association, New York.

Meyer, J. C. (2000). Humor as a double-edged sword: Four functions of humor in communication. *Communication Theory, 10,* 310–331.

Mitchell, D. B. (1981). Are we gonna do anything fun? *English Journal, 70,* 24–25.

Morreall, J. (1983). *Taking humor seriously.* Albany: State University of New York Press.

Morreall, J. (1991). Humor and work. *Humor, 4,* 359–373.

Neuliep, J. W. (1991). An examination of high school teachers' humor in the classroom and the development of an inductively derived taxonomy of classroom humor. *Communication Education, 40,* 344–355.

Raskin, V. (1985). *Semantic mechanisms of humor.* Boston: Reidel.

Rosenthal, D. B. (1981). A primer of domestic mathematics. *Mathematics Teacher, 74,* 224–226.

Rossel, R. D. (1981). Word play: Metaphor and humor in the small group. *Small Group Behavior, 12*(1), 116–135.

*Sadowski, C. J., Gulgoz, S., LoBello, S. G. (1994). An evaluation of the use of content-relevant cartoons as a teaching device. *Journal of Instructional Psychology, 21,* 368–371.

Smith, R. E., Ascough, J. C., Ettinger, R. F., & Nelson, D. A. (1971). Humor, anxiety, and test performance. *Journal of Personality and Social Psychology, 19,* 243–246.

Sternthal, B., & Craig, C. S. (1973). Humor in advertising. *Journal of Marketing, 23,* 12–18.

Stuart, W. D., & Rosenfeld, L. B. (1994). Student perception of teacher humor and classroom climate. *Communication Research Reports, 11,* 87–97.

Tamborini, R., & Zillmann, D. (1981). College students' perceptions of lecturers using humor. *Perceptual and Motor Skills, 52,* 427–432.

Townsend, M. A., & Mahoney, P. (1981). Humor and anxiety: Effects on class performance. *Psychology in the Schools, 18,* 228–234.

Tribble, M. E. (2001). *Humor and mental effort in learning.* Unpublished doctoral dissertation, University of Georgia, Athens.

*Vance, C. M. (1987). A comparative study on the use of humor in the design of instruction. *Instructional Science, 16,* 79–100.

*Van Giffen, K. (1990). Influence of professor gender and perceived use of humor on course evaluations. *Humor, 3,* 65–73.

Wakshlag, J. J., Day, K. D., & Zillmann, D. (1981). Selective exposure to educational television programs as a function of differently paced humorous inserts. *Journal of Educational Psychology, 73,* 27–32.

Wandersee, J. H. (1982). Humor as a teaching strategy. *The American Biology Teacher, 44,* 212–218.

Wanzer, M. B., Booth-Butterfield, M., & Booth-Butterfield, S. (1995). The funny people: A source-orientation to the communication of humor. *Communication Quarterly, 43,* 142–154.

Wanzer, M. B., & Frymier, A. B. (1999). The relationship between student perceptions of instructor humor and student's reports of learning. *Communication Education, 48,* 48–62.

Weinberger, M. G., & Gulas, C. S. (1992). The impact of humor in advertising: A review. *Journal of Advertising, 21,* 35–59.

Welker, W. A. (1977). Humor in education: A foundation for wholesome living. *College Student Journal, 11,* 252–254.

White, G. W. (2001). Teachers' report how they used humor with students' perceived use of such humor. *Education, 122,* 337–347.

Zijderveld, A. C. (1983). The sociology of humor and laughter. *The Journal of the International Sociological Association, 31*(3), 1–103.

Zillmann, D. (1981). Disparagement humor. In P. E. McGhee & J. H. Goldstein (Eds.), *Handbook of humor research: Vol. 1. Basic issues* (pp. 85–107). New York: Springer.

*Ziv, A. (1976). Facilitating effects of humor on creativity. *Journal of Educational Psychology, 68,* 318–322.

Ziv, A. (1988). Teaching and learning with humor: Experiment and replication. *Journal of Experimental Education, 57,* 5–15.

19

Exploring the Relationship Between Listening Comprehension and Rate of Speech

Raymond W. Preiss
University of Puget Sound

Barbara Mae Gayle
Saint Martin's University

For four decades researchers have investigated whether reducing the amount of time devoted to delivering any given message produced a more efficient educational process. The idea was to identify the rate of speech that maintained student comprehension levels without allowing the student's mind to wander. Basically, the significance of studying accelerated speech rate effects involved a quest to maximize the amounts of material that could be presented and learned due to increased content knowledge requirements in most disciplines and fields. The research conducted so far suggests there is a threshold in terms of speech rate to optimize listening recall and retention. Yet, research results vary in terms of their identification of optimal rates of speech compression to maximize learning.

The purpose of this study is to determine how listening comprehension is influenced by the rate of speech. This chapter begins by reviewing pertinent research. The results of this narrative review are followed by a meta-analysis of 34 empirical tests on the rate of speech and listening comprehension and a discussion of the findings' implications.

LITERATURE REVIEW

Listening has been defined "as the process of comprehending spoken language" or the "normal mode for accessing spoken messages" (Sticht, 1972, p. 285). One way to reduce listening time is to accelerate the words per minute (wpm) rate, which is often referred to as compressed speech. Experimental studies on listening comprehension and rate-controlled speech explored whether rate-controlled materials can be tailored to maximize learning (Barabasz, 1968; Beatty, Behnke, & Froelich, 1980). Researchers also investigated whether student aptitude may necessitate varying the presentation rate of learning materials (Goldhaber, 1970; Woodcock & Clark, 1968) or whether the individual's age or gender influences the rate at which information is presented to optimize recall (Stine, Wingfield, & Poon, 1986; Tunn, Wingfield, Stine, & Mecsas, 1992). Each of these areas of research and their findings are explored next.

Compressed Speech and Comprehension

Researchers explored listeners' ability to comprehend materials at various rates of presentation. They hypothesized that listening comprehension would be most effective at normal speaking rates (the rate at which a speaker reads aloud a continuous prose text). Yet, several researchers suspected the threshold for effective listening comprehension could be extended with extra effort at higher rates of speech. Sticht (1972) argued that the relationship between rate of speech and listening comprehension resembled an inverted U. He maintained that listening comprehension decreases at speech rates below normal due to lack of listener attention and at above-normal speaking rates when extra effort is no longer adequate to cope with incoming information. Overall, results failed to overwhelmingly support these hypotheses, as the findings were mixed.

Several researchers found no significant differences in listening comprehension at various rates of speech. Gill (1975) and Hagaman (1976) discovered that students who listened to compressed speech did statistically no better or worse on comprehension tests than those who listened to normal speech. For Gill (1975), the comparison was made among 125 wpm, 174 wpm, and 223 wpm, whereas Hagaman (1976) made comparisons between 150 wpm and 190 wpm. Sticht (1968a) found that no significant differences in recall occurred in the compressed speech conditions ranging from 75 wpm to 222 wpm, and Barabasz's (1968) research suggested that reducing the time of a college lecture by one third through accelerated speech did not adversely impact either recall or retention as he explored reducing a normal lectures from 21 minutes to 14 minutes and from 18 minutes to 12 minutes. Taken together, these studies suggest that accelerating the rate of speech does not compromise listening comprehension.

Other researchers suggest that accelerated speech is not as effective in fostering listening comprehension as normal speech rates. Reynolds's (1976) and Adelson's (1975) results indicated that normal speech rate (175 wpm) is more conducive to learning than compressed speech (275 wpm). These studies indicate that optimal recall and retention is only possible at normal rates of speech (around 150 wpm–175 wpm).

However, researchers revealed a threshold in the amount of increase in speech rate possible to maintain listening comprehension. For example, Nelson (1948) did not identify a significant difference between the rate of presentation and comprehension, but pointed out that higher recall scores did occur at 125 wpm and gradually decreased until the lowest recall scores were recorded for the 225 wpm presentation. Similarly, McConville (1982) discovered that attention increased at 275 wpm in comparison with 175 wpm, but comprehension decreases slightly and both attention and comprehension decreased greatly when compression reached 375 wpm. More directly, Sticht's (1969) research revealed that the rate of speech was the greatest contributor to the decline in comprehension observed at higher accelerated rates (a 40% compression of normal speech) and Goldhaber and Weaver (1968) revealed a significant decrease in comprehension between the rates of 175 wpm and 325 wpm in their research.

Foulke (1966) found that recall decreased rapidly after 253 wpm and Foulke (1968) discovered that comprehension was not seriously affected until the word rate extended beyond 300 wpm. He hypothesized that even though word intelligibility (the ability to recognize words and phrases) remained high in both of his experiments, the reduction in perception time needed to decode the incoming information adversely effected listening comprehension. Thus, these studies support the idea that normal speech enhances listening comprehension and that comprehension scores can only be sustained if accelerated rates are contained below the 300 wpm rate.

Similarly, several studies revealed that slower than normal rates of speech may also impede listening comprehension. Sticht (1968a) found that a significant decrease in comprehension scores occurred between the 75 wpm, no compression condition and the 100 wpm, no compression condition. He suggested that it is the rate of speech, not the method of compression, that interferes with listening comprehension. Both McConville's (1982) and Rossiter's (1971) results confirm the idea that too slow a rate of speech also impedes listening comprehension. McConville (1982) revealed that attention levels are similar at 75 wpm through 175 wpm, whereas comprehension decreased at 75 wpm. Rossiter (1971) found that comprehension of compressed speech declines significantly at rates slower than 175 wpm. Although the cause of decreased comprehension in this instance is likely a lack of attention, whereas in accelerated rates it appears to be an inability to process information at higher rates, the result of decreased recall and retention is the same. Yet, not all researchers support this claim. Riding (1979) discovered reducing presentation rate (79 wpm) improved recall.

Participant Aptitude, Listening Comprehension, and Rate of Speech

Another explanation for the degree of comprehension loss when speech rates are accelerated explored participant aptitude. The idea here is that intellectual potential is likely more responsible for listening comprehension scores than increased speech rates. In one experiment, Corey (1977) discovered that participants with high intellectual aptitude performed better at 175 wpm than at higher or lower rates and participants with lower intellectual aptitude performed best at 150 wpm. In another experiment, he found that the high-intellectual-aptitude group learned almost double the amount of information than participants with lower intellectual aptitude at faster speech rates and that when a low association response was required, low-intellectual-aptitude participants did best at normal rates. Overall, Corey (1977) suggested that adjusting compression rates can meet needs of a variety of intellectual aptitudes.

On the other hand, Sticht's (1968b) research discovered no difference in listening performance for high-, average-, or low-aptitude individuals. He found that all participants' comprehension scores declined when the speech rate was increased from 175 wpm to 425 wpm. In a later study, Sticht and Glasnapp (1972) revealed that low-aptitude men learned the easier material better than the difficult material as a function of decreased speech rate. High-intellectual-aptitude men learned material best around 175 wpm and lost disproportionately more material of low-association strength than did low-intellectual-aptitude men when the speech rate was increased from 175 wpm to 325 wpm.

The lack of consistency in results continued as other researchers explored participant aptitude, listening comprehension, and rate of speech. In their study, Woodcock and Clark (1968) discovered that highly intelligent individuals have their best comprehension scores at 128 wpm, but the comprehension drops to an all-time low at 278 wpm and then increases up to 378 wpm before decreasing dramatically at 428 wpm. These results were similar for both the average and low IQ individuals and for the 1-week later retention scores. These authors argued that comprehension could be increased for lower IQ students by using slower rates of speech and claimed that the most efficient rates for high IQ learners are 228 wpm and 328 wpm, although 178 wpm resulted in higher test scores. Woodcock and Clark argued that calculating efficiency rating is more telling than comprehension scores alone. The results of the efficiency index suggest that 228 wpm to 328 wpm are the most efficient rates to present information when you consider the amount of learning per unit of time. Taken together, these studies on participant aptitude are unclear. It is hard to calculate the exact rates of speech to enhance learning for high, average, or low intelligence.

Intervening Variables in Listening Comprehension and Rates of Speech Research

Researchers have extended the investigation of the relationship between listening comprehension and rate of speech. The exploration of intervening or mediating variables such as method of compression, sex, or age, produces mixed results. Several researchers explored whether specific circumstances intervene to promote comprehension when speech rates are accelerated. Sticht (1968a) explored (75 wpm, 100 wpm, 155 wpm, 222 wpm) whether the method for accelerating speech was partially responsible for the variation in comprehension scores. He found that recall was not enhanced when word duration was decreased and the time between words was increased, but found that syntax, inflection, and phraseology cues improved comprehension. Yet, Foulke (1966) found that the method of compressing speech had little impact on learning. Thus, it is unclear if the method of speech compression or accelerating speech influences learning potential.

Researchers have also explored whether augmenting the message or providing reasons to listen influence listening comprehension when the rate of speech is accelerated. Beatty et al. (1980) investigated whether incentives to listen enhance comprehension at higher wpm rates. These authors provided extra credit for enhanced performance on comprehension tests and discovered that extrinsic motivation had a positive effect on recall. There was not a decline in comprehension scores for the incentive groups that could be attributed to the accelerated speech rate (140 wpm, 210 wpm, and 280 wpm) in the presentations. However, Fairbanks, Guttman, and Miron (1957) discovered that even augmenting one version of an accelerated speech passage (141 wpm and 201 wpm) produced little differences in comprehension. Olson (1985) found that visually augmenting compressed speech is more effective than the speech is without that augmentation. Where this augmentation does not occur both normal and compressed messages were equally effective. Normal presentation rates (150 wpm) are more effective than compressed rates (250 wpm), but when material is technical in nature augmentation does not help a great deal. Olson argued that compressed speech works best when instructional efficiency is desired. These studies suggest that the relationship between rate of speech and learning is more complex than originally surmised.

Using another approach, researchers explored the type of information and whether training individuals to accommodate higher rates of speech would enhance listening comprehension capabilities. Meadows (1978) varied the type of information introduced. When the rate of oral message presentation was varied from 175 wpm to 265 wpm, sizable differences were found for tests concerning inferences but not for tests that concerned facts and ideas. Goldhaber (1970) suggested that comprehension levels for the participants in his experiment might improve if they were trained to listen to faster rates of speech (165 wpm, 330 wpm). Taken together, these results suggest that mediating factors could increase individual comprehension scores when the speech rate is accelerated.

In an effort to resolve differences, Adelson (1975) explored listening comprehension in terms of the stimulus material, the rate of speech, and the efficiency index. The length of the stimulus materials used appeared to be a critical factor. Time-compressed materials (275 wpm) suffered a proportionately larger loss of comprehension than did the normal rate (175 wpm) when educationally realistic materials were used. Adelson argued that Woodcock and Clark's (1968) efficiency index fails to take into consideration the number of items not learned, the difficulty of the items, and a criterion of acceptable comprehension stated in advance. She argued that relying on the efficiency model encouraged learning less provided that less time is spent on actual learning, and that it shifted the focus from best practices to how to spend less time and educate more people. Adelson (1975) argued that encouraging skimming materials, not deep learning, does not help determine the relationship between listening comprehension and accelerated speech rates. Thus, Adelson's (1975) research called for additional modifications in studying accelerated speech and learning.

Another variable that researchers explored to explain how recall and retention vary with compressed speech is age. Some studies explored the variation among younger individuals. Other studies compared and contrasted younger participants' listening abilities and older adults' listening abilities. Goldhaber's (1970) research suggested that there was no significant difference between academic level and rate of speech (165 wpm, 330 wpm). Junior high school listeners outperformed college freshman and sophomores perhaps because they were more eager to learn. Riding (1980) found large differences in recall due to speech rate (150 wpm and 198 wpm) between 7 years, 10 years, 12 years, and 15 years old. Ten- and 12-year-olds were only slightly different. Thus, comparisons among younger participants produced mixed results.

Studies exploring listening comprehension and speech rate effects on older adults also produced mixed results. Stine et al. (1968) matched older adults and younger participants by education and verbal ability. The older adults suffered in sentence recall when speech rate was increased beyond normal limits

(200 wpm, 300 wpm, 400 wpm) and with increasing prepositional density. The authors speculated that the reason for these findings may be the recognition of incoming speech, memory functioning, or the efficiency in processing skills that vary from younger adults. There also may be some qualitative difference in information processing in older individuals, but no age, rate, and level interaction occurred. Similarly, Tunn et al.'s (1992) study supported slowing speech processing among elderly, because faster rates disrupted comprehension and recall (140 wpm, 182 wpm, 280 wpm). In their study, young people had better recall than the elderly, but the age difference in task management was not exacerbated by a faster rate of speech. However, Schmitt and Carroll (1985) discovered that speaking slower to older adults did not improve comprehension scores, unlike some previous studies (175 wpm, 60% compression rate). Overall, the results assessing the rate of speech effect on older adults' comprehension are inconsistent.

Additionally, some researchers have explored the effect of gender on the relationship of compressed speech and listening comprehension. Schmitt and Carroll (1985) found no significant difference between men and women. However, Riding (1980) found that girls who were 15 years old (as compared to younger girls) were more adversely affected by increased speech rates. These authors discovered, as did Riding and Smith (1981), that recall was best for both boys and girls following slow presentation passages with related sentences adjacently positioned. All the girls in Riding's (1980) study had superior comprehension scores when the passage was arranged with related details separated and rate was slow. Boys, on the other hand, obtained better comprehension scores when the speech rate was faster. Similarly, Goldhaber and Weaver (1968) discovered that males outscored females in listening comprehension at all levels of compressed speech. They surmised that the subject might have appealed to males more or women are less interested in ideas than men. In another study, Riding and Smith (1981) identified that the presentation rate had a significant effect on recall and discovered a significant interaction among sex, type of presentation, and recall. Repetition did not improve learning for boys but did enhance recall for girls. It appears that sex has some effect on listening comprehension and rate of speech research findings but no clear pattern has emerged.

The focus has been on determining the ideal listening comprehension conditions. When a relationship appears between listening comprehension and the rate of speech it is characterized most often by the ability to comfortably comprehend materials in the "normal" range of speech or because of the extra effort required to comprehend materials presented at faster rates of speech. However, the results are contradictory. Some researchers identify specific rates of speech that enhance listening comprehension and others find no significant difference in listening comprehension scores dependent on the speech rate. These findings merit further investigation to answer the question of how powerful the relationship is between listening comprehension and speech rate.

METHOD

Collecting quantitative research studies about a phenomenon and converting results into a common metric can resolve statistical inconsistencies and test for homogeneity of effects. Experimental studies of oral advanced organizers were retrieved using the computer-based retrieval system ERIC, Education Abstracts, Academic Universe, PsychINFO, Dissertation Abstracts, Business Abstracts, and Communication Index. The reference section of each manuscript collected also was searched for additional studies involving oral advanced organizers.

Acceptable manuscripts had to: (a) investigate listening comprehension and rate of speech; (b) contain a quantitative analysis of the rate of speech's effect on listening comprehension; and (c) provide enough information to allow conversion of results into a common metric for comparison. The 25 manuscripts contained 28 separate studies that met these criteria. Each acceptable manuscript was coded for the year completed, types of learners tested, number of participants, publication status, compression method, and comprehension test method.

Statistical Analysis

The summary statistics of each study were converted to correlations so that the magnitude of outcomes attributable to student learning with advanced organizers could be quantified. The correlations were weighted for sample size and then averaged. Each average correlation was assessed to determine if the variance in the observed sample correlations was larger than expected by random sampling error (Hedges & Olkin, 1985). To detect a moderator variable, the sum of the squared error was tested using a chi-square test. A nonsignificant chi-square indicates that the amount of variability is probably the result of chance, whereas a significant chi-square indicates that the amount of variability may be the result of some type of moderating variable.

RESULTS

Over half of the average effect sizes for each of the 28 experiments were above −.40 (see Table 19.1). The overall average effect size ($r = -.417$) for the 3,274 participants was moderate (see Table 19.2). These results indicate that listening comprehension decreases as rate of speech increases.

The chi-square, $\chi^2(27, N = 3,274) = 138.03, p < .05$, was significant, indicating the presence of one or more moderating variables. The search for

TABLE 19.1
Effect Size Relationship Between Rate of Speech and Listening Comprehension

Author	Year	Sample Size	Effect Size
Adelson	1975	200	−.435
Barabasz	1968	118	−.009
Beatty et al.	1980	180	−.192
Corey	1977		
Experiment 1		204	−.402
Experiment 2		138	−.629
Fairbanks et al.	1957	142	−.631
Foulke	1966	123	−.380
Foulke	1968	360	−.565
Friedman & Johnson	1968	52	−.359
Gill	1975	60	−.220
Goldhaber	1970	40	−.458
Goldhaber & Weaver	1968	240	−.632
Hagaman	1976	67	.000
McConville	1982	20	−.885
Meadows	1978		
Experiment 1		92	−.215
Experiment 2		92	−.090
Nelson	1948	250	−.211
Olson	1985	250	−.313
Reynolds	1976	74	−.418
Riding	1979	78	−.603
Riding & Smith	1981	120	−.314
Rossiter	1971	222	−.257
Schmitt & Carroll	1985	28	−.560
Sticht	1968b	135	−.620
Sticht	1969	87	−.682
Stine et al.	1968		
Experiment 1		48	−.859
Experiment 2		12	−.868
Woodcock & Clark	1968	54	−.480

TABLE 19.2
Overall Average Effect Size Rate of Speech and Listening Comprehension

Average effect size	$r = -.417$
Number of studies	$k = 28$
Number of participants	$N = 3,274$
Chi-square	$\chi^2 = 138.03$

moderating variables is compounded by the variety of measures used to assess listening comprehension and the number of methods used to compress speech as well as the rate considered normal by each study. In addition, there is the issue of whether all materials are suited for oral communication

DISCUSSION

The results of this study suggest that compressed speech adversely effects listening comprehension. It appears that the difference between a conversational rate of speech and accelerated speech is a significant decrease in recall and retention. Collectively the average effect size lends credence to Foulke and Sticht's (1969) claim that understanding "spoken language implies the continuous registration, encoding, and storage of speech information and these operations require time" (p. 60). As these authors argued, the increased rate of speech does not allow enough processing time for incoming materials to ensure information retrieval. Apparently as Carver (1973) suggested, an individual's "decrease in thoughts understood ... drops" because "little or nothing is ... comprehended" (p. 124) above the normal rate of speech threshold. The idea is that it takes a specific amount of time to store information for easy retrieval and accelerated speech inhibits short-term memory processing and long-term memory storage.

Additionally, these results suggest that the failure to establish what constitutes a normal rate of speech and thus develop a standard comparison makes it difficult to determine the rate of speech threshold, high or low, that optimizes learning. The lack of studies exploring both participant aptitude and material difficulty also make determining the maximal rate of speech to enhance listening comprehension difficult.

The implications for classroom communication are clear. Compressed speech may be efficient but it is not effective regardless of participant aptitude, age, sex, and so on. The results of this study suggest that normal lecture rates are more conducive to student learning. This message is especially important given the new emphasis on the use of compressed video in distance education. Compressed video is "a means of delivering instruction that allows for two-way audio and video interaction between instructor and students at a remote site" (Magiera, 1994, p. 273). Research thus far on compressed video suggests student satisfaction with this form of presentation (Bynum, Cranford, Irwin, & Denny, 2002; Carter, 2001), although one study measuring student performance at both the transmission and receiving sites claims that compressed video did not impact student learning (Magiera, 1994). Researchers in this area might construct their inquiry to consider student aptitude, the difficulty level of the information presented, the educational relevance of the information presented and tested, and various demographic variables if they hope to make the findings easier to explicate. Until then, however, the findings of this study suggest that compressed video is less likely to be conducive to listening comprehension than normal lectures.

REFERENCES

References marked with an asterisk indicate studies included in the meta-analysis.

*Adelson, L. (1975). Comprehension by college students of time-compressed lectures. *The Journal of Experimental Education, 44,* 53–60.

*Barabasz, A. F. (1968). A study of recall and retention of accelerated lecture presentation. *Journal of Communication, 18,* 283–287.

*Beatty, M. J., Behnke, R. R., & Froelich, D. L. (1980). Effects of achievement incentive and presentation rate on listening comprehension. *Quarterly Journal of Speech, 66,* 193–200.

Bynum, A. B., Cranford, C. O., Irwin, C. A., & Denny, G. S. (2002). Participant satisfaction with a school telehealth education program using interactive compressed video delivery methods in rural Arkansas. *Journal of School Health, 72,* 235–243.

Carter, A. (2001). Interactive distance education: Implications for the adult learner. *Journal of Instructional Media, 28,* 249–261.

Carver, R. P. (1973). Effect of increasing the rate of speech presentation upon comprehension. *Journal of Educational Psychology, 65,* 118–126.

*Corey, J. M. (1977). *An investigation of auditory learning in relation to mental aptitude, signal distortion, and speech compression.* Unpublished doctoral dissertation, University of Southern California, Los Angeles, CA.

*Fairbanks, G., Guttman, N., & Miron, M. S. (1957). Auditory comprehension in relation to listening rate and selective verbal redundancy. *Journal of Speech and Hearing Disorders, 22,* 23–32.

*Foulke, E. (1966). Comparison of comprehension of two forms of compressed speech. *Exceptional Children, 33,* 169–173.

*Foulke, E. (1968). Listening comprehension as a function of word rate. *Journal of Communication, 18,* 198–206.

Foulke, E., & Sticht, T. G. (1969). Review of research on the intelligibility and comprehension of accelerated speech. *Psychological Bulletin, 72,* 50–62.

*Friedman, H. L., & Johnson, R. L. (1968). Compressed speech: Correlates of listening ability. *Journal of Communication, 18,* 207–218.

*Gill, L. R. (1975). *The effect of compressed speech and interim activity on comprehension.* Unpublished doctoral dissertation, Oklahoma State University, Stillwater, OK.

*Goldhaber, G. M. (1970). Listener comprehension of compressed speech as a function of the academic grade level of the subjects. *Journal of Communication, 20,* 167–173.

*Goldhaber, G. M., & Weaver, C. H. (1968). Listener comprehension of compressed speech when the difficulty, rate of presentation, and sex of the listener are varied. *Speech Monographs, 35,* 20–25.

*Hagaman, J. G. (1976). *A comparison of the effectiveness and efficiency of learning from multi-media programmed instruction at fixed and learner selected rated compressed speech.* Unpublished doctoral dissertation, Michigan State University, East Lansing, MI.

Hedges, L., & Olkin, I. (1985). *Statistical methods for meta-analysis.* Orlando, FL: Academic.

Magiera, F. T. (1994). Teaching managerial finance through compressed video: An alternative for distance education. *Journal of Education for Business, 69,* 273–278.

*McConville, J. R. (1982). *An arousal interpretation of the effects of change in rate of speech on listeners' attention.* Unpublished doctoral dissertation, Indiana University, Bloomington, IN.

*Meadows, C. L. (1978). *Task-specific comprehension of compressed speech.* Unpublished doctoral dissertation, Indiana University, Bloomington, IN.

*Nelson, H. E. (1948). The effect of variation of rate on the recall by radio listeners of "straight" news. *Speech Monographs, 15,* 173–180.

*Olson, J. S. (1985, January). *A study of the relative effectiveness of verbal and visual augmentation of rate-modified speech in the presentation of technical materials.* Paper presented at the annual convention of the Association for Educational Communications and Technology, Anaheim, CA. (ERIC Document Reproduction Service No. ED 256329).

*Reynolds, H. M. (1976). *The effects of rates of comprehension.* Unpublished doctoral dissertation, Southern Illinois University-Carbondale, Carbondale, IL.

*Riding, R. J. (1979). Tell me once, tell me slowly: Repetition versus speaking slowly as methods of improving children's learning. *Research in Education, 21,* 71–77.

Riding, R. J. (1980). Listening comprehension: The effects of sex, age, passage structure and speech rate. *Educational Review, 32,* 259–267.

*Riding, R. J., & Smith, D. M. (1981). Sex differences in effects of speech rate and repetition on the recall of prose in children. *Educational Psychology, 1,* 25–260.

*Rossiter, C. M. (1971). Rate-of-presentation effects on recall of facts and ideas and on generation of inferences. *AV Communication Review, 19,* 313–324.

*Schmitt, J. F., & Carroll, M. R. (1985). Older listeners' ability to comprehend speaker-generated rate alteration of passages. *Journal of Speech and Hearing Research, 28,* 309–312.

Sticht, T. G. (1968a). *Some interactions of speech rate, signal distortion, and certain linguistic factors in listening comprehension.* (Rep. No. HumBRO–PP–39–68). Alexandria, VA: George Washington University. (ERIC Document Reproduction Service No. ED 099932)

*Sticht, T. G. (1968b). Some relationships of mental aptitude, reading ability, and listening ability using normal and time compressed speech. *Journal of Communication, 18,* 243–258.

*Sticht, T. G. (1969). *Learning by listening in relation to aptitude, reading, and rate-controlled speech* (HumBRO Tech. Rep. 69–23). (ERIC Document Reproduction Service No. ED 037666)

Sticht, T. G. (1972). Learning by listening. In V. H. Winston (Ed.), *Language comprehension and the acquisition of knowledge* (pp. 285–314). New York: Wiley.

Sticht, T. G., & Glasnapp, D. R. (1972). Effects of speech rate, selection difficulty, association strength, and mental aptitude on learning by listening. *Journal of Communication, 22,* 174–188.

*Stine, E. L., Wingfield, A., & Poon, L. W. (1986). How much and how fast: Rapid processing of spoken language in later adulthood. *Psychology and Aging, 1,* 303–311.

*Tunn, P. A., Wingfield, A., Stine, E. A., & Mecsas, C. (1992). Rapid speech and divided attention: Processing rate versus processing resources as an explanation of age effects. *Psychology and Aging, 71,* 546–550.

*Woodcock, R. W., & Clark, C. R. (1968). Comprehension of a narrative passage by elementary school children as a function of listening rate, retention period, and IQ. *Journal of Communication, 18,* 259–271.

20

A Meta-Analysis of the Educational Benefits of Employing Advanced Organizers

Raymond W. Preiss
University of Puget Sound

Barbara Mae Gayle
Saint Martin's University

Educators design their lessons in ways that help students organize, comprehend, and retain new, unfamiliar, and complex material. One way to facilitate student performance is to provide an advanced preview of the material to be learned and organize the lecture content in ways that are consistent with the preview. The approach is consistent with Ausubel's (1960) belief that conceptual previews that are high in generalizability and inclusiveness should increase student learning. The use of conceptual previews has been termed *advanced organizers* (AOs), devices that Ausubel (1968) described as "appropriately relevant and inclusive introductory materials" (p. 148). These previews would be presented in advance of learning and at higher levels of abstraction, generality, and inclusiveness than the material learned.

According to Mayer (1979), one technique for using AOs is to employ comparative AOs, where the preview reinforces existing knowledge structures and facilitates understanding of subsequent information. A second technique is to employ expository AOs or previews that provide new information that promotes comprehension of subsequent new information. The two forms of AOs (comparative and expository) have been operationalized as oral, written, and mixed oral and written conceptual statements. Also, the material following the AO (the material to be learned) has been presented in oral and written form. The overarching principle is consistent, however. Abstract, inclusive conceptual previews promote learning of subsequent material.

A systematic review of the AO research reveals a rather fragmented and contradictory body of literature. Some studies confirm the effectiveness of AOs in increasing student retention and recall (e.g., Adejumo & Ehindero, 1980; Barron, 1986), whereas other studies suggest there is no tangible improvement in student performance (e.g., Christie & Schumacher, 1976; Kirkman & Shaw, 1997). Some studies support the efficacy of Ausubel's (1960) subsumption theory in explaining how AOs function (e.g., Ausubel & Fitzgerald, 1961; Mayer, 1979; Stone, 1983), whereas others credit reception and assimilation mechanisms for AO effectiveness (e.g., Barnes & Clawson, 1975; Glover, Bullock, & Dietzer, 1990). Only one study investigating the efficacy of AOs has separated oral and written AOs (Luiten, Ames, & Ackerson, 1980). The purpose of this study requires reviewing the overall summary of research (oral and written formats) on AOs as well as exploring the effectiveness of oral AOs in promoting student comprehension, recall, and retention.

After reviewing the extant literature, the focus of the chapter turns toward explaining the methods that were used for locating AO studies and computing effect sizes. Next, the results from the meta-analyses are presented and conclusions and limitations are discussed. We conclude by suggesting avenues for future research and making observations about the practical implications of the meta-analysis.

LITERATURE REVIEW

More than 40 years ago, Ausubel (1960) argued that "the cognitive structure is hierarchically organized in terms of highly inclusive concepts under which are subsumed less inclusive subconcepts and informational data" (p. 267). He suggested that new information is "incorporated into cognitive structure in so far as it is subsumable under relevant existing concepts" (Ausubel, 1960, p. 267). Mayer (1979) clarified the explanation of how AOs function by reasoning that AOs allow learners to commit more information to memory because they provide the foundation on which other information can rest. Thus, AOs are concepts that are introduced prior to a unit of study at the highest level of generality and inclusiveness and serve as devices that create a predisposition to learn (Ausubel, 1960; Ausubel & Fitzgerald, 1961; Barnes & Clawson, 1975).

Many studies have sought to identify the conditions under which AOs are optimally effective. In the next sections we summarize the results of the overall AO studies and focus on the effects of oral AOs. This area is of special significance, as it may provide tools for improving lecture comprehension and classroom effectiveness.

Summary Studies

Studies exploring the efficacy of Ausubel's (1960) subsumption theory examined whether AOs link what is to be learned with what is already known. These studies attempt to verify that AOs facilitate student comprehension, retention, and recall, and assume that instructors are capable of constructing and delivering AOs to diverse student populations.

Barnes and Clawson (1975) categorized 32 studies in an effort to explore the contradictory results in the AO literature. Employing mostly prose-oriented AO research, Barnes and Clawson identified 12 studies that indicate the efficacy of AOs in aiding student performance and 20 studies that suggested that AOs were not effective in enhancing student performance. Using a box score method, the authors found AOs were more effective when the subject matter studied was religion rather than science, social science, or mathematics. Also, AOs had slightly more impact on higher ability-level students than lower and moderate ability-level students. These researchers found no evidence of AO efficacy related to the length of the study, the grade level of the students, the type of organizer, or the cognitive level of the organizer.

Mayer (1979) extended on Barnes and Clawson's (1975) research by reviewing 44 AO studies to test several theoretical explanations and assess the ability of AOs in enhancing student learning. At the first level of analysis, he found that in 10 studies AOs enhanced learning. In 13 studies, however, AOs increased student performance only under certain circumstances, such as for poorly organized texts or for participants who had limited prior knowledge and experience in the subject area. Mayer (1979) argued that a "standard" AO gives learners a small advantage, especially when the material to be learned is somewhat familiar, the students are knowledgeable, or when the test does not assess knowledge transfer. He also found that in the 10 studies comparing a modified AO with postorganizers, AOs worked in mathematics, perhaps by providing a conceptual framework for the content. However, interpreting the seven studies in which postorganizers worked better than modified AOs proved more difficult, as no clear pattern emerged. Thus, Mayer (1979) concluded in this instance, "the locus of the effect is at encoding rather than retrieval" (p. 161). Finally, Mayer's review indicated that AOs can be designed to help inexperienced learners process new information, aid less effective cognitive learners, and aid in knowledge transference.

In the 1980s two studies abandoned the box count method employed by Barnes and Clawson (1975) and Mayer (1979). These authors employed meta-analysis to review the efficacy of AOs in increasing student learning. Luiten et al. (1980) meta-analyzed 115 published and nonpublished studies and examined possible moderating variables such as grade level, subject area studied, type of organizer, and learner ability. These authors found an overall small effect size $d = .21$ for learning, and the effect size increased over time for retention (from .19 after 2 days to .38 after 22 days). The effect size for learning was larger for college students ($d = .26$) and special education students ($d = .28$) than for secondary ($d = .17$) or primary ($d = .17$) students. For retention, the primary grades had a higher effect size ($d = .33$) than either the college students ($d = .21$) or secondary students ($d = .26$). AOs were more effective in learning in social studies ($d = .34$) than in biological ($d = .11$) or physical ($d = .15$) sciences or mathematics ($d = .10$). For retention, AOs were more effective for physical sciences ($d = .50$) than for social sciences ($d = .26$), biological sciences ($d = .18$), or mathematics ($d = .17$). Finally, AOs had greater overall effect for high-ability learners ($d = .23$) than moderate- ($d = .08$) or low-level ($d = .13$) learners.

When Luiten et al. (1980) separated written AOs from oral ones, they found a greater overall effect size for oral AOs ($d = .37$) than for written ($d = .17$) ones. They also discovered that grade level had an effect on the learning associated with oral AOs. The effect size for college students ($d = .68$) was greater than that for special education ($d = .37$), primary grades ($d = .34$), or secondary grades ($d = .11$).

Stone (1983) conducted a second meta-analysis of AO studies. She investigated 29 manuscripts with 112 effects meta-analytically. Her results identified a large overall (written and oral) effect size ($d = .66$), suggesting that AOs promote student performance. Stone's results indicate that written ($d = .43$) and written and illustrated ($d = .52$) AOs are less effective than other forms of AOs such as aural, games, and so on ($d = .83$) in promoting learning. Her findings indicate that expository ($d = .80$), nonsubsuming ($d = .71$), concrete ($d = .80$), and generalized ($d = .78$) AOs enhance learning. Additionally, AOs that were designed from the material to be learned ($d = .71$) and AOs that mix concepts with processes ($d = .67$) were more effective in promoting comprehension, retention, and recall.

Stone (1983) also examined the effect of learner characteristics and conditions. She found higher effect sizes for science and mathematics ($d = .72$), formulaic evaluations ($d = .70$), junior high students ($d = 1.39$), females ($d = 1.02$), moderate-ability learners ($d = .27$), low-level prior knowledge ($d = .32$), and longer length of the study ($d = 1.12$). She also investigated "the interactions between concepts and processes and AO operational level" and concluded "perhaps problem solving or active processing by the learner is essential when the AO is abstract, but not when it is concrete" (p. 197).

These studies summarizing both written and oral AOs were contradictory. It appears that under certain circumstances and with specific designs, AOs do promote an increase in student performance. However, it also is apparent that AO results are not broadly generalizable to all learning subjects and situations. Also, there has been very little investigation of oral AOs apart from written and mixed-format AOs. The next portion of the literature review examines oral AOs and their relationship to enhancing learning.

Oral-Oriented Advanced Organizer Studies

The studies investigating the overall efficacy of oral AOs in enhancing student performance reveal contradictory findings. Researchers produced studies that endorsed AOs' ability to increase retention and recall, studies that identify specific conditions under which AOs increase student learning, and studies that found that AOs produce no significant increase in student performance.

Eight studies revealed unequivocal support for the role oral AOs play in enhancing comprehension, recall, and retention. Alexander, Frankiewicz, and William (1979) explored the use of nonwritten AOs because they believed they were most adaptable to the classroom. These authors found that AOs facilitated learning and long-term retention. Barron (1986) used a tape recording as an AO and concluded that student achievement was enhanced through the use of oral AOs. He also found that achievement was higher when the oral AO was matched to the learning style of the student. Lawton (1978) discovered that oral AOs produced more learning than occurred in a traditional class. Herron (1994) found that the oral AO before viewing a video in a foreign language increased student learning, and Kahle and Rastovac's (1976) research revealed that learning of carefully selected and sequenced genetics information was enhanced by oral AOs. Even preschool children were able to improve their learning following oral AOs (Lawton & Blue-Swadener, 1979; Lawton & Burk, 1988). Finally, Wong (1972) discovered that college students' short-term and long-term achievement were enhanced through the use of oral AOs.

Other researchers identified the specific or limited circumstances under which oral AOs increase student performance. Adejumo and Ehindero (1980) investigated both the effect of experimenter-generated oral AOs and student participation in constructing AOs using high school students in Nigeria. These authors found that students in the higher level classes recorded better performance using oral AOs that served as idea-oriented scaffolding for the retention of new material. They also found that lower level classes performed better when they participated in the construction of the AO materials.

Blackhurst's (1979) research, on the other hand, suggested that oral AOs were not more effective than traditional teaching but were more effective than a control group that used neither an oral AO nor a traditional approach. Kahle's (1978) investigation revealed that when AOs were combined with behavioral objectives, a significant increase in student achievement occurred. His study results also indicated that when an oral AO was utilized in a meiosis (science) lesson, increases in student performance were observed in the delayed retention test but not in the immediate final exam. In their first experiment, Towsend and Clarihew (1989) found that oral AOs increased student performance for those who had strong prior knowledge but the effect was not as pronounced for those who had weak previous knowledge. In Experiment 2, these authors discovered that the effectiveness of oral AOs was enhanced by pictures.

A third group of studies located no significant increase in student learning or performance through using oral AOs. Christie and Schumacher (1976) found that participants who did not receive an oral AO recalled more than those receiving the AO. Peleg and Moore (1982) found that AOs were detrimental to learning when presented orally. Kirkland, Byrom, MacDougall, and Corcoran (1995) found special education eighth-grade students' learning was not enhanced through the use of an oral AO. Kirkman and Shaw (1997), Bricker (1989), Vickrey (1971), and Kahle and Nordland (1975) each discovered that there was no significant increase in student performance based on the use of an oral AO. Bertou, Clasen, and Lambert (1972) found that neither AOs or postorganizers enhanced student learning.

Taken together, these studies suggest that the optimal use of oral AOs has yet to be clearly defined. Given the contradictory findings after more than 40 years of research, it is reasonable to explore the efficacy of oral AOs in enhancing student learning.

METHOD

Collecting quantitative research studies about a phenomenon and converting results into a common metric can resolve statistical inconsistencies and test for homogeneity of effects. Experimental studies of oral AOs were retrieved using the computer-based retrieval system ERIC, Education Abstracts, Academic Universe, PsychINFO, Dissertation Abstracts, Business Abstracts, and Communication Index. The reference section of each manuscript collected also was searched for additional studies involving oral AOs.

Acceptable manuscripts had to: (a) investigate oral AOs and student performance; (b) contain a quantitative analysis of the oral AO's effect on comprehension, retention, and recall; and (c) provide enough information to allow conversion of results into a common metric for comparison. The 19 manuscripts contained 20 separate studies that met these criteria. Each acceptable manuscript was coded for the year completed, types of learners tested, number of participants, publication status, and student learning.

Statistical Analysis

The summary statistics of each study were converted to correlations so that the magnitude of outcomes attributable to student learning with AOs could be quantified. The correlations were weighted for sample size and then averaged. Each average correlation was assessed to determine if the variance in the observed sample correlations was larger than expected by random sampling error (Hedges & Olkin, 1985). To detect a moderator variable, the sum of the squared error was tested using a chi-square test. A nonsignificant chi-square indicates that the amount of variability is probably the result of chance, whereas a significant chi-square indicates that the amount of variability may be the result of some type of moderating variable.

Moderating Coding

Four common categories emerge from the research as potentially affecting the ability to judge the overall effectiveness of the oral AOs (Luiten et al., 1980; Stone, 1983). The moderator coding focused on the type of sample, the topic of oral AO, the publication status, and the achievement test timing. Participants in each study were coded as being in the following groups: educable mental retarded (EMR), preschool, primary grade, junior high, high school, or college student. The topic of the oral AO was categorized as science, social science, behavior, and English or foreign language. The achievement test timing was coded as happening immediately after the lesson, happening several days later, or an average of the immediate and the delayed achievement test. Finally, the publication status was coded as being published or unpublished manuscript.

RESULTS

Overall, the individual effect sizes range from very small to very large (see Table 20.1). The average effect size for 20 studies employing 1,937 participants was small ($r = .226$). AOs were associated with learning. The chi-square, $\chi^2 = 125.64, p < .05$, was significant, indicating the presence of one or more moderator variables (see Table 20.2).

The moderator search focused on the type of sample (see Table 20.3), the topic of oral AO (see Table 20.4), achievement test timing (see Table 20.5), and publication status (see Table 20.6). For the sample population, the average effect size (see Table 20.7) was larger for younger children (preschoolers $r = .617$, primary $r = .442$) than for high school students (r = .173), college students (r = .094), and EMR students (r = .087). The nonsignificant chi-square tests (see Table 20.7) for each sample population suggest it is unlikely that additional moderators or outliers could account for the variance.

TABLE 20.1

Effect Sizes for Studies Investigating the Relationship Between the Use of Oral Advanced Organizers and Student Achievement

Author	Year	Sample Size	Effect Size
Adejumo & Ehindero	1980	120	+.217
Alexander et al.	1979	270	+.661
Barron	1986	126	+.388
Blackhurst	1979	90	+.333
Bricker	1989	18	+.530
Christie & Schumacher	1976	64	−.123
Herron	1994	38	+.344
Kahle	1978	103	+.122
Kahle & Nordlund	1975	317	.000
Kahle & Rastovac	1976	116	+.187
Kirkland et al.	1995	68	−.239
Kirkman & Shaw	1997	32	−.121
Lawton	1978	120	+.236
Lawton & Blue-Swandener	1979	27	+.717
Lawton & Burk	1988	28	+.520
Peleg & Moore	1982	96	−.029
Towsend & Clarihew	1989	52	+.223
		42	+.345
Vickrey	1971	85	−.064
Wong	1972	123	+.368

TABLE 20.2

Overall Average Effect Size

Average effect size	r = .226
Number of studies	k = 20
Number of participants	N = 1,937
Chi-square	χ^2 = 125.64

TABLE 20.3
Individual Effect Sizes For Sample Type

Author	Preschool	Primary School	High School	College	EMR
Adejumo & Ehindero			+.217		
Alexander et al.		+.661			
Barron			+.388		
Blackhurst					+.333
Bricker		+.530			
Christie & Schumacher		−.123			
Herron				+.344	
Kahle				.000	
Kahle & Nordland			+.187		
Kahle & Rastovac			+.122		
Kirkland et al.					−.239
Kirkman & Shaw			−.121		
Lawton		+.236			
Lawton & Blue-Swandener	+.717				
Lawton & Burk	+.520				
Peleg & Moore			−.029		
Towsend & Clarihew		+.223			
		+.345			
Vickrey				−.064	
Wong				+.368	

Note. EMR = educable mentally retarded.

The moderator search for the oral AO topic revealed a higher effect size for social science ($r = .411$) than for science ($r = .152$), social behavior ($r = .206$), and English and foreign languages ($r = -.017$). The chi-square tests were not significant (see Table 20.8), indicating a low probability of additional moderating variables.

The moderator search for the student achievement test timing (see Table 20.9) revealed a larger effect size for the delayed test ($r = .363$) than the immediate testing procedure ($r = .170$) or for the studies reporting an average score for both the immediate and delayed test ($r = .260$). Caution must be exercised in interpreting these findings because only two studies reported separate delayed test scores. Yet, all the chi-square tests were not significant, indicating a low probability of further moderating variables (see Table 20.9).

TABLE 20.4
Individual Effect Sizes for Oral Advanced Organizer Topics

Authors	Science	Social Science	Behavior	English or Foreign Language
Adejumo & Ehindero	+.217			
Alexander et al.		+.661		
Barron	+.388			
Blackhurst		+.333		
Bricker	+.530			
Christie & Schumacher		–.123		
Herron				+.344
Kahle	.000			
Kahle & Nordland	+.187			
Kahle & Rastovac	+.122			
Kirkland et al.				–.239
Kirkman & Shaw	–.121			
Lawton		+.236		
Lawton & Blue-Swandener			+.717	
Lawton & Burk			+.520	
Peleg & Moore			–.029	
Towsend & Clarihew	+.223			
	+.345			
Vickrey				–.064
Wong		+.368		

The moderator search for publication status (see Table 20.10) indicated that unpublished studies had a larger effect size ($r = .327$) than the published studies ($r = .210$). However, the chi-square tests indicate a significant result for the unpublished studies, suggesting an outlier or moderating variable was accounting for a substantial amount of the variance (see Table 20.10).

DISCUSSION

The findings of this study indicate that oral AOs play a small but meaningful role in promoting student learning. It appears that oral AOs may provide an architecture or scaffolding that can support the integration and understand-

TABLE 20.5
Individual Effect Sizes for Achievement Test Timing

Authors	Immediately	Delayed	Averaged
Adejumo & Ehindero			+.217
Alexander et al.			+.661
Barron	+.388		
Blackhurst	+.333		
Bricker	+.530		
Christie & Schumacher	−.123		
Herron	+.344		
Kahle			.000
Kahle & Nordland			+.187
Kahle & Rastovac	+.122		
Kirkland et al.	−.239		
Kirkman & Shaw			−.121
Lawton	+.236		
Lawton & Blue-Swandener	+.717		
Lawton & Burk	+.520		
Peleg & Moore	−.029		
Towsend & Clarihew	+.223		
	+.345		
Vickrey	−.064		
Wong		+.368	

ing of subsequent information and complex concepts. The encoding function of oral AOs appears to function somewhat differently than has been thought. The context in which the oral organizer facilitates student learning varies from the contexts reported in previous meta-analyses. Those meta-analyses examined both oral and written AOs.

First, our meta-analysis on oral AOs isolated improved student learning for younger, less experienced students. This finding raises questions about the role of prior or existing knowledge on a topic. In the studies using oral AOs with preschoolers to enhance their understanding of appropriate social behavior, one might assume some prior understanding of good or bad behavioral expectations. Perhaps the oral AO actually built on the prior understanding of the preschoolers as much as it provided the foundation for future knowledge. The other issue that may confound these findings could be the

TABLE 20.6
Individual Effects for Publication Status

Authors	Published	Nonpublished
Adejumo & Enhindero	+.217	
Alexander et al.	+.661	
Barron		+.388
Blackhurst		+.333
Bricker		+.530
Christie & Schumacher	−.123	
Herron	+.344	
Kahle	.000	
Kahle & Nordland	+.187	
Kahle & Rastovac		+.122
Kirkland et al.		−.239
Kirkman & Shaw		−.121
Lawton	+.236	
Lawton & Blue-Swandener		+.717
Lawton & Burk		+.520
Peleg & Moore	−.029	
Towsend & Clarihew	+.223	
	+.345	
Vickrey	−.064	
Wong		+.368

TABLE 20.7
Average Effect Size for Sample Type

	Preschool	Primary School	High School	College	EMR
Average effect size	.617	.442	.173	.094	.087
Number of studies	2	6	6	4	2
Number of participants	55	566	593	123	158
Chi-square	.03	8.2	.76	9.65	.21

Note. EMR = educable mentally retarded.

TABLE 20.8
Average Effect Size for Oral Advanced Organizer Topics

	Science	Social Science	Behavior	English or Foreign Language
Average effect size	.152	.411	.206	−.017
Number of studies	9	5	4	2
Number of participants	926	667	151	191
Chi-square	2.72	1.76	13.39	5.20

TABLE 20.9
Average Effect Size for Achievement Test Timing

	Immediately	Delayed	Averaged
Average effect size	.170	.363	.260
Number of studies	13	2	5
Number of participants	915	165	885
Chi-square	2.19	.102	4.31

TABLE 20.10
Individual Effect Sizes for Publication Status

	Published	Nonpublished
Average effect size	.210	.327
Number of studies	11	9
Number of participants	1,320	615
Chi-square	3.81	40.11

actual differences in the oral AOs themselves. The studies reviewed for this manuscript revealed oral AOs that were one sentence in length to 50 minutes long. Clearly, these differences in the length and types of oral AOs must impact the findings on the efficacy of oral AOs.

Second, the results suggest that oral AOs were more effective in building scaffolding for social sciences topics rather than science and math. It is likely that some topic areas are easier to build on than others, especially if sequentially sequenced principles are involved. Perhaps in this study, students found oral AOs focusing on cultural differences in society or studying the facets of the U.S. Congress more palatable than genetics or the workings of the eye. These findings may also be partially confounded by the type of achievement test used and the specificity of the information recalled.

The third set of findings suggests that oral AOs are more powerful in enhancing student learning on delayed performance tests. It may be that carefully constructed oral AOs do increase long-term recall more than short-term recall because they "enhance" students' memories for the material being presented. This reasoning was advanced by Glover et al. (1990), who suggested that a "spacing" effect creates the opportunity for students to review stored information, whereas immediate recall requires access to "to-be-learned" information that has not been properly stored. Although Glover et al. (1990) admitted that AOs are only partly analogous to the idea that repeated encounters with the same information enhances accessibility to that information, they suggested that the completeness of the encoding process is better facilitated by the delay in testing and by rereading or rehearing the AO before the test. Clearly, more research is needed to investigate these potential relationships.

Finally, the results concerning the publication status of oral AO manuscripts suggest there are moderating variables that have inflated the effect size of the unpublished studies. These findings highlight the need for future research on the efficacy of oral AOs in enhancing student learning.

The educational implications of oral AOs are not crystal clear. However, this current study confirms the effectiveness of this device in enhancing student learning under certain circumstances and specific conditions. The conditions isolated in this meta-analysis differ from the circumstances and conditions identified in earlier meta-analyses. We agree with Dinnel and Glover (1985) that conceptual vagueness and poor operationalization may be confounding efforts to aggregate findings. These authors remarked that "there is no clear agreement within the field on what makes a good organizer .... Until a consensus exists ... it seems likely that conflicting results will continue to be reported" (Dinnel & Glover, 1985, p. 520). We suggest one conceptual improvement must be separating oral AOs from written and mixed AOs.

It is also evident that three independent meta-analyses have produced competing, even contradictory effect sizes on important issues associated with learning. The problem is associated with violating a fundamental principle of meta-analytic reviews: transparency. The two earlier meta-analyses did not publish the citations for primary studies used in calculations. This means that each new meta-analytic reviewer must collect new samples of AO research as the basis for claims. For an independent meta-analysis to replicate earlier meta-analytic studies, analysts must be able to examine each study, validate coding decisions, and replicate calculations. By distributing complete citations for all studies used in this meta-analysis, we hope to focus the discussion on the conceptual ambiguities lamented by Dinnel and Glover (1985). Inconsistencies among the three meta-analyses will be reconciled when reviewers can scrutinize findings on a study-by-study basis. Until that time, the best available evidence based on 43 years of research is that oral AOs are associated with a small, meaningful increase in learning and retention.

REFERENCES

References marked with an asterisk indicate studies included in the meta-analysis.

*Adejumo, D., & Ehindero, S. (1980). Facilitating learning of science-oriented textual material in a developing country: Study in the use of organizers. *Science Education, 64*, 397–403.

*Alexander, L., Frankiewicz, R. G., & Williams, R. E. (1979). Facilitation of learning and retention of oral instruction using advanced and post organizers. *Journal of Educational Psychology, 71*, 701–707.

Ausubel, D. P. (1960). The use of advanced organizers in the learning and retention of meaningful verbal material. *Journal of Educational Psychology, 51*, 267–272.

Ausubel, D. P. (1968). *Educational psychology: A cognitive view.* New York: Holt, Rinehart & Winston.

Ausubel, D. P., & Fitzgerald, D. (1961). The role of discriminability in meaningful verbal learning and retention. *Journal of Educational Psychology, 52*, 266–274.

Barnes, B. R., & Clawson, E. U. (1975). Do advance organizers facilitate learning? Recommendations for further research based on an analysis of 32 studies. *Review of Educational Research, 45*, 637–659.

*Barron, R. H. (1986). *The relationship between contrasting advanced organizers and achievement of students with different sensory modality preferences and aptitude in a high school biology laboratory.* Unpublished doctoral dissertation, University of Georgia, Athens, GA.

*Bertou, R. E., Clasen, R. E., & Lambert, P. (1972). An analysis of the relative efficacy of advanced organizers, post organizers, interspersed questions and combinations thereof in facilitating learning and retention from a televised lecture. *Journal of Educational Research, 65*, 329–333.

*Blackhurst, A. E. (1979). *Effect of oral advanced organizer on the learning and retention of EMR adolescents.* East Lansing, MI: Consortium on Auditory Learning Materials for the Handicapped. (ERIC Document Reproduction Service No. ED 102754)

*Bricker, E. J. (1989). *The effect of advanced organizers in the teaching of science.* Kean College of New Jersey, in Union and Hillside Townships. (ERIC Document Reproduction Service No. ED 313682)

*Christe, D. J., & Schumacher, G. M. (1976). Some conditions surrounding the effectiveness of advanced organizers for children's retention of orally presented prose. *Journal of Reading Behavior, 7*, 299–309.

Dinnel, D., & Glover, J. A. (1985). Advanced organizers: Encoding manipulations. *Journal of Educational Psychology, 77*, 514–521.

Glover, J. A., Bullock, R. G., & Dietzer, M. L. (1990). Advanced organizers: Delay hypotheses. *Journal of Educational Psychology, 82*, 291–297.

Hedges, L. V., & Olkin, I. (1985). *Statistical methods for meta-analysis.* Orlando, FL: Academic.

*Herron, C. (1994). An investigation of the effectiveness of using an advanced organizer to introduce video in the foreign language classroom. *The Modern Language Journal, 78,* 190–198.

*Kahle, J. B. (1978, October). *A comparison of the effects of an advanced organizer and/or behavioral objectives on the achievement of disadvantaged biology students.* Paper presented at the annual meeting of the National Association for Research in Science Teaching, Washington, DC. (ERIC Document Reproduction Service No. ED 164272)

*Kahle, J. B., & Nordland, F. H. (1975). The effect of an advanced organizer when utilized with carefully sequenced audio–tutorial units. *Journal of Research in Science Teaching, 12,* 63–67.

*Kahle, J. B., & Rastovac, J. J. (1976). The effect of a series of advanced organizers in increased meaningful learning. *Science Education, 60,* 365–371.

*Kirkland, C. E., Byrom, E. M., MacDougall, M. A., & Corcoran, M. D. (1995). *Using advanced organizers with learning disabled students: Research on learning disabilities. Social competence writing, and new technologies.* (ERIC Document Reproduction Service No. ED 390379)

*Kirkman, G., & Shaw, E. (1997, October). *Effects of an oral advanced organizer on immediate and delayed retention.* Paper presented at the annual meeting of Mid-south Education Research Association, Memphis, TN. (ERIC Document Reproduction Service No. ED 415263)

*Lawton, J. T. (1978). Effects of advanced organizer lessons on children's use and understanding of the causal and logic "Because." *Journal of Experimental Education, 46,* 41–46.

*Lawton, J. T., & Blue-Swandener, E. (1979). *Effects of expository and guided self discovery advanced organizer lessons on preschool children's learning of logical concepts.* Washington, DC: National Institute of Education. (ERIC Document Reproduction Service No. ED 167292)

*Lawton, J. T., & Burk, J. (1988). *Effects of advanced organizer instruction on preschool children's prosocial behavior.* (ERIC Document Reproduction Service No. ED 300 121)

*Luiten, J., Ames, W., & Ackerson, G. (1980). A meta-analysis of the effects of advanced organizers on learning and retention. *American Educational Research Journal, 17,* 211–218.

Mayer, R. E. (1979). Twenty years of research on advanced organizers: Assimilation theory is still the best predictor of results. *Instructional Science, 8,* 133–167.

*Peleg, Z. R., & Moore, R. F. (1982). Effects of the advance organizer with oral and written presentation on recall and inference of EMR adolescents. *American Journal of Mental Deficiency, 86,* 621–626.

Stone, C. (1983). A meta-analysis of advance organizer studies. *Journal of Experimental Education, 51,* 194–199.

*Towsend, M. A. R., & Clarihew, A. (1989). Facilitating children's comprehension through the use of advance organizers. *Journal of Reading Behavior, 19*(1), 15–35.

*Vickrey, J. F. (1971). An experimental investigation of the effect of "previews" and "reviews" on retention of orally presented information. *Southern Speech Journal, 3,* 209–219.

*Wong, M. R. (1972, April). *Additive effects of advanced organizers.* Paper presented at the annual meeting of the American Educational Research Association, Chicago. (ERIC Document Reproduction Service No. ED 065471)

21

Relationship of Teaching Evaluations to Research Productivity for College Faculty

Mike Allen
University of Wisconsin–Milwaukee

One of the comments I heard over and over again as an assistant professor was that time spent on teaching was time spent away from research. Although teaching was considered something important, when it came time for tenure evaluation at a research institution like the University of Wisconsin–Milwaukee, the only item on the curriculum vita that mattered would be published research, books, and refereed articles. Currently, I am in my second term on the University Tenure and Promotion Committee and I have yet to hear the word *teaching* mentioned in the committee meeting as a basis for decision. Not only is teaching not a basis for decision, but the activity receives no discussion during the tenure and promotion process. Essentially, the only real element ever discussed by the members of the committee has been the adequacy (quantity and quality) of the published or funded research.

Many friends I have in the discipline work at smaller private institutions (Concordia College, Lewis and Clark College, Marquette University, University of Puget Sound, University of Portland, Wake Forest University, etc.). They tell that a major emphasis for tenure and promotion involves excellence in the classroom. Many institutions would like to see published work by faculty but view the primary mission of the scholars as instruction. I have heard stories of tenure and promotion committees pouring over teaching evaluations on a class-by-class basis, semester by semester, and asking departments and instructors to justify particular marks for particular classes for specific semesters, considering a six- to eight-course-a-year teaching load for 5 years, that would be about 30 to 40 classes that are taught prior to tenure. For so-called teaching institutions, the mission focuses on teaching as an absolute necessity; research, although not a luxury, is certainly considered a commodity not as essential for the faculty.

The comments (and attitudes) of many faculty and members of institutions generate a sense of zero-sum association between the assumptions of the two activities (research and teaching) based on a limited resource: time. The assumption is that a fixed amount of time for professional activity exists and that a person must divide that time among a number of activities. The further assumption is that time spent on teaching or research does not reinforce or contribute to improving the other activity. Therefore, a person in the role of a professor must make a choice about how to allocate time among the various activities. At UW–Milwaukee, a tenured faculty member may request a change in the assumptions about a research emphasis and ask to devote more time to teaching. This release from research expectations incurs an increase in teaching responsibilities. Permitting persons to choose an identity or an intellectual pursuit serves to reinforce the perception that the two aspects of academic existence are inconsistent with each other. The division for senior (tenured) scholars permits and reinforces the sense that the two activities are separate and to some degree mutually exclusive activities.

This view has been examined empirically to find if there exists a trade-off in terms of the time spent on one activity reducing time spent on the other activity. The empirical examination (Olson & Simmons, 1996) of the relationship between time spent on teaching and research demonstrates a large negative correlation ($r = -.54$). As time spent on one activity increases, time spent on the other activity diminishes. This finding indicates that at the level of the individual faculty member the two activities are seen as inversely related. Faculty members view time as a fixed commodity and the division between the two activities is something negotiated in the sense of deciding how to divide efforts between the two types of activities. This published study reinforces the idea that the faculty must divide their roles between teaching and conducting research. This study serves to reinforce empirical evidence that the presumption of time as a fixed commodity represents a real view of most faculty.

The core argument goes on to state that the two activities represent a division of value and emphasis such that the focus on either activity creates a disincentive and a psychological barrier to participation in the other activity. The real contradiction may stem from the perception of what the nature of each activity implies for the individual's commitment to time allocation.

Research productivity for college faculty is regularly assessed and communication has a number of compilations that rate faculty on research productivity (Hickson, 1990: Hickson, Stacks, & Amsbary, 1989, 1992, 1993; Stacks & Hicks, 1983). The productivity ratings include individual faculty as well as assessments of research productivity at the departmental level. Almost all of the productive research faculty list doctoral institutions as the place of employment, as these organizations generally emphasize research.

The generation and use of the rating systems have raised some controversy (Blair, Brown, & Baxter, 1994; Erickson, Fleuriet, & Hosman, 1993). The objections are that other perspectives on the life of a faculty member and the contributions from other means are not considered. The criticisms have been validated by the authors of the original reports; however, the issue remains that tenure and promotion committees (like the one on my campus) demand some yardstick to provide comparison for scholars. I recently got a call from a provost about a tenure case I reviewed. The provost wanted to know what "national" standards existed in communication for tenure and promotion for publication. The provost referred to several disciplines with such standards. Interestingly, the standards only addressed research productivity and not teaching excellence. There is a movement to provide documentation or standards for teaching excellence, which is part of the scholarship of teaching and learning (SoTL) movement. However, even staunch advocates of SoTL admit that the generation of evaluation criteria and standards are still forthcoming and currently nonexistent. This creates a dilemma for the understanding and inclusion of standards that should reflect institutional design that would generate the optimal outcomes sought for teaching effectiveness. The question of time allocation must deserve consideration and exploration because the issue of SoTL quickly becomes the demonstration that involvement or concern about SoTL will increase the effectiveness of teaching or count as research. Whether institutional structures will accept the potential dual benefits of this effort or simply assign a value to the effort remains unresolved.

The real argument is not against the publication of the material that compares scholars and institutions based on research productivity. The argument is against tenure and promotion standards that are weighting research too heavily without full consideration of the other duties of faculty. In addition, the publication of that material favors or recognizes the institutional priorities of what is probably a small fraction of academic institutions. The problem, however, is not the authors who use that system, but rather the failure of the enterprise to articulate and elaborate alternatives to that method of counting.

The problem is that often the academy tends to dichotomize or set forces in opposition that generate forces and focus of opposition. Unfortunately, the resolution of the dispute requires that institutions, much like individuals in forming a relationship, find ways to take what are initially elements in competition and combine or integrate them into a holistic approach of the university or college (Allen et al., 1996). The solution requires that a framework be developed that views the duties or expectations of the scholar not in competition, but rather as mutually reinforcing.

However, beyond the simple opposition must come room for consensus and a multiplicity of standards and techniques of evaluation. Can departments, institutions, and disciplines embrace and endorse multiple standards of excellence? The real challenge is whether the pressures in higher education can find a way to be seen as maximizing the outcomes sought in collaboration rather than viewing the outcomes in competition. The usual tenure and promotion case separates the activities of research, teaching, and service into separate categories and views the responsibilities and outcomes separately. Another view would put the three elements not in opposition, but rather holistically in terms of how each separate part of the job for the scholar serves to reinforce or improve the other elements of the task. The tradition of separation between the elements creates the perception that the duties of the faculty member fall into separate, discrete, and unconnected spheres rather than holistic elements that mark the development of a professional identity as a scholar.

The outcome of the updated meta-analysis in this chapter simply provides information on one set of relationships that affect not only communication departments, but the entire fabric of our institutions. The issues of the connection between teaching and research are not parochial or local issues that affect only some institutions or a few faculty in particular disciplines. The concern about the nature of the integration is central to communication departments in particular because of the need for communication departments to integrate theoretical, applied, and performance concerns.

METHOD

Literature Search

A previous meta-analysis does exist on this topic (Feldman, 1987) in addition to the one by me (Allen, 1996). The literature was searched using ERIC to update the literature since 1996 (using the combination of the keywords *research productivity* and *teaching*) to provide additional sources of information that could be added to this report. One advantage of meta-analysis is that the subsequent publication of additional studies simply provides an additional entry to the database, much like receiving a late survey questionnaire that can be added to the data. Olson and Simmons (1996) pointed out that after the original burst of research, the publication of Feldman (1987) essentially diminished research on the issue. The only publication added since the Allen (1996) summary was the data in Noser, Manakyan, and Tanner (1996). Essentially, since the publication of meta-analysis by Feldman and Allen, little research has been conducted on the connection. This may reflect the impact of what happens when meta-analyses are published; however, as argued in the conclusion, this is a dangerous and unsettling set of circumstances. The understanding of a relationship, although desirable and a step forward, does not provide much information about the process and a background of representing why the relationship exists. I believe that additional research is essential in examining the dynamics of the relationship to provide the possibility of encouraging and creating an environment that would maximize both outcomes. The decline in research indicates that little additional exploration is ongoing that would provide information useful to improving outcomes sought by the various institutions.

Data were corrected for identified artifacts (restriction in range and measurement error due to attenuation). The use of corrections permits individual investigators to compare future findings by eliminating a source of error that varies from investigation to investigation. The averaging process across studies involved the use of weighting on the basis of sample size for the particular estimate. Rosenthal (1984) recommended that such a procedure can create a noncomparability problem because the meta-analysis provides an "ideal" situation that the individual experimenter cannot replicate. The result is that meta-analysis estimates will always differ from the individual estimates of investigators. This position was rejected because the alternative, averaging effects without corrections, is to average across studies with individual variability that is a combination of artifact (which differ in quality and magnitude across the sample of studies) and sampling error. Because the corrections are applied at the level of the individual study, any investigator can perform the corrections on the individual investigation and compare the average to the average provided by the meta-analysis. Additionally, many programs that conduct statistical analyses (e.g., LISREL and AMOS) routinely perform various corrections in the default options without advising the investigator. The real issue in correcting for artifacts should be the explicitness and understanding of the nature of the corrections rather than a universal rule against such corrections. The need for corrections is increased when one considers that extant literature concludes that the artifacts are in fact errors that systematically change the accuracy of the estimate of the relationship. When a scientist can correct for a known errors, I believe that such errors should be removed whenever possible.

Coding for Moderators

The coding for potential moderator conditions generally examines the techniques used to operationalize the variables of teaching effectiveness or research productivity. One issue raised in almost any setting is the nature of the particular operationalization used to measure the construct under investigation. An examination of the possible differences that exist related to the measurement instrument provides some evidence of whether particular operationalizations are the basis for persons concluding that the research is inconsistent.

The other source of moderator analysis was the year of data collection. The year of data collection analysis should reveal whether a consistent trend for a change in the relationship exists over time. A common theme heard in the academy is that the requirement for published research has consistently increased over the decades. Assuming that a zero-sum relationship exists between teaching and research, the impact should be a correlation (negative) that grows with time. As additional time is spent by a faculty member on research, the expectation should be that the size of a negative correlation should increase over time. As time spent on research increases, the quality of the teaching evaluations should decrease. This analysis was not included here only because the addition of one study does not provide enough information to change results reported by Allen (1996). That report indicates no trend since the correlation prior to 1960 was high ($r = .209$), lower in the 1970s ($r = .095$), higher in the 1980s ($r = .112$) and finally lower post-1980 ($r = .068$).

Teaching productivity was divided on the basis of the particular measure of teaching evaluation that the investigation used: (a) student evaluations, (b) peer evaluations, or (c) nomination or receipt of teaching award. Two forms of measurement of teaching were employed in the designs (combinations of various ratings, and amount of time spent in teaching-related activities), but those appeared in only one investigation and were considered insufficient to report separately as a measurement device. Each form of evaluation indicates the perspective of a particular indicator of quality. Clearly, student satisfaction with instruction is a source of evaluation of teaching because the student serves as the consumer affected by the quality of teaching. Similarly, students are in the best position to compare the effectiveness of various instructors because each student usually takes classes from multiple instructors at the same time as well as multiple instructors over time. Peer evaluations provide a different perspective on teaching quality related to content and professional expectations. Peer evaluations can consider the needs of an instructor to meet requirements for certification, rigor in grading, and evaluation of work, as well as appropriateness of assignments and selection of reading materials. Students lack the background to provide a professional-level evaluation. Teaching awards indicate evaluations related to professional expectations, student evaluations. In addition, they provide a better comparison to other instructors at an institution or at other institutions. Finally, teaching-related activities indicate the desire on the part of the instructor for self-improvement or the level of commitment and time spent handling instructional activities.

Research productivity was measured using a variety of methods: (a) number of published works, (b) grant contracts, (c) number of citations to authored works, (d) peer or chair rating of research productivity, (e) time spent on research, (f) awards earned for research quality, (g) combinations of grants and publications, and (h) the research creativity of the scholar as rated by other faculty at the institution. The research productivity measures that were used in two or fewer studies (number of grant contracts, amount of time spent on research, number of awards earned for research, combination of grants and publications, and research creativity of the scholar as rated by other faculty) were not included in this analysis. The statistical summary of these measures is available in Allen (1996).

Statistical Analysis

The technique used was the variance-centered form of meta-analysis developed by Hunter and Schmidt (1990). This process of meta-analysis involves three steps: (a) transformation and correction of data from the original reports; (b) estimating an average effect, using the correlation coefficient in this report, that is weighted on the basis of sample size; and (c) examining the level of variability among the observed effects relative to that expected due to random sampling error as well as systematic sources of variability (often called moderator variables). A central issue in meta-analysis is the generation of more accurate estimates for the population parameter by combining multiple samples.

RESULTS

The results generate a positive average correlation between the level of teaching evaluations and the measures of research productivity (see Table 21.1). The overall finding is that there is a positive relationship between positive teaching evaluations and research productivity (average $r = .106$, $k = 47, N = 65,263$) and the findings are not based on a homogenous set of findings, $\chi^2 (df = 46, N = 65,263) = 116.99, p < .05$.

Consideration of potential moderating influences deals with issues like the measurement of teaching quality and how the measures of research productivity were constructed. Another potential source of influence considered was the year of data collection and whether any discernible trends were evident over time. The addition of only one investigation provides little to change the results from the previous published work by Allen (1996).

TABLE 21.1
Summary of Results

	Average r	k	N	χ^2
Overall	.106	47	65,263	116.99*
Teaching measure				
Student evaluations	.085	38	11,515	88.33*
Peer evaluations	.320	6	685	19.76*
Teaching award	.110	5	53,337	2.70
Research measure				
Number of publications	.109	32	62,845	63.56*
Number of citations	−.032	5	1,036	6.85
Peer or chair evaluations	.124	7	858	6.40

*$p < .05$.

Analysis Considering the Method of Teaching Evaluation

Considering the evaluation method used for teaching provides some issues for future consideration. Student evaluations demonstrate a positive association between the report of student satisfaction and faculty research productivity (average $r = .085, k = 38, N = 11,515$) and the findings are not based on a homogenous set of findings, $\chi^2 (df = 37, N = 11,515) = 88.33, p < .05$.

The findings are similar for the use of peer evaluations of teaching and research productivity (average $r = .320, k = 6, N = 685$) and the average correlation demonstrates heterogeneity, $\chi^2 (df = 5, N = 684) = 19.76, p < .05$. The size of the effect is larger than for student evaluations. This possibly indicates that peer faculty could either be biased evaluators favoring the researcher or bring a greater understanding of the content and implications of the choices of the instructor. The net effect is that the faculty views the effect as larger; however, the number of investigations and size of the sample indicates more sampling error as a potential explanation.

The use of teaching awards demonstrates an effect that agrees with the overall average effect (average $r = .110, k = 5, N = 53,337$) and the findings are based on a homogeneous set of findings, $\chi^2 (df = 4, N = 53,337) = 2.70, p < .05$. However, although the number of studies is not large (five), the number of faculty involved in this set of investigations (more than 50,000) is extremely large. The reliance on one large study with an enormous sample size drowns out the influence of the other studies and more research should be conducted to test the veracity of the single investigation.

Analysis Considering the Method of Measuring Research Productivity

The first type of measurement of research productivity counted the number of published works by the faculty member. The correlations between that measure and teaching evaluations was positive and indistinguishable from the overall average (average $r = .109, k = 32, N = 62,845$) and the findings are based on a heterogeneous set of findings, $\chi^2 (df = 31, N = 62,845) = 63.56, p < .05$.

Examining research productivity in terms of the number of citations produced the only negative correlation observed (average $r = -.032, k = 5, N = 1,036$) and the findings are based on a homogeneous set of findings, $\chi^2 (df = 4, N = 1,036) = 6.85, p < .05$. Given the small number of studies (five) it is difficult to create meaningful inferences because the average has a high level of sampling error. The average does indicate something about the possibility of research that is more foundational or important, requiring more time and perhaps diminishing or interfering with the ability to provide quality teaching.

The peer rating of research demonstrates a consistent effect with the overall average relationship of teaching evaluation and research productivity (average $r = .124, k = 7, N = 858$) and the findings are based on a homogenous set of findings, $\chi^2 (df = 6, N = 858) = 6.40, p < .05$.

DISCUSSION

Rather than a negative correlation, the results of this summary indicate that the view of teaching and research should be one of complementary or reinforcing sets of skills and other sets of issues rather then inconsistent priorities. The tension felt between the two activities may simply indicate the stress of requiring excellence along many dimensions rather than two activities that are mutually inconsistent with each other in terms of skills and effort. Clearly, the meta-analysis provides very strong and clear evidence against scholars or administrators arguing that the two activities should be viewed in direct competition and inconsistent with each other. The analysis indicates that no such general inconsistency can be maintained in the face of the available research on this issue.

The meta-analysis concludes that a positive correlation exists between teaching evaluations and research productivity (see Table 21.2). Using the Binomial Effect Size Display developed by Rosenthal (1984), a correlation of .10 translates into a 22% increase in predictability. Rosenthal pointed out that typically "small" correlations have been incorrectly dismissed as unimportant, despite the fact that many such correlations may have enormous

TABLE 21.2
Binomial Effect Size Display of Results

		Percentage of Faculty With Teaching Evaluations	
		Below the Mean	Above the Mean
Faculty with research records that are	Above the mean	45%	55%
	Below the mean	55%	45%

Note. This is true assuming an average correlation of $r = .10$ and median splits on for categorization. The use of the Binomial Effect Size Display indicates a 22% increase in prediction that a faculty member with good teaching evaluations is also one above average in terms of a research record.

importance when applied to the substance of a particular problem or situation. The context of this issue, set in the higher educational environment of the college and university, remains important. The findings indicate that the demand or search for excellence in multiple dimensions of evaluation provides requirements that are not inconsistent with each other. Rather, the relationship between excellence in the two activities, for whatever reason, is reinforcing or positive rather than negative. Consider the long-term implications of a 20- or 30-year career and the impact of what may seem to be a relationship not obvious over a given year but additive and cumulative. This suggests a set of foundational issues for the academy.

The results should not be surprising at one level; many of the skills that go into good teaching should be skills consistent with good research. Persons successful at one end of the agenda should be successful in the other arena. Both arenas require the use of skills at explaining issues to persons with less expertise and in some cases disinterest in the topic. Publication requires good writing, skillful explanation, and some persuasion, which pushes the author to convince both an editor and some reviewers that the manuscript is worthy of publication. The additional benefit is firsthand experience in dealing with the subject matter, and the efforts may pay off in improved understanding of the material. The research imperative requires not only mastery of the material but the ability to contribute to the development of that literature.

The general literature dealing with teaching evaluations has been subjected to a series of meta-analyses by Feldman (1979, 1983, 1984, 1986). These meta-analyses cast doubt on a number of the myths that many faculty have about the "Neilson" ratings generated through the use of student evaluations. The meta-analyses provide some good evidence that many of the fabled explanations for high teaching evaluations are not supported. The work by Feldman explores many of the myths and problems typically associated with the use of student evaluations to generate information on the quality of instruction. Essentially, Feldman concluded that the available body of literature supports the validity and freedom from many other influences of teaching evaluations conducted by students. This body of work provides evidence for continued use and reliance on student evaluations to assess instructional quality.

One weakness in this and other reviews is the lack of consideration about student learning. Although the effectiveness measures of teaching in this report consider satisfaction, the issue of whether research productivity is related to cognitive learning is unknown. A central argument is whether a scholar engaged in research and teaching would generate higher test scores that measure student achievement. Additional research should be conducted that explores the relationship of teacher research productivity to some objective measure of learning rather than the perception of student satisfaction. The question of the relationship of student learning (measured in some objectified manner in relationship to demonstrable outcomes) creates a different set of expectations for the relationship to research productivity. The assumption is that a scholar engaged in research should provide more accurate and recent information on a topic to the student; therefore, the student should perform better on tests related to competence in the mastery of the material.

Another chapter in this volume (Witt, Wheeless, & Allen, chap. 10) demonstrates that teacher immediacy, although generating a high correlation ($r = .50$) with affective learning, has a small relationship to cognitive learning ($r = .05$). The outcome measures in this review are not unimportant, but there should be little confidence that cognitive outcomes are equally as positively related. It is quite possible that the cognitive outcomes would demonstrate a higher set of relations if knowledge about content should be considered something that would contribute to increased learning on the part of the students.

A concern is about the nature of research institutions and faculty teaching. Consider that many institutions would like research faculty to obtain extramural funding in the form of contracts and grants (Burgoon, 1988, 1989). Grant funding is usually used to buy the teaching portion of the contract of the faculty member from the institution to permit concentrated time on the research. Most doctoral programs have a teaching load that is two courses per semester (four courses for the year, typically with at least one of them a small graduate course), whereas the private small college or the nonresearch state institution has a teaching load of four courses per semester (eight per year). Additionally, the doctoral programs use teaching assistants for lower level (and sometimes upper division) courses. Research faculty are in the classroom less and with fewer students than faculty at nonresearch institutions. Another outcome is that persons with higher teaching evaluations are typically not found in the classroom, or found less often than other faculty. The result creates an interesting paradox for the role of teaching and research at academic institutions that emphasize the research role of the professor. The outcomes sought by focusing on research productivity are institutional designs that would take the best teachers and effectively minimize their influence as teachers. Noser et al. (1996) indicated that economics faculty members' attitudes toward research productivity were influenced by the combination of individual and institutional characteristics (priorities).

The one exception to that, documented by Kyvik and Smeby (1994), remains the relationship of graduate student supervision to research productivity. This relationship may indicate the natural tendency of graduate students to gravitate toward faculty advisers that share research interests and often data sets. The result is that graduate students may serve as a motivating force for faculty and push them to success by providing energy and a sense of urgency that older faculty members may not feel. Similarly, faculty more active in research may be viewed as more energetic and more knowledgeable and therefore more attractive to graduate students. The activity may generate a stronger sense of affinity and result in an increased level of productivity for both the graduate students and faculty members.

The preceding paragraph reveals the implications of institutional priority on financing based on research excellence as opposed to quality of teaching. The problem is that the quantification of teaching in a manner that contributes to financial viability has not been demonstrated in a manner that permits administrators to provide outcomes demonstrated remuneratively. The arguments made by those interested in the scholarship of teaching and learning provide for a different possibility related to outcome. Suppose that the faculty member is interested in the teaching and learning of the student. The affiliation or work in research related to learning the particular content of the faculty member may provide both research and student improvement. This potential effect deserves consideration and attention as the move toward the issues dealing with scholarship and teaching becomes perceived as interrelated and requires solutions that emphasize both teaching and learning within the institution.

For private institutions, the heavy dependence on tuition as a source of revenue forces much more consumer- or client-centered activity. Many public institutions rely on tuition for a portion of their operating revenue and have less incentive or receptivity to student-related issues. The center of financial issues may reflect the concern that each type of institution has or should have with the particular outcome. Given tighter budgets in this new century, the need for a sense of consumer responsiveness on the part of institutions may drive the process toward more teaching, or at least student satisfaction with teaching. If external funding sources dry up and grant funding becomes more difficult to obtain, the return to the classroom of some of these faculty is inevitable.

The question is whether the relationship can be changed by various institutional design or reward schemes. If institutions provide more direct awards for teaching excellence or research success, one would expect performance in these areas to be affected because the faculty is expected to emphasize areas rewarded and valued by the institution. This permits administrations and faculty to target or direct the nature of performance by creating the fundamental foundation of what is evaluated. Future research should examine the impact of various institutional frameworks on the output of faculty across a variety of measures.

The current trend in the academy centers on the SoTL. Cynical persons find the adoption of any trendy issue in the academy as one with about the same longevity in popularity as a rap song. The fundamental issue in generating a longer change must come from knowledge about how persons learn (as well as a real understanding of how instructors actually teach). Any influence on the quality of instruction (positive or negative) that reflects institutional priorities deserves attention. The more promising avenue is finding and articulating methods of taking what at the surface may be inconsistent goals and generating institutional models to propose ways of combining these procedures to generate higher quality outcomes for both processes.

The conclusion that we should reach is that research productivity and good teaching are not inconsistent with each other. In fact, the evidence indicates the converse, that good teaching and research productivity tend to reinforce each other and contribute to effectiveness in both endeavors. This conclusion does not mean that the connection is inevitable (clearly creating a job environment where it is impossible to do both would negate this connection); however, the normal relationship demonstrates the impact of a mutually reinforcing set of conditions.

The reconsideration that we need to make is how research and teaching end up mutually serving to reinforce goals rather than viewing them inevitably as trade-offs. This requires consideration at multiple levels for issues of how institutions define responsibilities and evaluate the productivity of faculty. Although we understand the direction and nature of the relationship, little is known about how this relationship exists and why the outcome becomes formulated in this manner. The next step forward in the research on this issue requires focus on explicating that relationship to maximize the value of the faculty in meeting institutional objectives.

REFERENCES

Allen, M. (1996). Research productivity and positive teaching evaluations: Examining the relationship using meta-analysis. *Journal of the Association for Communication Administration, 7*, 77–97.

Allen, M., Berchild, J., Bernhart, K., Domain, M., Gilbertson, J., Geboy, L., et al. (1996, May). *Dialectical theory: Testing the relationship between tensions and relational satisfac-*

tion. Paper presented at the annual meeting of the International Communication Association, Chicago. (ERIC Document Reproduction Service No. ED 394 164)

Blair, C., Brown, J., & Baxter, L. (1994). Disciplining the feminine. *Quarterly Journal of Speech, 80,* 383–406.

Burgoon, M. (1988). Extramural funding or extracurricular research: That is the choice. A research editorial. *Western Journal of Speech Communication, 52,* 252–258.

Burgoon, M. (1989). Instruction about communication: On divorcing Dame Speech. *Communication Education, 38,* 303–308.

Erickson, K., Fleuriet, C., & Hosman, L. (1993). Prolific publishing: Professional and administrative concerns. *Southern Communication Journal, 58,* 328–338.

Feldman, K. (1979). The significance of circumstances for college students' ratings of their teachers and courses. *Research in Higher Education, 10,* 49–172.

Feldman, K. (1983). Seniority and experience of college teachers as related to the evaluations they receive from students. *Research in Higher Education, 18,* 3–124.

Feldman, K. (1984). Class size and college students' evaluations of teachers and courses: A closer look. *Research in Higher Education, 21,* 45–116.

Feldman, K. (1986). The perceived instructional effectiveness of college teachers as related to their personality and attitudinal characteristics: A review and synthesis. *Research in Higher Education, 24,* 139–213.

Feldman, K. (1987). Research productivity and scholarly accomplishments of college teachers as related to their instructional effectiveness: A review and exploration. *Research in Higher Education, 26,* 227–298.

Hickson, M. (1990). Profiling the chairs of prolific speech communication departments. *Association for Communication Administration Bulletin, 73,* 4–14.

Hickson, M., Stacks, D., & Amsbary, J. (1989). An analysis of prolific scholarship in speech communication, 1915–1985: Toward a yardstick for measuring research productivity. *Communication Education, 38,* 230–236.

Hickson, M., Stacks, D., & Amsbary, J. (1992). Active female scholars in communication: An analysis of research productivity. II. *Communication Quarterly, 40,* 350–356.

Hickson, M., Stacks, D., & Amsbary, J. (1993). Active prolific scholars in communication studies: Analysis of research productivity. II. *Communication Education, 42,* 224–233.

Hunter, J., & Schmidt, F. (1990). *Methods of meta-analysis: Correcting error and bias in research findings.* Thousand Oaks, CA: Sage.

Kyvik, S., & Smeby, J. (1994). Teaching and research: The relationship between the supervision of graduate students and faculty research performance. *Higher Education, 28,* 227–239.

Noser, T., Manakyan, H., & Tanner, J. (1996). Research productivity and perceived teaching effectiveness: A survey of economics faculty. *Research in Higher Education, 37,* 299–321.

Olson, D., & Simmons, S. (1996). The research versus teaching debate: Untangling the relationships. *New Directions for Institutional Research, 90,* 31–39.

Rosenthal, R. (1984). *Meta-analytic procedures for social research.* Beverly Hills, CA: Sage.

Stacks, D., & Hicks, M. (1983). An analysis of doctoral degree-granting institutions and number of articles published by their graduates. *Association for Communication Administrative Bulletin, 43,* 47–52.

V

Meta-Analysis and Interactional and Instructional Processes in the Classroom

22

The Contributions
of the Scholarship
# of Teaching and Learning

Barbara Mae Gayle
Saint Martin's University

Kreber and Cranton (2000) asserted that the scholarship of teaching and learning (SoTL) enhances the reflection process by drawing attention to one's teaching. They stressed the interdependence of pedagogical, instructional, and curricular knowledge culminating in efforts put forth to study one's teaching. Feezel and Welch (2000) concurred, arguing that the scholarship of teaching and learning "affects teacher's choice of classroom activities, goals behind various class methods, and the ways in which they are used" (p. 252). Thus, "the scholarship of teaching begins with what a teacher knows, and then transforms and extends that knowledge through systematic study and critical reflection" (Litterst & Tompkins, 2001, p. 9). Results of the SoTL research reveal a growing body of findings employing a multiplicity of methods to enhance educators' pedagogical, instructional, and curricular knowledge. Although each SoTL scholar explores the efficacy of her or his own classroom, important implications can be drawn across studies for other educators and for those pursuing future research based in the meta-analytic reviews in this volume.

FINDINGS ASSOCIATED WITH PEDAGOGICAL KNOWLEDGE

Brandt and Perkins (2000) contended that pedagogical knowledge includes knowing how to construct learning environments based on understanding how students learn. Some SoTL research has focused on enhancing the instructor's ability to select the most engaging and challenging methods for increasing student learning based on learning theory, whereas other SoTL findings have centered on how students' ability to learn could be enhanced. Most results suggest that varying traditional pedagogical practice can enhance an educator's understanding of how students learn. For example, altering traditional teaching methods to include more engaging pedagogical learning processes enhanced student feelings of ownership in the learning process (Phillips, 2000; Qualters, 2001), produced more student satisfaction with peer collaboration (Qualters, 2001), and led students to believe what they learned was more useful (Hodges & Harvey, 2001; Qualters, 2001; Salvatori, 2000). On the other hand, Winter, Lemons, Brookman, and Hoese (2001) cautioned educators to carefully structure inquiry-based learning opportunities because they may interfere with student learning if the structure requires students to assume too much independent knowledge construction. The issue appears to be how much structure is necessary to maximize learning. Theilheimer (2003) reasoned that there is a fine line between insufficient structure and being overly prescriptive so that no critical or independent thought is possible.

Several researchers claim that structuring opportunities for learning enhances the capacity for student understanding. Maier (2002) reported that structured activities increase engaged participation by students, and Linkon (2003) and Tingley (2003) found that appropriate scaffolding enhanced students' ability to understand complex concepts. The organized environment in these instances helped students develop strategies for anchoring the theoretical or abstract constructs they were studying. Smith (2001) contended that carefully structuring assignments and classroom time can help student teachers conceptually understand the information they will one day teach themselves. Jacobs (2001) illustrated how to maximize "at-risk" student learning through structuring active learning techniques during a lecture. Thus it appears that implementing structured learning practices based on pedagogical theory can promote student engagement in the learning process.

SoTL researchers also explore the pedagogical efficacy of engaging students in specific learning techniques. Malone (2002) contended that incorporating previously or newly acquired experiences into the learning environment increases students' ability to participate in inquiry-based learning. Similarly, Cooperstein (1999) observed that learning to think mathematically required engagement in novel problems and Wu (2003) and Osborne (2000) suggested that modeling a behavior enhances the likelihood of student understanding. Taking a slightly different approach, Bennett (2003) asserted that personalizing the professor's image as a pedagogical practice motivates classroom discussions. He found that devoting as little as 10 minutes to discussing a professor's experience or views on the subject matter or some external interests promoted the classroom environment needed to enhance student question asking. Finally, Salem and Michael's (2001) work suggested that monitoring online discussions provides the instructor a wealth of information about student learning processes. It appears that carefully designed or monitored learning facilitates the pedagogical effectiveness of learning techniques. This logic is consistent with Cerbin's (1998), Salvatori's (2000), and Hodges and Harvey's (2001) research suggesting that promoting deep understanding requires some pedagogical adjustments.

Structuring the course environment to meet student needs involves the educator's pedagogical knowledge and understanding of the learning environment. Linkon (2003) observed that designing online modules helps professors clarify their thought process as they probe different ways of structuring learning for their students. Also, Web-based opportunities allow students to determine why some answers are better than others (Bernstein, 2003). Ambers (2003) found that structuring group interactions in a large enrollment class by student sex promoted student learning. Sims (2001), on the other hand, reported that practice-based learning could be enhanced through the use of narratives. This author discovered that sharing complex stories without telling students what they were supposed to learn enhanced students' ability to engage in inductive and creative thinking. Smith (2001) and Goddu (2003) observed that scaffolding was related to student learning capability. Smith (2001) noticed that structuring the course to make students more experienced in scientific inquiry required the creation of a learning community. Goddu (2003) contended that making the process of interdisciplinary thinking more visible required concrete participation in Web-based media. Thus, it appears that structured pedagogical techniques improve the use of class time and student thinking.

A mitigating factor in designing courses may involve the student learner needs and how those needs are associated with effective pedagogy. Curry (2003) noticed that students' critical thinking ability varied according to the status of the student learner. Novice learners had limited thinking capacity, whereas expert, engaged learners could represent multiple perspectives, take ownership of their interpretation, and display intellectual agility. Similarly, Tingley (2003) discerned that novice learners made overly broad generalizations and jumped too quickly to obvious interpretations. Bass (2001) reported that some students leapt to certainty, were reluctant to imagine questions relying on their own knowledge base, and did not know how to withhold judgment and be flexible in their interpretations. Schick (2002) observed that good students were occasionally uncomfortable with the ambiguity inherent in inquiry-based learning. This difficulty was more serious for apathetic students, who actually hindered the work of other students. Finally, Shick (2003) found that some students thrive regardless of the methodology or pedagogy employed. Overall, learning outcomes appear to vary depending on a student's capacity to learn and the limitation of specific pedagogical techniques.

To answer the question of under what conditions professors could alter a student's capacity to learn, some researchers addressed the precise impact of a specific learning strategy. Hodges and Harvey (2001) discovered that problem-based learning enhanced the intellectual development of students. Aries (2002) observed that immersion in a service learning experience could transform "transitional knowers" into "independent knowers." Sloan and Swenson (2003) discovered that encouraging a process of both teaching and learning about a topic area could transform students' thinking. Finally, Daley's (2002) work revealed that students' ability to produce cognitive maps enhanced their learning capability. It seems clear that specifically designed pedagogy can impact students' deep understanding and that there are many routes to academic success.

Taken together, the studies focusing on pedagogical knowledge provide educators with insights that can be used to guide student learning. Additionally, these studies show the promise inherent in curricular modifications. Careful reflection on teaching techniques and classroom conditions based on sound pedagogy can result in designed improvements in student learning.

FINDINGS ASSOCIATED WITH INSTRUCTIONAL KNOWLEDGE

Instructional knowledge involves a deep understanding of the methods used to promote student learning. Developing a broad repertoire of teaching strategies or instructional methods may help facilitate the learning needs of a variety of students. In fact, scholars found that creating a variety of activities and flexible learning opportunities increased most students' motivation to learn (Barkley, 2003; Lewis & Hayward, 2003). The research summarized here indicates that dynamically increasing student learning involves planning a variety of learning activities before, during, and after classroom interactions.

Some of the research exploring instructional practices focused on the use of collaborative and active learning strategies in creating successful learners. Fedler (1996) discovered that active, inductive, cooperative learning helped students in his chemistry classroom achieve a deeper level of understanding. Students achieved a greater sense of being a member of a learning community and made better use of office hours. Likewise, de Caprariis, Barman, and Magee (2001) verified that collaborative learning exercises improved student learning in a geology class. Milner-Bolotin and Suinicki (2000) reported that students were better able to connect scientific principles to their everyday life and more motivated to learn due to project-based activities that encouraged students to ask and refine questions. Kilgore's (2003) work supported this conclusion, indicating that learning how to formulate your own question is a significant first step in the learning process.

Long's (2003) work also explored active learning strategies. She used brainstorming technique to enhance students' thought processes and observed it was more effective than giving students specific examples to enhance critical thinking. Darden (2002), on the other hand, found that concrete examples were more helpful when dealing with abstract concepts. She discovered that using modeling activities as examples helped 50% of her students successfully visualize the genetic process. However, Kern (2000) cautioned that active learning techniques like role playing may increase students' understanding, but interfere with their overall conceptual recall. Similarly, Corbalan (2003) cautioned educators that active learning techniques are not 100% successful. The author asserted that digital-oriented activities, although helpful, should be purposely employed and limited to no more than 20 minutes at a time. The logic here is that learner success is dependent on the way a specific instructional technique is operationalized in the classroom.

Other researchers explored the use of videos or visual images as a type of graphic example (Benson, 2002; Calloway-Thomas, 2002; Jaffee, 2003; Stephen, 2002). These studies indicate that visual images enhance understanding, perhaps by providing a structure or a mnemonic that triggers student recall. Stephen (2002) discovered that the use of film improves both the depth and breadth of students' understanding. Benson (2002) found that watching videos enhanced student understanding of basic concepts, increased their science literacy, and created a positive attitude toward scientists. Theilheimer (2003) observed that visual aids such as Microsoft PowerPoint serve as organizing devices that build links to learning that are not possible in traditional pedagogical approaches. Calloway-Thomas (2002) reasoned that visual features are powerful mnemonics that can heighten student understanding. She believed that film images may be easier for students to understand and remember. Jaffee (2003) reported that students enjoy looking at visual images, but cautioned that students lack the ability to interpret the historical meanings. Jaffee urged educators to design strategic course structures that enhance contextual thinking. Kilgore (2003) supported this view, maintaining that using visual images requires planning beyond showing the image itself. She believed that visual images often produce a quick "I see" response. Without significant and well-structured follow-up, very little long-term learning can be expected. Overall, these scholars suggest that increasing cognitive involvement with the subject matter, whether it is through enhanced visuals or active learning strategies, can enhance cognitive processing if the learning context is properly structured.

Several other scholarship of teaching and learning scholars have investigated structuring a variety of pre- and postclassroom activities designed to enhance student learning; including quizzes, reading activities, and writing exercises. Robinson (2003), Nimmrichter (2003), Dym (2003), and Gaudry-Hudson (2003) all discovered that online quizzes were good preparatory activities to increase student learning. Nimmrichter (2003) found that students appreciated the instant feedback from online quizzes and used those quizzes to review for tests. She also observed that she could use quiz performance to adjust her instructional plans to meet students' needs. Dym's (2003) research indicated that open-book, online quizzes often motivated students to read course materials more thoroughly and study more extensively for tests. However, Dym was unable to identify a significant gain in exam scores. Gaudry-Hudson (2003) and Robinson (2003) also established a link between quizzes and prereading assignments. Both authors maintained that these activities enhanced classroom discussions.

It is also possible that classroom activities increase awareness of educational goals and strategies. Bass (2001) and O'Connor (2003) explored whether some active learning strategies increased student consciousness about their reading. O'Connor (2003) used student-created Web sites to enhance students' critical thinking and their ability to employ textual evidence to support an argument. O'Connor found evidence of associative and incremental thinking in the process of constructing Web sites. Consistent with Goddu's (2003) findings, O'Connor (2003) claimed that additional preparation time was needed to allow students to thoroughly read the text and deeply analyze that text. Bass's (2001) work concentrated on identifying the reading protocols used by students. He discovered that even though students were open to more expansive reading techniques, they were largely unable to defer interpretation of a passage long enough to complete the passage. On the other hand, Robinson (2003) suggested that making connections to popular culture enhanced students' reading ability. Robinson reasoned that links to popular culture allowed students to identify with the material being read. In summary, it appears that activities designed to adapt to student preferences can stimulate students' learning opportunities.

There is also a body of literature indicating that engaging students in written assignments can promote students' analytic skills. Yen (2003), Wyandotte (2001), and Bertrand (2002) concentrated on writing experiences. Ambrosio (2003), Clapp-Itnyre (2001) and Ingebretsen (2003) investigated writing in journals. Yen (2003) reported that using a computer-designed writing program required her students to read the text more carefully, to practice the process of analyzing literary passages, and to study longer. When Wyandotte (2001) engaged her students in writing about archetypes to analyze texts, she observed that the response papers helped students connect the readings to their own lives and created a deeper ownership of the literature being studied. Similarly, Smith (2001) discovered that writing exercises helped preservice teachers explore their own learning experiences. Bertrand's (2002) students gained confidence and increased their French language proficiency after completing multiple writing exercises in French. Similarly, Salvatori's (2000) students found that writing about moments of difficulty created ways of understanding and coping with differences. Finally, Hammerness, Darling-Hammond, and Shulman (2000) maintained that reading theory in context with writing and sharing enabled student teachers to think like more experienced teachers.

Writing in journals also seemed to enhance student mastery of course materials. Ambrosio (2003) uncovered that online journaling increased student learning, whereas Clapp-Itnyre's (2001) student responses were mixed due to the work required in producing the preclass, in-class, and postclass entries required. However, the journaling process in Clapp-Itnyre's course enhanced the depth of student understanding. Even though Ingebretsen (2003) could not establish a link between journaling and final exam achievement, he observed that students more frequently selected the journal assignment rather than the periodic essay or research paper assignments as ways of demonstrating their understanding of course content. Similarly, Duffy (2000) contended that journals help educators identify how students are assimilating course content.

Taken together, these studies suggest that structuring preparatory and postclassroom activities can provide a variety of ways of approaching course concepts and increase student mastery of course curriculum. These findings also suggest that students' analytic capabilities can be enhanced by well-crafted experiences.

A related area of investigation focuses on instructional techniques that structure classroom discussions or small-group interactions to enhance student learning. Fieto (2002) reported that creating an intellectual community helps students give "careful thought to the issues and ideas before them as well as consideration and support to those who accompany them on their journey." These communities involve "complementary social and cognitive" (p. 7) components shared by participants. Like Fieto, several scholars observed that building trust among classmates and being motivated to interact were necessary prerequisites for stimulating discussions (Bulcroft, Werder, & Gilliam, 2002; Gayle, 2002, 2003; Stephen, 2003). Malone (2002) and Fieto (2002) believed that sharing perspectives on complex issues promotes creative thinking. Bulcroft et al. (2002) noted that learning environments should foster connections across complex ideas to build the learning community. Leveen (2003) maintained that student completion of specific exercises enhanced their participation in class discussion, and Gayle (2002; Gayle, Martin, Mann, & Chrouser, 2002) reported that a student's ability to alter attitudes or beliefs was directly affected by her or his willingness to actively participate in interpreting complex topics and deliberating on complicated issues. For Gayle (2002; Gayle et al., 2002), the promotion of discussion was as much about students listening to diverse perspectives with an open mind as it was about their actual participation in classroom discussions. None-the-less, this line of inquiry suggests that interactive discussions on complex topics enhance student creativity and understanding.

In a related area, several SoTL scholars investigated the efficacy of computer-mediated discussions among their students. Salem and Michael (2001) used Web-based threaded discussions to enhance problem solving conversations in their calculus class. They reported substantial success in generating problem-solving interactions. Stephen (2003), Berggren (2003), Megraw (2003), and Cohen (2003) all used online discussions to enhance student learning. Although these authors found that students willingly participated in discussions, the investigations were not able to establish a strong association with increased learning. In fact, Berggren (2003) maintained that electronic discussions may fail if students decide not to participate in favor of face-to-face communication.

There is also evidence that online discussions are generally effective in promoting course material understanding. For example, Ugoretz (2003) found that students who were willing to take responsibility for online discussions were not afraid of giving a factually correct answer. These students also used the discussion to create a more personal connection with the course material. He maintained that these online discussion behaviors create a deeper understanding than was observed in other course work. Adrian (2003) and Robinson (2003) also addressed the issue of answering online questions. Robinson (2003) discovered that faculty answering online questions enhanced the level of student analysis. Adrian (2003) used a handheld device to let students record their positions on a topic before discussing their response and why they chose it. Her results revealed no clear link between student participation in the discussion and test-taking proficiency. Thus, the research investigating online and face-to-face discussions indicates that many factors beyond mere participation influence student learning.

Scholars studying small-group interactions focused on the discussions and the activities occurring among subsets of students rather than the class as a whole. Goodwin (2003) argued that debating promotes small-group communication and discussion. This position is consistent with Malone's

(2002) analysis. Kilgore (2003) noticed that small-group work encourages students to increase the complexity of their responses to course material, and Maier (2002) observed that during group work, students focused on finding the right answers to complex problems, corrected superficial errors, practiced using new terminology, and aided one another's critical thinking. Similarly, Malone (2002) indicated that opportunities to collaborate with others on research projects lead to a deeper understanding of course materials and fostered self-sustaining abilities in assessing one's own work. Jacobs (2001) concluded that working with other students helps develop problem-solving skills for "at-risk" chemistry students and Kelly (2003) reported that collaborative group activities motivate students because they obtain new insights from others or work harder to avoid being embarrassed by their peers. Moskal (2002) urged caution, however, and reported evidence that group work during class can be overdone, fail to leave enough time for clarifying questions, and inhibit student learning. Overall, small-group activities appear to be generally successful in motivating student learning. This line of research suggests that peer groups can aid in the mastery of course materials if the classroom activities are properly structured.

In summary, it appears that regardless of the instructional technique employed to facilitate or enhance student learning, the success of the technique relies on structuring or scaffolding the technique to fit the curriculum. As a result, maximizing student learning requires well-considered pedagogical practices implemented in a teacher-structured instructional context.

FINDINGS ASSOCIATED WITH CURRICULAR KNOWLEDGE

Because educators must be able to assess the ability of their course objectives to meet curricular standards, they must adjust their courses to maximize academic outcomes and articulate what should constitute an important aspect of the overall curriculum. Some SoTL research has focused on developing this curricular knowledge. The results of this line of inquiry suggest that intentionally applying curricular knowledge is intricately related to course design, implementation decisions, and classroom delivery.

Instructor reflection on aspects of course design has been explored by several researchers. Cottrell and Jones (2003) analyzed how instructors designed courses for SoTL initiatives and noticed that these instructors reflected on their course design to emphasize student learning and its improvement. Albers (2003) reasoned that constructing a syllabus serves as both a pedagogical tool and an artifact of scholarship that benefits both the professor and the students. She contended that the instructor benefits by providing hiring and review committees with a picture of his or her research. The scholarly reflection involved in course design benefits students because the syllabus provides a way to organize, direct, and integrate learning. Taking a slightly different approach, Hunt (2003) explored the success of midsemester feedback in enhancing student–teacher course design. Hunt found that students and educators experienced enhanced communication as a result of midsemester evaluations. Together, these investigations on curricular knowledge indicate that both course evaluations and course design decisions influence student learning.

It also appears that implementing technology in the curriculum affects delivery decisions and the structure of the course. Barkley (2003) discovered that students preferred a structure of multimedia instruction that produced blended versions of an online course with opportunities for enhanced face-to-face interactions. Arbaugh and Duray (2002), on the other hand, found that large MBA classes negatively assessed learning and satisfaction with online experiences. They also determined that students were more satisfied with online courses if they perceived some kind of flexibility in the curriculum or if they had experienced an online course in the past. Russo (2002) found that students were more engaged in online learning when the curriculum was designed to enhance their ability to interact interpersonally with classmates. Thus, factors other than mere online pedagogical delivery techniques seem to affect student satisfaction and learning in new, technology-based courses.

Knowledge about students' responses to curricular implementation has also developed as a result of SoTL research. Several researchers investigated the effects of intentionally structuring curriculum. Bender (2002) found that tailoring curriculum improved the rate of nonscience majors' overall science literacy at a rate similar to that of science majors. Also, Bower (2002) noticed that math anxiety affected classroom performance and student information processing ability. He maintained that taking time to involve students in understanding their own learning process had a positive impact on their overall performance. Simlarly, Sleeter (2003) reasoned that education students could be instructed to identify global constructs in a multicultural curriculum and use these generative ideas to plan their own curriculum. Burman (2001) studied a family nurse practitioner (FNP) curriculum and recommended incorporating complementary and alternative medicine into the FNP course content to enhance student learning outcomes. Finally, Fukami (2000) suggested that implementing curricular changes takes more time, but the quality of student understanding and assignments increases. These studies suggest that curriculum design can be enhanced by carefully applying specific curricular knowledge to a variety of contexts.

Taken together, studies on curricular knowledge underscore the necessity of educators understanding the interaction among course delivery, planning, and implementation. It appears that curriculum knowledge underlies student learning and faculty reflection. The scholarship of teaching and learning research illustrates the viability of studying one's own classroom in enhancing an instructor's pedagogical, instructional, and curricular knowledge. As Shulman (2000) argued, the SoTL research is "learning-focused, domain-specific and oriented toward analyzing the educative experiences and outcomes that institutions support" (p. 52). SoTL encourages "the convergence of disciplinary knowledge, pedagogical practice, evidence of learning, and theories of learning and cognition" (Bass, 1999, p. 9).

CONCLUSIONS

Readers will quickly ascertain the connection between meta-analytic reviews and the SoTL. Empirical reviews summarize and assess the record of empirical investigations. SoTL applies findings from an instructors' classroom to provide benchmarks for interpreting curricular success. Educators designing state-of-the-art classrooms must begin building their curricula on the best available evidence, and meta-analyses are the preferred summaries for establishing generalizations about classroom practices, processes, and outcomes. At the same time, SoTL advances a philosophy of introspection, reflection, and assessment that will lay the foundation for future research. Meta-analytic reviews of the instructional literature must be guided by insights grounded in the classroom experience and SoTL can provide that foundation.

This is a healthy collaboration for both scientists and pedagogues. Scientists will discover a wealth of insights and hypotheses embedded in the SoTL literature. Pedagogues will discover stable generalizations that advance curriculum development and provide a platform for future innovations. This relationship is dynamic and mutually reinforcing, as success in the classroom is rooted in existing research and new developments in the classroom will prompt additional empirical summaries.

REFERENCES

Adrian, L. (2003). *The impact of technology on student discussion and learning.* Retrieved December 31, 2003, from Georgetown University, Visual Knowledge Project, http://lumen.georgetown.edu/vkp/posters/public/index.cfm?fuseaction=poster.display&posterID=29

Albers, C. (2003). Using the syllabus to document the scholarship of teaching. *Educational Administration Abstracts, 38*(3), 305–308.

Ambers, R. K. R. (2003). Effects of using single-gender group exams in a large, introductory geology class. *The Journal of Scholarship of Teaching and Learning (JoSoTL), 3*(2), 1–12.

Ambrosio, F. (2003). *Dante and the journey to freedom.* Retrieved December 31, 2003, from Georgetown University, Visual Knowledge Project, http://lumen.georgetown.edu/vkp/posters/public/index.cfm?fuseaction=poster.display&posterID=72

Arbaugh, J. B., & Duray, R. (2002). Technological and structural characteristics, student learning and satisfaction with Web-based courses: An exploratory study of two on-line MBA programs. *Management Learning, 33*(3), 331–347.

Aries, J. (2002, June). *Second language acquisition: Oral proficiency and service-learning in Spanish.* Paper presented at The Carnegie Foundation for Advancement of Teaching, Summer Session for Carnegie Scholars, Menlo Park, CA.

Barkley, E. F. (2003). *Using the scholarship of teaching and learning to transform a general education music course.* Retrieved December 31, 2003, from the Carnegie Foundation for the Advancement of Teaching's Knowledge Media Laboratory, http://kml2.carnegiefoundation.org/html/gallery.php

Bass, R. (1999). The scholarship of teaching: What's the problem? *Inventio, 1*(1), 1–9.

Bass, R. (2001). *Reading the US cultural past: Designing a course for flexible performance.* Retrieved December 31, 2003, from Georgetown University, Visual Knowledge Project, http://lumen.georgetown.edu/vkp/posters/public/index.cfm?fuseaction=poster.display&posterID=1

Bender, H. (2002, June). *Science as a human activity: Investigations of the achievement of genetic literacy by non-science majors in the human genetics classroom.* Paper presented at the Carnegie Foundation for the Advancement of Teaching, Summer Session for Carnegie Scholars, Menlo Park, CA.

Bennett, C. (2003). *Advanced mathematics for secondary teachers: Course portfolio.* Retrieved December 31, 2003, from the Carnegie Foundation for the Advancement of Teaching's Knowledge Media Laboratory, http://kml2.carnegiefoundation.org/html/gallery.php

Benson, S. (2002, June). *Using a non-print teaching platform in a general science course.* Paper presented at the Carnegie Foundation for the Advancement of Teaching, Summer Session for Carnegie Scholars, Menlo Park, CA.

Berggren, P. (2003). *Incremental learning: The arts in New York City.* Retrieved December 31, 2003, from Georgetown University, Visual Knowledge Project, http://lumen.georgetown.edu/vkp/posters/public/index.cfm?fuseaction=poster.display&posterID=40

Bernstein, D. (2003). *Peer review of teaching—Course portfolio.* Retrieved December 31, 2003, from the Carnegie Foundation for the Advancement of Teaching's Knowledge Media Laboratory, http://kml2.carnegiefoundation.org/html/ gallery.php

Bertrand, D. (2002, June). *Value-added writing: A transformational experience all around.* Paper presented at the Carnegie Foundation for the Advancement of Teaching, Summer Session for Carnegie Scholars, Menlo Park, CA.

Bower, N. W. (2002). Development of a simple mathematical predictor of student performance in general chemistry. *The Journal of Scholarship of Teaching and Learning (JoSoTL), 3*(1), 4–13.

Brandt, R. S., & Perkins, D. N. (2000). The evolving science of learning. In R. Brandt (Ed.), *Education in a new era, ASCD yearbook* (pp. 159–183). Alexandria, VA: Association for Supervision and Curriculum Development (ASCD).

Bulcroft, K., Werder, C., & Gilliam, G. (2002). Student voices in the campus conversations. *Inventio, 4,* 18–20.

Burman, M. E. (2001). *Making sense of complementary and alternative medicine: Analysis of a family nurse practitioner program.* Retrieved December 31, 2003, from the Carnegie

Foundation for the Advancement of Teaching's Knowledge Media Laboratory, http://kml2.carnegiefoundation.org/html/gallery.php

Calloway-Thomas, C. (2002, June). *I've got the word in me and I can sing it, you know: Using representative illustrations as modes of enhancing student learning.* Paper presented at the Carnegie Foundation for the Advancement of Teaching, Menlo Park, CA.

Cerbin, W. (1998). *Problem-based learning in an educational psychology class.* Retrieved December 31, 2003, from the Carnegie Foundation for the Advancement of Teaching's Knowledge Media Laboratory, http://kml2.carnegiefoundation.org/html/gallery.php

Clapp-Itnyre, A. (2001). Three-part journaling in introductory writing and literature classes: More work with more rewards. *The Journal of Scholarship of Teaching and Learning (JoSoTL), 1*(2), 2–13.

Cohen, A. (2003). *Can computer bulletin boards replace traditional class meetings?* Retrieved December 31, 2003, from Georgetown University, Visual Knowledge Project, http://lumen.georgetown.edu/vkp/posters/public/index.cfm?fuseaction=poster.display&posterID=34

Cooperstein, B. (1999). *Learning to think mathematically.* Retrieved December 31, 2003, from the Carnegie Foundation for the Advancement of Teaching's Knowledge Media Laboratory, http://kml2.carnegiefoundation.org/html/gallery.php

Corbalan, R. (2003). *New technologies and the teaching of a foreign language.* Retrieved December 31, 2003, from Georgetown University, Visual Knowledge Project, http://lumen.georgetown.edu/vkp/posters/public/index.cfm?fuseaction=poster.display&posterID=24

Cottrell, S. A., & Jones, E. A. (2003). Researching the scholarship of teaching and learning: An analysis of current curriculum practices. *Innovative Higher Education, 27*(3), 169–181.

Curry, R. (2003). *Developing "engaged learners" in the film studies classroom.* Retrieved December 31, 2003, from Georgetown University, Visual Knowledge Project, http://lumen.georgetown.edu/vkp/posters/public/index.cfm?fuseaction=poster.display&posterID=111

Daley, B. J. (2002). The scholarship of teaching and learning: Facilitating adult learning. *The Journal of Scholarship of Teaching and Learning (JoSoTL), 3*(1), 16–23.

Darden, A. (2002, June). *Using modeling activities to facilitate the development of abstract thinking in genetic students.* Paper presented at the Carnegie Foundation for the Advancement of Teaching, Menlo Park, CA.

de Caprariis, P., Barman, C., & Magee, P. (2001). Monitoring the benefits of active learning exercises in introductory survey courses in science: An attempt to improve the education of prospective public school teachers. *The Journal of Scholarship of Teaching and Learning (JoSoTL), 1*(2), 32–44.

Duffy, D. K. (2000). Resilient students, resilient communities. In P. Hutchings (Ed.), *Opening lines: Approaches to the scholarship of teaching and learning* (pp. 23–30), Menlo Park, CA: The Carnegie Foundation for the Advancement of Teaching.

Dym, J. (2003). *The effectiveness of weekly online computer quizzes in helping students learn content.* Retrieved December 31, 2003, from Georgetown University, Visual Knowledge Project, http://lumen.georgetown.edu/vkp/posters/public/index.cfm?fuseaction=poster.display&posterID=50

Fedler, R. M. (1996). Active-inductive-cooperative learning: An instructional model for chemistry. *Journal of Chemical Education, 73*(9), 832–836.

Feezel, J., & Welch, S. A. (2000). What is new or different about the scholarship of teaching? *Journal of the Association for Communication Administration, 29,* 250–256.

Fieto, J. A. (2002, June). *Exploring intellectual community.* Paper presented at the Carnegie Foundation for the Advancement of Teaching, Summer Session for Carnegie Scholars, Menlo Park, CA.

Fukami, C. V. (2000). Looking through a different lens: Inquiry into a team-taught course. In P. Hutchings (Ed.), *Opening lines: Approaches to the scholarship of teaching and learning* (pp. 31–40). Menlo Park, CA: The Carnegie Foundation for the Advancement of Teaching.

Gaudry-Hudson, C. (2003). *The impact of Web-based technologies on teaching practices.* Retrieved December 31, 2003, from Georgetown University, Visual Knowledge Project, http://lumen.georgetown.edu/vkp/posters/public/index.cfm?fuseaction= poster.display&posterID=89

Gayle, B. M. (2002). How can we teach students to critically evaluate their own stance and seriously consider divergent view points? *National Teaching and Learning Forum, 12*(1), 1.

Gayle, B. M. (2003). *Communicating responsible citizenship: Exploring social class differences through service learning* (Final report for Systems of Service: Building Systemwide Continuums of Service grant, Oregon Campus Compact). Portland, OR.

Gayle, B. M., Martin, D. M., Mann, S., & Chrouser, L. (2002). Transforming the public speaking classroom: A scholarship of teaching and learning project on civil public discourse. *Journal of Northwest Communication, 31,* 1–26.

Goddu, T. (2003). *From world's fairs to on-line museums: U.S. culture in the gilded age.* Retrieved December 31, 2003, from Georgetown University, Visual Knowledge Project, http://lumen.georgetown.edu/vkp/posters/public/index.cfm?fuseaction= poster.display&posterID=179

Goodwin, J. (2003). Student's perspectives on debate exercises in content area classes. *Communication Education, 52,* 157–163.

Hammerness, K., Darling-Hammond, L., & Shulman, L. (2000). *Learning from cases.* Retrieved December 31, 2003, from the Carnegie Foundation for the Advancement of Teaching's Knowledge Media Laboratory http://kml2.carnegiefoundation.org/ html/gallery.php

Hodges, L. C., & Harvey, L. C. (2001, June). *Exploring how students learn organic chemistry.* Paper presented at the Carnegie Foundation for Advancement of Teaching, Summer Session for Carnegie Scholars, Menlo Park, CA.

Hunt, N. (2003). Does mid-semester feedback make a difference? *The Journal of Scholarship of Teaching and Learning (JoSoTL), 3*(2), 13–20.

Ingebretsen, E. (2003). *Evaluating the relationship between technologies and evaluation.* Retrieved December 31, 2003, from Georgetown University, Visual Knowledge Project, http://lumen.georgetown.edu/vkp/posters/public/index.cfm?fuseaction= poster.display&posterID=93

Jacobs, D. (2001). *Cooperative learning in general chemistry.* Retrieved December 31, 2003, from the Carnegie Foundation for the Advancement of Teaching's Knowledge Media Laboratory, http://kml2.carnegiefoundation. org/html/gallery.php

Jaffee, D. (2003). *Visualizing history.* Retrieved December 31, 2003, from Georgetown University, Visual Knowledge Project, http://lumen.georgetown.edu/vkp/posters/ public/index.cfm?fuseaction=poster.display&posterID=34

Kelly, M. (2003). *Making collaboration visible.* Retrieved December 31, 2003, from Georgetown University, Visual Knowledge Project, http://lumen.georgetown.edu/ vkp/posters/public/index.cfm?fuseaction=poster.display&posterID=9

Kern, B. B. (2000). Using role play simulation and hands-on models to enhance students' learning fundamental accounting concepts. *The Journal of Scholarship of Teaching and Learning (JoSoTL), 1*(1), 8–24.

Kilgore, S. (2003). *Visualizing American cultures.* Retrieved December 31, 2003, from Georgetown University, Visual Knowledge Project, http://lumen.georgetown.edu/vkp/posters/public/index.cfm?fuseaction=poster.display&posterID=35

Kreber, C., & Cranton, P. A. (2000). Exploring the scholarship of teaching. *The Journal of Higher Education, 71*(4), 476–495.

Leveen, L. (2003). *Putting the text in context, final version.* Retrieved December 31, 2003, from Georgetown University, Visual Knowledge Project, http://lumen.georgetown.edu/vkp/posters/public/index.cfm?fuseaction=poster.display&posterID=670

Lewis, L. K., & Hayward, P. A. (2003). Choice-based learning: Student reaction in an undergraduate organizational communication course. *Communication Education, 52,* 148–156.

Linkon, S. (2003). *Making interdisciplinary visible.* Retrieved December 31, 2003, from Georgetown University, Visual Knowledge Project, http://lumen.georgetown.edu/vkp/posters/public/index.cfm?fuseaction=poster.display&posterID=4

Litterst, J. K., & Tompkins, P. (2001). Assessment as the scholarship of teaching. *Journal of the Association for Communication Administration, 30,* 1–12.

Long, B. (2003). *Do examples inhibit creativity?* Retrieved December 31, 2003, from Georgetown University, Visual Knowledge Project, http://lumen.georgetown.edu/vkp/posters/public/index.cfm?fuseaction=poster.display&posterID=138

Maier, M. (2002, June). *You can learn a lot by listening.* Paper presented at the Carnegie Foundation for Advancement of Teaching, Summer Session for Carnegie Scholars, Menlo Park, CA.

Malone, L. (2002, June). *Peer critical learning: CASTL final report.* Paper presented at the Carnegie Foundation for Advancement of Teaching, Summer Session for Carnegie Scholars, Menlo Park, CA.

Megraw, R. (2003). *Reading the American landscape.* Retrieved December 31, 2003, from Georgetown University, Visual Knowledge Project, http://lumen.georgetown.edu/vkp/posters/public/index.cfm?fuseaction=poster.display &posterID=110

Milner-Bolotin, M., & Svinicki, M. D. (2000). Teaching physics of everyday life: Project-based instruction and collaborative work in undergraduate physics courses for nonscience majors. *The Journal of Scholarship of Teaching and Learning (JoSoTL), 1*(1), 25–40.

Moskal, B. M. (2002). Improving the instruction of engineering calculus: Responding to student feedback. *The Journal of Scholarship of Teaching and Learning (JoSoTL), 3*(1), 24–37.

Nimmrichter, S. (2003). *The impact of Web-based technologies on teaching practices.* Retrieved December 31, 2003, from Georgetown University, Visual Knowledge Project, http://lumen.georgetown.edu/vkp/posters/public/index.cfm?fuseaction=poster.display&posterID=90

O'Connor, P. (2003). *Hypertext monsters: Student Web pages and associative thinking.* Retrieved December 31, 2003, from Georgetown University, Visual Knowledge Project, http://lumen.georgetown.edu/vkp/posters/public/index.cfm?fuseaction=poster.display&posterID=94

Osborne, R. E. (2000). A model for student success: Critical thinking and "at risk" students. *The Journal of Scholarship of Teaching and Learning (JoSoTL), 1*(1), 41–47.

Phillips, M. T. (2000). A case study of theory, voice, pedagogy, and joy. In P. Hutchings (Ed.), *Opening lines: Approaches to the scholarship of teaching and learning* (pp. 73–81), Menlo Park, CA: The Carnegie Foundation for the Advancement of Teaching.

Qualters, D. M. (2001). Do students want to be active? *The Journal of Scholarship of Teaching and Learning (JoSoTL), 2*(1), 51–60.

Robinson, S. D. (2003). Using computer-mediated communication to enhance in-class discussions and comprehension in undergraduate literature class. *Inventio, 5*(1). Retrieved from http://www.doit.gmu.edu/inventio/articlepopup.asp?pID= spring03&sID_=robinson

Russo, T. (2002, June). *Learning online with invisible others: The rule of relational communication behaviors on learning and attitudes.* Paper presented at the Carnegie Foundation for Advancement of Teaching, Summer Session for Carnegie Scholars, Menlo Park, CA.

Salem, A., & Michael, R. (2001). *Conversations: Making student thinking visible.* Retrieved December 31, 2003, from the Carnegie Foundation for the Advancement of Teaching's Knowledge Media Laboratory, http://kml2.carnegiefoundation.org/html/gallery.php

Salvatori, M. R. (2000). Difficulty: The great educational divide. In P. Hutchings (Ed.), *Opening lines: Approaches to the scholarship of teaching and learning* (pp. 23–30). Menlo Park, CA: The Carnegie Foundation for the Advancement of Teaching.

Schick, S. (2002). *Using new media to initiate student-centered learning in a mass media class.* Retrieved December 31, 2003, from Georgetown University, Visual Knowledge Project, http://lumen.georgetown.edu/vkp/posters/public/index.cfm?fuseaction= poster.display&posterID=60

Sims, S. L. (2001). Preparing teachers and students for narrative learning. *The Journal of Scholarship of Teaching and Learning (JoSoTL), 1*(2), 1–14.

Shulman, L. S. (2000). From Minsk to Pinsk: Why a scholarship of teaching and learning? *The Journal of Scholarship of Teaching and Learning (JoSoTL), 1*(1), 48–53.

Sleeter, C. (2003). *Multicultural curriculum, ideology, and perspective.* Retrieved December 31, 2003, from Georgetown University, Visual Knowledge Project, http:// lumen.georgetown.edu/vkp/posters/public/index.cfm?fuseaction=poster.display& posterID=34

Sloan, R. S., & Swenson, M. (2003). "Doing" phenomenological research: Connecting nursing, education, research, and professional practice. *The Journal of Scholarship of Teaching and Learning (JoSoTL), 3*(2), 34–40.

Smith, D. (2001). *Making a new song about science.* Retrieved December 31, 2003, from the Carnegie Foundation for the Advancement of Teaching's Knowledge Media Laboratory, http://kml2.carnegiefoundation.org/html/gallery.php

Stephen, E. (2002). *Journeys far from home.* Retrieved December 31, 2003, from Georgetown University, Visual Knowledge Project, http://lumen.georgetown.edu/ vkp/posters/public/index.cfm?fuseaction=poster.display&posterID=34

Theilheimer, R. (2003). *Meshing it all together: First semester early childhood students making sense of new ideas about children, families, and schooling.* Retrieved December 31, 2003, from Georgetown University, Visual Knowledge Project, http:// lumen.georgetown.edu/vkp/posters/public/index.cfm?fuseaction=poster.display& posterID=59

Tingley, S. (2003). *Reading visual texts.* Retrieved December 31, 2003, from Georgetown University, Visual Knowledge Project, http://lumen.georgetown.edu/vkp/posters/ public/index.cfm?fuseaction=poster.display&posterID=34

Ugoretz, J. (2003). *Casting wider and digging deeper science fiction online.* Retrieved December 31, 2003, from Georgetown University, Visual Knowledge Project, http://lumen.georgetown.edu/vkp/posters/public/index.cfm?fuseaction=poster.display&posterID=82

Winter, D., Lemons, P., Brookman, J., & Hoese, W. (2001). Novice instructors and student-centered instruction: Identifying and addressing obstacles to learning in the college science laboratory. *The Journal of Scholarship of Teaching and Learning (JoSoTL), 2*(1), 14–42.

Wu, H. J. (2003). *Case study made easy, finally!* Retrieved December 31, 2003, from Georgetown University, Visual Knowledge Project, http://lumen.georgetown.edu/vkp/posters/public/index.cfm?fuseaction=poster.display&posterID=147

Wyandotte, A. (2001). A special gift: Archetypes in ancient literature as a reflection of readers' "language understandings." The *Journal of Scholarship of Teaching and Learning (JoSoTL), 1*(2), 1–14.

Yen, J. (2003). *Making learning visible in literary analysis.* Retrieved December 31, 2003, from Georgetown University, Visual Knowledge Project, http://lumen.georgetown.edu/vkp/posters/public/index.cfm?fuseaction=poster.display&posterID=133

23

How Does Meta-Analysis Represent Our Knowledge of Instructional Communication?

Stacy L. Young
Timothy G. Plax
Patricia Kearney
California State University, Long Beach

Learning happens in many locations. It occurs in the classroom when teachers present information, engage student participation, provide feedback, and cocreate the classroom climate. It happens during office hours when students seek out additional guidance or social camaraderie, and when teachers create an opportunity for that to occur. Learning can be seen when teachers go home to be self-reflexive about their performance and the extent to which their goals for the class are being achieved; students also continue the learning process during their "off time" by honing their study skills. Outside of the classroom, both teachers and students continue to advance their learning, whether through continued research to stay abreast of current findings or through participation in extracurricular activities. Indeed, learning begins even before teachers or students set foot in the classroom—it happens in the construction and design of the course, as well as in students' selection in taking one class in lieu of another. In short, the construct of learning, just like communication, is a dynamic and ongoing process. Who then is better equipped to reflect on the topic of learning than experts in the field of communication? Using a common methodological framework, the authors in this volume shed light on what we know about instructional communication and where we can go from here.

A COMMON METHODOLOGICAL FRAMEWORK: META-ANALYSIS

A meta-analysis is a set of statistical procedures designed to combine data and assess results across primary studies that address a common topic. Hunter and Schmidt (1990) stated that the purpose of meta-analysis is to provide "some means of making sense of the vast number of accumulated study findings" (p. 37). Although this methodology was originally not very well received in the research community, it is "an idea whose time had come" (Hunt, 1999, p. 13). Indeed, virtually every field of study from hard sciences to social sciences has seen a rise in popularity in using this approach.

Meta-analyses serve several vital functions in social science research. First, they can provide answers to important research questions, particularly when results of primary studies conflict. It is not uncommon for primary research studies to make conclusions that are counter to previous scholarship. For instance, some research suggests that giving students verbal praise can enhance learning (Brophy, 1999), whereas other findings contradict this premise by arguing that praise can be an ineffective strategy, especially if it is overused (Emmer, 1988). By providing a synthesis of prior scholarship on a particular topic, meta-analyses can facilitate a clearer understanding of conflicting research results.

In short, meta-analyses help organize the proverbial research closet, and by doing so, they highlight the knowledge that we have and what is missing. In other words, the second benefit of meta-analyses is that they provide a cumulative assessment of current scholarship and they reveal what remains to be studied. This strength enables meta-analyses to not only uncover future research directions, but also to provide scholars with the opportunity to identify what we know and how certain we can be with research conclusions. As a result, researchers can avoid reinventing the wheel or regurgitating scholarship that does not significantly advance knowledge or efficiently utilize valuable research resources.

Finally, meta-analysis is a fruitful tool for theory development and refinement. By synthesizing data as well as revealing what needs further exploration, meta-analyses can demonstrate how well research findings correspond with various theoretical perspectives. They can provide a test for existing theories or they can offer guidance for theory construction.

Despite the benefits of this approach, meta-analysis has received its fair share of criticism. One of its staunchest critics, H. J. Eysenck (1978), called meta-analysis "an exercise in mega-silliness" (p. 517). Others, like Sohn (1995) and Gallo (1978), have also been quite vocal in critiquing this methodology. More specifically, Eysenck (1984) argued that meta-analysis can confuse issues, disregard important problems, and generally hamper scientific progress by deriving meaningless conclusions. Based on Hunter and Schmidt's (1990) discussion as well as criticisms raised by its opponents, those who question the value of meta-analyses generally note four primary concerns: (a) availability bias; (b) garbage in, garbage out; (c) comparing apples to oranges; and (d) being variable analytic.

Although all studies are limited by their samples, this issue is particularly relevant when using meta-analysis to test claims. The inclusion or exclusion criteria for studies as well as the research databases utilized to locate findings unavoidably leads to bias in sampling. In particular, although not always the case, meta-analyses tend to rely on published studies to obtain data. Arguably, published studies may differ from unpublished studies in meaningful ways. For instance, studies that do not uncover significant relationships between variables or significant differences between groups are less likely to get published than those that do. As a result, published studies may present a skewed picture of research findings, portraying overall results as largely statistically significant.

Because meta-analyses are constrained by their samples, if the primary studies were not rigorously conducted, this methodological sloppiness can carry over into the analysis of these findings. This criticism has been referred to as the "garbage in, garbage out" issue (Hunt, 1999). In short, using poorly designed studies or combining weak studies with strong ones leads to a confusing picture of the data at best; at worst, the result is a false or obscure depiction of what the data are really trying to portray.

Not only how the studies were conducted but also what they investigated is important to consider when evaluating meta-analyses. As Hunt (1999) explained, "both the multicausal nature of social science phenomena and the imperfect comparability of the measures of effect limit what social science meta-analyses can yield" (p. 113). Meta-analyses using studies that do not explore like phenomenon or that have significantly different operationalizations of the same variable (i.e., comparing apples to oranges) may produce meaningless results. Because empirical research attempts to make generalizations about a population based on a sample, this goal is only possible to the extent that meta-analyses utilize studies examining the same phenomenon measured in a similar fashion (i.e., comparing apples to apples).

Finally, even meta-analyses studying comparable phenomenon may be criticized for emphasizing variables as the primary point of focus. Wellman (1988) argued that researchers in general who study social phenomena tend to rely too heavily on variable analytic research. This shortcoming is particularly relevant in meta-analyses where often the focus is on a variable or variables of interest as opposed to using a theory as a guiding framework. Because solid empirical research should be theoretically grounded, meta-analyses sometimes fall short of being theory driven.

The criticisms put forth about meta-analyses can typically be grappled with in the design and implementation of the study, as well as through various statistical analyses. Numerous scholars (e.g., Hall & Rosenthal, 1991; Hunter & Schmidt, 1990) provide guidance on the type of statistical analyses that can be computed to handle a variety of issues that may arise while analyzing data via meta-analysis. Hall and Rosenthal (1995) also offered input on how to conceptually develop and conduct meta-analyses, arguing that the three key principles are accuracy, simplicity, and clarity. The meta-analyses in this book work hard to be accurate, simple, and clear. They serve as impressive models of how meta-analyses should be conducted. In the next section, we discuss what these meta- analyses collectively tell us about the field of instructional communication.

WHAT WE KNOW

The chapters presented in this volume do a good job of maximizing the strengths of meta-analyses and handling the limitations of this methodology. Meta-analyses offer a state-of-the-art review on a given topic. Indeed, many chapters herein highlight the theoretical advancements, the future research directions, and the practical implications of current scholarship on instructional communication.

Theoretical Implications

Because meta-analyses provide a synthesis of current empirical findings, they enable scholars to assess how research contributes to theoretical advancement. Several of the chapters vividly illustrated the role their findings had in enhancing understanding of various theories. Broadly speaking, the theoretical perspectives covered in these meta-analyses can be classified into cognitive, behavioral, and motivational-emotional perspectives.

Cognitive Perspective. A cognitive approach to learning focuses on how people acquire, store, and access knowledge; it emphasizes perception, memory, language, and various other cognitive functions (Neisser, 1967). The theories in this book that would fall within this perspective explored the acquisition and recall of knowledge, as well as the important role of perceptions. Information can be gleaned in a variety of ways. Media richness theory (Daft & Lengel, 1986; Fulk, Schmitz, & Steinfield, 1990; Lengel & Daft, 1988; Trevino, Daft, & Lengel, 1990) posits that rich media can convey more information than lean media; in other words, the greater number of cues associated with a channel should relay more information than one with fewer cues. Similarly, dual coding theory (Paivio, 1991) argues that information presented in both pictures and words should facilitate its recall. Interestingly, neither Timmerman and Kruepke (chap. 6, this volume) nor Allen, Bourhis, Mabry, Burrell, and Timmerman (chap. 14, this volume) fully supported these premises. Instead, they discovered that too many cues may distract from the message and that people's individual preferences about channels played a significant role in the learning outcome. So although more sophisticated presentations of information may be engaging, it is possible to have too much of a good thing. Likewise, how information is stored can affect the learning process. According to the subsumption theory (Ausubel, 1960), new information is comprehended and retained insofar as it can be subsumed under existing knowledge structures. Preiss and Gayle (chap. 20, this volume) on advanced organizers speak directly to the importance of framing new information in terms of already acquired knowledge and to providing a clear structure or road map of material to be covered. Making clear connections between concepts and using succinct channels to transit information appears to be key in information retention and recollection.

Behavioral Perspective.   The behavioral perspective examines observable behaviors and evaluates them in relation to environmental influences (Watson, 1930). In terms of instructional communication, a behavioral perspective would explore how the context and the interactants themselves shape learning. Several theories covered in this book provide insight on the role situational expectations have in shaping students' educational experiences. For instance, the interactive model (Deaux & Major, 1987) contends that situational pressures and expectations promote sex-typed behavior. Jones, Dindia, and Tye (chap. 12, this volume) found that teachers had more interactions in general and more negative interactions in particular with male students as opposed to female students. They suggested that this may have more to do with expectations about behavior rather than the behavior itself; in other words, teachers may anticipate that males will be more unruly than females and as a consequence teachers more actively involve males to offset the potential class disruption. In a similar vein, speech accommodation theory (Giles, Mulac, Bradac, & Johnson, 1987) states that people adjust their communication behavior to adapt to the perceived style of their interactional partner. Teachers and students, then, may alter their patterns of communication to be more similar to each other. If, as the similarity attraction principle (Byrne, 1971) maintains, people like others who are similar to them, accommodating one's speech to match the audience may promote a sense of liking or closeness. Thus, it is not surprising that Witt, Wheeless, and Allen (chap. 10, this volume) discovered that teacher immediacy (overall, nonverbal and verbal) improved perceived and affective learning, but not cognitive learning. In other words, students who believed their teachers displayed high levels of immediacy behaviors felt like they learned a lot (i.e., perceived learning) and were pleased with the learning process (i.e., affective learning); however, there were no marked differences in actual knowledge gained (i.e., cognitive learning). Teachers, then, who are immediate are more attractive—in the sense that they make learning enjoyable—but, based on their findings, a good time in the classroom does not necessarily transfer to an improved learning outcome.

Spielberger and Vagg's (1995) transactional process model may offer some insight into why a positive environment in the classroom may not necessarily translate into higher grades for students. One factor that may affect students' academic performance (e.g., grades) is their test anxiety. Their model specifically focuses on test anxiety and suggests that students' efforts expended well before an exam and the behaviors and cognitions during an exam may contribute to test anxiety (or vice versa). Preiss, Gayle, and Allen (chap. 7, this volume) confirmed that high test anxiety was linked to low academic motivation, poor study skills, and decreased self-esteem. They also revealed that programs designed to thwart test anxiety, such as systematic desensitization or skills training, may be largely ineffective. They argued that the routine, everyday behaviors of students are at the root of the problem. In other words, the actions that students take on a day-to-day basis to synthesize, retain, and recall information have a significant influence on their learning outcomes. Again, these findings reinforce the notion of learning as an ongoing process occurring on many levels in various places.

Motivational-Emotional Perspective.   The motivational-emotional perspective emphasizes how people's emotions shape their motivations and these motivations in turn influence their processing of information (Simon, 1967). For instance, the approach–avoidance theory (Mehrabian, 1981) states that people move closer to objects they like and move away from objects they do not like. This concept was exemplified by Witt et al. (chap. 10, this volume). Moreover, Pintrich and Schunk (2002) identified several factors that may impact the motivation–emotion connection for students, such as expectations about failure, perceived value of a task, attributions of controllability, modeling of others' behavior, goal orientation, intrinsic motivation (i.e., self-efficacy), and emergent motivation (i.e., self-esteem). Each of these important issues is addressed in this book. Whether talking about the transference value of mediation (Burrell, Zirbel, & Allen, chap. 8, this volume) and debate (Berkowitz, chap. 4, this volume), exploring the adverse effects of text anxiety (Preiss et al., chap. 7, this volume) and communication apprehension (Bourhis, Allen, & Bauman, chap. 13, this volume), or identifying the benefits of entertaining (Martin, Preiss, Gayle, & Allen, chap. 18, this volume) and well-informed (Allen, chap. 21, this volume) teachers, it is clear that how students feel, how they think, and what they are motivated by have very real and serious ramifications for their educational success.

Future Research Directions

Although several chapters did not discuss their contribution to theoretical advancement, every chapter identified specific areas of future scholarship based on its particular topic. After reviewing their future research suggestions, a common pattern seems to emerge. Throughout the volume, the authors call for more scholarship on the conceptualization of learning and on the role of interaction in shaping it.

Learning. Bloom (1956) identified three types of learning: psychomotor, affective, and cognitive. Psychomotor learning refers to skills that involve physical movement and mental activity. Affective learning deals with students' feelings about the educational experience. Cognitive learning pertains to the actual information gained. Cognitive learning is the most frequently assessed type of learning and can be measured by looking at performance outcomes or by students' perceptions about how much they think they have learned; this second type of cognitive learning measurement is referred to as perceived learning. Two chapters in particular (e.g., Martin et al., chap. 18, this volume; Witt et al., chap. 10, this volume) dealt with these different types of learning, and they discovered that teacher behaviors, such as humor and immediacy, can improve perceived and affective learning but they can, at times, detract from cognitive learning. In other words, humor and immediacy create an enjoyable learning environment but they may distract from students' ability to retain information. Humorous class discussions, then, may be a pleasure to hear, but may leave students confused about what information is serious or important. Likewise, teachers who are highly immediate may cause students to forget the purpose of the classroom experience—they may view the class period as quality bonding time and not necessarily information-gathering time. It should be noted that these findings are counter to the motivational theory advanced by Christophel (1990) and Frymier (1994), which contends that immediacy behaviors increase student motivation, which in turn increases student learning. Rodriguez, Plax, and Kearney's (1996) study also suggests a similar relationship; however, they argued that affective learning (which theoretically subsumes the motivation construct) is a central causal mediator for cognitive learning. Yet, the chapters in this volume suggest that having too much fun in the classroom can actually thwart the learning process.

These findings raise several meaningful questions for future scholars. First, researchers in general need to specifically delineate how learning is being measured and why this decision was made. Is the learning measurement instrument self-report, exam grades, assignment grades, or performance on a research-related task? Each of these measurements of learning may in fact be tapping different aspects of the learning construct. Likewise, although presumably exam and assignment grades should be measuring cognitive learning, they may be confounded by a variety of issues, including text anxiety of students, the preexisting knowledge base from which students are working, the typically restricted range of scores on these assessments, and the varying levels of learning that can occur (e.g., high level or low level).

Another factor to consider based on these findings is how teachers can create an effective balance between the various types of learning. In an ideal world, students would enjoy their cognitive development; in other words, they would both have fun and get smart (i.e., the "edutainment" model of education). In reality and as the findings herein suggest, sometimes one aspect gets sacrificed for the other. Yet, it seems clear that both teachers and students would benefit if scholars explored the many forms of learning and the various ways in which each type can be cultivated without detracting from the others. Obviously, it is important for students to gain information from their studies (i.e., cognitive learning), but it should also be meaningful for teachers to help instill a love of learning (i.e., affective learning) so that students want to continue to improve their knowledge base even after they have their diploma in hand. Future scholarship needs to explore all types of learning, because even though the findings herein do not support this, we maintain that motivated, affectively based learners will be better life long learners.

Interaction.   One way students can become motivated is through their interactions. Whether interacting with the material (Gayle, Preiss, & Allen, chap. 17, this volume; Preiss & Gayle, chap. 19, this volume), various media channels (Allen et al., chap. 14, this volume; Shapiro, Kerssen-Griep, Gayle, & Allen, chap. 5, this volume; Timmerman & Kruepke, chap. 6, this volume), their peers (Berkowitz, chap. 4, this volume; Burrell et al., chap. 8, this volume), or their instructors (Jones et al., chap. 12, this volume; Witt et al., chap. 10, this volume), the value of interaction in and out of the classroom remains pivotal to the learning process. It is not the instructor or the student who independently makes or breaks the educational experience; rather it is their interaction together that matters. As Staton (1992) explained, the learning environment is continuously interactive, whether through the negotiation of roles and rules for teachers and students, through the management of classroom discussions, or through the socialization into the discipline, school, or department. Yet, as Waldeck, Kearney, and Plax (2001) noted, this aspect is often neglected and its influence warrants further investigation. An in-depth understanding of instructional communication will remain elusive until the important role of interaction is fully explored and its practical ramifications are discussed.

Practical Applications

Indeed, scholars of instructional communication pursue this line of inquiry not only to contribute to theory and to advance scholarship, but also to enhance their own instructional practices. The meta-analyses in this book provide teachers with guidance on how they can improve their communication in and out of the classroom. Based on the empirical evidence discussed in this book, the three ingredients to success seem to be preparation, presentation, and practice.

Preparation.   Planning ahead is vital to promoting student achievement. For instance, Preiss et al. (chap. 7, this volume) advised instructors to schedule assignments with minimal opportunity to procrastinate and sequence them in order of difficulty so that students can gain a sense of accomplishment. In the chapter on advanced organizers, Preiss and Gayle (chap. 20, this volume) suggested that not only using previews during lecture but also setting up material to build off of previously covered information can assist students with retention and recall of information. Additionally, Berkowitz (chap. 4, this volume) argued that more critical thinking assignments should be integrated into communication courses, because they are both empowering for students and create a connection or common thread across the curriculum. Allen et al. (chap. 14, this volume) also noted that designing courses that match students' learning preferences can maximize their performance and satisfaction with the course. These ideas provide some insight on what teachers can do to enhance learning before they enter the classroom.

Presentation.   Communication in the classroom is of paramount importance, because it not only revolves around the discussion of material, but also works to create the climate for which learning takes place. When discussing course concepts, the authors suggest that teachers use a normal rate of speech (Preiss & Gayle, chap. 19, this volume), incorporate desktop presentational programs in conjunction with active learning strategies (Shapiro et al., chap. 5, this volume), provide hard copies of information and use video presentations sparingly as they can be distracting (Timmerman & Kruepke, chap. 6, this volume), and ask higher order questions of students (Gayle, Preiss, & Allen, chap. 17, this volume). To develop a positive classroom climate, teachers should be attentive to how their prior expectations or preconceived notions may influence student–teacher interactions (Jones et al., chap. 12, this volume); they should work ardently to reduce students'

communication apprehension through skills training, systematic desensitization, cognitive modification, or some combination thereof (Bourhis et al.,
chap. 13, this volume); and they should consider incorporating humor
(Martin et al., chap. 18, this volume) and being immediate (Witt et al., chap.
10, this volume) to make the learning experience more enjoyable—although not necessarily more fruitful, as both studies purported.

   Practice.   Enabling students to carry what they have learned in the classroom and apply it in their everyday lives is arguably the most important mark
of educational success. Three chapters in particular state in no uncertain
terms the value of transference—meaning taking concepts covered in the
classroom and integrating them into real-life experiences (or vice versa). If a
school does not have service learning programs (e.g., peer mediation or debate), efforts should be undertaken to establish these. The meta-analyses
conducted by Burrell et al. (chap. 8, this volume) as well as Berkowitz (chap.
4, this volume) provide noteworthy support for the effectiveness of various
co-curricular and extracurricular activities; they have the potential to benefit the participants, the school, and the community at large. These opportunities for involvement enable students to hone their communication skills
and connect classroom content to the world outside of it. Likewise, Allen
(chap. 21, this volume) argued that activities outside of the classroom can
enhance instructional effectiveness. Specifically, he stated that there should
be a marriage between scholarship and teaching; although the two activities
are often placed in competition with each other, they are in fact mutually reinforcing. Just as students should be encouraged to engage in communica-
tion-relevant extracurricular activities, teachers also should use their
extracurricular activities (i.e., research) to inform their teaching. Research
and instruction go hand in hand.

WHAT REMAINS TO BE SEEN

The preceding discussion highlights the important work that can be done
with meta-analysis. We view it as an important tool that can help advance
our understanding of instructional communication. Like any tool, however,
it must be handled properly and it is not suited for all tasks. The next section
addresses what is missing from the meta-analyses covered in this book.
   Many of the authors in this book took painstaking efforts to grapple with
the limitations or criticisms put forward about this methodological approach. For instance, some authors identified results from published versus
nonpublished data sets and tested for differences between the two groups.
They also clearly explicated their inclusion and exclusion criteria for studies
and chose not to utilize studies that were poorly designed or did not provide
sufficient statistical information to be included in the analysis. The clarity of

explanation for these choices can provide other scholars with a model to follow in conducting their own meta-analyses.

However, one of the shortcomings that emerged in evaluating the chapters was that several of them were atheoretical. We view this omission as a significant oversight. The goals of empirical scholarship in general are to predict and explain—not merely to describe. One of the primary functions of meta-analyses is theory development. Indeed, Hunter and Schmidt (1990) argued that meta-analyses provide "the empirical building blocks for theory" (p. 40). Meta-analyses that do not discuss how they extend, develop, or even contradict certain theoretical premises have missed an important opportunity to truly advance knowledge. We believe they have fallen into the realm of being variable-analytic. The resulting outcome is an interesting portrayal of how a variable relates to other variables, and although intriguing, meta-analyses that neglect a discussion of theory are simply providing a description of a puzzle piece without illustrating how that piece fits into the puzzle as a whole.

Likewise, we believe it is meaningful to acknowledge what was not covered in this book. Although no one document can cover it all, there are various prominent areas of instructional scholarship that did not receive attention in this book. For instance, the role of power dynamics in the classroom was not addressed. French and Raven (1959) considered power to be the ability to influence people to do something they would not have done had they not been influenced. Power arguably impacts all aspects of the learning environment (Richmond & McCroskey, 1992). It shapes how teachers manage the classroom environment (Kearney, Plax, Richmond, & McCroskey, 1984, 1985). It affects in-class communication (Richmond, 1990). It is particularly meaningful in student–teacher interactions (Staton, 1992; Winograd, 2002). Therefore, investigating the influence of power on the learning process is an important area worthy of consideration.

The dark side of instructional communication also was not explored. This broad area of research includes a variety of topics emphasizing the negative aspects or the unpleasant side of the instructional context. For instance, this body of work has explored the stress associated with classroom discipline for teachers (Lewis, 1999), the misbehaviors in which they engage (Boice, 1996; Kearney, Plax, Hays, & Ivey, 1991), students' reactions to those misbehaviors (Berkos, Allen, Kearney, & Plax, 2001), and teachers' negative emotional expressions (McPherson, Kearney, & Plax, 2003). Additionally, students' aggressive emotional displays (Lesebo & Marshall, 1999; O'Donnell & White, 2001), as well as how teachers respond to students' misbehaviors, has been studied (Kearney, Plax, & Sorensen, 1988; Plax, Kearney, & Tucker, 1986), along with students' resistance to these control and compliance-gaining attempts (Kearney & Plax, 1992; Kearney, Plax, & Burroughs, 1991). If, as Spitzberg and Cupach (1994) suggested "the dark, difficult, disruptive, and distressing elements of social interaction deserve close empirical scrutiny" (p. 316), these aforementioned examples provide a brief glimpse of the vast array of studies on the dark side of instructional communication that warrant further investigation.

Of course, there are other areas of inquiry that remain to be explored via meta-analysis. The point is that this volume provides a snapshot of the instructional communication field—by including some parts, others are cut out of the picture but are still worthy of exploration.

Meta-analysis, in fact, may not be the right tool for all occasions. There are certain areas of instructional scholarship that may not lend themselves well to being examined with this methodological approach. Naturally, the large and informative body of qualitative research on instructional communication, for instance, cannot be synthesized with meta-analytic procedures. Additionally, areas of inquiry that have not yet amassed a significant set of data, such as extra class communication, are ill-prepared for meta-analysis at this time. Conducting a meta-analysis, like any other methodological choice a researcher makes, should be guided by how the question to be studied can best be answered.

The most important question we face as scholars and practitioners of instructional communication is this: How can we best serve our students? These are challenging times—many of us are teaching an array of classes with more students and fewer resources. As a result, we must spend our time and energy wisely both in the classroom and outside of it. Despite the constraints under which we are working, we still want to create student-centered, learning-enhanced educational opportunities for our students. The meta-analyses presented in this book provide some guidance in answering these questions. Overall, they make important strides in addressing the theoretical advancements, the future research directions, and the practical implications of current scholarship on instructional communication.

As Hale and Dillard (1991) and Hunt (1999) argued, meta-analyses should not be viewed as the definitive word on a particular body of scholarship; rather they should be viewed as a means of taking stock and of identifying future research directions. What the meta-analyses in this volume do particularly well is to uncover what remains to be investigated. In the methodological toolbox, meta-analysis is like a tape measure—it allows us to see the distance we have come and where we need to go. This volume, in short, serves as a call to action for scholars, because without primary studies, meta-analyses will have no data. There continues to be a need for theoretically driven, methodologically sophisticated, and substantively significant scholarship on instructional communication. Just like communication, learning is a dynamic and ongoing process—and what we know about this line of research, as measured by these meta-analyses, is that we have come a long way, but there is still more to be learned.

REFERENCES

Ausubel, D. P. (1960). The use of advanced organizers in the learning and retention of meaningful verbal material. *Journal of Educational Psychology, 51,* 267–272.

Berkos, K. M., Allen, T. H., Kearney, P., & Plax, T. G. (2001). When norms are violated: Imagined interactions as processing and coping mechanisms. *Communication Monographs, 68,* 289–300.

Bloom, B. S. (1956). *A taxonomy of educational objectives.* New York: Longman.

Boice, R. (1996). Classroom incivilities. *Research in Higher Education, 37,* 453–486.

Brophy, J. (1999). Toward a model of the value aspects of motivation in education: Developing appreciation for particular learning domains and activities. *Educational Psychologist, 34,* 75–85.

Byrne, D. (1971). *The attraction paradigm.* New York: Academic.

Christophel, D. (1990). The relationships among teacher immediacy behaviors, student motivation, and learning. *Communication Education, 39,* 323–340.

Daft, R. L., & Lengel, R. H. (1986). Organizational information requirements: Media richness and structural design. *Management Science, 32,* 554–571.

Deaux, K., & Major, B. (1987). Putting gender into context: An interactive model of gender-related behavior. *Psychological Review, 94,* 369–389.

Emmer, E. (1988). Praise and the instructional process. *Journal of Classroom Interaction, 23,* 32–39.

Eysenck, H. J. (1978). An exercise in mega-silliness. *American Psychologist, 33,* 517.

Eysenck, H. J. (1984). Meta-analysis: An abuse of research integration. *Journal of Special Education, 18,* 41–59.

French, J. R. P., Jr., & Raven, B. H. (1959). The bases of social power. In D. Cartwright (Ed.), *Studies in social power* (pp. 150–167). Ann Arbor: University of Michigan.

Frymier, A. B. (1994). A model of immediacy in the classroom. *Communication Quarterly, 42,* 133–144.

Fulk, J., Schmitz, J. A., & Steinfield, C. (1990). A social information model of technology use. In J. Fulk & C. Steinfield (Eds.), *Organizations and communication technology* (pp. 117–140). Newbury Park, CA: Sage.

Gallo, P. S. (1978). Meta-analysis: A mixed metaphor. *American Psychologist, 33,* 515–517.

Giles, H., Mulac, A., Bradac, J. J., & Johnson, P. (1987). Speech accommodation theory: The first decade and beyond. In M. L. McLaughlin (Ed.), *Communication yearbook 10* (pp. 13–48). Newbury Park, CA: Sage.

Hale, J. L., & Dillard, J. P. (1991). The uses of meta-analysis: Making knowledge claims and setting research agendas. *Communication Monographs, 58,* 463–471.

Hall, J. A., & Rosenthal, R. (1991). Testing for moderator variables in meta-analysis: Issues and methods. *Communication Monographs, 58,* 437–448.

Hall, J. A., & Rosenthal, R. (1995). Interpreting and evaluating meta-analysis. *Evaluation & The Health Profession, 18,* 393–407.

Hunt, M. (1999). *How science takes stock: The story of meta-analysis.* New York: Russell Sage.

Hunter, J. E., & Schmidt, F. L. (1990). *Methods of meta-analysis: Correcting error and bias in research findings.* Newbury Park, CA: Sage.

Kearney, P., & Plax, T. G. (1992). Student resistance to teacher control. In V. P. Richmond & J. C. McCroskey (Eds.), *Power in the classroom: Communication, control, and concern* (pp. 85–100). Hillsdale, NJ: Lawrence Erlbaum Associates.

Kearney, P., Plax, T. G., & Burroughs, N. F. (1991). An attributional analysis of college students' resistance decisions. *Communication Education, 40,* 325–342.

Kearney, P., Plax, T. G., Hays, E. R., & Ivey, M. J. (1991). College teacher misbehaviors: What students don't like about what their teachers say and do. *Communication Quarterly, 39,* 309–324.

Kearney, P., Plax, T. G., Richmond, V. P., & McCroskey, J. C. (1984). Power in the classroom IV: Teacher communication techniques as alternatives to discipline. In R. Bostrom (Ed.), *Communication yearbook 8* (pp. 724–746). Newbury Park, CA: Sage.

Kearney, P., Plax, T. G., Richmond, V. P., & McCroskey, J. C. (1985). Power in the classroom III: Teacher communication techniques and messages. *Communication Education, 37,* 54–67.

Kearney, P., Plax, T. G., & Sorensen, G. (1988). Experienced and prospective teachers' selection of compliance-gaining messages for "common" student misbehaviors. *Communication Education, 37,* 150–164.

Lengel, R. H., & Daft, R. L. (1988). The selection of communication media as an executive skill. *The Academy of Management Executive, 2,* 225–232.

Lesebo, J., & Marshall, A. (1999). Dealing with angry students: A qualitative study with implications for school counselors. *Professional School Counseling, 3,* 91–100.

Lewis, R. (1999). Teachers coping with the stress of classroom discipline. *Social Psychology Education, 3,* 155–171.

McPherson, M., Kearney, P., & Plax, T. G. (2003). The dark side of instruction: Teacher anger as classroom norm violations. *Journal of Applied Communication, 31,* 76–90.

Mehrabian, A. (1981). *Silent messages* (2nd ed.). Belmont, CA: Wadsworth.

Neisser, U. (1967). *Cognitive psychology.* Englewood Cliffs, NJ: Prentice-Hall.

O'Donnell, R., & White, G. P. (2001). Teaching realistic consequences to the most angry and aggressive students. *Middle School Journal, 32,* 40–45.

Paivio, A. (1991). Dual coding theory and education. *Educational Psychology Review, 3,* 149–210.

Pintrich, P., & Schunk, D. (2002). *Motivation in education: Theory, research, applications.* Englewood Cliffs, NJ: Prentice-Hall.

Plax, T. G., Kearney, P., & Tucker, L. (1986). Prospective teachers' use of behavior alteration techniques: Reactions to common student misbehaviors. *Communication Education, 35,* 32–42.

Richmond, V. P. (1990). Communication in the classroom: Power and motivation. *Communication Education, 39,* 181–195.

Richmond, V. P., & McCroskey, J. C. (Eds.). (1992). *Power in the classroom: Communication, control, and concern.* Hillsdale, NJ: Lawrence Erlbaum Associates.

Rodriguez, J. I., Plax, T. G., & Kearney, P. (1996). Clarifying the relationship between teacher nonverbal immediacy and student cognitive learning: Affective learning as the central causal mediator. *Communication Education, 45,* 293–305.

Simon, H. A. (1967). Motivational and emotional controls of cognition. *Psychological Review, 74,* 29–39.

Sohn, D. (1995). Meta-analysis as a means of discovery. *American Psychologist, 50,* 108–110.

Spielberger, C. D., & Vagg, P. R. (Eds.). (1995). *Test anxiety: Theory, assessment, and treatment.* Washington, DC: Taylor & Francis.

Spitzberg, B. H., & Cupach, W. R. (1994). Dark side denouement. In W. R. Cupach & B. H. Spitzberg (Eds.), *The dark side of interpersonal communication* (pp. 315–320). Hillsdale, NJ: Lawrence Erlbaum Associates.

Staton, A. Q. (1992). Teacher and student concern and classroom power and control. In V. P. Richmond & J. C. McCroskey (Eds.), *Power in the classroom: Communication, control, and concern* (pp. 159–176). Hillsdale, NJ: Lawrence Erlbaum Associates.

Trevino, L. K., Daft, R. L., & Lengel, R. H. (1990). Understanding manager's media choices: A symbolic interactionist perspective. In J. C. Fulk & C. Steinfield (Eds.), *Organizations and communication technology* (pp. 71–94). Newbury Park, CA: Sage.

Waldeck, J. H., Kearney, P., & Plax, T. G. (2001). Instructional and developmental communication theory and research in the 90s: Extending the agenda for the 21st century. In W. Gudykunst (Ed.), *Communication yearbook 24* (pp. 207–230). Newbury Park, CA: Sage.

Watson, J. (1930). *Behaviorism.* Chicago: University of Chicago.

Wellman, B. (1988). Structural analysis: From method and metaphor to theory and substance. In B. Wellman & S. D. Berkowitz (Eds.), *Social structures: A network approach* (pp. 19–61). New York: Cambridge University.

Winograd, K. (2002). The negotiative dimension of teaching: Teachers sharing power with the less powerful. *Teaching & Teacher Education, 18,* 343–362.

24

Why SoTL Matters: Knowing What We Need to Know to Make Sure Our Students Learn What They Need to Know to Succeed as Citizens

James L. Applegate
Kentucky Council on Postsecondary Education

Teaching and learning: two words that sound like they go together but, in the history of higher education, efforts to document the link between the two have been embarrassingly anemic and typically relegated to second-class status in the academy's research community. Our focus has been on teaching, the "sage on the stage," and our understanding of the relationship of teaching and learning largely grounded in anecdotal evidence and academic folklore. Even in psychology, where learning generally has been a core theoretical concept, applications to the work we do in the classroom have been limited.

Now, the question of what kind of teaching strategies in what disciplines most effectively produce learning in what kind of students has taken on new significance. Our students are more diverse than ever before. Over two thirds are classified as non-traditional, making the teaching–learning connection more obviously problematic. In addition, parents, students, political leaders, and business leaders have accepted higher education's argument that what we teach—critical thinking, communication, mathematics—is essential to a successful 21st century economy and society and to better lives for people. So they are demanding students learn these things and we be able to document that the students are learning. The need for higher education and the demand for accountability are especially strong for traditionally underrepresented groups of students: students of color, economically disadvantaged and underprepared students, first-time college goers, and adult learners who all desperately need these skills to overcome the barriers to success society places before them.

So we have won the argument that what we do matters and now we are being held accountable to do it well: Enter the scholarship of teaching and learning. We have traditionally spoken of scholarship and teaching: two separate and never equal parts of our mission. However, the scholarship of teaching and learning (SoTL) demands that we employ the full resources of our research expertise to examine the teaching–learning relationship. It also requires that we value that work, treating it as equally important as other forms of scholarship (Boyer, 1990; Glassick, Huber, & Maeroff, 1997).

To take SoTL seriously is to understand that teaching is a means to an end, and that end is to engage students, graduate and undergraduate, traditional and nontraditional, on-campus and off-campus, in active learning. To be a scholar of teaching and learning means more than being a good teacher. Teaching scholars are committed to experimenting with new practices, assessing those practices, engaging in peer review of their scholarship, and sharing successful practices with the teaching community so that they improve not only their own teaching but the practice of teaching generally.

As this volume indicates, communication is uniquely positioned to help higher education find its way to fully engaging SoTL. Unlike many disciplines, we have a long tradition of scholarly work in instructional communication and communication education that lays the framework for continuing this work under the rubric of SoTL. Communication is, after all, the process through which teaching and learning are linked across every discipline. So communication scholars are in a position not only to advance SoTL through instructional and communication education research directly focused on the classroom but, in addition, to connect SoTL questions to the best of general communication theory. Communication research on communication anxiety, gender and race, attention processes, listening, message behavior, and a host of other source, receiver, and interaction variables all are relevant to our understanding of learning. Some of the best chapters in this volume do exactly that. Jones, Dindia, and Tye (chap. 12, this volume), for example, link the best of current gender research to learning, treating gender as an interactive variable. Their results help us go beyond traditional coding of teacher and student behavior and popular stereotypes about gender differences and better understand the relationship between gender and learning. Burrell, Zirbel, and Allen (chap. 8, this volume) similarly apply communication scholarship on conflict mediation to management of the classroom environment.

A recently published volume by Carnegie provides examples of how the scholarship of teaching and learning is being integrated across many disciplines (Huber & Morreale, 2003). A blueprint for the application of SoTL to the communication discipline is included in that volume. However, this volume shows how communication contributions to SoTL are clearly important to SoTL work across the disciplines. It builds on earlier volumes arguing for the relevance of SoTL to learning research by providing an on-the-ground research effort that brings to life the conceptual potential for SoTL only outlined in most previous volumes.

The conversation about teaching today is rich with discussions of new strategies to enhance learning. The creation of learning communities, problem-based learning, interdisciplinary perspectives, and service learning are all at the center of a new scholarly agenda for graduate and undergraduate teaching. These new practices add to the demands on the SoTL to document if and how these different approaches to pedagogy actually enhance learning. If we are to meet this challenge, we must redefine our role as teachers and include ongoing, peer-reviewed research assessing the predictors of student learning as part of that role. We must be lifelong learners as well as teachers in this endeavor.

This volume is another indication that SoTL work is maturing in communication and in the academy. Using meta-analytic techniques it brings together large bodies of research literature to answer questions and identify issues for future research that will help us better teach students. Its meta-analytic strategy is timely because we need to pull together what has been done under various research rubrics to understand what now needs to be done to advance SoTL. These essays identify what we know and what we need to know to best use technology in teaching, design teacher preparation and professional development programs, and create assessments that accommodate the learning styles of increasingly diverse populations of students. Their focus on quantitative research provides a needed expansion of SoTL work beyond narrative, descriptive, and critical research, allowing for the triangulation of research results that characterize established research domains. Finally, it puts another chink in the wall that has divided teaching and research in higher education and prevented us from applying our best work to one of our most important outcomes: student learning.

In fact, Allen's (chap. 21) analysis suggests that good teaching and research productivity reinforce each other. His analysis not only debunks the dichotomization of these activities but also raises important policy issues for university reward systems that want to walk the walk of promoting both good teaching and research productivity.

TECHNOLOGY AND LEARNING

Campuses are making enormous investments in technology to support teaching and faculty development efforts to ensure its effective use. Good scholarship in this area will have an enormous impact on student learning and build support from campus leadership as it provides administrators guidance in how to manage this investment wisely in difficult budgetary times.

As is so often the case when we actually do the research to answer the question of what types of technology for what types of material with what types of students enhance learning and justify the investment, the answers are complicated. Timmerman and Kruepke's (chap. 6, this volume) review suggests differential results for computer-assisted, asynchronous, and traditional methods of instruction. Significant investment in more sophisticated technologies may not increase learning in many cases. Effects may vary across subject matter. Allen, Bourhis, Mabry, Burrell, and Timmerman's (chap. 14, this volume) analysis reviews work comparing distance learning and face-to-face learning contexts, suggesting among other things that important student learning style variables (internal vs. external local of control) may moderate learning outcomes as well as faculty attitudes. Their suggestion that we need to move to multiple pedagogical strategies adapting to multiple student learning styles makes sense but further complicates our research task.

The technology-related meta-analyses here take, as they should, student learning as their primary outcome variable. This work can and should be integrated with initiatives like the PEW funded work on Course Redesign that integrates learning and cost variables in an effort to address the "value-added" question so important to policy decisions about technology and teaching (see review in Twigg, 2003, and project description at www.center.rpi.edu/PewGrant).

TEACHER QUALITY

In survey after survey legislators and governors, when asked to define the most important work done by postsecondary education, put K–12 teacher education and teacher quality at the top of the list. In addition, postsecondary education is devoting increasing resources to faculty development and doctoral education reform. These efforts seek to better equip college faculty to meet the demands placed on them by new communication technologies, students who are more ethnically and socioeconomically diverse, new forms of pedagogy, more sophisticated learning assessments, and teaching that better engages students with the needs of the 21st century economy and society.

So what is it that we are to give to K–12 and postsecondary faculty as a part of our teacher education and faculty development work to help them do their job? What we must tell them is what the SoTL tells us that they need to know based on solid research, not faddish suggestions based on the political ideology of the day. Little of what goes on in postsecondary classrooms and, I would argue, not much of what we teach K–12 faculty or future post-secondary colleagues in doctoral programs, is informed by that kind of systematic research effort.

The chapters in this volume addressing classroom interaction and teacher effectiveness provide a wealth of information that every aspiring K–12 teacher and college faculty member should know. These represent just a small sampling of what we as scholars of teaching and learning need to provide one another to improve our ability to ensure that every student knows what they need to know and is able to do all that will enable them to succeed.

WHY SoTL MATTERS

At the risk of sounding more polemic than academic, let me conclude by returning to the argument for why SoTL is so important, why we must never lose sight of its ultimate goal. SoTL is not primarily about making us better teachers. It is about making our students better citizens and improving the quality of their lives.

To say we live in difficult times may be the understatement of all time. Today the United States is on high alert for terrorist attacks. Thousands of innocent Iraqis, Americans, and citizens in countries around the world have died in recent years, victims of terrorism and war: the ultimate evidence of the inability of people to think and communicate well informed by a sense of history and a global consciousness. This provides evidence that somewhere our link to an ethical and humane means of working together as humans has been broken.

Hate and fear of human difference is rampant, fueled by nationalism, religious fanaticism, homophobia, xenophobia, and a terribly large array of other phobias based on who people are. Environmental degradation threatens the planet and is a symptom of the cancer of unbridled consumption by those whose focus on private gain has blinded them to what is in the public good and the good of future generations. Large parts of the human family have lost hope and are dying by the thousands as the economic gulf between the haves and have nots widens at a frightening pace and anything resembling a middle class slips into the abyss.

The loss of our social capital and the atrophy of the skill world citizens need to build communities are depriving us of the ability to overcome our differences and solve mutual problems. Robert Putnam's (2001) *Bowling Alone* and an array of other studies clearly document that we are losing sight of the concept of a democratic public as John Dewey eloquently articulated that concept. We have far less motivation to express our differences civilly around recognition that our fates are inextricably intertwined. And we increasingly lack the skills and knowledge to engage in that kind of dialogue: critical thinking skills, communication skills, and the ability to bring a sense of history and a global consciousness to the conversation. These are the very things that we as faculty are charged to bring to the table as public intellectuals and what we must provide in the education of our students.

Although this last threat posed by lost social capital may sound less dire than the other threats I mentioned, it is the one that, if not met, will keep us from successfully addressing the others. We cannot engage in meaningful dialogue about environmental degradation if we do not have the motivation and skills to create and maintain the social capital necessary to conduct such difficult discussions. We cannot find common ground in the midst of our cultural differences if we cannot dig below the surface to find what links us as humans.

So much depends on marshaling the resources of postsecondary education (more than $50 billion a year in the United States alone) to engage these threats that no effort to ensure our success is too great, no sacrifice too much. Sometimes what we do on a daily basis with our students may seem small in the face of threats of the scale we face. However, our work can help society meet these threats. Imagine hundreds of thousands of faculty doing their job well with millions of students around the globe and those same faculty generating libraries full of useful knowledge. We can produce the knowledge we need to address the threats that confront society and a world citizenry that is capable and motivated to put that knowledge to work for the common good. By acting together locally we can, together, contribute globally.

We must turn from the vision that has led us to see ourselves, and sell our students, on education as an engine for private gain. We must rediscover our role and help our students to see their role in serving the public good. We also must climb down from our role as a sage on the stage and embrace the responsibilities of a scholar of teaching and learning using the knowledge we gain to be a guide on the side helping our students take charge of their own learning.

We must help our students see that although there is no shame in wanting an education to live the good life, that it is also the case that the privilege of an education obligates one to a life of doing good.

Our undergraduate programs must assess the effectiveness of practices like service learning and implement those that contribute to the goals of fostering civic engagement, and the preparation of students to become successful workers and citizens. In short, our programs must motivate students to create social capital and find the best ways to provide the skills to do so.

We must develop teaching practices that reach out to a broader, more diverse base of students of all ages, including adults, many of whom already have been driven from our system once. We must do this because we recognize that every person we leave behind in postsecondary education is a life likely lost to economic degradation and social isolation, and certainly more vulnerable to the hateful and narrow appeals of bigots, terrorists, and imperialists.

We must refocus and all understand that our role is no longer to "weed out" those who are not "college material," but to "grow up" all of our students so they can live decent lives and, as citizens, sustain a decent and humane society. To succeed in the latter role we must generate and implement SoTL.

Our graduate programs must outgrow the privileged MBA and the ivory tower PhD. I invite you to visit the University of Texas Web site. Look at what is being done in their "intellectual entrepreneurship" program that helps graduate students understand how they can and should invest the intellectual capital they acquire in every graduate discipline from microbiology to sociology in problems that matter where that investment pays the kind of dividends that matter (www.utexas.edu/ogs/public/what.html). Or visit the Re-Envisioning the Ph.D. site at the University of Washington site (www.grad.washington.edu/envision) or the Responsive Ph.D. program on the Woodrow Wilson Foundation Web site (www.woodrow.org/responsivephd) and discover models for graduate education that will truly prepare the next generation of faculty who will populate all of our institutions to be scholars of teaching and learning.

Jurgen Habermas, the German philosopher, said that we should strive for a world in which "the gentle force of the better idea will prevail" because of its betterness and because people have the critical thinking skills, the communication skills, the sense of history, the global perspective, and the civic commitment that allows them to discover and honor its betterness (Habermas, 1970; also see McCarthy, 1982). That is what our educational resources must produce to ensure the survival of human society.

From biology and chemistry, to psychology and communication, to English and the arts, we must reject the vision of "the well frog." The well frog lives its life at the bottom of a well (for us it is a disciplinary or institutional well). It believes that all there is to the sky is what it can see from the bottom of its well. We must break out of that well and discover the connection of our work to the creation of a society that is healthier physically, economically, and socially.

It is sometimes said that society has problems whereas universities have departments and disciplines. We must overcome both institutional and disciplinary divisions to address the problems that society faces.

The motivation for the work of the scholar of teaching and learning should be fueled by the best of human imagination. Let us imagine communities free of hate where people have the cognitive and communicative capacity to embrace the rich opportunities of human diversity; where a child of color is spared the toxic effects of racist attacks; where young gay men are not beaten and left to die strapped to a fence post in Wyoming; where African Americans are not dragged to horrible deaths behind pick-up trucks in Texas; and where the horrific images of death and destruction so vividly burned in our consciousness from September 11, 2001, and more recently in Baghdad are replaced with a vision and a commitment to civility and community.

Let us imagine our generation and future generations of faculty and higher education leaders prepared by engaged doctoral programs, assuming the responsibilities of public intellectuals mobilizing their efforts in the interest of a civil, equitable, and humane society conscious of its responsibilities to its future.

Imagine the hundreds of thousands, even millions, of students and faculty across the world fully engaging their teaching and research work in efforts to improve public policy, elevate communities, and improve lives.

There has seldom been a time when society has cried out more for our knowledge and our commitment to solve its most pressing problems. We must join together to meet that challenge and fulfill the promise of education. We must not falter. We must not fail in ensuring that America does not destroy its democracy to save it and that the world community does not founder on selfish consumption, hate, and fear.

We all have a role to play in this. Students must commit to education for the public good as well as private gain. As faculty we must better engage our teaching and research with improving lives. At the ground level, that means building on work like that presented in this volume to understand how to best teach every student what he or she needs to know and be able to do to succeed individually and as world citizens. Our goal is not to indoctrinate but to equip our students to be critical consumers of all doctrines as they forge their own way in the world. Someone once wisely pointed out that no one ever washed a rented car. We care for and commit to what we own. Our research must tell us how to teach so what we teach is owned by our students, not expertise rented from us to acquire a credential. Then they become lifelong learners committed to using their knowledge for the common good.

Wayne Gretzky, a philosopher on the ice, once said that success depends not on skating to where the puck is but to where it will be. As educators and educational institutions we can affect where that puck will go in the 21st century. By embracing the work demonstrated in this volume and doing the difficult job that confronts us, we can make sure that our students, present and future, and we are there to catch it when it arrives, to catch it and guide it toward that place envisioned by Habermas where the gentle force of the better idea prevails.

REFERENCES

Boyer, E. (1990). *Scholarship reconsidered: Priorities of the professoriate.* Princeton, NJ: Carnegie Foundation for the Advancement of Teaching.

Glassick, C. E., Huber, M. T., & Maeroff, G. I. (1997). *Scholarship assessed: Evaluation of the professoriate.* San Francisco: Jossey-Bass.

Habermas, J. (1970). Toward a theory of communicative competence. In H. P. Dreitzel (Ed.), *Recent sociology No. 2: Patterns of communicative behavior.* New York: Macmillan.

Huber, M. T., & Morreale, S. (Eds.). (2003). *Disciplinary styles in the scholarship of teaching and learning.* Menlo Park, CA: The Carnegie Foundation.

McCarthy, T. (1982). *The critical theory of Jurgen Habermas.* Cambridge, MA: MIT Press.

Putnam, R., (2001). *Bowling alone: The collapse and revival of American community.* New York: Simon & Schuster.

Twigg, C. A. (2003, July–August). Improving quality and reducing cost. *Change, 35*(4), 22–23.

25

What to Do in the Classroom? Evaluating the Advice

Mike Allen
University of Wisconsin–Milwaukee

Raymond W. Preiss
University of Puget Sound

Nancy A. Burrell
University of Wisconsin–Milwaukee

The issues involved in decisions that any instructor makes in any class-room can impact the effectiveness of that instruction. For example, the decision to videotape the speeches in a public speaking classroom involves a set of choices or requirements. The decision to videotape requires material resources (cameras), human resources (instructors trained in the use of the cameras), and a commitment on the part of the instructor (to incorporate student viewing of the material). The critical question is whether or not this expenditure of resources improves student learning or not (in this case a meta-analysis demonstrates that videotaping speeches improves student learning; Bourhis & Allen, 1998). The meta-analysis provides an answer to the question about whether or not to expect an improvement by changing educational practice. In theory, the purpose of departments and colleges of education should be the preparation and inspiration of persons for effective instruction. Documenting that such improvement takes place and continues to take place remains an important but unanswered question.

The entire movement of the scholarship of teaching and learning (SoTL) is the assumption that studying the connection between teaching (a process) and learning (the desired outcome) should provide the potential for improvement. The term *best practices* often describes the use or providing examples of experienced and successful applications that instructors can incorporate in their respective fields. The problem with such approaches is that often the representations are simply anecdotal evidence provided by an instructor regarding the beliefs about a technique. Usually the hard evidence of student learning related to the effectiveness of the particular practice is lacking.

Each possible strategy or technique (use of Microsoft PowerPoint, computers, advanced organizers, etc.) provides one possible tool that an instructor can use to improve learning. Each method requires varying amounts of effort on the part of the instructor to prepare and incorporate the potential approach. The problem is that often it is difficult to know in advance which, if any, of the methods can expect improvement. As important, the instructor has little information on the relative size to which the various methods can expect to improve the learning in the classroom. Meta-analyses generate solid evidence about whether or not some procedure or teaching aid improves an outcome as well as the relative size of the impact of the various approach. The information provides a basis for educators to decide how to best improve the efforts of instruction. Time spent preparing for lectures with little improvement in instruction means that the time could be better spent on a different set of preparations. Meta-analysis should empower teachers to make informed decisions about the potential choices available for instruction.

Arguments exist over the appropriateness and effectiveness of virtually any potential classroom procedure or instructional aid. The choice of the tactic needs to be driven by a combination of principles about how the classroom should be conducted, the ability of the instructor to undertake the strategy, and the evidence of the believed effectiveness of the effort. To devote time to some instructional exercise (both in preparation and in execution) requires a belief that some desired outcome emerges from this effort. The justification for the particular choice needs to come from a reasoned position of the instructor. Meta-analyses aid that process of choice by providing useful information on the instructional effectiveness of that strategy.

The problem for most instructors is the sense of the overwhelming number of choices available and the uncertainty of the outcomes associated with each strategy. We are faculty and the barrage of constant messages and promises of more effective instruction serve sometimes to overwhelm the ability to begin to incorporate or evaluate the choices. It seems that every year or perhaps on a 3-year cycle another set of recommendations comes from gurus brought in from the outside to provide some advice to various instructors. We have participated in literally dozens of workshops or sessions and very seldom does the presenter provide direct and measurable evidence for the effectiveness of the particular method. The result is an interesting set of potentially new approaches provided, advice about implementation, and the suggestion to innovate or experiment by incorporating these ideas. The problem is that ultimately the bottom line becomes the willingness of the individual instructor to use students as guinea pigs to experiment with some educational intervention. Although educational practices need to remain dynamic and fresh, the change in approach should be grounded in the belief and evidence that the change benefits the students.

The commentary and search for better teaching materials has involved the application meta-analysis (Allen & Preiss, 1990, 2002) and represents nothing radical. The assumption behind the application of meta-analysis to pedagogy simply reflects the need for any person to accurately reflect the state of the scientific knowledge. The assumption is that for any instructor to use a state-of-the-art teaching technique ultimately requires knowing the state of the art (particularly the implications of the practice in terms of outcome). It is impossible for anyone to know that state of the art without summarizing the available evidence. Evaluation of the existing evidence provides a basis for understanding the level of improvement (if any) that the choice an instructor makes results in for the student learning outcomes desired.

A number of workshops we have attended have pointed out that the educational outcomes sought or offered by the instructional methods are often not directly measurable. Although we appreciate that claim, by the same token, then no evidence can be found to support that any positive outcome ever occurs. This may cause a bit of an eventual re-evaluation of the aspect of education, whether having a student go through a process in the belief that a desirable outcome emerges, particularly when that outcome cannot be measured and the method cannot be evaluated. The search for demonstrable outcomes and the relationship between the method used in the classroom represents the increased need to exhibit accountability to those funding institutions as well as those attending (and graduating) the institution. We believe that the ability of teaching methods to be sustained as viable methods ultimately requires the ability to provide evidence of consistent success in learning. The goal is to provide a means to end the cycling and recycling of ideas under new labels and provide for a more consistent basis for teaching driven by the findings of the research on what constitutes effective methods. The eventual accumulation of data should provide the basis for the generation of more inclusive and powerful theories about learning that spur even better understanding of the process to generate improved methods. The process does not require that one size fits all. For example, if learning styles of individuals require different approaches to the material, then an instructor could assess the learning styles of the individual and tailor the educational material to maximize his or her potential.

The real benefit is that by establishing or identifying what methods work, the subsequent research can begin the process of improving that method and creating an understanding about why that particular method generates desirable outcomes. In addition, practices that are discriminatory or undesirable (like treating males and females differently or responding to different students on the basis of race) become identifiable and appropriate training or methods of change can be considered. The impact of the various differences in instructor classroom behavior can be considered and recommendations for more effective behavior become subject to evaluation. Consider that the next generation of research and subsequent meta-analyses receive guidance from the addition of these analyses. The key is that the process of accumulation of results (not the recycling of method and labels) provides an improved basis so the process of educational pedagogy actually can improve. A great deal of cynicism exists about the status of education departments in colleges and universities. The failure of this apparatus to provide a demonstration of beneficial impact on the quality of education may end. The key is that the process of scientific demonstration provides either support or refutation for the practices of some members of the institution. The process ultimately elevates the student outcome as the source of evaluation rather than some prior ideology or theory. The effect is a raising of standards for educational practice that would not consider it appropriate to simply tell instructors to "experiment" on students in the classroom as a possibility for improving learning outcomes.

Any writer may choose not to employ scientific methods in making a claim; many other methods of making claims exist that do reflect scientific method or make claims to generalizable knowledge. However, other types of claim making cannot benefit or claim support from scientific method or findings. The problem is that once a writer, scholar, or teacher decides to use a particular method, any conclusions produced by that method should bind the claims that the person makes. Scientific evidence presents a claim to both a kind of objectivity as well as universality. The person using the information therefore becomes ensnared by the assumptions and implications of the method, as well as the findings of the method. Scholars not wishing to accept these outcomes could quite legitimately reject these methods and find another means or method to support the conclusions offered.

Change simply reflects the ultimate acceptance that the net result of scientific investigations is, in fact, scientific knowledge. Arguments about the ethical implications and the need to continue the diligence of practicing the art of teaching still remain. However, in the same way that medicine is an art (that uses scientific understanding to improve outcomes), teaching should be increasingly viewed as an art that can and should incorporate scientific methods as a means for improving practice. That creates a tension between the practitioners of the art of teaching and the knowledge known about teaching. The question is whether educational practitioners can implement what is known about effective educational techniques.

UNDERSTANDING THE APPROACH TO KNOWLEDGE

We view the fundamental goal of scholarly inquiry as the production and public dissemination of knowledge. For us, to say a person claims real knowledge of a subject is to state that the sum total of information and position both permits action, understanding, description, and provides the basis for reflection. The depiction in Fig. 25.1 illustrates our view regarding the issues of knowledge (for previous discussions of this view see Allen & Preiss, 1998, 2002). Essentially, the argument forwards that a person to have knowledge must be able to describe, understand, acknowledge, and ultimately act. The problem is that knowing something is true does not necessarily involve that any particular action be implemented. For example, the justification for an

ELEMENTS OF KNOWLEDGE

Horizontal axis—Purpose/Type of Conclusion
Vertical axis—Level of Decision Making Methodology

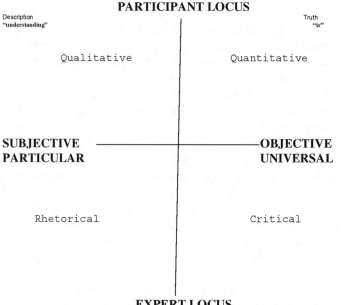

FIG. 25.1.   Elements of knowledge.

action requires an ethical component that goes beyond the simple knowing of something as true. A scientist may be able to demonstrate that successful cloning of a human is possible, but that does not entail that society should practice cloning. Einstein demonstrated that it was theoretically possible to build an atomic bomb, but his equations did not provide the necessary engineering to create the actual bomb.

Effective teaching not only requires knowing that advanced organizers are effective but the additional knowledge about how to make advanced organizers for the particular class. One cannot simply offer a "fill in the blanks" format to a teacher and expect to immediately produce positive outcomes. The combination of quantitative scientific information and qualitative descriptive understanding is necessary for effective implementation of any pedagogical strategy (Huxman & Allen, 2004). The investigations that evaluated the impact of advanced organizers contain knowledge that reflects an understanding of the community and material that permitted the development and use of the advanced organizer. The investigator involved in a study that examines a nonverbal communication course understood the elements of the content and the logic of the material and the lecture well enough to create a meaningful organizer. That knowledge about the course related to creating effective organizers requires particular understanding of the students and the material to be effective.

The issues of application require a combination of both ethnographic and quantitative knowledge to justify the time spent in development of materials and for the use of student time. However, when the instructor understands the process of creation as applied to the particular course as well as the belief that the development and introduction of advanced organizers will improve the educational outcomes, the process of education improves. Knowing that empirical research supports this endeavor also relieves the instructor from simply "experimenting" on the students in the hope that the process improves. The previous experience of other instructors in other courses provides the basis for a rational and reasoned choice to use these materials.

This process requires more than knowing that using advanced organizers increases learning. A total approach would view the knowledge that advanced organizers are effective as one element of knowledge. However, knowing that advanced organizers help students does not provide any information about how to create an advanced organizer. We have encountered instructors who recognize that some procedure improves learning but do not use it because of ethical or ideological objections to the procedure. So, knowing that advanced organizers improve learning might still not result in use if the instructor objects to the use of the tool. The problem is that relying on the "facts" to suppose that outcomes are obvious or inevitable ignores other real and legitimate concerns. Those concerns involve the ability to implement the particular solution in the context of the particular class. In addition, ethical objections may indicate that a procedure, no matter how demonstrably effective, may not result in the use of the method. For example, even if corporal punishment were demonstrated to be effective, many instructors and schools would refuse to use the method of discipline because of the objections to the ethics of using physical punishment in an educational setting. No research about the effectiveness or method of implementation can ever answer or provide evidence about the resolution to ethical issues raised about the appropriateness of particular procedures.

To work in an educational setting, in the classroom with students, requires knowledge about the effectiveness of practice, the ethics of practice, and the understanding of the particulars of the course and the students. An educator needs to identify those procedures and techniques that improve outcomes sought by the system. The implementation of that knowledge requires the ability to engineer a successful application to the task at hand. At the same time, knowing that some action will produce desirable consequences still requires that the means of generating those outcomes falls within the actions perceived as ethical by the actor. One might be able to obtain superior educational outcomes by offering physically painful punishments for failure, but most would reject the use of physical punishment or torture as an acceptable means to improve learning. Effectiveness is only one element of the evaluation, but assuming that the issues addressed in most of the reviews in this volume provide less immediate ethical dilemmas, the desire by instructors for improved educational outcomes should be enough of a motivation for implementation of the various procedures, assuming the instructor already possesses a level of knowledge to permit such application.

Scientific knowledge can provide simple but important evaluations. For example, finding out that advanced organizers assist and improve the learning in a course is not an unimportant conclusion to reach. The reason this conclusion is important is that advanced organizers require planning and some time to develop. Given the choices that exist for any instructor about how to effectively use preparation time and that time as a resource is limited, the decision to make and use advanced organizers can be evaluated as a potential option by an instructor. Knowing what outcomes are anticipated provides a baseline for the evaluation of the procedure. Knowing that distance education generates the same level of satisfaction and performance for students is important (Allen et al, 2002; Allen et al., 2004). However, that does not mean that one can take any course material, any instructor and assume that the material and instructor will immediately be as effective in the technological environment of distance learning. Much consideration, care, and planning of a different kind is required to succeed in the new environment with the challenges that the process brings.

Knowing that advanced organizers will improve learning does not mean that they will magically appear. The instructor still must generate the organizer and the particular organizer must reflect the outcomes and the structure of the course. Advanced organizers require a process of creation and application that the meta-analysis will be unable to provide. Meta-analysis is important because the results provide evidence and an argument for a person to undertake the effort. Evidence indicates that the effort produces a payoff in the form of improved learning for the course. What the meta-analysis does not do is provide the means or the advice on how to construct the advanced organizer.

The next step in the research could be the examination or comparison of different kinds of advanced organizers and some additional advice provided about how to refine and improve the effectiveness of the particular tool. However, even the new form of the advice will enlarge or improve the information by saying that, "advanced organizers that use visual aids are more effective than advanced organizers without incorporating visual aids." The new advice provides additional and useful information, but again the same challenges exist for creating and providing that information for any course. Every improved understanding and advice still leaves much room for application and creation. Instructors can improve the advanced organizer but the process of application requires the fundamental act of creation.

CRITERIA FOR TEXTBOOK EVALUATION

A simple but important criterion for the evaluation of a textbook is the accuracy of the representations of the existing empirical literature. A textbook should be in the position of offering advice to the reader that intends to improve practice. A reasonable criterion is that when giving advice that the basis for the expectation for improvement come from a collection of experiences that have demonstrated desirable consequences for the practice. Empirical research represents really nothing more than a collection of various experiences that are systematically collected and examined. The level of standardization and use of statistics permits a more direct comparison of those experiences and provides for simple methods of accumulation. The textbook offering a review of the literature should therefore provide as accurate and comprehensive a summary of the available empirical literature as possible. One necessary basis for action should be that the scholar is using the most authoritative scientific information. The textbook author should be in the position of offering, whenever available or possible, the best available and most accurate synthesis of the material.

Meta-analyses provide a kind of baseline to evaluate the statements provided to the instructor about the impact of various approaches or the reality of classroom instruction. For example, suppose a textbook author in instruction suggests that teacher immediacy behavior provides improved cognitive learning. The current meta-analysis disputes that finding and suggests that there is little association or improvement when teachers use higher levels of immediacy in the classroom on cognitive learning. The result is that the instructor's training as well as time and effort spent in acquiring a particular skill does not result in improved cognitive learning. In this case, the textbook's statement, in our opinion, is inconsistent with the existing meta-analysis and represents simply ineffective and erroneous advice. The textbook in these conditions is simply offering advice inconsistent with existing and known scientific evidence.

Meta-analysis simply represents a better method of accumulating and evaluating research results (Cooper & Hedges, 1994; Hunter & Schmidt, 1990; Preiss & Allen, 1995). Hedges (1987) pointed out that the "hard" sciences have used forms of meta-analysis to permit examination and reduction of variability in outcomes of empirical investigations. Hedges demonstrated that the variability of outcome in "hard" science is actually slightly greater than that in the "soft" sciences. What differentiates the two approaches to knowledge is not whether the scholarship deals with the physical sciences or the social sciences, but rather the mechanism for evaluation of inconsistent empirical results. The move toward meta-analysis in this view means that the social sciences begin to reflect the procedures and potentially the outcomes of those generated by the natural scientists.

Textbook authors often are considering hundreds of possible statements or possibilities. The issue dealing with immediacy might occupy only a small portion of a text on teaching in the classroom. Given a textbook will probably consider dozens, if not hundreds of such topics, the number of individual studies combined across all these topics could run easily into the thousands. A textbook author cannot reasonably be expected to read all of this literature and generate accurate conclusions, particularly when other narrative reviews of the same topic reach differing conclusions. The result is a relatively haphazard, random, and incomplete search of the literature that often lacks specificity as well as estimates of the magnitude of the effect. Not only is a conclusion important, but distinguishing between larger and smaller associations would also be desirable.

One example of this is the issue of gender difference research where a large number of meta-analyses point to few differences (Hyde & Plant, 1995). The review of issues in communication (Canary & Hause, 1993) involved a call for a reconsideration of the assumptions of gender differences because meta-analyses almost always reject the view of large gender differences existing. A number of possible explanations and applications of this view exist (Allen, 1998) that might permit a different conclusion to emerge. However, the point is that teaching about gender cannot simply assume that there are a large number of gender differences. In short, the most current and accurate summaries of research should be reflected in the content of courses. The failure to incorporate the new content within a review of the material means that the representations remain inconsistent with available research summaries. Gender representations, particularly in popular texts, remain one of the most misrepresented literatures in the social sciences (see examination of Tannen by Goldsmith & Fulfs, 1999).

Textbooks can gain large benefits from meta-analysis when the body of research is large. A meta-analysis provides a bottom-line summary about the state of the research, and when combined with theoretical modeling and the examination for potential outliers and moderators, can generate the best and most accurate summary of the existing research. The key is that a meta-analysis can eliminate or reduce Type II error (false negatives) and identify the existence of Type I error (false positives). This provides a mechanism for instructors to utilize research in a systematic and authoritative manner, rather than relying on the subjectivity, inconsistency, and lack of systematic evaluation typically the result of classic narrative or vote-counting reviews. When the question is a relatively simple one about the choice between competing models of instruction or whether the implementation of some practice results in improvement, results of a meta-analysis should be most instructive and useful.

This implies that textbook authors now have a shortcut to a clear examination of the research in the discipline. Rather than gathering a mere sample of what can often be dozens of studies with inconsistent and incoherent results when syntheses are attempted, a meta-analysis can provide a simple and authoritative summary of the relationships under investigation. The results of a meta-analysis provide a state-of-the-art analysis that a textbook author can use to make more sweeping and simple statements about the state of the research. Such statements are necessarily the outcome of a comprehensive and systematic procedure and should be embraced as a solution to the inconsistent and often chaotic state of research findings (brought on by a 5% Type I error rate and a 50% Type II error rate). A textbook author cannot offer clear advice when the basic research literature provides a fragmented and complex picture of the findings.

The move toward a science ultimately is based on an acceptance of the methodology that produces claims. That acceptance of a method when combined with an assumption of replication and stability means that induction becomes the preferred method of establishing empirical claims. This means that the scientific enterprise is driven by the search for and the explanation of empirical consistencies. When the instruction and education of students requires that the material used represents the state of the world in terms of facts that have been accepted as established by the community, then the curriculum is established as scientific.

For example, more than 100 investigations exist that demonstrate that a public speaking course reduces the level of communication apprehension (Allen, Hunter, & Donohue, 1989). To argue that public speaking courses

risk traumatizing and potentially increasing the level of communication apprehension is inaccurate. This does not mean that some particular small seg-
ment of identifiable students might benefit more from some other
procedure, only that the expectation of instructors should be that enrolling
in a public speaking course will prove beneficial (even for the highly apprehensive student). The difference between what persons may fear is potentially a problem versus the accumulated evidence gained from experience is
what meta-analysis addresses. The finding supports the conclusion that a
public speaking course produces one demonstrable outcome, the reduction
of communication anxiety felt by the student, in addition to other desirable
improvements.

EVALUATION OF THE TEXTBOOK ADVICE

The various textbooks were evaluated on the basis of the conclusions offered about issues in this book subject to a meta-analysis (see Tables 25.1
and 25.2). When the textbook made a statement, that statement was evaluated as either consistent ($+$), inconsistent ($-$), or could not be determined
(0). If the textbook did not make a statement about the issue no evaluation
took place, and a blank is left in Table 25.2 indicating no statement was
made about the particular issue.

The attempt is not to provide an exhaustive or complete evaluation of
the entire set of claims made by a textbook. Instead, the benchmark becomes the particular set of meta-analyses included in this text. The score-
card in effect provides a simple attempt to evaluate the veracity of the
nature of the empirical claims about the status of instruction across the
available materials. Rather than viewing the critique as a serious attempt to
provide an evaluation of individual textbooks, the goal is more at a macro-
level to examine how the discipline provides a general view of the educational process and the accuracy of that view when compared with the
available research.

Using seven textbooks, there were a total of 112 (7×16) possible codings
that could occur. A total of 21 relevant parts of the textbooks were assessed
with 17 conclusions consistent with the meta-analysis and 4 inconsistent.
As with other previous analyses (Allen & Preiss, 1990, 1998, 2002) the most
frequent outcome was noninclusion of the particular topic. This particular
issue is of some concern because many of the topics of these meta-analyses
are the subject of much research by members of the field. This reflects a partial disconnection between what research is conducted in the field and what
textbook authors view as important issues.

The majority of representations (17 out of 21) were consistent with the
available research. The most frequent and accurate representation was that
for interaction with gender in the classroom. The meta-analysis reaffirmed

TABLE 25.1
Summary of Chapter Findings

1. Advanced organizers—Advanced organizers demonstrate an improvement in student learning.

2. Communication apprehension—High levels of communication apprehension predict lower levels of academic achievement, and less quantity and quality of participation in communication and speaking assignments. However, communication apprehension can be reduced through a variety of methods that work best in combination.

3. Computer-assisted instruction—Use of CAI is associated with improved student learning in courses.

4. Distance learning—Use of distance learning when compared to face-to-face learning demonstrates similar levels of satisfaction and student learning.

5. Gender in classroom—Some evidence exists of differential treatment in that males typically receive more total and more negative interaction with instructors than females.

6. Humor in classroom—Humor is associated with higher levels of student satisfaction but not higher levels of student learning.

7. Location of child care—The site of child care (home or day care) is not associated with positive or negative development of a child. Similar outcomes are generated regardless of the placement of the child.

8. Research productivity and teaching evaluation—A positive relationship exists between college-professor-published research and higher levels of teacher evaluations by students.

9. Race in classroom—Minority students interact less with instructors but have higher levels of negative interaction. There is a relationship between the level of positive view of one's own racial group and positive academic outcomes.

10. School-based conflict resolution—Mediation programs in schools have a high rate of solution to conflict, with the solutions generating high levels of satisfaction for participants. Mediation programs reduce school disciplinary problems.

11. Teacher immediacy—Higher levels of teaching immediacy in the classroom are predictive of higher levels of affective learning but have no relationship to the level of student learning.

12. Thinking critically—Argumentation, debate, and public speaking all improve the critical thinking skills of the students.

13. Question asking—Question asking by students increases student learning and the higher the level of cognitive questioning, the better the learning.

14. Test anxiety—A negative correlation exists between level of test anxiety felt and procrastination, academic self-efficacy, study habits, and test-wiseness.

15. PowerPoint use—Use of Microsoft PowerPoint slightly improves measures of student learning, although larger improvement existed in the natural sciences.

16. Speech rate—A negative correlation was found between speech rate and listening comprehension.

TABLE 25.2
Textbook Analysis

Meta-Analysis	Author of Text						
	Burton & Dimbleby (1990)	Christ (1994)	Eggen & Kauchak (2004)	Garcia et al. (2001)	Joyce & Weil (1996)	Vangelisti et al. (1993)	Zemelman et al. (1998)
1.			+	+			
2.						+	
3.			+	−		+	
4.				−		+	
5.			+	+	+		
6.						+	
7.							
8.			+	+			
9.			+	+			
10.							
11.						−	
12.							
13.			−	+		+	
14.			+				
15.							
16.							

what most persons believe about instructor interaction differences when comparing males and females. However, only three of the seven textbooks mentioned this issue. Given the potential significance of this issue, it is surprising that the majority of textbooks did not review or consider it. No issue had more than one negative rating (computer-assisted instruction, distance learning, immediacy, and question asking). Only one book (Garcia, Spalding, & Powell, 2001) had more than one negative rating and these were both about the use of technology (computer-assisted instruction, distance learning). Essentially, both negative ratings occurred because the authors did not view technology as something that could effectively substitute for or assist instructors. The number of caveats, not present in the current literature, created unwarranted cautions and restrictions on the use of the educational techniques.

The negative rating for the book edited by Vangelisti, Daly, and Friedrich (1998) came from the statement, "no teacher variable has been shown to contribute more consistently to students' motivation and learning than nonverbal immediacy" (p. 276). The first part of the statement is clearly supported by an average correlation of .50 between teacher immediacy and affective learning. However, the correlation between teacher immediacy and cognitive learning is far less substantial. The result is that although the statement is partially correct, it is not correct for the outcome most instructors would rate as most important.

The analysis essentially provides a preview into the future of textbook writing, not only for communication and classroom educational issues, but across the curriculum. As meta-analysis gains acceptance as a scientific procedure, the results will eventually be a greater standardization of content and improvement in the practice and theorizing about any substantive discipline. The ability to offer precise and useful advice begins to grow, as does the ability to refine and test that advice.

The overall assessment is that textbooks dealing with classroom and instructional issues are doing relatively well in representing research. The books are doing less well in incorporating that research into the presentations. Greater attention to existing meta-analyses (the reference sections of the articles contained virtually none) would provide for greater accuracy as well as greater scope of advice.

LESSONS LEARNED

The challenge for the next set of textbooks of subsequent generations will be the focus on improving instructional advice. We are confident that as the number of meta-analyses grows and the findings become refined and elaborated that specificity and applicability of the instructional advice will increase. The question is whether the teaching profession will capitalize on the evidence and try to improve the instruction provided to students. Bostrom (2003) pointed out that often advancing thinking and research requires changing the worldview and the dialogue existing between various methods. The use of meta-analysis should never be viewed as a denial or in struggle with other methods. Instead, the view should be toward an integration of the various methods to accomplish a task.

The single biggest criticism to probably make of current instructional texts is the lack of advice about the effectiveness of various instructional methods. The tendency exists to outline or describe the process of implementation of various pedagogical choices but provide little examination or consideration of the effectiveness of the method advocated. Essentially, the tendency is to provide curriculum information about how to implement or describe the process of undertaking some classroom practice. The problem is that given the wide variety of potential choices, little is done to provide evidence or a review of the potential impact (positive or negative) of the particular choice made by the instructor.

Teaching represents, much like medicine, an art, not a science. However, the practice of medicine is not unconnected or uninterested in scientific knowledge. The practice of medicine requires and employs a great deal of scientific knowledge. However, the knowledge is not applied without consideration of the particular circumstances of the patient and the available resources. In other words, medicine should not be simply and mechanically applied. The medical doctor must function using an art of interpretation and application that goes beyond the mechanical and unthinking application of a procedure. At the same time, threats of malpractice stem from failure to use the latest or best procedure for the specific circumstances. The art of teaching, like medicine, must balance the needs for scientific application (and the inherent risk of mechanical application without consideration of circumstance) and the need for individual interpretation (and the risk of failure to apply the best practice as evidenced by scientific study). Like the doctor, the teacher must find a method of striking the correct balance between the two elements to create effective outcomes.

Too often, in our experience, teaching improvements have focused on fads or trends that tend to disappear when the new trend or terminology appears (and the old terminology or technique becomes "old"). Although energy and interest are important in sustaining the activity of teaching over the long term, the inevitable move toward better and improved models of instruction does not appear all that confident an enterprise. The advice provided seems to reflect often various ideological dispositions that come and go with the seasons and the need to develop a new method or approach to instruction. The problem was that the trend in educational improvement did not provide a mechanism to evaluate the proposed changes when compared with more traditional methods. When there exists no basis for comparison, the individual instructor must make a choice among techniques, and the list of techniques or possibilities continues to expand in numerous directions. The state of the art in teaching knowledge was and continues to remain disjointed and unorganized. It reflects divisions with little sense of movement toward unity or even comparative evaluation. Without any basis for making a comparison, there is no basis for relatively rational decision making among competing alternatives. The current set of teaching instructional materials pays little attention to comparing or evaluating the effectiveness of the various alternatives.

Over the longer term, meta-analysis will provide a better and more foundational basis for evaluation of the efforts to improve instruction. Relying on empirical evidence accumulated across time and context, the ability to provide advice with a greater certainty of effect, both now and in the future, appears warranted. There is much cynicism about colleges and departments of education in the university and the contribution to instructional improvement provided to elementary, secondary, and higher education. Once there is an acceptance that firm advice can be provided and curriculum and practices can in fact be evaluated against known standards and suggestions for improvement offered, the process of objectification begins.

Objectification is often discouraged because teaching is considered an art and not a science. Yet, at the same time, the use of tests and suggestions about outcomes learning (math, reading, science, foreign language, etc.) invoke the application of standards that although argued about, involve accreditation and measurement of outcomes. The issue is not the introduction of a mechanical process. Instead, the move is toward a greater understanding of the process and the outcomes associated with instruction.

We suggest that the battle over the objectification of educational outcomes has already been decided. The question now is simply what instructional methods demonstrate superior approaches at generating those particular outcomes. Meta-analysis operates as a scientific means to evaluate the effectiveness of those various outcomes. It is not the only means of evaluation, nor can meta-analysis evaluate all possible outcomes. However, as long as learning outcomes can be identified and objectified, the evaluation of instructional effectiveness becomes possible.

The findings of the impact of various educational practices carry not only issues of efficacy of particular methods. The finding that students receive differential treatment in the classroom from instructors suggests potential ethical problems that may require consideration and potentially intervention. The next set of research requires careful consideration about the status of communication in the classroom and the impact of the various practices. The ability to reflect on the process of communication in the classroom means that future teachers and students can continue to benefit by the ongoing research programs by numerous scholars. The goals of the phrase "leaving no child behind," although rooted in a political environment, reflect the honest desire of instructors to make positive impact on students. Can the academic community take the research and permit instructors to take advantage of this knowledge to provide successful application to classroom settings?

REFERENCES

Allen, M. (1998). Methodological considerations when examining a gendered world. In D. Canary & K. Dindia (Eds.), *Handbook of sex differences and similarities in communication: Critical essays and empirical investigations of sex and gender in interaction* (pp. 427–444). Mahwah, NJ: Lawrence Erlbaum Associates.

Allen, M., Bourhis, J., Mabry, E., Emmers-Sommer, T., Titsworth, S., Burrell, N., et al. (2002). Comparing student satisfaction of distance education to traditional classrooms in higher education: A meta-analysis. *American Journal of Distance Education, 16*, 83–97.

Allen, M., Hunter, J., & Donohue, W. (1989). Meta-analysis of self-report data on the effectiveness of public speaking anxiety treatment techniques. *Communication Education, 38*, 54–76.

Allen, M., Mabry, E., Mattrey, M., Bourhis, J., Titsworth, S., & Burrell, N. (2004). Evaluating the effectiveness of distance learning: A comparison using meta-analysis. *Journal of Communication, 54*, 402–420.

Allen, M., & Preiss, R. (1990). Using meta-analysis to evaluate curriculum: An examination of selected college textbooks. *Communication Education, 39*, 103–116.

Allen, M., & Preiss, R. (1998). Evaluating the advice offered by the tool users. In M. Allen & R. Preiss (Eds.), *Persuasion: Advances through meta-analysis* (pp. 243–256). Cresskill, NJ: Hampton.

Allen, M., & Preiss, R. (2002). An analysis of textbooks in interpersonal communication: How accurate are the representations? In M. Allen, R. Preiss, B. Gayle, & N. Burrell (Eds.), *Interpersonal communication research: Advances through meta-analysis* (pp. 371–388). Mahwah, NJ: Lawrence Erlbaum Associates.

Bostrom, R. (2003). Theories, data, and communication research. *Communication Monographs, 70*, 275–294.

Bourhis, J., & Allen, M. (1998). The role of videotaped feedback in the instruction of public speaking: A quantitative synthesis of published empirical literature. *Communication Research Reports, 15*, 256–261.

Burton, G., & Dimbleby, R. (1990). *Teaching communication.* New York: Routledge.

Canary, D. J., & Hause, K. (1993). Is there any reason to research sex differences in communication? *Communication Quarterly, 41*, 129–144.

Christ, W. (Ed.). (1994). *Assessing communication education; A handbook for media, speech, & theatre educators.* Hillsdale, NJ: Lawrence Erlbaum Associates.

Cooper, H., & Hedges, L. V. (1994). Research synthesis as a scientific enterprise. In H. Cooper & L. Hedges (Eds.), *Handbook of research synthesis* (pp. 3–14). New York: Russell Sage Foundation.

Eggen, P., & Kauchak, D. (2004). *Educational psychology* (6th ed.). Upper Saddle River, NJ: Pearson/Merrill/Prentice-Hall.

Garcia, J., Spalding, E., & Powell, R. (2001). *Contexts of teaching: Methods for middle and high school instruction.* Upper Saddle River, NJ: Merrill/Prentice-Hall.

Goldsmith, D., & Fulfs, P. (1999). "You just don't have the evidence": An analysis of claims and evidence. In M. Roloff (Ed.), *Communication yearbook 22* (pp. 1–50). Thousand Oaks, CA: Sage.

Hedges, L. V. (1987). How hard is hard science, how soft is soft science? The empirical cumulativeness of research. *American Psychologist, 42*, 443–455.

Hunter, J., & Schmidt, F. (1990). *Methods of meta-analysis: Correcting research findings for artifact and bias.* Beverly Hills, CA: Sage.

Huxman, S., & Allen, M. (2004). Scientists and storytellers: The imperative pairing of qualitative and quantitative approaches in communication research. In S. Iorio (Ed.), *Qualitative research in journalism: Taking it to the streets* (pp. 175–192). Mahwah, NJ: Lawrence Erlbaum Associates.

Hyde, J., & Plant, E. (1995). Magnitude of psychological gender differences: Another side to the story. *American Psychologist, 50*, 129–161.

Joyce, B., & Weil, M. (1996). *Models of teaching* (5th ed.). Boston: Allyn & Bacon.

Preiss, R., & Allen, M. (1995). Understanding and using meta-analysis. *Evaluation and the Health Profession, 18,* 315–335.

Vangelisti, A. L., Daly, J. A., & Friedrich, G. W. (Eds.). (1998). *Teaching communication: Theory, research, and methods.* Mahwah, NJ: Lawrence Erlbaum Associates.

Zemelman, S., Daniel, D., & Hyde, A. (1998). *Best practice: New standards for teaching and learning in America's school* (2nd ed.). Portsmouth, NH: Heineman.

Author Biographies

Mike Allen (PhD, Michigan State University, 1987) is Professor and Chair of the Department of Communication at the University of Wisconsin-Milwaukee. His more than 100 published works deal with issues of HIV/AIDS education and prevention, drug use, persuasion, and other sources of social influence. His work has appeared in *Health Education and Behavior, Human Communication Research, Journal of Personal and Social Relationships, Law and Human Behavior,* and *Communication Education.* He is co-editor of *Persuasion: Advances through Meta-analysis* and *Interpersonal Communication Research: Advances through Meta-analysis.*

Jim Applegate (PhD, University of Illinois, 1978) is Vice President for Academic Affairs for the Kentucky higher education system. He previously served as Professor and Chair of Communication at the University of Kentucky and as President of the National Communication Association, the world's largest association of communication scholars, and the Southern Communication Association. He has been named an American Council on Education Fellow and a distinguished alumnus of his program at the University of Illinois. He has authored numerous publications studying factors that contribute to increased communication ability in children and adults. As a consultant, Dr. Applegate has conducted over 200 seminars for private sector, educational and government organizations designed to improve communication practices and solve communication problems.

Sandra J. Berkowitz (PhD, University of Minnesota, 1994) is an Associate Professor in the Department of Communication and Journalism at the University of Maine. In addition to research on critical thinking and communication pedagogy, her research focuses on how ideology

423

structures social practices, particularly the discourse of the U.S. Jewish community. Her work has been published in journals including *Communication Monographs* and *Communication Studies*.

John Bourhis (MA, University of Arizona, 1980) is a Professor in the Department of Communication at Missouri State University. For the past 8 years he has served as the director of a large, multisection course in public speaking. He has authored several books and articles in public speaking, communication education, and organizational culture.

Isabelle Bauman (PhD, University of Wisconsin-Madison, 1991) is an Assistant Professor in the Department of Communication at Missouri State University. Her training and research are in cognitive approaches to interpersonal communication, with particular emphasis on issues related to understanding and misunderstanding in conversation. Most of her work is in the social scientific tradition, but she has also been heavily influenced by critical and interpretive approaches to theorizing.

Lisa Bradford (PhD, Arizona State University, 1993) is a Assistant Professor in the Department of Communication at the University of Wisconsin-Milwaukee. Her research interests focus on intercultural and interpersonal communication; issues related to values, issues of identity; strategic embarrassment with adolescents and young adults; and Latinos and European Americans' perceptions of competence. She is currently working on a study that examines how European Americans evaluate competent communication behavior in four contexts: intracultural–social, intracultural–task, intercultural–social, and intercultural–task.

Nancy A. Burrell (PhD, Michigan State University, 1987) is a Professor at the University of Wisconsin-Milwaukee. Professor Burrell's research centers on managing conflict in family, workplace, and educational contexts. She has published in *Human Communication Research, Communication Monographs* and *Management Communication Quarterly*. She is currently investigating the impact of workplace bullies to design dispute systems for organizations. She is a co-editor of *Interpersonal Communication Research: Advances through Meta-analysis*.

Erica Cooper (MA, University of Wisconsin-Milwaukee) is a doctoral candidate at Indiana University. She has a fellowship in the Preparing Future Faculty Program. Her research focuses on the development and maintenance of racial identity. She has published in *Communication Research Reports* and has presented papers at the National Communication Association annual conference.

Derek Cortez (MS, University of Portland, 2002) is ABD at University of Texas at Austin in organizational communication. His research interests focus on organizational communication and leadership. He is currently serving as Executive Administrator of Summit Academy.

Kathryn Dindia (PhD, University of Washington, 1981) is a Professor in the Department of Communication at the University of Wisconsin-Milwaukee. She has served on the editorial board for *Journal of Social and Personal Relationships, Human Communication Research, Journal of Applied Communication, Journal of Communication,* and *Women's Studies in Communication.* She co-edited the volumes *Sex Differences and Similarities in Communication* and *Communication in Personal Relationships.* Dindia has published approximately 30 articles and book chapters, including articles in *Psychological Bulletin, Human Communication Research, Journal of Social and Personal Relationships,* and *Personal Relationships.*

Barbara Mae Gayle (PhD, University of Oregon, 1989) is Professor and Vice President of Academic Affairs at Saint Martin's University. Selected as a 2001–2002 Carnegie Scholar, Gayle is published in *Women's Studies in Communication, Journal of Applied Communication, Management Communication Quarterly,* and *Communication Research Reports.* She is a co-editor of *Interpersonal Communication Research: Advances through Meta-analysis.*

Denis Grimes (MA, Wake Forest University) is a doctoral candidate at the University of Wisconsin-Milwaukee. His work focuses on communication and the resolution of personal identity and institutional requirements. His work has been published in the *Howard Journal of Communications* and he has presented papers at the National Communication Association annual conference.

Patricia Kearney (EdD, West Virginia University, 1979) is Professor of Communication Studies and recipient of the Distinguished Scholar Award at California State University, Long Beach. Her research and teaching, both theoretical and applied, focus on communication in the instructional process. The Editor of *Communication Education* and a member of several other journal editorial boards, Kearney has written a variety of textbooks and industrial training packages, and she has published more than 100 research articles, chapters, and commissioned research reports and instructional modules. She is listed among the 100 most published scholars and among the top 15 published female scholars in her discipline.

Jeff Kerssen-Greip (PhD, University of Washington, 1997) is an Associate Professor in the Department of Communication Studies at the University of

Portland. His scholarship examines the effects of intercultural contact and how "facework" in instructional communication helps sustain engaging learning environments, productive teaching–learning relationships, and intrinsically motivated learners. His research is published in *Communication Education*, *The Western Journal of Communication*, *Communication Research*, *College and University*, the *Journal of the Northwest Communication Association*, and in several book chapters.

Susanne M. Jones (PhD, Arizona State University, 2000) is an Assistant Professor in the Department of Communication Studies at the University of Minnesota, Twin Cities. Her areas of research include comforting communication and emotional support, the communication of emotion, and nonverbal communication. Her articles have been published in *Human Communication Research*, *Communication Monographs*, *Communication Research*, and *Sex Roles*.

Kristine A. Kruepke (MA, University of Wisconsin-Milwaukee, 2003) is currently employed as a Trainer for U.S. Cellular in Waukesha, WI. Her research examines communication processes of temporary employees and how organizational identification influences these individuals' intent to stay with a client organization.

Edward Mabry (PhD, Bowling Green State University, 1972) is an Associate Professor in the Department of Communication at the University of Wisconsin-Milwaukee. His research interests focus on communication in face-to-face and mediated groups, effects of communication technology on groups and organizations, and communication and instructional technology. His work appears in the American Journal of Higher Education, Say Not to Say: New Perspectives on Miscommunication, and New Directions in Group Communication.

Diane Martin (PhD, Utah, 2001) is an Assistant Professor in the Pamplin School of Business at the University of Portland. Her current research focuses on theoretical and social dimensions of marketing and communication, with an emphasis on gender, humor, and consumption. Her research has been published in numerous edited books, and in several journals including the *Journal of Applied Communication Research*, *Southern Communication Journal*, and the *Journal of Business Ethics*.

James C. McCroskey (EdD, Pennsylvania State University, 1966) is a Professor of Communication Studies at West Virginia University. His major areas of research are instructional communication, organizational communication, communication traits, and communibiology. He has published over 200 articles and book chapters and over 30 books and revisions, as well as over 30 instructionally related books.

Linda L. McCroskey (PhD, University of Oklahoma, 1998) is an Associate Professor of Communication Studies at California State University, Long Beach. Her major areas of research are intercultural communication, organizational communication, instructional communication, and communication theory.

Timothy G. Plax (PhD, University of Southern California, 1974) is a Professor and Executive Director of the Hauth Center at California State University, Long Beach. He has served on the faculty at the University of New Mexico and West Virginia University. His experiences include 6 years as a member of the Executive Staff at Rockwell International Corporation and 25 years as a consultant for numerous fortune 500 corporations. He has published over 150 manuscripts and is listed among the 25 most published scholars in his discipline.

Raymond W. Preiss (PhD, University of Oregon, 1988) is a Professor of Communication Studies at the University of Puget Sound. He is a co-author *Persuasion: Advances through Meta-analysis* and *Interpersonal Communication Research: Advances through Meta-analysis*. His work has appeared in *Human Communication Research, Communication Quarterly, Management Communication Quarterly*, and *Communication Research Reports*.

Craig Rich (MS, University of Portland, 2003) is a graduate teaching fellow and doctoral student in the Department of Communication at the University of Utah. His research focuses on the interrelationships of gender, sexuality/queer, and power within organizational and interpersonal communication. His work has appeared in the *Southern Communication Journal*.

Virginia P. Richmond (PhD, University of Nebraska, 1976) is a Professor of Communication Studies at West Virginia University. Her major areas of research are nonverbal communication, instructional communication, organizational communication, and communication traits.

Elayne Shapiro (PhD, University of Minnesota, 1992) is Chair and Associate Professor in the Department of Communication Studies at the University of Portland. Her research interests include computer-mediated communication, interpersonal communication, and organizational communication. Her research appears in several book chapters, the *Journal of the Northwest Communication Association*, and the *Journal of Technology Studies*.

Jennifer Stanley (MA, University of Wisconsin-Milwaukee) is currently working at the Center for International Education, University of Wisconsin-Milwaukee. Her work focuses on the means of finding solutions to cultural conflict. She has presented papers at the Central States Communication Association annual conference.

C. Eric Timmerman (PhD, University of Texas, 2001) is an Assistant Professor in the Department of Communication at the University of Wisconsin-Milwaukee. His research focuses on organizational communication, communication technology, and distance education. His work appears in *Communication Monographs, Management Communication Quarterly,* and *Communication Studies.*

Lindsay M. Timmerman (PhD, University of Texas, 2001) is an Assistant Professor in the Department of Communication at the University of Wisconsin-Milwaukee. Her research focuses on communication in romantic relationships and families. She has examined issues that include romantic jealousy, long-distance relationships, family secrets, and pre-marital commitment. Her work has appeared in *Communication Monographs, Communication Quarterly,* and *Communication Studies.*

Stacy Tye-Williams (MA, University of Wisconsin-Milwaukee, 2003) is a doctoral student at the University of Nebraska-Lincoln. She received her MA along with a Certificate of Mediation and Negotiation. She has published a co-authored piece in *Communication Studies,* and her current research interests include emotional labor and workplace bullying.

Lawrence R. Wheeless (PhD, Wayne State University, 1970) is a Professor at the University of North Texas in the Communication Studies Department. Dr. Wheeless has held offices in international and regional professional communication associations and has served in numerous editorial positions for those organizations, including Editor of *Communication Quarterly.* His scholarship includes the publication of 12 book chapters, 3 books, and over 50 scholarly journal articles. Twelve of his 92 scholarly papers presented at meetings of professional associations have received awards.

Paul L. Witt (PhD, University of North Texas, 2000) is an Assistant Professor in the Department of Communication Studies at Texas Christian University. In addition to teaching courses in instructional communication, theory, and intercultural communication, he also serves as Director of Graduate Studies for the department. His research has been published in *Communication Education, Communication Monographs, Communication Quarterly,* the *Southern Journal of Communication,* and *Communication Reports.*

Stacy L. Young (PhD, University of Texas at Austin, 2000) is an Associate Professor of Communication Studies at California State University, Long Beach. Her research and teaching explore communication interactions that are difficult, distressing, or disruptive in instructional and in relational contexts. She is a member of the *Communication Education* editorial board and a reviewer for several other interdisciplinary journals. Her numerous publications address topics of interest to a broad audience in the communication, psychology, and educational fields.

Cindy Zirbel (MA, University of Wisconsin-Milwaukee) is currently a member of the investment team at Edward T. Jones. Her research focuses on the applications of conflict resolution skills to resolving conflict in schools. Her work has been published in *Conflict Resolution Quarterly* and *Communication Research Reports* as well as presentations at the National Communication Association annual conference.

Author Index

Subject Index